THE NEW NATURALIST
A SURVEY OF BRITISH NATURAL HISTORY

BRITISH THRUSHES

The aim of this series is to interest the general reader
in the wild life of Britain by recapturing the enquiring
spirit of the old naturalists. The Editors believe that
the natural pride of the British public in the native fauna
and flora, to which must be added their concern for
their conservation, is best fostered by maintaining a
high standard of accuracy combined with clarity of
exposition in presenting the results of modern scientifiic
research.

THE NEW NATURALIST

BRITISH THRUSHES

ERIC SIMMS, D.F.C., M.A.

COLLINS
ST JAMES'S PLACE, LONDON

William Collins Sons & Co Ltd
London · Glasgow · Sydney · Auckland
Toronto · Johannesburg

TO

JEANNE AND LEWIS GORDON

First published 1978
© Eric Simms 1978
ISBN 0 00 219670 0
Made and Printed in Great Britain by
William Collins Sons & Co Ltd Glasgow

CONTENTS

PLATES

EDITORS' PREFACE

ERIC SIMMS is well known to New Naturalist readers, as the author of the very successful volume *Woodland Birds*. This contains many references to the thrushes, which are essentially denizens of woods and forest, though they are particularly familiar to man in Britain because of the way they are able to exploit his gardens, hedgerows and farms. However, we believe that the group is of such interest that it deserves a book to itself, and we are very gratified that Eric Simms agreed to write it.

As readers of *Woodland Birds* well know, Eric Simms is skilful at communicating his enthusiasm for, as well as his knowledge of, the birds he has so painstakingly observed over a great many years. He is perhaps best known for his careful studies of suburban birds, of which the black-bird, described here, is one of the commonest. But he has also followed his subjects into their other, perhaps more natural, habitats in many parts of Britain and overseas. He modestly disclaims being an expert on the thrushes, and he pays tribute to the work of other leading authorities, particularly Dr David Snow. However, he has been able to combine their researches with his own observations, producing a work which makes this group of birds appear as living members of our native fauna.

Serious ornithologists will welcome the many tables, including much meticulously recorded data about the biology and ecology of the different species. Such information could have been included in such a way that the less well-informed student would have found the text indigestible. Here the reader will find no such difficulty. Eric Simms has produced an eminently readable volume, and one which will make us all observe the British thrushes with a new and deeper understanding.

AUTHOR'S PREFACE

THIS book is the culmination of a lifetime of interest in an attractive and familiar group of birds. Yet it was with both a feeling of inadequacy and a sense of elation that I embarked on the writing of a book about the family of thrushes. To some extent the former was assuaged by my respect for the pioneer work of Dr David Snow, much of which was embodied in his delightful *A Study of Blackbirds*, first issued in 1958, and in a number of highly perceptive and stimulating scientific papers published over more than two decades. Dr Snow not only very generously approved my use of his unique material in the preparation of my own book but also, despite his present preoccupation with the *Turdus* species of South America, kindly agreed to read the manuscript as well. My diffidence was also to some extent dispelled by another generous offer – this time from Dr Leo Batten, bird populations expert at the British Trust for Ornithology, to allow me to consult his very instructive unpublished thesis on blackbird population dynamics. I am very conscious of the debt that I owe to these ornithologists who both made very many helpful comments on the text. Finally, I must thank Robert Gillmor for his delightful drawings of thrushes.

For some of the background material I have widely consulted *The Handbook of British Birds* by H. F. Witherby, F. C. R. Jourdain, N. F. Ticehurst and B. W. Tucker, *The Birds of the British Isles* by Dr David Bannerman and G. E. Lodge, the *Atlas of European Birds* by Dr K. H. Voous, *The Status of Birds in Britain and Ireland* prepared by the Records Committee of the British Ornithologists' Union, *The Atlas of Breeding Birds in Britain and Ireland* compiled by Dr J. T. R. Sharrock for the BTO and the IWC, and *Breeding Birds of Britain and Ireland* by John Parslow. A glance at the selected bibliography will show how much I depended too on the published work of the late Dr David Lack. I am also grateful to the Editors of *British Birds* and *Bird Study* for permission to reproduce maps, diagrams, figures, tables and sonagrams that have appeared in their journals.

I have also consulted several authors who have studied certain species of thrush outside the British Isles. Accounts of the blackbird in Czechoslovakia by J. Havlin and in Switzerland by J-P. Ribaut, of the mistle thrush in Germany by F. Peus and of the redwing in Finland by H. Tyrväinen have proved of very great value. There were well over 600 entries in the full bibliography and for reasons of space it was only possible to include a selection in the present volume. I have, however, made

11

arrangements to lodge copies of the full bibliography with both the Edward Grey Institute at Oxford and the British Trust for Ornithology at Tring.

I am very conscious of the debt that I owe to many organizations and individuals who have without real exception always granted me most generous facilities, undertaken research, answered questions and pursued various esoteric lines of enquiry on my behalf. The British Trust for Ornithology has proved, as it has always done in the past, a veritable tower of strength. I wish to express my appreciation to its recent Director, Dr J. J. M. Flegg, for many personal kindnesses, to Dr J. T. R. Sharrock, Organizer and Compiler of the new *Atlas*, for advice and help in the reproduction of six of the *Atlas* maps, to Robert Spencer for guidance on the ringing returns and for his approval of my inclusion of several maps of thrush and chat recoveries, and to David Glue for his agreement to my use of two diagrams that appeared in a joint paper that he wrote with Dr Flegg on the breeding of the ring ouzel.

The Nature Conservancy Council and its officers have always been most courteous and prompt in giving advice and help in my research. I must, however, make special mention of Richard Balharry, the warden of the NCC for the east of Scotland – an old friend and delightful companion in the hills – who showed me many kindnesses for which I am grateful.

I am especially indebted to Roger Durman who is engaged on a study of ring ouzels in the Pentland Hills in Midlothian. He not only willingly put at my disposal the material that he has gathered so far in his invaluable researches into a rather neglected species, but he suggested that I might also quote from his analysis of ring ouzel recoveries and migrations which he had prepared for publication in *Bird Study*. This is indeed assistance of a very special and valued kind. I would also like to thank Barry Spence, the warden of Spurn Bird Observatory, for his help with ring ouzel weights and wing measurements.

Professor W. H. Thorpe very kindly agreed to the reproduction of the sonagrams of song and sub-song of five of the thrush species, based on sound recordings by Ludwig Koch, John Kirby and myself. Richard Savage generously provided me with a tape copy of one of his fine ring ouzel recordings from Dartmoor, and Joan Hall-Craggs of the Sub-Department of Animal Behaviour at Cambridge kindly converted it into a sonagram for inclusion in this book. Patrick Sellar gave me invaluable guidance as to the availability of recent thrush recordings while Ronald Kettle at the British Library of Wildlife Sounds explored the shelves of the collection for material suitable for my purpose. I would also like to thank the Venerable P. H. T. Hartley for his permission to publish a table from one of his instructive papers in the journal *British Birds*.

This would also seem to be an appropriate place to put on record the value of observations, sometimes acquired only after long and diligent hours of study, sometimes simply isolated incidents, which have been published and preserved in this way only through the application and efforts of ornithologists and birdwatchers who might easily not have bothered. Many of the records could have remained merely memories in one individual's recall but instead they were made available to us all.

This is the second New Naturalist volume which I have been privileged to undertake. Following *Woodland Birds* it has enabled me to look in greater depth at some of those bird species which figured so prominently in the earlier volume. Professor Kenneth Mellanby and Eric Hosking also read the text and Michael Walter and Robert MacDonald kept a kindly and helpful watching brief on behalf of the publishers.

Each kind of thrush reveals a remarkable perfection of form, colour and performance, each 'a sweet melodious bird' as William Shakespeare approved them. In *A Midsummer Night's Dream* the Bard found both thrush and blackbird a deep source of inspiration. For myself, living in the twentieth century, they have proved no less.

INTRODUCTION

THIS is a book about the thrushes of the British Isles – a group of birds many of which are not only familiar to and well-loved by us who live there but are also known to most of the inhabitants of western Europe. Our common and wide-ranging blackbird is the *merel* of the Dutch, the *merle noir* of the French, the *koltrast* of the Swedes and the *amsel* of the Germans. The name 'thrush' itself seems to have arisen from the Middle English or Anglo-Saxon, and probably from the word 'throstle'. Here there is kinship with the Middle English 'throstel', the German 'drossel', the Swedish 'trast' and the Icelandic 'throstur'. The origins of some of the other popular names are uncertain but it seems likely that 'ouzel' is derived from either the Middle English 'osel' or Anglo-Saxon 'osle' (compare the German 'amsel'), 'fieldfare' from the Middle English 'feldfare' or Anglo-Saxon 'feldeware'. The name 'mavis' or 'mavish' – a common one for the song thrush and occasionally for the mistle thrush – may have arisen from the French 'mauvis'.

The thrushes have been with us for a very long time, probably from the Upper Pliocene several million years ago. More than one-third of our native breeding birds originated from the cold, temperate and sub-tropical regions of the northern part of the Old World. Our very well-established bird communities of woodland and farmland have arisen very largely from this fauna with the thrushes important members. I have already traced in *Woodland Birds* the origins of the birds of forest habitats and I do not propose to embark on a detailed study in the present volume. However, many of the thrush species could have been found in the riverine plant-growth that was characteristic of the steppe-like countryside bordering the edge of the tundra in the Ice Age. There is little profit from speculation about the origins of individual species but redwings and fieldfares must have been components of the bird communities of those birch forests that arrived in Britain during the Pre-Boreal Phase following the retreat of the tundra. Mistle thrushes may have come from the dry, unglaciated regions from southern Europe to Turkestan. They could have entered with the broad-leaved forests or they may have been inhabitants of the early coniferous woodlands and spread from them into the deciduous.

Song thrushes were in Britain in Mindel glacial times and possibly redwings as well. The redwing has been recorded as a fossil from Early Ice Age Somerset and Late Ice Age Devon, Derbyshire and Ireland.

15

Blackbirds as well as redwings and song thrushes appear in the fossil record from Early to Late Ice Age, while both mistle thrushes and field-fares were found on Late Ice Age sites. Although there is no fossil evidence for the ring ouzel, it is a species which may have come to us from the dry hill strip that ran from the Mediterranean east to the Kirghiz Steppes. In a later period song thrush remains were found in the ruins of the Roman city of Calleva Atrebatum, now known as Silchester. The Romans regarded fieldfares and redwings very highly as delicate eating and kept thousands of them in aviaries where they were fattened on a paste formed of bruised figs and flour; the birds were almost deprived of light, fattened and then sold for three denarii each.

After Roman times there is something of a gap in the historical record. The Dark Ages witnessed the acceleration of the forest clearances that were to alter and eventually shape the lives of many passerine birds, including the commoner thrush species. The Anglo-Saxons of the eighth century expressed admiration for the song thrush as a performer and the blackbird and mistle thrush were also known to them. The fieldfare appears in the literature in the ninth century but the ring ouzel is not apparently mentioned by name before the middle of the fifteenth century nor the redwing before about 1600.

The continuing history of the six breeding British thrush species has been a dynamic and a fascinating one. Towards the end of the eighteenth century Gilbert White barely mentioned the blackbird except for its song and period of singing, and Thomas Bewick found it solitary, elusive and a bird of dense thickets. In the mid nineteenth century it was still a bird of woodland and was not known as a nesting bird near houses. Gilbert White closely observed the pugnacious qualities of the nesting mistle thrush as well as its berry-eating propensities and he recorded the song periods of both blackbird and song thrush, the vulnerability of the red-wing to prolonged cold weather, the habit of fieldfares of roosting on the ground and the inland migrations of the ring ouzel. Although many of White's observations are as true today as when he chronicled them, there have also been great changes since his time – the steady decline in recent years of the song thrush, the acquisition of both redwing and fieldfare as breeding species and more regular winter visitors to urban and suburban areas, the decrease in the number of ring ouzels nesting in Ireland and the remarkable advance of the blackbird on to outlying islands and to greater heights on the hills as well as into gardens, town parks and squares. Some of these expansions of range or habitat, like the move of the mistle thrush in the nineteenth century into more open environments including those of parks and city centres, have been observed in western and central Europe as well.

As the forests disappeared, hedgerows that arrived with the Enclosures began to absorb many of the woodland birds and the Common Birds

PLATE 1. SONG THRUSHES. *Above*, the alert ready-to-fly stance of the song thrush. *Below left*, a typical nest-site in an evergreen with well-developed young; *right*, a less common nest-site on the ground among bracken on the Isle of Mull.

PLATE 2. SONG THRUSHES. *Above*, earthworms form a large part of the diet of both adults and young. *Below*, a male song thrush feeds an incubating female with an earthworm.

Census has shown that on farmland the blackbird is the commonest species, forming between 10% and 20% of the population after the exclusion of rook, starling, woodpigeon and house sparrow. In the great overgrown hedges of forest trees in Ireland with their rich field layer the commonest birds that I found were song and mistle thrushes. Now with more efficient agriculture geared to profitable operation many of the hedges have been grubbed up with serious effects on the populations of small songbirds, and in the past they have also been subjected to the pressures of toxic chemicals, greater mechanization and shifting seasons for the harvests. And other changes have taken place since Gilbert White lived and observed his countryside. His century saw an increase in the planting of native broad-leaved and exotic European conifers by private landowners. The growth in industrialization and the building of towns made more inroads into Britain's overstrained woodland resources during the latter part of the nineteenth century and the situation was aggravated during the Great War of 1914–18. To make up these staggering losses the Forestry Commission was set up and soon was planting conifers, mainly alien species, on moorland and marginal ground. When the thicket plantations are ten years old or more blackbirds and song thrushes reach their peak often in regions where a decade before there were perhaps skylarks, meadow pipits, red grouse and a few waders such as curlew, snipe or lapwing.

There is today a growing concern about the health and balance of all our different environments. Research has been undertaken to see how best their variety and richness can be sustained or improved for the benefit of both birds and men. In 1975 I carried out an ecological survey of a disused railway line in north London, which had become a natural linear park, in order to evaluate those areas which needed to be preserved, or planted up, and those where some development might be tolerable. Twenty-three per cent of the total number of breeding pairs was formed by blackbird, song thrush and mistle thrush. Britain's suburbia has become a kind of Shangri-La for the once shy and retiring blackbird and its greatly increased breeding distribution and density in the suburbs reflect the advantages that man's way of life has brought it. Yet many parts of suburbia are changing, and not, I am afraid, always for the better. Municipal insensitivity and lack of imagination, combined with pre-set ideas of 'landscaping' housing estates, have brought no benefit to the birds and have sometimes had positively adverse effects. The presence in numbers of blackbirds and song thrushes must be a very good guide – an indicator, if you like – to the richness and satisfying nature of an environment for man himself. I look upon the thrushes with interest and affection since many are remarkably plastic in their behaviour and some are capable of turning events and developments to their positive advantage.

One of my treasured possessions are the four volumes of Sir William

Jardine's *The Natural History of the Birds of Great Britain and Ireland*, dated 1839. Jardine wrote perceptively about the habits of the various species of thrush but it was his introduction to them which impressed me, not only by its elegance of expression but also for its crystallization of the strong appeal that this family has for me. He wrote: 'The true Thrushes, in all their members, taken collectively and in adaptation to their general habits, shew considerable perfection. The parts are adapted for extensive locomotion, either in walking or perching, or during flight; many perform long migrations, and extensive flights are taken even in those countries where the climate does not render this annual removal necessary. They are nearly omnivorous; a great part of their sustenance is sought for upon the ground, particularly during that season when insects are not indispensable for the welfare of their broods, and their feet and tarsi are admirably formed for walking and inspecting the various places where their food is then chiefly to be found.'

Their rightful place is in our gardens, in the deep woodlands or our leafy parkland, on the wind-trimmed mountainsides, in the moonlight or freshness of dawn borne high on the strength and splendour of their appointed purpose. For this reason I find the sight of redwings in tiny cages in, say, the October markets in Arles infinitely distressing, just as I deplore the growing use of air guns in Britain and the employment of our blackbirds and song thrushes as living targets. We seem to be losing ground in conservation and education where a decade or so ago the future seemed more promising and assured.

In the last one hundred years ornithology in Britain has expanded fan-like into a great delta of activity. The development of bird ethology with its exact disciplines and demands has embraced many different groups and species. Films, still photography, tape recording, mist-nets, computers, statistics, the calculation of energy flows, the construction of 'models' have supplemented the collection of data, the examination of living birds, skins and bird parasites, the trapping and ringing of birds and the plotting of their recoveries in the continuing search for knowledge. There is still room, however, for the observer who gets to know an area well and its avian inhabitants intimately, who records clearly and critically what he sees, and who can recognize the changes that are continually taking place around him. That may seem like a sermon but the most valued comment made by any reviewer of my previous books was that 'he has made Dollis Hill his Selborne', since here in north-west London I have carried out a twenty-six-year-long continuous study of a bird community.

A great deal has been written and published about the six British breeding thrushes both within the United Kingdom and outside it, especially the ecology, ethology and population dynamics of the blackbird. Less has been made available about the other species, in particular the ring ouzel. It would be quite impossible in a book of this length, however, to cover in detail all the varied aspects of the life of these birds. I have therefore sought to compose a series of essays designed to reflect what is known about the British thrushes – their range and distribution, ecology, plumages and moults, food and feeding habits, display, voice, breeding behaviour, population dynamics, roosting habits, and migratory journeys and patterns. There is also a chapter devoted to an account of Britain's vagrant large thrushes. This is followed by the final chapter which reviews the range, ecology and breeding of the smaller chat-like thrushes and makes some reference to the vagrants as well. In some instances it seemed logical for easier reference to summarize what is known for individual species – for example, on range and habitats – but most of the remaining material is treated on a comparative basis. Where this is intended, I have assembled both observations and findings that have appeared in scientific journals up to early 1976, and this synthesis may perhaps cast some light on the likenesses and differences in the species. Although I have been interested in the thrushes for more than forty years, there are certain aspects of their lives which have had a special appeal – voice, breeding, habitats and their visible migrations. The book is therefore an amalgam of personal observations and research inter-woven with many other studies and isolated records. The journal *British Birds* is a rich quarry for single items of observation and has supplied many in this book; they are listed in the full bibliography now at the BTO and the EGI.

It will be readily apparent that many questions remain unanswered. What regulates populations of thrushes to different levels in different years? Why did blackbird populations fall *before* the exceptionally cold winter of 1962–63? What is the difference in survival to be expected between partially migratory and wholly sedentary members of the same species? What controls the low density of breeding mistle thrushes? Why are redwings and fieldfares now entering towns in mild as well as severe winters? What is the true proportion of male ring ouzels that actually incubates eggs? There are many more. One can make some educated guesses as to the possible answers but proof remains a matter for the future. We still know very little about the dynamic relationships between thrush species and we are also very ignorant about their relationships with the various other organisms with which they share their respective environ-ments. Ecosystems, particularly in woodland, are very complex and it is extremely difficult to unravel the great tangled skein of interrelationships.

None of Britain's breeding thrushes now nest in truly natural habitats. Even the ring ouzel may find his moorland home burned but to com-pensate for this adverse biotic effect he may now nest on hill-farm pastures, on the edges of new conifer plantations and even in disused man-made structures. The other five species have all appeared to feed in my own garden or near-by Gladstone Park in north-west London, less than six

miles from Marble Arch, and three of them breed there as well. Their
adaptability in the face of uncompromising modern trends in agriculture
and town planning is a matter for rejoicing. Let us hope that these
attractive and intriguing birds, which bring us so much pleasure and
more rarely a little irritation to the market gardener, will continue to
hold out against our most determined efforts to despoil and develop the
land.

CHAPTER I

THE WORLD'S THRUSHES

THRUSHES are one of the most widely distributed of all groups of small birds. They appear on every continent and penetrate north beyond the Arctic Circle and south across the tropics to Cape Province in Africa and Cape Horn in South America. It is possible to find some species on a number of remote oceanic islands. During my excursions around the world I have been captivated by the vigorous warblings of an olive thrush in a Nairobi garden, by the flight calls of a fieldfare in the Swiss Alps, by the fluent song of a blackbird in an English oakwood and by the striking adornments of an eastern robin on a New Brunswick lawn. All these birds are members of the central *Genus* of thrushes – *Turdus*. Their smaller relations have almost as wide a spread across the world and have brought me great pleasure as well – white-browed robin-chats in Kenya, scrub robins in Uganda, bluebirds in the United States, black wheatears in Spain and European robins in my own back garden.

The thrushes are thus a very cosmopolitan group of birds. The name 'Thrush' is generally applied to those species that are placed in the sub-family *Turdinae* of the *Muscicapidae* – a family of the sub-order *Oscines* of the great order of perching birds known as the *Passeriformes*. The *Oscines* are formed from a wide mixture of primarily Old World insect-eating song-birds equipped with ten primary flight feathers.

In his comprehensive review of the thrushes S. Dillon Ripley (1952) agreed with such earlier authorities as M. Seebohm and R. B. Sharpe, E. Hartert, and E. Mayr and D. Amadon that the true thrushes had been correctly placed in the sub-family *Turdinae*. They were quite closely allied to the Old World warblers – the *Sylviinae* – but they differed from them by not undergoing a double moult and by having in nearly all cases spotted plumages in their young. In the majority of species the thrushes also have a booted tarsus with an undivided horny covering rather than a scutellate one with large and often overlapping scales.

The sub-families are generally separated by the features listed in Table 1. A typical thrush can best be described as of medium size and, in human terms, perky and alert, and with often a pleasing and sometimes complex song. The bill may vary from slender to stout, the tongue is blade-like and there are, of course, ten primaries of which the first is often rather short. There may be bristles around the gape and nostrils. The tail, particularly in European species, tends to be square-ended, but it can also be curved or tapered and can vary in length from short to quite long.

Table 1. Thrushes and Some Other Sub-Families of the Muscicapidae

Sub-Family	Tarsus	Double Moult	Plumage of Juveniles
Muscicapinae (Old World Flycatchers)	Weak, scutellate	Uncommon	Spotted
Turdinae (Thrushes, Wren-Thrushes, Chats, Robins etc.)	Booted or scutellate	Uncommon	Spotted
Timaliinae (Babblers, Wren-Tits)	Scutellate	Uncommon	Unspotted
Sylviinae (Old World Warblers)	Primarily scutellate	Usual	Unspotted

The feet are strong and well developed, and the tarsi are sturdy. The birds can hop and run well and can fly fast. In fact, many species perform quite long migrations.

The moult is a simple one and takes place in the late summer and autumn. In the case of White's thrush (*Zoothera dauma*), of one of the *Monticola* rock thrushes and of some of the wheatears there can also be a partial moult. In their colouring thrushes range from black or brown to various greens, blues, rusts and various shades of grey. They are land dwellers and many show a preference for arboreal habitats, while others can be found in savannah and even waterside environments. They are adapted to a wide range of habitats from the bare tundras south through more temperate regions into the belts of equatorial rain forest. Some live in close association with man's farmlands, homesteads and towns, and perhaps at a greater density in some urban or suburban areas than in their original habitat. They are mainly insectivorous but many kinds will also eat fruit. Some thrush species are particularly well adapted to eating snails and earthworms.

Nests are often built in trees and shrubs, on rock faces, in holes, outbuildings and among clumps of tough grass. The typical thrush nest is a cup formed from grass, moss and leaves, sometimes compacted with mud, and in town habitats birds may take advantage of the rejectamenta arising from man's untidy way of life. In most instances the female takes on the responsibilities of constructing the nest and incubating the eggs, which are pale, clear and usually spotted, and also the brooding of the young. The male also takes his turn in feeding the nestlings. The period of incubation lasts about a fortnight and the nestlings remain in the nest for about the same period of time, but in the Arctic regions, where daylength is greater than it is further south, the length of time spent by the young birds in the nest may be reduced.

The largest number and the greatest complexity of forms among thrushes occur in the Old World which suggests that the birds are primarily of Palaearctic origin. Africa would also seem to be a likely centre, especially for the small chat-like thrushes. From Eurasia thrushes have dispersed into the New World, Australia and Polynesia, while distinctive thrush species have evolved on a number of islands. Thrushes were missing from the area of the Antarctic and New Zealand but some European species have been released in Australasia and spread to many small islands.

The sub-family *Turdinae*, which includes the British thrushes, consists of just over three hundred species. Two species have certainly become extinct in the last two hundred years. These are Kittlitz's thrush (*Zoothera terrestris*), which lived on Peel Island in the Bonins, and the Raiatea thrush (*Turdus ulietensis*). One species is probably extinct – the Grand Cayman thrush (*Turdus ravidus*) – while several others like the Teita olive thrush (*Turdus abyssinicus*), the Seychelles magpie-robin (*Copsychus sechellarum*) and the *Phaeornis* thrushes of Hawaii qualify for the list of endangered bird species in the Red Data Book of the IUCN. More than a score of fossil species is known.

It is convenient to divide the three hundred turdine species into two large groups or tribes – the small chat-like thrushes and the larger true thrushes. The former is made up of small birds, generally less than eighteen cms long, which are often secretive or shy by nature and can differ considerably in appearance from the large true thrushes. They tend to be adorned with more exotic plumages and to have more slender legs; the European robin (*Erithacus rubecula*) seems to us to possess legs too thin and brittle to support its weight.

The chat-like thrushes often reveal a more varied breeding behaviour than the true thrushes and their songs tend to be less bold and striking. The name 'Chat' is derived from the harsh calls that many of these birds employ. It is in this group that the very early forms of the sub-family seem to have emerged; here there are more relict species and a higher degree of differentiation than among the true thrushes. It is perhaps interesting to note that it is in this varied group of birds that those exceptional instances of unturdine characters are most likely to occur – unspotted young, scutellate tarsi and so on. Some genera resemble the flycatchers and others the Old World warblers but, diverse though they may be, Ripley maintained that 'they seem to stand closer together as a group, distinct from the larger, more compactly evolved true thrushes'.

The chat-like thrushes are very familiar in the tropics and, since the largest development has taken place in Africa, they may well have evolved there. The very primitive kinds are the wren-like *Brachypteryx* shortwings of south-east Asia and the shy *Zeledonia* wren-thrush of the high forests of Panama and Costa Rica. These relict forms of both the Old and the New World are sedentary birds of thick jungle. The scrub robins (*Drymodes*) of Australia and New Guinea are also rather primitive species and with the *Cercotrichas* scrub or bush robins of Africa may have helped to form the reservoir of rather warbler-like birds from which many new groups were to evolve. These might well include the Old World *Erithacus* robin and the *Luscinia* nightingales, blue robins, bush robins and bluethroats, as well as a complex set of African *Cossypha* robin-chats, *Alethe* forest robins, magpie-robins (*Copsychus*), Asiatic forktails (*Enicurus*), cochoas and the Hawaiian thrush (*Phaeornis*). The North American sparrow-sized bluebirds (*Sialia*) of open woodlands and the sweet-voiced solitaires (*Myadestes*) of the New World tropics may have had similar origins. The remaining sub-divisions of the chat-like thrushes appear more uniform and ordered and embrace the red-rumped or red-tailed *Phoenicurus* redstarts of the Palaearctic, the primarily African and rather dull *Cercomela* blackstarts, rock and desert chats, the black, brown or white small *Saxicola* chats of open country like the stonechat (*S. torquata*) and whinchat (*S. rubetra*), the red- or white-rumped *Oenanthe* wheatears of dry ground, the Indian robin (*Saxicoloides fulicata*) and the African *Myrmecocichla* cliff, sooty or black chats. The chat-thrushes tend to produce somewhat bigger clutches than the larger true thrushes but otherwise their breeding biology is not very different.

There remains now the second group – that of the true thrushes – and this is of immediate concern since it includes the six species to which this book is primarily devoted. It comprises the familiar genus *Turdus* – a rather cosmopolitan central group consisting of some sixty species of which about a third can be found in the Palaearctic Region. The six common thrushes of the British Isles are all members of this genus – song thrush (*Turdus philomelos*), mistle thrush (*T. viscivorus*), blackbird (*T. merula*), ring ouzel (*T. torquatus*), redwing (*T. iliacus*) and fieldfare (*T. pilaris*).

Clustered around the genus *Turdus* are several other related groups. These include the medium-sized Old World *Monticola* rock thrushes; these are mostly blue with mixtures of reds and browns and live on cliffs and boulder-clad slopes. A large and ancient group is that of the *Zoothera* ground thrushes which occur widely through the Old World tropics; they also include White's thrush (*Z. dauma*), which sometimes straggles west to Britain from Asia, as well as the isolated varied thrush (*Z. naevia*) of western America and the Aztec thrush (*Z. pinicola*). There are other genera such as the whistling thrushes of south-east Asia; one of the better known examples is that of the handsome, dark blue whistling thrush (*Myiophoneus caeruleus*) which sings plaintively among the torrents and mountain streams. There are also one or two species of other genera in New Guinea and the Celebes. Two interesting birds of true thrush classification are the *Cichlherminia* forest thrush of the West Indies and the starchy (*Nesocichla eremita*) with three sub-species each of which is restricted to an island in the Tristan da Cunha group. The starchy is a typical thrush with some features in keeping with those of *Cichlherminia* and with others that suggest a relationship with a bird of the *Turdus* genus in the Falkland Islands.

The New World is noteworthy for its nightingale-thrushes of the genus *Catharus*. These include such fine singers as the olive-backed or Swainson's thrush (*C. ustulatus*) and the hermit thrush (*C. guttatus*) whose songs often delighted me in the eastern United States. To the south the thickets of the Central American forests echo with the simpler refrains of other species of *Catharus* such as the russet nightingale-thrush (*C. occidentalis*) and the orange-billed (*C. aurantiirostris*).

The great central genus *Turdus* includes those birds which we regard as typical thrushes – birds of similar shape, about twenty to thirty cms long, and with roughly similar kinds of song. Examples might include the blackbird, fieldfare, American robin (*T. migratorius*), bare-eyed thrush (*T. nudigenis*) of the West Indies and South America, the great thrush (*T. fuscater*) of the Andean mountain scrublands and the mountain black-bird (*T. poliocephalus*) of the Pacific. The genus is best developed in the Old World and besides the six major European species which are featured in the present volume there are around a score in Asia. There is only one species in North America – the American robin – but the genus has established itself firmly to the south with another score of species from Mexico and the West Indies south to Tierra del Fuego and the Falkland Islands. The rufous-bellied thrush (*T. rufiventris*) is common in the city parks of Rio de Janeiro, the clay-coloured (*T. grayi*) occurs in Central America, the white-eyed (*T. jamaicensis*) in the Caribbean and the austral thrush (*T. falcklandii*) in the Falkland Islands. More than a dozen species can be found in the Ethiopian Region and here I have seen the kurrichane thrush (*T. libonyanus*), the African bare-eyed thrush (*T. tephronotus*) and the ground-scraper thrush (*T. litsitsirupa*) in a small area of Tanzania.

Cichlherminia and the starchy reached the New World and Tristan respectively by an early invasion. The origin of the starchy on Tristan is a matter for conjecture and it would seem that most of the birds of that island group did not originate from Africa. Birds of forest and woodland edge such as *Catharus* then arrived in the Americas and these birds seem to be intermediate between the nightingale/robin groups of the Old World and the true thrushes. Another invasion left two *Zoothera* species stranded in Mexico and western North America. The greatest movement, however, was an impressive sweep of true thrushes of the genus *Turdus* across Eurasia and the Americas bringing with it the most highly de-veloped members of the sub-family. Since they are strong fliers and active, adaptable birds, the true thrushes have been rather more successful than their relations – the warblers and flycatchers – in spreading across the face of the earth – a movement that has not yet come to its end.

Tables 2–4 on pages 27–30 list the world's thrushes, some popular names and the genus *Turdus*. Now follow the chief characters in this book:

TRUE THRUSHES

Turdus philomelos	Song Thrush
Turdus viscivorus	Mistle Thrush
Turdus merula	Blackbird
Turdus torquatus	Ring Ouzel
Turdus iliacus	Redwing
Turdus pilaris	Fieldfare

but the following vagrants will also find a place:

Turdus obscurus	Eye-browed Thrush
Turdus ruficollis	Black-throated Thrush
Turdus naumanni	Dusky Thrush
Turdus sibiricus	Siberian Thrush
Turdus migratorius	American Robin
Catharus minimus	Grey-cheeked Thrush
Catharus ustulatus	Olive-backed (or Swainson's) Thrush
Catharus guttatus	Hermit Thrush
Catharus fuscescens	Veery
Zoothera dauma	White's Thrush
Monticola saxatilis	Rock Thrush
(*Monticola solitarius*)	(Blue Rock Thrush)

CHAT-LIKE THRUSHES

Erithacus rubecula	Robin
Luscinia megarhynchos	Nightingale
Phoenicurus phoenicurus	Redstart
Phoenicurus ochruros	Black Redstart
Saxicola rubetra	Whinchat
Saxicola torquata	Stonechat
Oenanthe oenanthe	Wheatear

and

Cercotrichas galactotes	Rufous Bush Robin or Bush Chat
Luscinia luscinia	Thrush Nightingale
Luscinia svecica	Bluethroat
Luscinia calliope	Siberian Rubythroat
Tarsiger cyanurus	Red-flanked Bluetail
Oenanthe isabellina	Isabelline Wheatear
Oenanthe deserti	Desert Wheatear
Oenanthe hispanica	Black-eared Wheatear
Oenanthe pleschanka	Pied Wheatear
Oenanthe leucura	Black Wheatear

Table 2. Genera of the World's Thrushes

Chat-like Thrushes

Stiphornis (Forest Robin)
Brachypteryx (Shortwings)
Zeledonia (Wren-Thrush)
Namibornis (Thrush-Flycatcher)
Cercotrichas (Scrub Robins)
Pinarornis (Sooty Rock Chat)
Chaetops (Rufous Rock Jumper)
Drymodes (Scrub Robins)
Pogonocichla (Bush Robins)
Erithacus (Eurasian Robin)
Sheppardia (Akalats)
Luscinia (Nightingales, Bluethroats etc.)
Tarsiger (Bluetail)
Cossypha (Robin-Chats)
Modulatrix (Spot-Throat)
Cichladusa (Morning Warblers)
Alethe (Forest Robins)
Copsychus (Magpie-Robins or Shamas)
Irania (White-throated Robin)

Phoenicurus (Redstarts)
Rhyacornis (Water Redstarts)
Hodgsonius (Hodgson's Shortwing)
Cinclidium (Blue Robins)
Grandala
Sialia (North American Bluebirds)
Enicurus (Forktails)
Cochoa
Myadestes (Solitaires)
Entomodestes (Solitaires)
Phaeornis (Hawaiian Thrushes)
Neocossyphus (Ant-Thrushes)
Cercomela (Desert or Rock Chats)
Saxicola (Small Chats)
Chaimarrornis (White-capped Water Redstart)
Myrmecocichla (Sooty Chats)
Oenanthe (Wheatears)
Saxicoloides (Indian Robin)
Pseudocossyphus (Madagascar Robin-Chat)

True Thrushes

Monticola (Rock Thrushes)
Myiophoneus (Whistling Thrushes)
Geomalia (Celebes Mountain Thrush)
Cataponera (Cataponera Thrush)
Amalocichla (New Guinea Thrush)
Zoothera (Ground Thrushes)
Nesocichla (Starchy)
Cichlherminia (Forest Thrush)

Catharus (Nightingale Thrushes)
Platycichla (Yellow-legged and Pale-eyed Thrushes)
Turdus (65 sp: 5 species breed regularly in British Isles and a sixth erratically. The two scarcest of the British breeders are also winter visitors and passage migrants. Five others have also occurred as vagrants or stragglers)

Table 2 above is revised from Dr S. Dillon Ripley's synoptic examination of the *Turdinae*. Not all taxonomists have agreed with his findings. Derek Goodwin (1957) believed that there was no justification for putting the water redstarts in the genus *Phoenicurus* or the single species *Pinarochroa sordida* in *Cercomela*, or *Platycichla flavipes* in *Turdus*. Edward S. Gruson (1976) did not retain *Turdus sibiricus* but he was not a taxonomist and I have done so as current British literature knows the Siberian thrush by that name. Dr C. G. Sibley (1968) has shown that comparisons of the electrophoretic pattern of egg-white proteins of the wren-thrush *Zeledonia coronata* with most other groups of passerine birds indicate that this species is not a thrush but possibly a member of the wood warblers (*Parulidae*).

Further conclusions will depend not only on such traditional considerations as external morphology and internal anatomy, cytology and tissue analysis, but also on the ecology, behaviour, voice and parasites of the living bird.

Table 3. Popular and Vernacular Names of the British Breeding Thrush Species

	Latin name	English popular names	French name	German name	Swedish name	Dutch name
MISTLE THRUSH	Turdus viscivorus	Missel-bird, Screech, Holm Screech, Shrite, Stormcock, Swine-Throstle, Norman Gizer, Mavish	Grive draine	Misteldrossel	Dubbeltrast	Grote lijster
SONG THRUSH	Turdus philomelos	Throstle, Tross-el, Mavi, Mavis, Mavish, Grey Bird, Whistling Thrush, Whistling Dick	Grive musicienne	Singdrossel	Taltrast	Zanglijster
BLACKBIRD	Turdus merula	Ouzel, Black Ouzel, Black Drush, Colly	Merle noir	Amsel	Koltrast	Merel
RING OUZEL	Turdus torquatus	Rock Ouzel, Tor Ouzel, Fell Ouzel, Moor or Mountain Blackbird	Merle à plastron	Ringdrossel	Ringtrast	Beflijster
REDWING	Turdus iliacus	Wind Thrush, Windle, Winnard	Grive mauvis	Rotdrossel	Rödvingetrast	Koperwiek
FIELDFARE	Turdus pilaris	Felf, Felfer, Felfer-bird, Felt, Pigeon Felt, Feltyfare, Bluebird, Blueback, Jack Bird	Grive litorne	Wacholderdrossel	Björktrast	Kramsvogel

	Latin name	English popular names	French name	German name	Swedish name	Dutch name
ROBIN	Erithacus rubecula	Redbreast, Redocke, Ruddock	Rouge-gorge	Rotkehlchen	Rödhake	Roodborst
NIGHTINGALE	Luscinia megarhynchos		Rossignol philomèle	Nachtigall	Sydlig näktergal	Nachtegaal
REDSTART	Phoenicurus phoenicurus	Firetail	Rouge-queue à front blanc	Gartenrotschwanz	Rödstjärt	Gekraagde roodstaart
BLACK REDSTART	Phoenicurus ochruros	Black Redtail	Rouge-queue noir	Hausrotschwanz	Svart rödstjäart	Zwarte roodstaart
WHINCHAT	Saxicola rubetra	Furzechat, Grasschat, Barkeyear	Tarier des prés	Braunkehlchen	Buskskvätta	Paapje
STONECHAT	Saxicola torquata	Furzechat, Blackcap	Tarier pâtre	Schwarzkehlchen	Svarthakad buskskvätta	Roodborsttapuit
WHEATEAR	Oenanthe oenanthe	Fallowchat, Chickell	Traquet motteux	Steinschmätzer	Stenskvätta	Tapuit

Table 4. The Genus *Turdus* and the Zoogeographical Regions of the World

Key: P=Palaearctic Region   N=Nearctic
      E=Ethiopian   T=Neotropical
      O=Oriental   C=Caribbean and Central America
      A=Australasian

Turdus abyssinicus	Rufous Thrush E
T. albicollis	White-necked Thrush TC
T. albocinctus	White-collared Blackbird PO
T. amaurochalinus	Creamy-bellied Thrush T
T. aurantius	White-chinned Thrush C
T. bewsheri	Comoro Thrush E
T. boulboul	Grey-winged Blackbird O
T. camaronensis	Black-eared Ground Thrush E
T. cardis	Grey Thrush PO
T. celaenops	Seven Islands Thrush T
T. chiguanco	Chiguanco Thrush T
T. chrysolaus	Red-bellied Thrush PO
T. dissimilis	Black-breasted Thrush PO
T. falcklandii	Austral Thrush T
T. feae	Fea's Thrush PO
T. fischeri	Fischer's Thrush E
T. fulviventris	Chestnut-bellied Thrush T
T. fumigatus	Pale-vented Robin TC
T. fuscater	Great Thrush T
T. grayi	Clay-coloured Thrush T
T. gurneyi	Orange Ground Thrush E
T. haplochrous	Unicoloured Thrush T
T. ignobilis	Black-billed Thrush T
T. iliacus	Redwing PO
T. jamaicensis	White-eyed Thrush C
T. kessleri	Kessler's Thrush PO
T. lawrencii	Lawrence's Thrush T
T. leucomelas	Pale-breasted Thrush T
T. libonyanus	Kurrichane Thrush E
T. litsitsirupa	Ground-Scraper Thrush E
T. maranonicus	Maranon Thrush T
T. merula	Blackbird POA
T. migratorius	American Robin NC
T. mupinensis	Verraux's Song Thrush PO
T. naumanni	Dusky Thrush PO
T. nigrescens	Sooty Robin C
T. nigriceps	Slaty Thrush T
T. nudigenis	Bare-eyed Thrush TC
T. oberlaenderi	Congo Thrush E
T. obscurus	Eye-browed Thrush PO
T. olivaceofuscus	Olivaceous Thrush E

T. olivaceus	Olive Thrush E
T. olivater	Black-hooded Thrush T
T. pallidus	Pale Thrush PO
T. pelios	African Thrush E
T. philomelos	Song Thrush PEA
T. piaggiae	Abyssinian Ground Thrush E
T. pilaris	Fieldfare PON
T. plumbeus	Red-legged Thrush C
T. poliocephalus	Mountain Blackbird OA
T. princei	Grey Ground Thrush E
T. ravidus	Grand Cayman Thrush C
T. reevei	Plumbeous-backed Thrush T
T. rubrocanus	Grey-headed Thrush PO
T. ruficollis	Red-throated Thrush PO
T. rufitorques	Rufous-collared Robin C
T. rufiventris	Rufous-bellied Thrush T
T. rufopalliatus	Rufous-backed Robin C
T. serranus	Glossy-back Thrush TC
T. sibiricus	Siberian Thrush PO
T. swalesi	La Selle Thrush C
T. tephronotus	African Bare-eyed Thrush E
T. torquatus	Ring Ouzel PE
T. unicolor	Tickell's Thrush PO
T. viscivorus	Mistle Thrush PO

CHAPTER 2

SONG THRUSH AND MISTLE THRUSH

I T is probable that these two rather similar and common species with their single-toned backs and spotted breasts are most readily confused by the layman, especially as their habitats may overlap and both may be found quite close to human dwellings. Both species occur in orchards, parks and gardens as well as various kinds of woodland and open moor. However, in many suburban areas where these two thrushes can be found the blackbird is often the commonest turdine species. It seems clear that the genus as a whole is preadapted to take advantage of a number of man-made environments and several species have moved away from their original forest homes into man-made habitats.

The song thrush is perhaps the most familiar thrush in western Europe. It is about 23 cm long – the mistle thrush is 4 cm longer – weighs about 74 gm and its vital statistics lie within the following limits: wing 111–121 mm, tail 77–90, tarsus 31–35 and bill 20–23. It can be recognized by its 'warm brown' back and upper parts with perhaps a suggestion of a reddish-brown suffusion on the head. The rump and upper tail coverts are paler and rather more olive in colour. A faint line runs from the base of the bill over the eye and there is also a narrow pale orbital ring. The feathers around the ear are a buffish gold edged with dark brown. The chin varies in colour from pale cream to buff and there are dark streaks on the upper throat. The lower throat and upper part of the breast are a deep yellow-brown with black-brown spots, rounded and fan-shaped in the autumn and V-shaped in the spring through subtractive wear, which decrease in number and finally disappear from the white lower breast and belly. The upper part of the bill is blackish brown and there is a brown tip to the lower mandible. The legs and feet are a pearly flesh colour and the iris is dark brown. The tail feathers are reddish brown and the outermost ones are shorter than the rest. This plumage is acquired by an autumn moult and it may be of interest to note that the details which I have just given have been confirmed at the time of writing after my inspection of an adult which I saw fly straight into one of the picture windows in my house. Summer birds tend to look paler and greyer on the back and less well spotted below; this is due to the abrasion of the feathers through wear.

In flight the song thrush reveals a glowing golden underwing and, if this can be seen by an observer – and it is not easy! – it is a very useful diagnostic feature. It helps to distinguish it from the redwing with its chestnut-red

PLATE 3. MISTLE
THRUSHES. *Left*, a mistle
thrush at a sheltered nest-site
among ivy close to the trunk
of a hawthorn. *Below*, a pair
of mistle thrushes at a
common and much more
open site out on a bough
where the nest has been
decorated with wool.

PLATE 4. MISTLE THRUSHES. *Above*, an unusual nesting site in a baler in a farm courtyard with well-grown young. *Below*, mistle thrushes come to drink at a man-made pool in a wood.

flanks and underwing. The mistle thrush is larger and greyer and has white tips to its outer tail feathers and a whitish underwing; these features usually show up in flight and the tail is often spread out. The large and boldly marked fieldfare has a blue-grey rump as an important distinguishing mark.

I find the song thrush to be an alert, charming and graceful bird with a retiring and unassertive demeanour. Yet it seems that these very features have allowed the song thrush or 'mavis' to be dominated by other members of the genus and to have held it back in its own struggle for survival. Song thrushes have a very upright stance and progress by a brisk run or a series of hops. Often they stand on our lawns with their heads cocked on one side as they look or listen for an earthworm near the surface. Their habit of using roads and stones as anvils to smash snails is well known. They fly in a very direct manner with little closure of their wings and they have been timed at around 48 kph. The mistle thrush appears to cruise at about 37 kph and it regularly closes its wings and dips in flight like the fieldfare.

The mistle thrush is a stout greyish bird. The chin and throat are buffish white with a small number of brownish wedge-shaped spots. The throat, upper breast and the rest of the underparts grade from yellowish-buff to whitish and are covered with large wedge-shaped spots becoming rounder towards the belly. The bill is a dark brown and the base of the lower mandible is yellowish in colour. The legs and feet are a pale yellowish brown and the iris is a darker brown. As in the song thrush the sexes have similar plumages. The adult is about 26·5 cm long with wing measurements falling within the limits of 145–164 mm, tail 100–117, tarsus 30–35 and bill 22–25. The full adult plumage is obtained by a complete moult between August and October. There is some variation between individuals in their plumage and one skin of a January bird in my collection shows considerable golden patches on the upper breast, flanks and along the edges of the secondaries which are certainly atypical.

The stance of the mistle thrush on the ground is also very upright with its head held well up and its tail kept down and sometimes flicked in a rather nervous fashion. It hops and runs well and behaves in a very much more assertive and confident way than its smaller relation. In the spring and summer it can be fearless in defence of its nest, launching prolonged attacks on predatory birds, cats, dogs and even man! William Yarrell in 1856 noted that, according to Pennant, the mistle thrush in Wales had acquired the name of Penn y Llwyn – 'the master of the copse'.

The mistle thrush has a very characteristic call – a harsh churring rattle. With the addition of some hoarse guttural croaks this is used as an excited scold which can reach a peak of intensity when the bird mobs an owl in daylight. A tape recording which I obtained in Berwickshire in October 1952 shows this very well. Other notes include a dry staccato

Table 5. Some Dimensions and Weights of Thrushes

SPECIES	Overall Length (App.)	DIMENSIONS (mm)					WEIGHT (gm)			
		Wing (♂)	Wing (♀)	Tail	Tarsus	Bill from Skull	Normal Range	Normal Mean	Low (starvation) Level Range	Low Mean
MISTLE THRUSH	265	143–164	143–162	100–117	30–35	22–25	95–130	118	66·7–76·7	72·0
SONG THRUSH	230	111–123	110–123	77–90	31–35	20–23 (Hebridean 22–24)	61–112	73·9	41·3–58·6	47·9
BLACKBIRD	255	116–135	118–128	95–110	32–34	23–27	75–140 male 83–134 female	92·7 108	51·9–79·3	64·3
RING OUZEL	240	134–150 (mean 141·2)	132–147 (mean 138·2)	101–110	33–35·5	23–25	88–125	107		
REDWING	207	111–122 (mean 116)	110–120 (mean 115)	76–85 (mean 79·9)	29–31	20–22	71–88	82	36·3–40·5	37·9
ICELAND REDWING	209	116–133 (mean 121·3)	120–128	mean 85·2	29–31	19–21	80–108	c. 86		
FIELDFARE	255	140–153	135–148	100–110	31–34	23–24·5	90–126	96–98	58·7–60·0	58·1

Compiled from *The Handbook of British Birds* (1946), Williamson (1957), P. Hope Jones (1962), Harris (1962), Ash (1964), and Batten, Durman, Spence and Simms (unpublished).

'Tuck-tuck-tuck' used in the breeding season and the effect of each note is emphasized by a jerk of the wing and the fanned tail. There is a sharp scream of distress but I have not heard the redwing-like 'seeih' which is reported in *The Handbook of British Birds*. The song thrush has a loud 'Tchuck-tchuck' note, which is less full bodied and higher in pitch than a similar note used by the blackbird, but it can be worked up into quite an alarm rattle. This call can be shortened to a 'Tchick' or 'Tic'. I have heard it in courtship and at roosting time and sometimes from individuals in dense vegetation, where the significance has not always been apparent. The song thrush also has a short 'Tsipp' flight call. I have heard this note from many night migrants and find it shorter and less 'wavy' than the flight call of the redwing but care is needed in separating the two species in flight. I have handled very many song thrushes and a proportion of them give the distress call – a high-pitched wavering scream – the same sound that I have heard when a short-eared owl has plucked a migrant song thrush out of the beams of the old Dungeness lighthouse.

In their songs the two species are very different. The song thrush has a territorial outpouring of simple clearly enunciated and musical notes and phrases delivered with vivacity, application and reiteration. Each note formed from several syllables is usually repeated a number of times but it is possible for a male to give only two repeats in eighty-five phrases. Mimicry may also occur in song thrushes. The mistle thrush has, on the other hand, a loud wild song of short stereotyped phrases, limited in originality and variety and repeated from fourteen to twenty-one times a minute – 'Tee-aw-tee-aw-tee' and so on. It carries for a greater distance

Male song thrush **in full territorial song**

than the notes of the song thrush and may be given from a high storm-tossed bough since the singer favours high song posts in trees. Both birds also sing a quieter, inward sub-song and this, and their territorial songs, will be examined in more detail in chapter 8.

FIG. 1. The breeding range of the song thrush. The dotted line marks southern limits of the wintering range.

The song thrush breeds over a wide area of Eurasia (Fig. 1). It is an abundant breeding species in the British Isles but it nests only occasionally in Shetland. There seems to have been something of a decline since about 1940 due perhaps to a succession of cold winters. Figure 2 shows the distribution in the British Isles. The song thrush is a bird of woodlands with a good shrub layer, thickets, hedgerows, parks and gardens but it may also appear in treeless districts. The Hebridean song thrush (*Turdus philomelos hebridensis*) is confined to the Outer Hebrides and the Isle of Skye where it lives on heather moors, in sheltered glens, and even by the seashore, but it comes closer to human habitations in the winter. This race is somewhat darker and more thickly spotted than the typical race and its notes seem perhaps softer, but I have found it difficult to identify in the field. Populations in the Inner Hebrides and other areas in western Scotland and Kerry seem to be intermediate between this race and *T. p. clarkei* which is found typically in the rest of the British Isles, northern and western France and southern Holland. The remainder of the song thrushes in France, southern and central Europe north to Germany and Denmark, south towards the Mediterranean and east to Czechoslovakia, the northern parts of Greece, Rumania and Bulgaria are themselves intermediate between *T. p. clarkei* and *T. p. philomelos* which breeds in almost all the rest of the range east

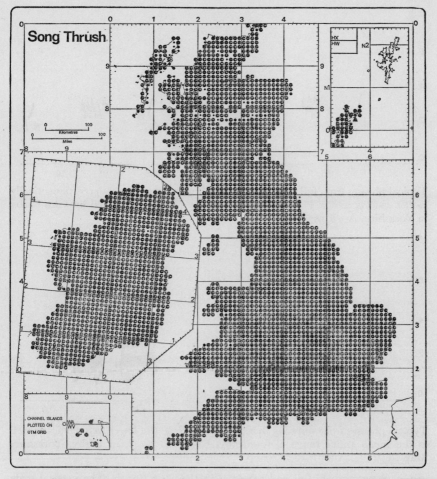

FIG. 2. The breeding range in the British Isles (on 10km Square Grid) of the song thrush. Large dots indicate confirmed breeding, medium dots probable breeding, and small dots possible breeding. (From *Atlas of Breeding Birds in Britain*, B.T.O./I.W.C. Updated to 1975.)

to Iran and Siberia. Both sub-species are rather sedentary. In autumn many Continental song thrushes appear in Britain on passage and from observations and some ringing studies it seems that some may remain for the winter. They seem shyer than our residents and to have greyer plumage but this may be a subjective opinion.

The mistle thrush has a somewhat similar breeding distribution to the song thrush but it reaches further south to the Mediterranean and North

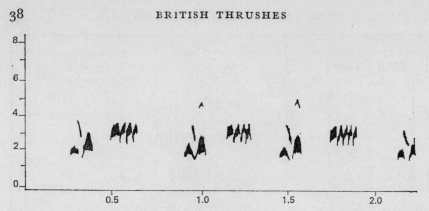

Typical phrases from full song of song thrush which can be rendered phonetically *tu-ittee, tu-ittee, tu-ittee.* Note the extreme purity of tone. Recorded by John Kirby in Yorkshire, April 1956.

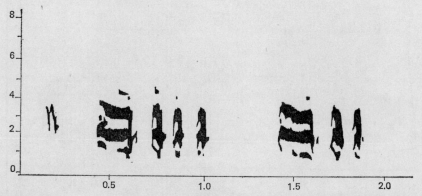

Typical phrases from sub-song of song thrush. Note the lower frequencies as well as the much wider range of frequency. Recorded by John Kirby, Yorkshire, May 1954.

FIG. 3. Sonagrams of full and sub-song in the song thrush. The vertical scale represents frequency in kHz; the horizontal time in seconds. (Reproduced from *British Birds*, Vol 51, 1958, by permission of Professor W. H. Thorpe.)

Africa and is established in Iran, Afghanistan and northern Baluchistan (Fig. 4). *Turdus viscivorus viscivorus* breeds throughout most of this range but there are distinct populations in north-west Africa (*T. v. deichleri*), the southern Crimea and Asia. In the southern part of its range the mistle thrush is a bird of mountain woodlands but it also occupies similar habitats to those of the song thrush. It particularly favours open woods and well-timbered parklands but can also be found in comparatively treeless regions. It is a numerous and widespread bird in the British

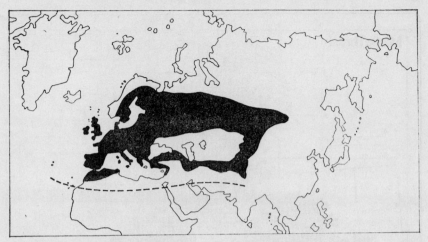

FIG. 4. The breeding range of the mistle thrush. The dotted line marks southern limits of the wintering range.

Isles. Figure 5 gives the distribution. It has greatly increased in numbers since about 1800. The movement by mistle thrushes from woodlands into parks, gardens, cultivated land and even city centres has been matched by similar trends on the Continent where the bird now shares the same habitats with song thrushes and blackbirds. The British population shows flocking tendencies in late summer, when birds gather in small numbers on farms and grassland, but it is primarily sedentary. However, British-ringed first-year birds have been recovered in France and Belgium (Snow 1969) (Fig. 40) and because of the lack of recovered ringed European birds it is not possible to say how many birds may come to Britain in the autumn and return in the spring – if, in fact, they do.

Despite its spread into new habitats and the widening of its range the mistle thrush's population density has remained low and even in apparently suitable regions the breeding density has failed to reach one-tenth that of song thrushes and blackbirds. In suburban Dollis Hill where I live the proportion of pairs in an area of 546 acres, or 202 hectares, is in the ratio of 1 pair of mistle thrushes to 12 pairs of song thrushes and 180 pairs of blackbirds (Fig. 32). We do not know why this should be because the bird appears in a wide variety of habitats. In an oakwood in Northamptonshire I found a proportion of 1 pair of mistle thrushes to 12 of song thrushes and 36 of blackbirds, while Wallace (1974) found the proportion on average in Regent's Park in London between 1959 and 1968 to be $1:6\frac{1}{2}:18\frac{1}{2}$. As Dr David Snow said in 1969 the mistle thrush 'remains a rather unknown, almost mysterious bird'. Certainly its comparatively

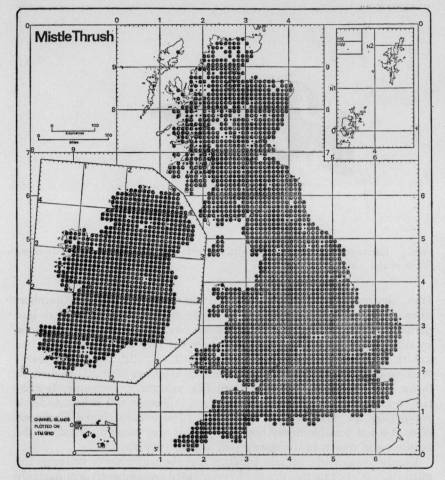

FIG. 5. The breeding range in the British Isles (on 10km Square Grid) of the mistle thrush. Large dots indicate confirmed breeding, medium dots probable breeding, and small dots possible breeding. (From *Atlas of Breeding Birds in Britain*, B.T.O./I.W.C. Updated to 1975.)

low numbers are nothing new having been commented on by Yarrell, Sir William Jardine and others in the nineteenth century. It seems to need a large home range and so few territories can be fitted into a given area. It is perhaps the absence of a staple winter food supply that is responsible for migration among mistle thrushes which were perhaps once sedentary in their habits. In some years the remaining residents may be at an advantage while in others it may be the partial migrants.

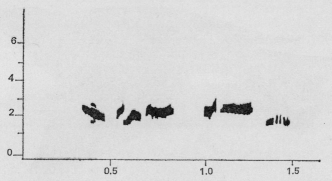

Typical phrases from full song of mistle thrush somewhat in the phonetic form *tee-aw-tee-taw-tee*. The notes are characteristically pure. Recorded by Eric Simms in Kent, March 1954.

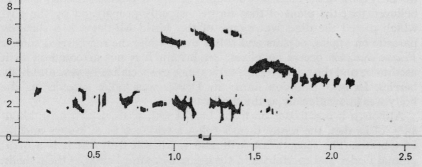

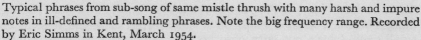

Typical phrases from sub-song of same mistle thrush with many harsh and impure notes in ill-defined and rambling phrases. Note the big frequency range. Recorded by Eric Simms in Kent, March 1954.

FIG. 6. Sonagrams of full and sub-song in the mistle thrush. The vertical scale represents frequency in kHz; the horizontal time in seconds. (Reproduced from *British Birds*, Vol 51, 1958, by permission of Professor W. H. Thorpe.)

Most song and mistle thrushes in northern and central Europe migrate for the winter while those in the west and south tend much more to remain in their breeding areas. Among the migrants birds from different breeding populations tend to gather in different areas and are likely to be pre-adapted to the local conditions that they find in their winter quarters. In France mistle thrushes can survive quite long cold spells if there is an adequate supply of mistletoe berries available. The name of the birds is, of course, derived from their habit of feeding on the berries. Gilbert White described this behaviour in 1788 and Thomas Bewick in 1797 reported that the mistle thrush, or shrite, 'feeds on various kinds of berries, par-

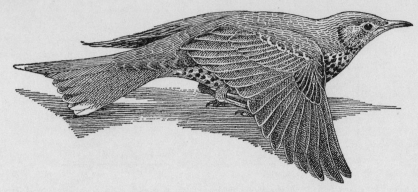

Mistle thrush in display showing white tips to fanned tail

ticularly those of the mistletoe, of which bird-lime is made. It was formerly believed that the plant of that name was only propagated by the seed which passed the digestive organs of this bird.' Mistletoe is a shrubby parasite on apples, poplars and other trees, while the red-berried species *Viscum cruciatum* occurs on olives. In Britain it is not as common as it used to be and the mistle thrush now seems to specialize in yew and holly berries. Its once common name in Devon was 'holm screech' as the holly was known locally as the 'holm tree'.

Although it is a feeder on fruit, berries and seeds, which form about 45% of its diet, the mistle thrush takes a wide range of insects and invertebrates. The song thrush will also relish soft fruit but it is a great animal feeder and specializes in taking snails, after breaking their shells. T. A. Coward (1920) writing about the mistle thrush noted that 'like the Song Thrush, it smashes snails on a stone anvil'. Although it feeds on small snails I have not once observed the use of an anvil in over forty years of watching. There are ecological differences between the closely allied species of thrush and their food and feeding habits will form the subject of chapter 7.

It is not too difficult to separate these two thrushes by their appearance and voice. As one becomes familiar with them there are differences in habitat and behaviour which begin to reveal themselves. The song thrush may be shy but it is less wary than the mistle thrush in winter. It can often be seen in the company of blackbirds on the grass, looking for worms but remaining close to evergreen or other thick cover to which it will return if danger threatens. It is not as noisy as its larger relation which favours tall trees and big expanses of grass rather than the shrubs and understory which attract the song thrush. When disturbed or alarmed the mistle thrush seeks the shelter of large trees or in open country takes to flight. It is often amongst the tallest trees that it selects its favourite song posts.

CHAPTER 3

BLACKBIRD AND RING OUZEL

In the northern Pennines is a rough hillside where more than thirty years ago I used to watch both blackbirds and ring ouzels living and nesting alongside each other. In this habitat shared by the two species of thrush, which are the subjects of this chapter, I found it was necessary to see each bird on its nest before being sure in my own mind to which species the nest and eggs belonged. Fortunately, each is sufficiently different in appearance and voice for identification, although one must beware of the occasional partially albinistic blackbird which sports a white collar and bears a superficial resemblance to the ring ouzel. Their basic breeding areas may also be sufficiently different for an observer to be fairly confident of his identification. The ring ouzel is a summer visitor to Britain and Ireland, and south-west Asia, and has a discontinuous distribution in the mountainous areas of Europe. On migration it may be seen passing through many regions. Gilbert White, who was greatly intrigued by the annual movements of ring ouzels on the sheep downs above Selborne, found them both 'very tame' and 'most punctual' arriving on passage about 13 April and 30 September each year.

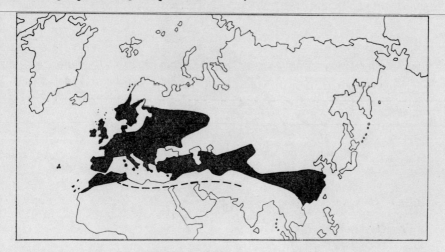

FIG. 7. The breeding range of the blackbird. The dotted line marks southern limits of the wintering range.

The blackbird is a common species in the British Isles, where there may well be ten million pairs. From a grand total of birds that I counted in nearly three hundred British and Irish woods I found that it was the fourth most abundant bird. It favours many kinds of habitat from deep woodland to hills and rocky coasts and is particularly well known to man.

The adult male blackbird is quite distinctive – the only all-black bird of Europe with a golden yellow bill. In fact, its plumage is a sooty black, glossy in character but quite without the iridescence of other black birds such as ravens and crows. The inner margin of the wing feathers is greyish in colour. This plumage is attained through a moult late in the year and the wings of some summer blackbirds show up brown through wear and tear. The length of the bird is about 25 cm putting it halfway between the song and mistle thrushes. The ring ouzel is a centimetre or so shorter. The other outstanding feature of the blackbird's appearance was noted by Shakespeare; in his time the bird was known as 'the ouzel' or 'ousel',

> The ousel cock so black of hue
> With orange tawny bill.

This showy bill is acquired during the bird's first winter. The legs and feet as well as the iris are dark brown in colour and the eyelid is also yellow. The length of most males' wings can vary from 117–134 mm, of the tail from 95 to 110, the tarsus 32–34 and the bill 23–27. The ring ouzel has somewhat longer wings.

Male blackbird in full territorial song

The female blackbird is a dark brown on the back of the head and the mantle but blacker on the back and rump. Hens from the southern parts of the European range seem to be greyer and darker in plumage. The chin is pale grey, the throat buffish-grey with streaks and the breast and under-parts an earthy brown with a number of unclear dark spots. The wing length tends on average to be a little shorter than that of the male. Normal males weigh about 95 gm in summer and females a little less but the limits can vary from about 75 to 140 gm. From July the juvenile black-birds of the year start to moult into their first but not finally complete adult plumage. The males have browner wings and the young females tend to carry paler, more reddish underparts but there can be considerable variation among them. We shall look again at the various plumages of the blackbird and other thrushes in chapter 6.

The adult male ring ouzel, or moorland blackbird as it has sometimes been called, is easily identified and separated from the male blackbird by the white crescent on its breast. Its plumage is also sooty black but each feather bears a greyish brown fringe and the secondaries and coverts have clear greyish edges and these fringes give the closed wing a much paler look; this is a useful guide in all plumages. With the white gorget, pale wing and different voice the ring ouzel can soon be recognized. The male's bill is yellowish and brighter in summer with a brownish black ridge and tip; the legs and feet are brown. The wing length lies between the limits 132–150 mm – rather longer than that of the blackbird, but in overall length the ring ouzel is shorter at 24 cm. The tail length varies from 101–110 mm, the tarsus from 33–35·5 and the bill 23–25 mm. The measure-ments of the female's wing are slightly shorter – between 132 and 147 mm.

The female ring ouzel is browner in colour than the male. The edges to the feathers on her upper parts are broader and browner while the feathers on the underparts have broader, whiter fringes; she therefore looks a paler bird in the field. The crescent on her breast is narrower and very much tinged with brown. Young females in their first autumn and winter may show little of the gorget but young males bear a resemblance to the adults.

Since both blackbird and ring ouzel generally occupy different habitats – perhaps the result of earlier competition – they tend to overlap only in certain fringe regions such as farm pastures and areas where the hill wood or plantation reaches up to the open moor, or perhaps when the summer-visiting ring ouzels are on their migration. The blackbird is very much a bird of cover, flying noisily into trees and shrubs when disturbed or frightened. It tends to keep low in a weak, rather undulating flight with barely any visible closing of the wings. High-flying migrants which I have watched usually demonstrated the wing closure in a slightly more obvious manner. On alighting the blackbird raises and fans its tail in a rather leisurely and relaxed way. The ring ouzel, on the other hand, has a more bold and rapid flight, suited to its wild and hilly home, with the bird flashing down the gullies, dipping low over the rocks and disappearing from sight as rapidly as possible. Anyone who has tried to watch ring ouzels knows how well they can take evasive action of this kind! As a ring ouzel lands on a rock face or boulder it often fans out its tail. The commoner of the two species also lowers its wings and if disturbed will flick its wings and tail nervously up and down; these movements are in my opinion much less marked in the mountain blackbird. But the ring ouzel is bouncy, spirited and very adventurous! Ring ouzels are generally shy and difficult to approach but, as Yarrell reported, they are 'bold and clamorous near the nest'. I have not been physically attacked by them, as C. Oldham once experienced, but they will readily and bravely take on some of the larger birds of prey after the manner of mistle thrushes.

On the ground the blackbird is less upright than the song and mistle thrushes with its tail carried lower and often parallel to the ground or even at a rising angle from it. It is alert and active and on the lawn can often be seen running or hopping, with each activity alternately employed as the bird hunts for earthworms. It is also a great 'tiffler' among leaf litter and dead grass, using both its bill and feet in short forward runs or more statically to turn over the dead vegetation. The ring ouzel is somewhat similar in its habits on the ground and I have come across the birds foraging among the grass and plants along the edges of mountain streams. It is essentially a bird of the open spaces of the wilder and more mountainous parts of the British Isles and frequently perches on exposed rocks. On migration when it is searching for berries it can be seen in trees and bushes; Gilbert White recorded a party 'haunting with the missel thrushes, and feeding on the berries of the yew tree' and I have also seen birds on brambles on the east coast of England. Birds may even occur in suburban areas and in recent years migrants have been seen in the outskirts of London.

The blackbird is often a very noisy bird – much more so than the song thrush with which it shares many of its habitats. There appear to be some seven call notes, in addition to the song and sub-song, which it requires for everyday life. One of the most regularly used is a low 'Tchook-tchook-tchook', given with the bill closed, which indicates a state of nervousness or mild alarm, and is used by both sexes. About one in ten of the females that have nested in a thick bush in my garden over a period of twenty-five years has used it both when building the nest and also approaching the site during incubation and feeding the young. The habit would seem to be biologically disadvantageous to the individual by attracting predators. Dr David Snow (1958) has pointed out that blackbirds will use this call in strange situations – 'for instance when searching for food in an enclosed space such as a balcony or back-yard, or in any place which involves an element of insecurity'. A hen feeding week-old young in my

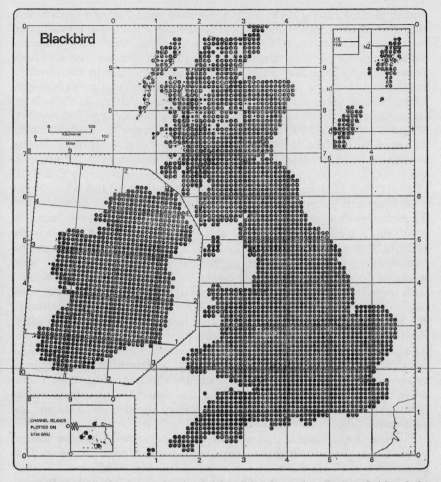

FIG. 8. The breeding range in the British Isles (on 10km Square Grid) of the blackbird. Large dots indicate confirmed breeding, medium dots probable breeding, and small dots possible breeding. (From *Atlas of Breeding Birds in Britain*, B.T.O./I.W.C. Updated to 1975.)

garden lost her mate and used the 'Tchook-tchook' call persistently without a break for three whole days. A musical variant of this call is used to give warning of the presence of a ground predator, especially a cat or even a human. Fledglings acknowledge this call by freezing and keeping silent.

The second well-known blackbird call is a very persistent 'Mik-mik-mik-mik', sometimes called 'chinking'. It is slightly metallic and rather higher pitched among males. It is a common sound among birds before they go to roost, at dawn and in the very excited mobbing and scolding of owls and cats. C. Chappuis (1969) has shown that this note gets appreciably deeper in pitch the further to the south the birds are found in their normal range. Thus the call is lower in Morocco than in the north of France and there is a cline of deepening notes in the regions in between. Chappuis has argued that the deeper calls travel further in those large territories which blackbirds occupy in the less densely crowded habitats of Spain or North Africa. I am not convinced that the lower-pitched calls do travel better. The 'Mik-mik' call reveals a raised level of aggression in the bird but a low drive towards attack. It may subside, as the situation improves, to the 'Tchook-tchook' call or it can rise in intensity to a shrill alarm rattle with a screaming crescendo, when the bird has been caught unawares, and punctuated at the end by a few 'Tchook-tchook' calls. There is also an aggressive 'seeee' given by both sexes with the beak just open; this is high-pitched, piercing and lasts about a second. In his study of blackbirds at Oxford Dr David Snow (1958) found that 'When the circumstances have been known, aggressive "seee" calls have always been uttered by combative and usually dominant birds in situations connected with the taking up and maintenance of territory'. Consequently, this note can be heard most regularly from January to June and in the autumn. Blackbirds will also employ another thin 'seee' note, but lower in pitch this time, with a pure tone and indefinite start and finish; it is used in the presence of an aerial predator but by its nature the call does not reveal the exact position of a blackbird, crouched and waiting, to its enemy. Other passerines use alarm calls which are similarly difficult to locate when hawks are about. Like Dr Snow I have found that woodland blackbirds seem to use this type of call quite often when their nests are approached.

Blackbirds also have a distress call – a high-pitched repeated scream which might possibly distract a predator, but rarely seems to do so. It is given when a bird is taken by a hawk and it is very familiar to all of us who have trapped, handled and ringed blackbirds. Birds caught in mistnets may scream together and this might confuse a predator trying to take one of the captured birds. We have seen in the last chapter that song thrushes have a similar distress call. Finally, there is a low-pitched 'Tseerk' call, used by birds in flight, including migrants, and by subordinate birds during the period in which territories are being taken up.

The ring ouzel has two familiar calls. The first is a clear piping 'Peeoo' – the basis of the song; it is shrill and very characteristically a thrush's note. There is also a sharp alarm – 'Tac-tac' or 'Tuc-tuc'. This is rather metallic and a little blackbird-like but it is deeper and mellower. To me this chat-like note is reminiscent of that of a wheatear. I have heard a chuckling rattle – 'Tchook-tchook-tchuc' – many times and this is

PLATE 5. BLACKBIRDS. *Above*, a male blackbird in characteristic stance with the yellow bill and orbital ring of its breeding plumage. *Below*, a male blackbird at a typical nest-site with downy young.

PLATE 6. BLACKBIRDS.
Above, the female blackbird
has distinct mottlings and a
paler throat than the male
but there is often wide
variation in colour. *Right*, a
female blackbird incubates
in a rather open site; there is
a deep foundation of mud to
the nest.

Ring ouzel pair in courtship display

sometimes elaborated and included in the song. This chuckle is well
illustrated by Sveriges Radio's recording of a Scandinavian bird. The
alarm, leading to flight in many cases, is a trilling 'Tchurree' and this can
be heard from birds on passage as well. This is presumably the call
described by the late Professor M. F. M. Meiklejohn, and reported in
The Handbook of British Birds, as resembling that of a dunlin but shorter
and harsher. Ring ouzels will also chase crows and ravens and utter a
fast screech.

The finest song of all the British thrushes is delivered by the blackbird
with its fluent and beautiful fluty notes, spoiled sometimes by a poor and
scratchy ending. For me it is the epitome of summer in a woodland glade
or a dusty suburban street. The notes flow in an easy continuous warble
lasting from two to eight seconds. They are mellower, more liquid and
generally lower in pitch than those of the song and mistle thrushes. The
sub-song is a quiet inward warble and together with the blackbird's song
will be examined fully in chapter 8.

The male ring ouzel has a simple fluting song formed from the loud
piping notes which are repeated from two to four times with a clear
interval between each. I have rendered the song of one bird in northern
England as 'Tchouee-tchouee-tchouee' and another in Ireland as 'Ter-
WEE, ter-WEE, ter-WEE' and there are many variations on the pipe.
Sometimes the fluty phrases are interspersed with the weaker, chuckling
notes that I described earlier in the chapter.

Blackbirds can be found breeding across the western and southern
Palaearctic and marginally into the Oriental Region; some of these birds
winter to the south (Fig. 7). *Turdus merula merula* breeds in the greater
part of the European area from the British Isles and Iberia as far as the
Urals in Russia but not in southern Russia and the Balkans. Migratory

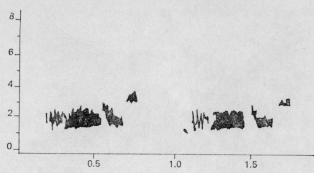

Typical phrases from full song of the blackbird. They can be represented phonetically as the syllables *tll-ew, tll-ui*. Note the fairly pure tone fundamental frequencies of the characteristic notes, restricted within a narrow range. Recorded by Eric Simms at Dollis Hill, London, April 1957.

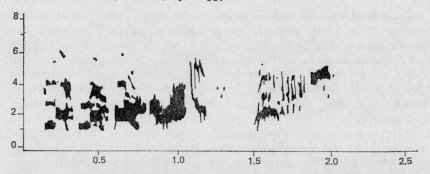

Typical phrases from sub-song of the same individual as above. The notes are impure, harsh-sounding and both higher and lower than those of the full range. Recorded by Eric Simms at Dollis Hill, April 1957.

FIG. 9. Sonagrams of full and sub-song in the blackbird. The vertical scale represents frequency in kHz; the horizontal time in seconds. (Reproduced from *British Birds*, Vol 51, 1958, by permission of Professor W. H. Thorpe.)

birds of *T. t. merula* winter south to the Mediterranean area and southeast Russia. There are other races in Madeira and the Canaries (*T. t. cabrerae*), the Azores (*T. m. azorensis*), southern Morocco to southern Tunisia (*T. m. mauritanicus*), the Balkans, Crete, the Crimea and Asia Minor (*T. m. aterrimus*) and across Asia from Syria and Israel to Mongolia and China. Birds which can be found in the north of the range and in mountainous regions are larger in size. As we have seen already, the blackbird is a bird of forested regions, parks and gardens, but it can also be found on islands and even desert palm oases. In the mountains it reaches the treeline and in the Himalayas, as Dr K. H. Voous (1960) has shown, the blackbird occurs in habitats 'which in the Caucasus and in the European mountains would be occupied only by the Ring Ouzel'. Similar habitats in North America and Japan to those filled by the blackbird are taken over by the American robin (*T. migratorius*) and the red-bellied thrush (*T. chrysolaus*) respectively.

FIG. 10. The breeding range of the ring ouzel. The dotted line marks southern limits of the wintering range.

The ring ouzel has a more restricted world range being a bird of the western Palaearctic with a scattered boreal-alpine distribution. It occurs in the summer most frequently in mountainous regions and less often on sea coasts and coastal islands (Fig. 10). It seems probable that the ring ouzel was originally a mountain bird but the ice sheets forced it to live at lower levels on the tundra. As the ice retreated, the tundra and steppes of central Europe were divided up into a northward moving region of tundra and dwarf shrubs and a zone of alpine meadows and scrub travelling into the higher mountain ranges. As a result the populations of ring ouzels became separated, leading eventually to the appearance of the northern and alpine sub-species. The northern sub-species *T. t. torquatus* breeds in the British Isles and Fenno-Scandia while the Alpine ring ouzel *T. t. alpestris* can be found nesting in the mountains of northern Spain, France, Italy across to the Balkans. *T. t. amicorum* breeds from eastern Turkey and the Caucasus across to Transcaspia and northern Iran. Both these races have very pale wings but *T. t. amicorum* has even more white on the fringes of the wing feathers and the greater coverts. The Alpine ring ouzel is a bird that I have seen on lightly wooded mountain slopes where it breeds among the firs and spruces. Its song is rather different and perhaps more powerful.

The blackbird is an abundant breeding species in the British Isles (Fig. 8). It has spread out of its early-nineteenth-century woodland home into farmland, gardens, cities and towns. It can live in a great variety of habitats. The ring ouzel is widely distributed on the hills and moorlands

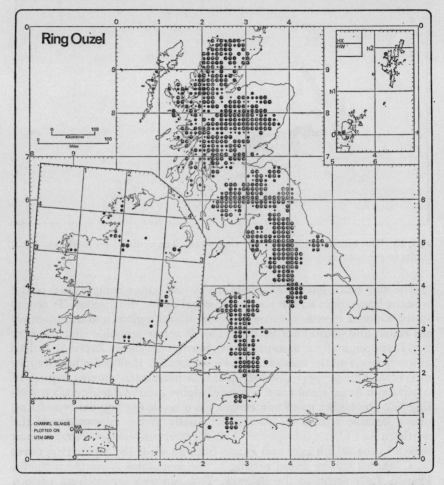

FIG. 11. The breeding range in the British Isles (on 10km Square Grid) of the ring ouzel. Large dots indicate confirmed breeding, medium dots probable breeding, and small dots possible breeding. (From *Atlas of Breeding Birds in Britain,* B.T.O./I.W.C. Updated to 1975.)

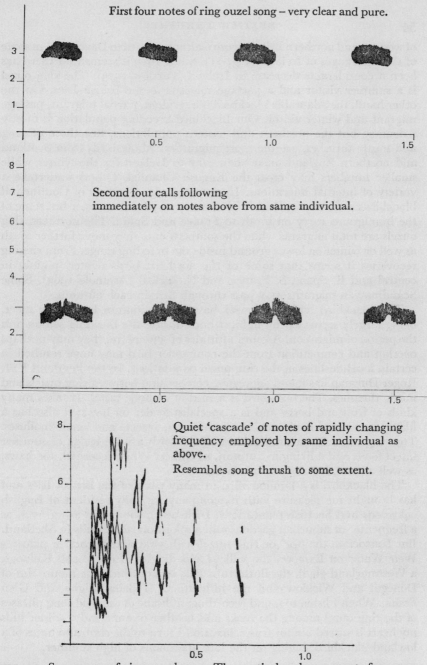

FIG. 12. Sonagrams of ring ouzel song. The vertical scale represents frequency in kHz; the horizontal time in seconds. All recordings made by Richard Savage on Dartmoor, June 1972. (Sonagrams specially prepared by Joan Hall-Craggs.)

of western and northern Britain from Caithness south to Devon and in some of the hill ranges of Ireland (Fig. 11). Since 1900 it seems that there has been a considerable decrease in Ireland (Parslow 1973). The ring ouzel is a summer visitor and a passage migrant to the British Isles. On the other hand, the adaptable blackbird is a resident, partial migrant, passage migrant and winter visitor. Our blackbird breeding population is mostly sedentary but the northern and eastern populations, like those of song and mistle thrushes, are the most migratory. Many birds from Scotland and northern England make their way to Ireland for the winter while smaller numbers may cross the English Channel. Others undertake a variety of internal migrations. In autumn large numbers of Continental blackbirds arrive in the British Isles, many stay for the winter but some of the immigrants carry on south to France and Spain. The northern ring ouzels are total migrants while the southern ones may move further south as well or winter on lower ground inside the breeding range. From ringing recoveries it seems that some of the northern birds winter 'mainly in central and E. Spain, S. France and N. Africa' (Ashmole 1962). Some Scandinavian migrants may pass through Britain each autumn.

The blackbird and ring ouzel have close affinities but rarely meet, being largely separated by habitat both during the breeding season and the period of migration. Around altitudes of 330 metres they may perhaps overlap and competition from the commoner bird may have resulted in certain local declines in the ring ouzel populations. In the Pentland Hills Roger Durman has found aggressive competition between ring ouzels and mistle thrushes. The blackbird is a bird of catholic tastes. It takes many kinds of fruit and berry and is a specialist feeder on haws; it also has a liking for animal food such as earthworms, insects and small molluscs. The ring ouzel has a similar kind of diet with a wide range of summer insect foods and a liking in autumn, as Gilbert White recorded, for haws, as well as yew, ivy and mountain berries.

The blackbird is a familiar bird in many parts of the British Isles and has brought me pleasure with its company as a shy resident of English oakwoods and Scottish plantations, Irish beechwoods and ash groves, as a frequenter of suburban gardens and a soloist on stone walls in Shetland. But I associate the 'tor' or ring ouzel with wild and attractive places – Weir Water on Exmoor, the valleys and dingles of the Welsh Rhinogs, a Westmorland ghyll, the Buttertubs Pass in Yorkshire, the mountains of Donegal and Wicklow and the hilly tracts of Beinn Eighe and Glen Feshie. When I listen to sound recordings at home of the wild song phrases of the ring ouzel among the rocks and heather of our windy, wilder hills my heart is stirred but for true relaxation I turn to the contralto notes of a lowland blackbird singing on the late afternoons of high summer.

CHAPTER 4

REDWING AND FIELDFARE

FOR most of us who live in the British Isles the redwing and fieldfare are best known as winter visitors or birds of passage. Only a few observers have been privileged to see them as rare or very rare British breeding birds. I know them best as birds of open country, flying and dipping in loose flocks over the damp winter pasture fields or assembling to roost in some dense shrubbery or covert. But I have also seen redwings as tired migrants arriving in September and fieldfares as stout birds of passage flying over north-west London. In January 1963 I was able with a BBC Television Film Unit to obtain shots for the news programme *Town and Around* of both redwings and fieldfares feeding on cotoneaster berries at the White City Station in London only a few feet from passing Central Line tube trains; these cold weather visitors stayed for several days and others came to feed in the snow on apples in my own garden at Dollis Hill.

The redwing looks rather like a small song thrush and at 21 cm in length it is, in fact, some two centimetres shorter. It is the smallest common European thrush and is somewhat darker on the back than most song thrushes. It can be recognized by the conspicuous and clear creamy white eye-stripe and the chestnut-red flanks and underwing. The upper parts

Redwing in characteristic stance on ground

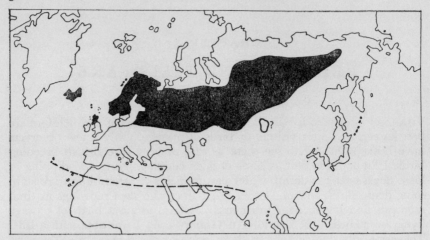

FIG. 13. The breeding range of the redwing. The dotted line marks southern limits of the wintering range.

are a warm darkish brown in colour; the ear coverts are even darker and have buff centres. The chin is whitish and sometimes streaked, the sides of the throat are heavily streaked, the whitish breast carries brown-tipped feathers and the belly is white. The underparts are streaked, not spotted. This plumage, which is common to both sexes, is acquired by a late summer moult.

The wing of the male redwing of the typical race lies normally between 113 and 119 mm in length. Many of the redwings coming to Britain for the winter have journeyed from Scandinavia but others come from Iceland. *Turdus iliacus iliacus* breeds from Scotland east across Russia and Siberia (Fig. 13). These birds winter in southern Norway, the British Isles, southern and central Europe, Asia Minor, Iran, the Mediterranean area and some even reach the Canary Islands and Madeira. *T. i. coburni* is restricted as a breeding bird to Iceland and the Faeroes. It comes as a winter visitor to the Hebrides, north-west Scotland and Ireland but some remain in Icelandic towns (Gudmundsson 1951).

The Iceland redwing is somewhat larger and darker than the typical race from Scandinavia. Many Iceland birds have longer wings – up to 133 mm – but there is some considerable overlap between the races and their wings may be as short as 116 mm. Kenneth Williamson (1951), who had had vast experience of Iceland redwings on Fair Isle, felt that it is undesirable to try and separate the races in the field. As a general guide he has suggested that any bird which shows the following features has a reasonable chance of being an Iceland bird: a strong olive wash on the sides of the flanks and breast, diffused spotting on the upper breast, a strong buffish suffusion over the lighter parts of the head and breast, under tail coverts with olive-brown centres and horn-brown legs rather than flesh-brown or flesh-pink. The bill is blackish brown and the iris dark brown in both races.

In its general behaviour the redwing resembles the song thrush but its delicate darker form helps to distinguish it. It moves in a typical thrush-like way with short runs or a series of hops followed by a pause. The red-

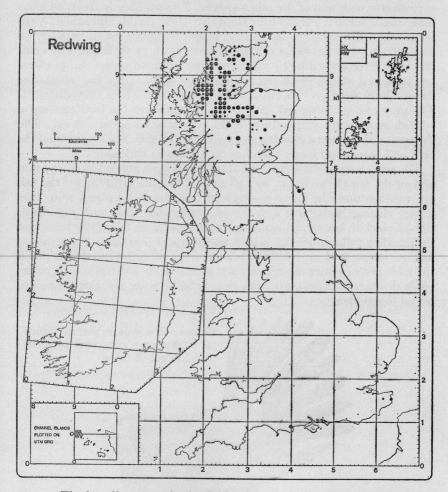

FIG. 14. The breeding range in the British Isles (on 10km Square Grid) of the redwing. Large dots indicate confirmed breeding, medium dots probable breeding, and small dots possible breeding. (From *Atlas of Breeding Birds in Britain*, B.T.O./ I.W.C. Updated to 1975.)

wing is a gregarious bird and can often be found in the company of field-fares and, more rarely in my experience, with song thrushes. The flight is strong and fairly fast – between 20 and 30 mph – with quick wingbeats and an alternate closing of the wings at short intervals. The path through the air is slightly undulating and the birds travel in loose open formations.

As I write I have in front of me skins from my collection of mistle thrush, song thrush and redwing. The small size of the redwing contrasts very clearly with that of the other species. The fieldfare is about 25·5 cm long; this is some 1·5 cm shorter than the mistle thrush and almost 5 cm longer than the redwing. In normal health fieldfares weigh between 90 and 126 gm while the redwing's limits range from 71 to 88 gm. The field-fare can be recognized by its pale blue-grey head, nape and rump, chest-nut back and almost black tail. It has some white under the wings, like the similarly sized greyish mistle thrush, but the voice is very different. The grey crown is streaked with black blotches and the bird also has a whitish superciliary stripe above a thin black band under the eye. The throat and breast are a glowing rusty yellow with thin black streaks on the chin and throat and larger blotches on the breast and flanks.

The wing length of the male fieldfare varies from about 140 to 153 mm and of the female from 135 to 148 mm. The general limits for the tail are 100–110 mm, the tarsus 31–34 mm and the bill 23–24·5 mm. Our winter visiting birds have a yellowish-orange bill with both mandibles tipped blackish brown. In summer the male has an all yellow beak and the female a yellow one with brown on the upper mandible. The legs and feet are brown and the iris dark brown. In general the female resembles the male but in winter the upper parts are browner and the mantle paler, while the dark blotches on the flanks are also browner and the throat and breast less golden.

Fieldfare in aggressive posture (based on a photograph supplied by Fritz Siedel/Frank W. Lane)

The fieldfare, or 'felt' as I have known it called in many parts of England, has a fairly direct flight at around 48 kph. The bird flies straight with a marked and regular closure of the wings but this flight is not as undulating as that of the other large thrush in the British Isles – the mistle thrush. Birds fly in a straggling open flock and are often accompanied by the smaller redwings. On the ground the fieldfare is alert and rather upright with the head often held well up. On their wintering grounds fieldfares are rather shy and wary, usually working upwind in the fields and, if disturbed, curving back in flight downwind with sharp alarm calls. If really concerned they will fly high up into tall trees and not make for low cover. I well remember seeing my first birds going high up into trees in Ladbroke Square in London when I was six years old. Often they sit facing the same direction, generally into wind

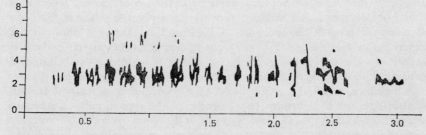

Typical phrases from full song of redwing. Recorded by Dr Ludwig Koch at Thingvallavatn, Iceland, June 1953.

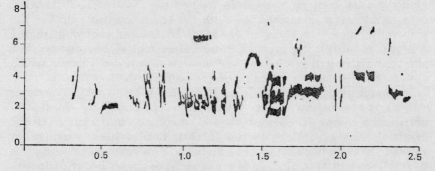

Typical phrases from sub-song of redwing in early morning chorus prior to departure. Here there is a big frequency range and the phrases are less well defined. Recorded by Eric Simms in Kent, March 1954.

FIG. 15. Sonagrams of full and sub-song in the redwing. The vertical scale represents frequency in kHz; the horizontal time in seconds. (Reproduced from *British Birds*, Vol. 51, 1958, by permission of Professor W. H. Thorpe.)

Both redwings and fieldfares mix freely on the pasture and root fields and it is a not uncommon sight in winter to see flocks of the two species feeding together and flying sociably from one piece of farmland to another. On their breeding grounds they often nest quite close to each other.

Both species can be readily separated by their calls as well as their relative size. The redwing's note, which I have heard from birds in flight by day and from migrants passing overhead at night, is a soft, thin 'See-ip' or 'Seeng', longer and more wavy than the 'Tsic' or 'Tsipp' note of song thrushes. J. N. Hollyer has suggested that the flight call of the Continental song thrush may be mistaken for that of the redwing but after checking on Continental birds I believe that with careful listening and discrimination the distinction can be made. The redwing also has an abrupt 'Tchup' or 'Tchep' call which I have heard from birds feeding among themselves and from birds arriving at their roost. Sound recordings that I obtained at a Staffordshire roost in December show the regular use of a sharp, crisp 'Chittuck' and 'Chittituck' variant and also what I described in *Voices of the Wild* as 'a rarely heard whinnying call which is rather like the prolonged distress call of the blackbird'. The 'Chittuck' calls are also employed as alarm notes on the breeding ground.

A fieldfare, which I watched and tape-recorded in a fenland tree in Cambridgeshire in February 1971, produced the typical call – a staccato sharp 'Ter-TCHACK-TCHACK-TCHACK' – at intervals of roughly twenty-five seconds; occasionally it injected a softer phrase – 'Tchuck-tchuck' – into the series of harsh notes. This desultory kind of calling is not uncommon from perched and perhaps only slightly uneasy birds. Flying parties keep up a constant flow of the 'TCHACK-TCHACK' calls. If the nest is threatened the birds use harsh churring calls like the pair which nested in Shetland in 1968. In another recording that I collected of birds flying over the Staffordshire mid-winter countryside I also captured a soft, gentle 'See' call as well as a rising 'Gezeek' which appears to be related to the call used by young birds.

In March 1963 and 1964 John Kirby made some very interesting recordings at a fieldfare roost in Yorkshire. These included the typical notes and a trilling 'Tchirrick-tchirrick' running on into what I call the fieldfare's 'twitter-warble' – a series of coarse swallow-like twitterings but without the wide pitch range of these birds. This subdued sub-song was then followed by several clear notes of rising pitch – 'Trit-trit-trit-trit'. The whole performance was sustained for minutes on end but with no great dynamic range. It suggested the home song on the breeding ground and recalled a sub-song that I heard one spring on Holy Island.

European fieldfares sing a high, tuneless 'Took-took-tcheree', 'Took-took-cherri-weeoo', and 'Took-took-took-cherri-wee-chee' and variants with occasional squeaks and softer versions of the hard typical call. This rather feeble effort is given both in flight and from a perch. The song of the redwing has become increasingly familiar in Scotland in recent years. There is considerable variation and dialects among redwing groups are common but a good example of the full song might be: 'Trui-trui-trui' or another 'Teetra-teetra-teetra', reedy and conversational with a quiet squeaky warble at the end. In recent years I have heard a number of full songs in Wester Ross – a pleasing addition to the bird songs of northern Scotland. We shall be looking at the song and the gay and spontaneous communal spring sub-song in chapter 8.

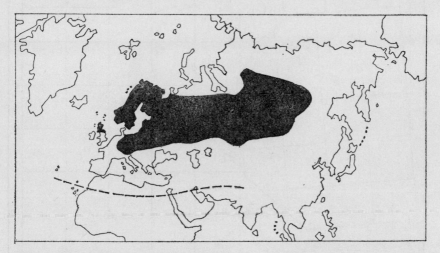

FIG. 16. The breeding range of the fieldfare. The dotted line marks southern limits of the wintering range.

Both the redwing and the fieldfare are Palaearctic species. The breeding distribution of the fieldfare is roughly similar to that of the redwing. Its main breeding area lies in northern Eurasia from Fenno-Scandia, Germany and Switzerland east to Russia and Siberia. The fieldfare also breeds sporadically in the British Isles and has colonies in Iceland and Greenland (Fig. 16). The more northerly populations move south for the winter to many parts of Europe and south-west Asia as well as Spain, Asia Minor and Iran.

Fieldfares leave their northern breeding grounds in late September and the first half of October; the main arrivals appear in the British Isles in October and during the first three weeks of November. Continental redwings start their migrations in late September as well with their main movements in October and the first half of November. Although both

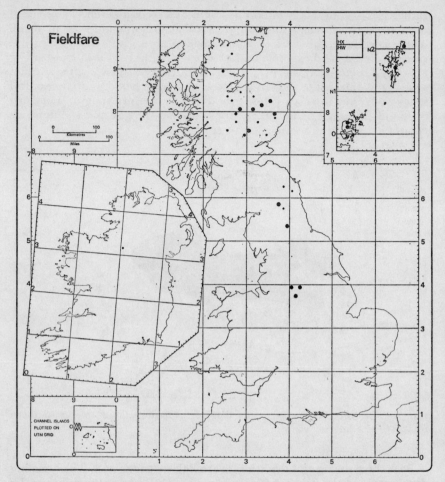

FIG. 17. The breeding range in the British Isles (on 10km Square Grid) of the fieldfare. Large dots indicate confirmed breeding, medium dots probable breeding, and small dots possible breeding. (From *Atlas of Breeding Birds in Britain*, B.T.O./ I.W.C. Updated to 1975.)

species are regular winter visitors many birds that we see in the British Isles are also passage migrants.

As a nesting species the redwing is very much a bird of mixed, rather open forests with alder, willow and birch, pine and spruce as well as town gardens, parks and similar habitats. The fieldfare can be found in similar situations but it tends to be rather a more social breeder. In winter both species favour open farmlands where they search for small animal life and vegetable and other plant foods. They take many berries but these seem to be less favoured by redwings except in bad weather. In adverse conditions I have often seen both species inside many towns and cities. They can also be seen migrating by day and travelling even over built-up areas far from their normal more rural environments. In October and November I often listen out at night for the soft whisper of redwing calls above the lights of London.

CHAPTER 5

RANGE AND HABITATS

In the preceding chapters I have given a very broad outline of the appearance, behaviour and environment of the common British thrushes. I propose to devote the whole of the present chapter to a deeper and wider survey of both the ranges and habitats of the different thrush species. Since this may have some value for reference purposes I am sub-dividing the chapter into six sections each of which is concerned with a single species. Each section will deal with the world range, the distribution in the British Isles and the kinds of habitat in which the bird may be found. Some species despite being territorial can also show a high degree of interspecific tolerance and this will, I hope, emerge as well.

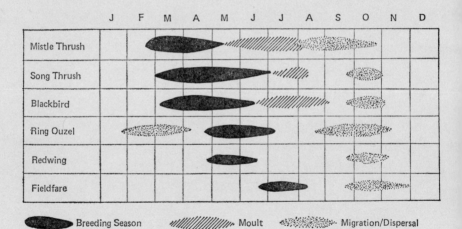

FIG. 18. Annual cycle of activity in Britain's thrush species.

THE SONG THRUSH

This is a bird of the Palaearctic; it is distributed through the temperate and boreal zones and many of the mountain regions. It can be found as far north as the July isotherm of 53°F, or about 69°N in Fenno-Scandia and as far south as 35°N in Iran. Song thrushes can be found east from

PLATE 7. RING OUZELS. *Above*, a male ring ouzel in fine breeding plumage showing the clear white crescent on the breast and the grey-edged secondaries and coverts that make the closed wing appear paler than the rest. *Below*, a male ring ouzel at a nest on hill grassland.

PLATE 8. RING OUZELS. *Above*, the female ring ouzel with more prominent light edgings to the feathers and a narrower breast crescent than the male; this is a typical breeding site under the shelter of a bank. *Below*, a ring ouzel's nest in a less usual tree-site in Derbyshire – a stunted alder.

the British Isles across Europe and Asia as far as Lake Baikal and western Siberia. In southern Europe the limits pass through northern Spain – I have seen birds in the Sierra de la Demanda – north Italy, northern Greece and they appear again in Asia Minor; here the song thrush is often a mountain bird making its way down to lower levels in the winter. *Turdus philomelos clarkei*, which occurs throughout most of the British Isles, can be seen in the Channel Isles, northern and western France, Belgium and southern Holland.

The song thrush is both resident and migratory and the northern populations tend to move southwards to the Mediterranean, North Africa and the Middle East. Both the British sub-species are basically sedentary but *T. p. hebridensis* has been recorded in England and even Algeria. Some British ringed *T. p. clarkei* have been recovered in western Europe as well as the Iberian Peninsula and the Balearic Islands. Song thrushes regularly winter in the Coto Doñana and birds have been reported as regular, sometimes abundant, in winter in Morocco, Tripolitania and some other parts of North Africa. The song thrush has been described as 'fairly common' in Iraq and 'a winter visitor in variable numbers' to Eritrea. Birds have also been reported in winter in the Canary Islands, Egypt, Sinai, Arabia and even the Sudan.

Song thrushes were introduced into Australia in 1863 and birds are now well established mainly in Victoria and the suburbs of Melbourne. Birds were also liberated in New Zealand between 1865 and 1867 and G. R. Williams described them in 1953 as 'common throughout'. Altogether thirteen passerine species are established in New Zealand and some of these have appeared on small islands in the Australasian seas, perhaps as a result of dispersal by strong winds. Many song thrushes nest among scattered shrubs in mountain valleys but others have succeeded in breeding on Sunday Island, Chatham Islands, Campbell Island, Snares Islands, Lord Howe Island, Auckland Islands and Norfolk Island; these range from 100 km to as much as 880 km from New Zealand.

In the British Isles the song thrush is an abundant bird but it has shown signs of a decrease in the last quarter of a century or more throughout most of its range. It has decreased markedly in the built-up areas of London since the beginning of the century. It breeds very occasionally in Shetland generally in the neighbourhood of trees.

The song thrush is essentially a bird of the woodlands, both deciduous and coniferous, as well as groves, clumps of trees and small woods with a good shrub layer, of thickets, scrub, hedgerows, orchards, parks and gardens. In Europe it can often be found where spruce is common but, according to Dr K. H. Voous, not where pine or birch are dominant. It can, however, be found singing in numbers in the sub-alpine birchwoods at Abisko in Lapland. In Slovakia song thrushes also breed through the spruce forests up to heights of about 1300 metres above sea level. The song

Table 6. Natural Habitats of European Thrushes in Breeding Season

	Mediterranean		Broad-leaved		Boreal		Montane Conifers		Tundra		Barren Rocks, Coast / Open, Tree-less Country
	Forest	Forest Edge	Forest	Forest Edge	Forest	Forest Edge	Forest	Forest Edge	Arctic	Alpine	
MISTLE THRUSH	●	●	●	●	●	●	●	●			●
SONG THRUSH			●	●	●	●	●	●			● (occ. Ireland)
BLACKBIRD	●	●	●	●	●	●	●	●			
RING OUZEL						●		●	●	●	●
REDWING					●	●		●	●		●
FIELDFARE					●	●		●	●		

thrush tends to avoid the densest parts of the northern taiga but it does occur with both Siberian jay and Siberian tit in the world's most northern pine forests at Porsangerfjord in Norway at about 70°N. It is generally commoner along the edges of the taiga, in woodland clearings and ecotones. It can be found in many suburban areas in western and central Europe but it is less of an urban bird than the blackbird; in gardens and parks in Scandinavia it is replaced by the redwing. It is only in this century that the Continental song thrush has become a familiar bird in gardens and parks in Germany. On the Pacific islands song thrushes have been found in a variety of habitats from forest and tall scrub to grassland and cultivated areas. In their winter quarters song thrushes can also be found in a number of different kinds of environment. In Eritrea birds appear at all altitudes on open moorland, in woodland, parks and coastal acacias. In Morocco they seem to favour *Ilex* and *Salicornia*. In southern Europe I have seen winter birds in vineyards and olive groves in small flocks of around a dozen birds.

After visiting several hundred woods in the British Isles I found the song thrush most frequently in the sessile oakwoods of Scotland and then in the Irish sessile and English pedunculate oakwoods. It is much less common in the sessile oakwoods of England and Wales. I found it not uncommon in beech and birchwoods in Ireland and Scotland and in young Irish conifer plantations but it was less so in ashwoods and the native pine forests of Speyside. When I came to visit Scottish and Irish thickets it was again scarcer. In many of the yew woods that I explored it was generally absent in summer although in autumn many birds come to feed on the berries. Richard and Kenneth Williamson gave the song thrush the percentage dominance of 2·25 in the yew woods at Kingley Vale. Song thrushes are also not uncommon in hedgerows and on farmland, where they may form from 3% to 5·3% of the bird community compared to 7% to 8·7% for the blackbird. Birds nest at Dollis Hill but they are no longer 'the commonest thrush' in Outer London as Charles Dixon claimed at the beginning of this century. The species is now often outnumbered by the blackbird in suburbia in the ratio from 17 to 27 to 1. The bird is scarce in Inner London but is commoner in the Royal Parks. From 1904–11 C. L. Collenette recorded 97 nests of the song thrush to 94 of the blackbird but after the First World War the balance changed to one of five blackbirds' to every song thrush's.

In Scotland and Ireland the song thrush can also be found in desolate treeless areas and I have seen males singing on rocks and boulders in competition with blackbirds and ring ouzels. The Hebridean song thrush favours open country, particularly wild moors with scrubby gorse, heather and willow scrub and I have watched birds in summer on peat hags, remote glens and on the edge of both fresh and salt water. In the winter birds of this island race wander regularly over the shore and appear

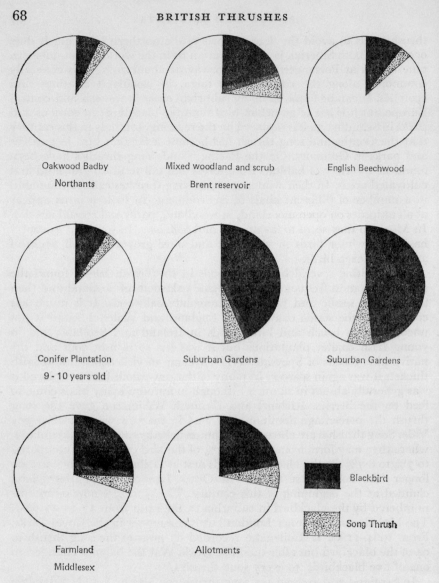

FIG. 19. Dominance (percentage of total pairs) for two thrush species (house sparrows excluded). (From Simms, 1971, 1975, and Batten, 1972.)

around the townships and farmsteads. In Orkney the song thrush is a nesting bird of gardens, woods and buildings, but it will feed on farmlands near by.

This member of the thrush family is distributed throughout the western and central Palaearctic both in the mountains and in the boreal, temperate and Mediterranean zones. To the north it reaches about the same level as the song thrush – that is, 69°N. *T. v. viscivorus* breeds from the British Isles, Portugal and Fenno-Scandia east to the River Ob and south to Iran. The populations in Corsica, Sardinia, north-west Africa and the southern Crimea are usually regarded as distinct. In Europe the northern range reaches south-east Norway, Sweden, Finland and Russia, the Kola Peninsula and to 63°N on the River Pechora and 64°N in the Urals. To the south the range embraces southern Spain, north-west Africa, Sicily, Greece, Asia Minor and the Lebanon. In Asia a larger, paler mistle thrush breeds from Turkestan and Transcaspia to Iran, northern Baluchistan, Afghanistan, east of the Yenisei, western Sinkiang and Altai. It is very much a bird of the grassy Russian steppes but there seems to be a large region – an island of emptiness – where the bird does not occur; it stretches from west of the Caucasus across the Kirghiz Steppes to Lake Baikal. In the east the breeding range is complemented by that of the dusky thrush – *T. naumanni* – a bird of dense coniferous woodland.

In north-eastern Europe the mistle thrush tends to be a forest bird but in the nineteenth century it spread from the mountainous woodlands into the European plains. In western and central Europe the bird became much more an inhabitant of parklands and towns, sharing these habitats with blackbirds and song thrushes. By the 1930s the mistle thrush had greatly increased and, although there has been considerable debate as to the origins of the 'parkland' populations, it would seem that like some of the other thrushes the mistle thrush was preadapted to parkland environments, which man was increasing all the time. The resident breeding race of the mistle thrush in the dry woodlands of north-west Africa ranges from Morocco east to Tunisia but the European race winters in the Mediterranean area as well. There are records from North Africa, the Azores and Palestine. Mistle thrushes from Sweden, Holland and Belgium seem to have fairly restricted winter quarters in western France. To the east a considerable movement of mistle thrushes has been recorded through Kurdistan in the autumn and the first bird was seen in Iraq in 1954.

In the British Isles the mistle thrush is a widespread and quite numerous species, breeding in every region except those of Shetland and the Outer Hebrides. It nests erratically in Orkney and rather sparsely in the extreme north and north-west of Scotland. This species greatly increased its range in the first half of the nineteenth century in England, Scotland and Ireland. The first nest was discovered in Ireland in 1807 and by 1850 the mistle thrush had colonized every county. The bird also spread in Scotland perhaps as the result of increasing afforestation. This widening of range

matches a similar movement on the Continent and both here and in the
British Isles there was a spread into parks, gardens and city centres. I
found that in many parts of Ireland the mistle thrush was commoner than
the song thrush and in treeless areas it would nest on walls, buildings and
sometimes on the ground. As late as 1929 only a few pairs were nesting
in Inner London but I watched pairs breeding in Ladbroke Square well
before the last war; the species now nests regularly in the squares and
Royal Parks and in 1975 I saw a pair in the grounds of Buckingham
Palace. At Dollis Hill the mistle thrush is a very marginal bird indeed.
After breeding is over birds tend to wander away from both rural and
urban nesting grounds.

We have already seen that in the British Isles the mistle thrush is a
bird of well-timbered parklands but it also occurs in both broad-leaved
and coniferous woodland, plantations, orchards, gardens and open
country. It is regular in the sessile oakwoods of Ireland, not quite so
common in English pedunculate woods and rather scarce in English
sessile oakwoods. It is quite plentiful in Irish beechwoods but less so in
those in England and Scotland. I have seen mistle thrushes in Scottish
alderwoods and English fen carrs and I have many records of birds in
English, Scottish and Irish birchwoods but fewer from Wales. I found
birds missing from or very uncommon in ashwoods. The mistle thrush can
be found in the old Scots pine forests of Speyside where it has been
described as common but my experience is that 'in the forest proper it
often keeps to the more secluded parts'. On the other hand it is a thrush
which I have often observed in mature Scots pine plantations as well as
those formed from Norway and Sitka spruce. It may also be seen in the
thickets and pole-stage conifer plantations as well.

In Europe mistle thrushes occur in open pinewoods and sub-alpine
coniferous forests and, in the southern parts of their range, in montane
oak and beechwoods. I did not find it common in the Alpine spruce forests
but it is regular in those of Slovakia up to a height of 1400 metres. In
southern France and Spain I found it to be very much a bird of mountains
and hillsides. In western and central Europe its habitats are similar to
many of those in Britain – broad-leaved woods, parkland and gardens
with tall trees and open grassland. After breeding birds will gather in
loose flocks on farm and other grassland; parties generally vary from
twenty to forty birds but I have occasionally seen some containing more
than a hundred.

THE BLACKBIRD

The blackbird is a Palaearctic faunal type occurring in both western and
southern parts of the region as well as in the northern Oriental. It lives
in the temperate, boreal and Mediterranean climatic zones, in mountain

areas and probably in 'the tropical winter-dry climatic zone' (Voous 1960).
The northern limit reaches the Faeroe Islands exceeding the July isotherm
of 55°F or 63°N, and birds have been pushing north in Finland. In fact,
blackbirds can be found from the Azores, Madeira, the Canary Islands,
north-west Africa, the Iberian Peninsula, the British Isles and central
Norway east to Russia, Asia Minor, Iran, Russian Turkestan, Sinkiang,
northern Afghanistan and Baluchistan to the mountains of the Himalayas,
Tibet and southern China. Chinese blackbirds are very similar to the
western European bird *T. m. merula* but mountain birds in Asia tend to
be large compared with the small blackbirds of the extreme west of western
Europe, and the Himalayan blackbird seems to have very close affinities
in its behaviour with the ring ouzel.

Blackbirds are largely resident but some populations like those of
Scandinavia are migratory and others partially so, and wintering birds
can be seen as far south as Egypt, southern Iraq, southern Afghanistan
and various parts of south-east Asia. Among the blackbirds of northern
Europe more females migrate than males. Blackbirds are regular winter
visitors to Algeria, Morocco and northern Libya, where they can be
heard in song in December, and to central Anatolia. Birds have also
appeared in the Balearics, Greenland, Iceland, Jan Mayen, Spitzbergen
and Bear Island. The blackbird is a winter visitor to Iraq but it may have
bred in the 1950s near Amadia.

The blackbird was introduced to Australia in 1864 and is now mainly
established in Victoria and Tasmania where it is quite common. Birds
were liberated two years earlier in New Zealand where they are widespread, having adapted themselves to the different timing of the southern
hemisphere seasons, and are nesting between September and December.
Their biology and behaviour in New Zealand have been well described
by L. Gurr (1954). Like the introduced song thrush the blackbird has
spread to groups of outlying islands ranging from 100 to 720 km from
New Zealand.

The blackbird is a very abundant species breeding throughout the
British Isles. It has spread from its original woodland habitat into gardens
and finally towns and cities. It was not until the 1830s that there were
records of birds appearing in or near gardens and towns but this habit
was restricted to the winter months. The spread into the larger towns in
Britain has taken place only in the last half century or so. The movement
of blackbirds into the cities of Holland began about the same time as in
Britain – in Denmark about 1890, Sweden 1900, Finland 1924 and
Kaliningrad 1933. Since that time more blackbirds have entered towns
and cities. In eastern Europe the blackbird is just beginning to penetrate
towns as the bird expands its easterly range. In Poland birds are becoming commoner in towns leaving only a low density in the woodlands. Birds
seem to begin by spending the early part of the year in towns but retiring

at night to roost in near-by woodland; this seems to be the common pattern before breeding actually begins. In Czechoslovakia and Poland town blackbirds are now four times as abundant as in the forests. In Britain the breeding density in the oakwoods at Wytham near Oxford was only one-tenth that of the density of blackbirds nesting in the Botanic Garden. There are many more per acre of Dollis Hill than per acre of Northamptonshire oakwood.

Blackbirds have spread out into the Scottish islands reaching Shetland in the 1870s and 1880s, and Foula in 1930. Perhaps the growing European breeding stock, aided by some climatic improvement, may have added to the number of blackbirds wintering in Shetland; in winter blackbirds are to be found on islands such as Papa Stour where they do not breed. There are birds especially around the crofts and townships, as well as a greater number of males than females. Elsewhere blackbirds are tending to nest higher in the new conifer forests and hillsides of England and Wales as well as becoming established in urban areas. In London's parks the blackbird is the commonest land species after the house sparrow.

Table 7. Man-made Habitats of European Thrushes

	Conifer Plan- tations	Farmland, Orchards	Villages	Gardens, Parks, Cemeteries	Dumps, Waste Land, Allotments	City Centres
MISTLE THRUSH	BW	BW	BW	BW		BW
SONG THRUSH	BW	BW	BW	BW	BW	BW
BLACKBIRD	BW	BW	BW	BW	BW	BW
RING OUZEL	B(fringes)	B(hill farms)				
REDWING	B(Scot- land)	W	W(occ.)	B(Scan- dinavia)	W	W(rare)
FIELDFARE	BW	BW	W(occ.)	B(Scan- dinavia)	W	W(rare)

B = Breeding
W = Present in winter
Occ. = Occasional

The blackbird is very much a bird of many different kinds of forested region with a dense shrub layer and softish ground which carries grass and a reasonable amount of leaf litter. In western and central Europe and in China it is often found in association with man's farmlands and gardens. It occurs from mixed broad-leaved and coniferous woods in the lowlands up to sub-alpine Continental forests. In Slovakia it can be found in spruce forests from 100 to 1200 metres above sea level. In Estonia it is the third commonest thrush after the song thrush and redwing; it is also a bird of the Russian steppes. In Asia Minor it is a shy bird living in scrub and thickets where its song is poor and unfulfilled. In New Zealand blackbirds can be found in mountain valleys at 660 metres and around 'lawns, flowerbeds and kitchen gardens'.

In *Woodland Birds* (1971) I gave the following survey of the blackbird's British habitats and I would like to quote it here; it is based on my survey of several hundred woodlands of many different types. 'I have found it to be the most abundant species in Irish ashwoods (RA 27) and hazel scrub. It was the second commonest bird in English and Scottish beech (RA 12) and Irish sessile oak, beech, and mixed broad-leaved woods (all RAs 11). It came third in the mixed broad-leaved woods of Scotland, the mixed broad-leaved/coniferous woods of Ireland and in the suburban area of Dollis Hill. Blackbirds were not uncommon in English pedunculate oak, English and Scottish sessile oak, alder, ash and birch as well as English and Irish yew, Irish birch and Scottish sycamore. The blackbird is regular in the late thicket stages and in mature Norway spruce, Sitka spruce and mixed conifer plantations in Britain and Ireland. In Ireland it is to be found in the early thicket stages where the proportion to song thrushes is about 3 to 2. The blackbird was very scarce in *Tsuga* plantations and missing not only from the old Caledonian forest of Speyside, but also from twelve mature Scots pine plantations north of the border. It is the commonest bird of lowland farmland. The densest populations of blackbirds occur in gardens, then in parkland, farmland and finally dense woodland where pairs are fewer and generally very retiring.' It is also a bird of commons, moorlands, hillsides and rocky coasts. This very adaptable and successful bird continues to flourish. In the area of Regent's Park, Battersea Park and Bloomsbury in London the population has trebled since 1951 resulting in a high competition for nest sites which have included building 'on drain pipes, ruined walls and window ledges, in street lamps and even on the traffic lights at a busy junction' (Cramp and Tomlins 1966). However, the population at Dollis Hill has changed little apart from a crash after the severe winter of 1962–63.

The breeding population in the British Isles is mainly sedentary but some birds from northern Britain winter in Ireland, others move around inside the country and some may cross the English Channel. European blackbirds may travel to France and Spain occurring in a wide range of habitats including vineyards, while others can appear in wooded or open country around the Mediterranean Sea.

This western Palaearctic thrush has a broken distribution throughout the boreal climatic zone, mountain regions and even temperate and tundra zones. It breeds in Europe and south-east Asia in three regions – the British Isles and Fenno-Scandia; the mountains of northern Iberia eastwards to southern Poland, south-west Russia and the Balkans; and from eastern Turkey and the Caucasus across Transcaspia to northern Iran. The limits range north from 36°N to 71°N. The typical ring ouzel can be found in suitable localities in Ireland, Highland Britain, in the western parts of Norway, thinning out into Finmark and the Baltic. It is scarce in parts of Lapland but it has been described as fairly common at Abisko. Exceptional nesting has taken place in France, Belgium, Holland and Denmark. The alpine race is very much a bird of the great massif of the high Alps and not of the lower hill ranges that occur in central Europe. It breeds also in the Pyrenees, Jura, Germany, Poland and other parts of central Europe and in the Balkans. As we have seen, the sub-species *T. t. amicorum* breeds from the Caucasus to Iran and possibly in Asia Minor as well.

Northern ring ouzels winter mainly in central and eastern Spain, southern France and North Africa. Of 850 ring ouzels ringed in Norway 21 were recovered in the south of France. Of course, birds may overwinter in Norway in a very good berry year and very occasionally in England as well. One of their regular winter haunts is in the Saharan Atlas on the northern borders of Algeria and Morocco where birds live in the cedar woods in company with other thrushes. Heim de Balsac discovered birds in some numbers in the Sud-Orannais north of the Sahara in the cedar forest and again feeding on junipers on the Djebel Guettar which rises to a height of some 500 to 800 metres. Small pools of rainwater, as described by Dr David Bannerman (1954), supplied water from rock crevice reservoirs while the birds relied on the juniper berries for food. A nestling ring ouzel ringed in Dumfriesshire was recovered from the Djebel Guettar which suggests that this was correctly identified as a winter home for the northern race. K. D. Smith (1965) found ring ouzels abundant in light conifer woods at 2000 metres in the High Atlas. They also appear to be regular in Majorca, Minorca and Corsica. The Alpine ring ouzel normally winters in the Mediterranean region and has been recorded in the Sudan. A ring ouzel was reported in 1954 in Iraq – the first record for the species – but I do not know its race.

The ring ouzel is quite widely distributed on the moorlands of western and northern Britain from Caithness to Devon and on the hill ranges of Ireland. Numbers do appear to have declined in the first half of this century, perhaps as a result of competition with the blackbird; here interspecific tolerance may have been lacking. Ring ouzels do not appear in the Outer and most of the Inner Hebrides, nor the Isle of Man. Numbers which went down in Scotland do not appear to have shown any recent signs of a recovery. Birds appear to be increasing in parts of south Wales, holding their own in north Wales, and decreasing in Radnor and Carmarthen. In England, Cornwall has been abandoned and perhaps other parts of the country as well after about 1900. In Ireland, after a decline from about the same date, ring ouzels now breed very locally in Co. Kerry, northern Tipperary, Cos. Wicklow, Waterford, Leix, Sligo, Fermanagh, Down, Derry, Tyrone and Donegal, and perhaps Limerick and Antrim. During a six-week tour of Ireland in 1967 the ring ouzels of Donegal, Down and some of the other counties were quite hard to find as I searched the rocky valleys of the uplands. There are only about a

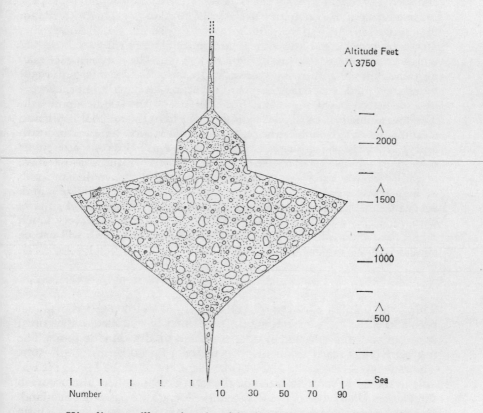

FIG. 20. Kite diagram illustrating the altitudinal distribution of ring ouzel nest records into 250 feet intervals. (Reproduced from *Bird Study*, Vol 22, 1975, by permission of Dr J. J. M. Flegg and David Glue.)

dozen pairs, for example, in the Mountains of Mourne. This decrease in Ireland may have been due to changes in climate.

In Ireland a typical summer home for the ring ouzel is a rather steep boulder-strewn gully at 270 metres or more. In Scotland I have watched pairs in Highland glens where a heather moor with small open patches of scree is divided by a cleft or gully as it slopes down towards a stream. In Derbyshire ring ouzels occur from 230 metres above sea level to around 330 metres and in small numbers even up to 660 metres. In Yorkshire the lower level is often about 430 metres but the diets are different in the two areas. In the northern Pennines in the early 1940s I found nests from 330 up to 530 metres. The Nest Record Cards of the British Trust for Ornithology show more than 80% of all reported nests as between 250 and 580 metres above sea level. Dr J. J. M. Flegg and David Glue (1975) analysed the habitats from the Record Cards; they found that 72% reflected a moorland environment, 8% hill farmland, 3% high woodland, 6% grassy hillside, 9% rocky hillside and 2% scrub. So, although ring ouzels are very much birds of moorland and hill, they will breed in areas which have been shaped and influenced by man. The northern race may also be found close to rocky shores. In Lapland C-F. Lundevall (1952) found most of the ring ouzels occurred in the low alpine belt but they were also often seen in the sub-alpine birch forest and the middle alpine belt. The low alpine belt consists of willow scrub, juniper and poor heath and swamp; the middle alpine belt contains boulder fields, bare earth, heath and grass, while the sub-alpine birch forest is fairly close or scattered, or consists of isolated trees or shrubs. The Alpine ring ouzel, as we have already seen, is a bird of high coniferous woods near the tree line or scrub at high levels, as well as alpine meadows with scattered boulders and, according to Dr Voous, 'preferably near mountain torrents and streams with wide grassy banks liable to flooding'. We do not know very much about the winter quarters of this race but it seems that birds will choose similar habitats around the Mediterranean.

THE REDWING

This – the smallest of the six thrush species – is a bird of Siberian faunal type and of the Palaearctic Region. It is primarily restricted to the boreal zone but may also be found in temperate and tundra climatic zones. The northern limits reach to about 70°N or the July isotherms of 46°–50°F. The redwing is classically a bird of the taiga but after the Ice Age it was able to extend its range to Iceland; the form breeding there also occurs in the Faeroes. The range of the European redwing runs east from Scotland, Norway, central and northern Sweden, Finland and Poland across Russia and Siberia as far as Lake Baikal, the Lena and the lower Kolyma. In the south the redwing's range extends to about 50°N. To these regions the

bird is only a summer visitor. Small numbers nest in Germany; other
isolated instances of breeding in central Europe – in Czechoslovakia,
Austria, Belgium and France, for example – suggest attempts at expansion
rather than survival as glacial relicts.

The redwing is chiefly a migratory species. Iceland birds appear on
passage and in winter in northern Ireland and Britain, sometimes in
western Europe and occasionally in Greenland, and on Bear Island and
Jan Mayen. In the British Isles they may overlap with European redwings. European birds winter in the south-western tip of Norway, the
British Isles and Continental Europe chiefly south and west of a line from
the Kattegat to Bulgaria, and on the islands of the Mediterranean. The
actual migration of Scandinavian redwings is rather spread out with birds
also reaching Italy and the central Mediterranean countries. Redwings
have also been reported in North Africa, Egypt, Asia Minor and north-
west India. Southern Spain is a regular winter resort but it seems that
redwings are rare in Cyprus and Malta but more frequent from Tunisia
westwards to Morocco. Heim de Balsac saw redwings in the cedar forests
on the slopes of Sidi Abdel-Kader in North Africa; they were common in
olive groves in Morocco (Smith 1965) and birds were seen in Iraq in
1954 for the first time.

Redwings ringed in the British Isles on passage have been recovered in
winter in Iberia, Sardinia, Italy, Greece, and the Lebanon while recoveries of foreign ringed birds in Britain showed sources of origin in
Iceland, Fenno-Scandia, the Baltic and Russia.

In recent years the redwing has come to be known as a breeding bird
in Scotland. The first nest was located in Sutherland in 1925 and between
that year and 1941 breeding was proved or thought to have taken place
in at least seven years in that county as well as in Inverness, Moray and
Shetland. Then there was a lull until 1953, after which for some years it
was thought that three or more pairs were nesting in almost every year in
Sutherland and Ross, and more erratically in Inverness and Shetland. In
1967 breeding was satisfactorily proved in all four counties and in the
following year Kenneth Williamson led a BTO Bird Census Expedition
to Wester Ross which discovered twenty redwing territories and found
evidence of nesting by ten pairs in the region of the Loch Maree basin.
In that same year I also heard territorial songs from more than a dozen
males in the same region where it was clear that an irregular breeder had
now become well established. By 1971–72 there were between 40 and 50
pairs mainly in Sutherland, Ross and Inverness but also in Moray,
Caithness and Shetland. In 1973 redwings were noted at only ten sites in
Banff, Inverness, Perth, Ross, Sutherland and Shetland with at least
four pairs nesting, but it is assumed that many sites were not reported
otherwise a marked decrease must have taken place. In 1974 there was a
total of 25 sites in Moray and the other six counties listed with perhaps

19 pairs breeding. There has therefore been a decrease since 1969–72 and birds were missing in 1974 from some areas occupied during that period. In 1975 there were 20 sites in six counties with 8 pairs proved to breed and at least 19 other singing males. A pair of redwings tried to nest in Kerry in Eire in 1951.

It is reasonable to assume that fluctuations in climate must have important influences on animals and plants and it is known that since the 1890s there has been an amelioration in the northern hemisphere. In the 1940s winter temperatures began to show a downward move and in the 1950s winter snow began to lie longer in the northern parts of Scotland and Shetland. Kenneth Williamson has shown how 'this relapse from warmth' continued into the 1970s. During the last twenty years or so other boreal species besides the redwing have colonized or recolonized the Scottish Highlands – snowy owl, goldeneye, Temminck's stint, wood sandpiper, shorelark and fieldfare – and Williamson has suggested that the explanation for the arrival of these birds is 'that returning migrants from southern and south-eastern Europe are displaced to Scotland in unusual strength by the easterly airstream on the south side of the Scandinavian anticyclone, and find a suitable habitat when their migration urge has been expended'.

In Britain we tend to think of the redwing's habitat as that favoured by birds wintering in the country – open pasture lands, stubble and root fields, open woods or thorn hedges. In the breeding season the European redwing is very much a bird of the taiga. Its summer home is typically the boggy spruce forests with ancient lichen-encrusted trees mingled with birch which stretch from Scandinavia to the Urals. In Scandinavia itself the bird is common where spruce and pine are plentiful and perhaps the dominant trees, but it is generally even more abundant in birch and mixed forests. In eastern Norway the redwing can be found in numbers in the fjeld-side birch woodlands and near-by conifer forests but it is less regular at the lower levels; in the west it may be as common by the fjords as at the higher altitudes. Beyond the Arctic Circle redwings breed both in the woods and the open country above the birch line. At Abisko C-F. Lundevall reported 'only a few redwings above the timber line and most of them in the subalpine birch forest belt'. Many redwing breeding sites are near water especially in flooded birchwoods. Away from the woodlands European redwings will also nest in damp scrubby thickets of sallow and juniper. In Iceland, where forest is missing, the island form will nest in birch scrub, where this is available, as well as among rocks like the ring ouzel, and even on buildings. In Scandinavia redwings will also find nesting places in parks and large gardens in the manner of the fieldfare.

As we have already seen, the British breeding redwings have a number of different habitats – State forests, mixed birch and conifer woods, hedges, bushes and evergreen shrubs around large and generally isolated private houses, the edges of oakwoods, and grassy regions with coppiced alders and gorse often near running water.

This extremely handsome and attractive thrush breeds in Europe from Germany, Austria, Hungary and Switzerland north to the Arctic Circle. In Scandinavia and the east it is more of a summer visitor whereas in central Europe it is generally present throughout the year. The fieldfare is almost entirely trans-Palaearctic and north-eastern Nearctic and it can be found in three climatic zones – the tundra, boreal and temperate. In the north its range does not reach much beyond the 50°F July isotherm. Fieldfares breed to 71°N in Norway and also in northern Sweden, Finland, Russia north to the Kara Sea, east to Perm and south to Kiev, Saratov and Orenburg. In Asia the range reaches east to the areas of Irkutsk and Yakutsk. The taiga-loving fieldfare has been extending its breeding range since the Ice Age westwards into Europe and, according to Dr Finnur Gudmundsson, it did not colonize Iceland as a breeding bird until 1950. The redwing had, of course, reached Iceland long enough ago to have permitted a new geographical form to have arisen.

A large flock of fieldfares was blown to Greenland, probably from Norway where, with an improvement in the climate, the birds had developed the habit of staying late until cold drove them out usually towards the British Isles. Such an exodus on 19 January 1937 was carried north-west by the strong winds originating from a depression situated unusually far to the south. Dead birds were found in Iceland, Jan Mayen and Ymer Island in east Greenland. Ten years afterwards, a flourishing colony of nesting fieldfares was discovered in the extreme south of Greenland where the climate was sub-arctic and comparatively warm. Fieldfares have also proved more successful than the redwing as colonists of central Europe. They began to breed in eastern Germany in the nineteenth century and occasionally also in western Germany. Now the species nests very locally and thinly throughout most of the two countries. Birds have bred in Switzerland since 1923 and Paul Géroudet has described how the fieldfare reached the Rheintal in 1925, Lake Neuchâtel by 1927 and in 1949 the basin of Lake Geneva. In less than thirty years this thrush advanced some 250 kilometres. By 1953 it was also nesting in the French Jura. Birds also breed in Poland, Hungary, Austria and Czechoslovakia and occasionally in the Faeroes and Holland. Denmark was colonized in the 1960s.

Fieldfares are chiefly migratory but their movements are often variable, may even take on 'invasion' qualities, and are apparently particularly subject to local weather conditions. Birds are reported wintering in Scandinavia and along the Baltic coasts and as far north as Leningrad in the European part of the Soviet Union and Krasnoyarsk in the Asiatic. Many birds move south to the British Isles, France and the countries of central and southern Europe. Fieldfares are rather rare in the Mediterranean region but birds have been observed in the Balearic Islands, Corsica, Sardinia, Sicily, Malta, Cyprus, north-west Africa and Egypt. Further to the east, birds also winter in southern Russia, Turkestan and Transcaspia and may even reach Iran and north-west India. The fieldfare is a vagrant to Anatolia and the Canaries.

In the British Isles this species is best known as a winter visitor and passage migrant but in recent years there has been a tendency for birds to remain later in the spring. I heard a bird singing one May on Holy Island and birds were also reported staying rather late – to May and June – in other parts of eastern England. The first breeding record in the British Isles occurred in 1967 in Orkney where a pair raised three young. In the following year came the first nesting in Shetland and in 1970 on the Scottish mainland when six young birds fledged from a nest in eastern Inverness-shire in June. By 1972 fieldfares were present at six known sites in Scotland. Since that year the published records show a few pairs breeding each year in north-east Scotland and in England. In 1975 birds were reported from six sites in two counties – Grampian and Staffordshire – with one pair proved to be breeding in the latter county.

Like the redwing the fieldfare is also a lover of the light mixed taiga especially along streams and by swamps. In the far north the woodlands will carry a considerable amount of birch and stretch into the sub-arctic zone; in Greenland the colony nests in birch and willow scrub that lies inland in the fjord region. Further south, the woods consist of pine, spruce, alder and birch with grassy environs. In Slovakia fieldfares range in the spruce forests from 100 to 1425 metres above sea level – the highest point reached by any of the four thrush species breeding in those woodlands.

Dr K. H. Voous also listed as European habitats 'Forest edges with upland, not alpine meadows, and clumps of trees (pine, spruce, birch) in quiet, cultivated areas'. Fieldfares also nest in parks and large public gardens in Scandinavia. In the British Isles the summer home of the breeding fieldfares is rather variable, ranging from open, crofting country in Shetland to more wooded country in the south. It will be interesting to see whether the colonization of the British Isles by the fieldfare will continue. Since 1950 there has been a notable growth in the number of species breeding in the British Isles. How long the climatic change, which has to some extent influenced this pattern, will go on is a matter for conjecture, but our ability to monitor these influences has also improved in recent years.

PLATE 9. REDWINGS. *Above*, a redwing at its rather shallow-built nest low down in a birch tree. *Below*, a redwing's nest on the ground in Norway. The characteristic creamy eye-stripe can be seen clearly in both individuals.

PLATE 10. FIELDFARE. This fieldfare is nesting in a birch tree in Norway. The present nest has been built on the remains of the previous year's structure.

CHAPTER 6

PLUMAGE AND MOULT

THE moulting of feathers in birds is essential if the animals are to remain healthy and to survive. Among the many important activities, besides that of actual flight, which are dependent upon the condition of the plumage are those of temperature regulation and the protection of the body. In addition to these obvious advantages to a species, the plumage that is assumed and periodically renewed helps in the recognition of each other by members of the same species, as well as highlighting sexual features which may be useful in display. In a crisis their feathers have even saved blackbirds and song thrushes, which have alighted on the sea and taken off again, while an adventurous mistle thrush was once seen swimming in a shallow pool. The feathers themselves are both unique to birds and typical of the class to which they belong. They are the extraordinarily complex and very specialized product of the epidermis, which lies above a thicker layer of skin, known as the dermis, and in which the muscles, nerves and blood vessels are housed.

The epidermis is formed from many layers of cells which as they divide keep pushing the older ones further away from the dermis with its life-support systems. The outer cells die and fill with keratin; this is a horny substance formed by their own metabolism. After being incubated for a short period the embryo of a bird begins to develop rows of tiny protuberances or pimples in well-marked patterns over its surface. Each tiny lump is the result of a rise in the epidermal cell multiplication rate and is, in effect, a feather 'germ'. It is soon transformed into a kind of pit containing a backward sloping cylinder. In the lower part of this tube occur the special cell growths that give the down feather form, moulded in keratin. As the cylinder grows it becomes ridged inside and these ridges contain the developing feather barbs. Other cells fuse together into two columns along each of the ridges; when these have become keratinized they will become the barbules, or lateral branches of the barbs, while processes on the barbules, known as barbicels, will become the hooks which engage with the barbicels of the next barbule to maintain the continuity of the feather or, in older birds, the vane. There is now a rather short quill from whose outer edge rises a coronet of barbs with short barbules. This forms the down feather. Some will go on being produced throughout the bird's life while others will be succeeded by adult feathers with vanes on each side of a central shaft.

Since the plumage and moults of the blackbird are perhaps best known

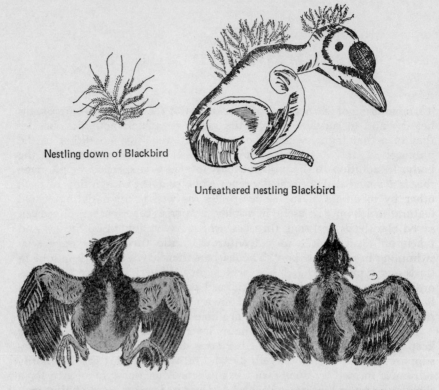

Nestling down of Blackbird

Unfeathered nestling Blackbird

Blackbird assuming nestling feathers from A History of British Birds by W. Yarrell 1856

FIG. 21. Nestling blackbirds.

among those of the British thrushes it would seem more logical to look at this species first. When a young blackbird is hatched in the nest it is remarkable for four features. It is altricial (incapable of locomotion), it remains in the nest (it is nidicolous), it is blind and it is very largely naked (it is psilopaedic). Gradually more down appears along certain characteristic tracts on the bird's surface. Figure 22 illustrates the down tracts that can be found in passerine birds. In the six British thrushes the down tracts are the inner supra-orbital, although rather scanty in the redwing, the occipital, the spinal, the humeral and the ulnar. In the mistle and song thrushes there are sometimes traces of an outer supra-orbital tract and the fieldfare and ring ouzel have short down in this region as well. In the ring ouzel there are sometimes short down tufts on the ventral tract. The down itself is buff-coloured and fairly long in both fieldfare and ring ouzel,

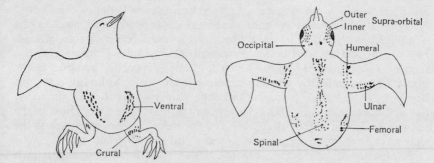

Mistle thrush   buffish white down, plentiful and quite long. Distributed inner and sometimes outer supra-orbital, occipital, spinal, humeral and ulnar regions. Interior mouth bright yellow, no tongue spots, and flange yellow.

Song thrush   golden buffish down and fairly long. Distributed inner supra-orbital, occipital, spinal, humeral and ulnar regions. Sometimes a few tufts at outer supra-orbital tract. Interior of mouth golden yellow, no spots and flange pale yellowish in colour.

Blackbird   rather sparse fairly long down, pale greyish-buff. Distributed inner supra-orbital, occipital, humeral, spinal and ulnar. Interior of mouth deep yellow, no spots and flange yellowish-white.

Ring ouzel   long plentiful buffish down. Distributed inner supra-orbital, outer supra-orbital (where rather short), occipital, humeral, ulnar, spinal, and short tufts on ventral. Interior mouth very deep yellow, no tongue spots and flange yellowish-white.

Redwing   long, rich down except scanty on inner supra-orbital region; fawn. Distributed also on occipital, spinal, humeral and ulnar regions. Mouth interior gamboge, no spots and flanges ivory.

Fieldfare   long, plentiful buffish down. Distributed outer supra-orbital, where short, inner supra-orbital, occipital, spinal, humeral and ulnar. Mouth interior yellow, no spots and flange yellowish-white.

FIG. 22. Down tracts on nestling thrushes.

fawn-coloured, long and plentiful in the redwing, buffish-white, quite long and well distributed in the mistle thrush, golden and fairly long in the song thrush, and pale greyish-buff and not very frequent in the blackbird. The inside of the nestlings' mouths is coloured in various shades of yellow and gold, and the external flanges by the bill are pale yellow in the mistle and song thrush, yellowish-white in the blackbird, ring ouzel and field-fare, and off white in the redwing.

The nestlings gradually assume the juvenile plumage usually when they are about a week old. Figure 21, reproduced from William Yarrell's *A History of British Birds* (1856), illustrates the upper and lower surfaces of a nestling blackbird. The juvenile blackbird is black-brown above, reddish brown and whitish buff underneath with dark-tipped feathers giving a blotchy appearance. When the juvenile plumage has been assumed in the blackbird it is generally possible to separate the sexes, although one must beware of considerable individual variation among juveniles. In the males the overall plumage as well as the primary flight feathers and those of the tail are darker in colour than those of the female. The markings of the wing coverts on the female are also paler and less obvious.

The juvenile mistle thrush has a buffish brown head and upper parts and as each feather has a whitish centre and darker tip the bird always looks to me very streaky and variegated; its appearance has sometimes led to its misidentification as a White's thrush. The chin and throat are unspotted and the rest of the underparts carry smaller spots than those to be seen on the adult. Juvenile song thrushes resemble the adults but there are buffish streaks on the upper parts, the spots on the underside are smaller, and the rump and upper tail coverts look rather paler. In the juvenile Hebridean song thrush the upper parts are darker than in the British bird and the streaks are more accentuated while the spots below are larger and also darker. At a first glance juvenile redwings look rather like juvenile song thrushes but, although there is very little chestnut on the flanks, they can be recognized by clear and prominent eye-stripes. The juvenile fieldfare is much duller than the adult with white shaft-streaks on the crown, nape and upper parts. Juvenile blackbirds and ring ouzels have a superficial resemblance, but the latter, although lacking the white gorget, are less red-brown in colour – more grey, in fact – and the underparts are more spotted and mottled with white shaft-streaks on the coverts.

Juveniles of the six species of British thrush moult their body plumage in late summer, changing all their feathers except for those of the tail and some in the wing. This newly acquired first-year plumage is not the same as the true adult plumage which will not be assumed for another twelve months. It is rather duller. The male blackbird is not so black, the wings are browner and there are traces of brown flecks on the breast, while the female has a redder plumage especially on the underside. When the wing is moulted some feathers are retained; these include the flight feathers, except for a few occasional inner secondaries, the alula or bastard wing, primary coverts and a certain number of the outer greater or secondary coverts (Fig. 23). The actual moult into the first-year plumage starts with the body plumage and wing coverts and ends with the head. The change of feathers on the head is achieved rather slowly so that for the last part of the moult the bird looks like an adult with a naked, ragged or flecked head. Dr David Snow called these individuals rather aptly 'vulturine'

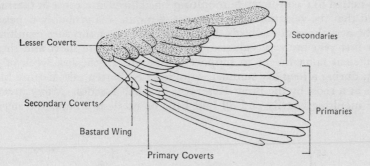

FIG. 23. Wing of typical first-year blackbird, showing unmoulted juvenile feathers (unshaded) and adult feathers (shaded). (Reproduced from *A Study of Blackbirds*, 1958, by permission of the author, Dr David Snow.)

young blackbirds and they often appear on my garden lawn during the dry overblown days of August. There is a lot of variation in the first-year plumage of male blackbirds and around my home I have seen some apparently almost adult, while others have looked more like mature females. This first moult lasts just over a month and the older juveniles start first. In Germany the more adult or advanced type of plumage has been called 'Fortschrittskleid' while the term 'Hemmungskleid' was employed for retarded plumage. Male blackbirds in retarded first-year plumage are known as 'Stockamsels'.

The first-year plumage of the other five thrush species is very close to that of the adults. The mistle thrush has a few pale shaft-streaks, the fieldfare is browner and not so grey, the song thrush resembles the adult except when any of the juvenile greater coverts still remain unmoulted, the redwing has a few white or buff tips on the secondary and greater coverts, and the ring ouzel male looks slightly duller and browner than the adult.

The actual time when the juvenile blackbird starts its moult seems to depend on the age of the bird and certain environmental factors such as food and daylength. Most juveniles go through their moult in August and September with the first birds of the year moulting first but not so significantly early as to indicate that the timing was solely dependent upon age. Dr Snow colour-ringed twenty-nine young blackbirds and observed the intervals between departure from the nest and the completion of the moult. In *A Study of Blackbirds* he wrote: 'For four which left the nest in April this interval ranged from 117 to 136 days, with an average of 127: for six birds which left the nest in July the interval ranged from 78 to 90 days, with an average of 86. For the nineteen which left the nest in May and June the interval averaged 112 days.' A. Richter (1972), who mist-netted 611 post-juvenile moulting blackbirds at a roost in Germany, found that the variation in and extent of moult was probably dependent on the actual age of the birds. Blackbirds and other thrushes moulting in their first year are very vulnerable if food supplies are short and there is insufficient nourishment to support the moult. In the last week of July 1975, during a long dry summer, I joined Leo Batten mist-netting blackbirds at a roost by the Brent Reservoir in north London. Many juveniles were moulting heavily and all had little or no flesh around the sternum

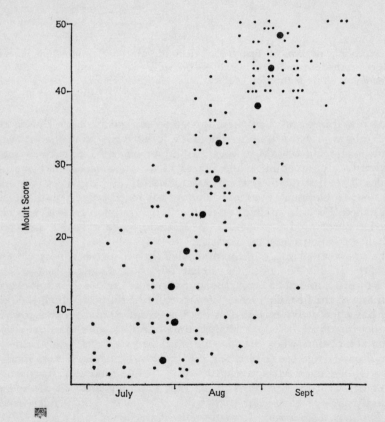

FIG. 24. Moult records of British song thrushes, all years. Each new primary feather is given a score of from 1 to 5, according to its stage of growth. Thus each individual whose primaries are in active moult can be given a primary score of from 1 to 49. Birds whose primary moult is complete score 50. Mean duration of moult in the individual has been estimated from the slope produced by plotting moult-score against date in all individuals. (Reproduced from *Bird Study*, Vol 16, 1969, by permission of Dr David Snow.)

and were underweight. For many weeks earthworms had not been available to any of the thrushes in suburban London. The beak and eye-rim of the first-year male blackbird are dark at first but then turn to golden yellow during the first winter. Females usually acquire their yellowish beaks in their first breeding season.

The next moult occurs in the second autumn of the thrush's life and this time all the feathers are moulted to produce the adult plumage. It has been known for some years that the timing and order of moult in birds is linked very closely to the ecological situation of each species. The British Trust for Ornithology has organized a Moult Enquiry since 1960 and details of individual birds in moult were entered on cards for analysis. The immediate aim of the enquiry was 'to gather information which would assist in distinguishing between adult and first-winter birds in late summer and autumn'. However, the data gathered had a much wider significance in studies relating the moult to breeding seasons and migrations. For the purposes of the enquiry, if in captured thrushes a system of scoring could be employed to give values to indicate the stage of the moult, it could also be used to plot the progress through the months. Each new primary was given a score of from one to five, according to its stage of growth, so that each individual bird whose primaries are being actively moulted can be given a 'score' of from one to forty-nine. Any bird which has fully completed its primary moult is entitled to a score of fifty.

Figure 25 gives the moult records of British blackbirds in 1967; moult scores, calculated in the way I have just described, are plotted against dates, grouped into five-day periods. Mean dates have been arrived at for each group of five scores and the mean duration of the moult has been estimated from the slope. As the slope is likely to flatten off near the fifty score the mean duration of the blackbird's moult has been estimated at eighty-five days. In 1967 nearly all the birds indexed began to moult in June or July; the extreme dates taking all years together were the fourth week of May and the third week of August. Generally blackbirds can be found in some stage of moult over a period of some five months. For many individual blackbirds the onset of its moult is directly influenced by the time at which its last attempt at breeding finishes. This may be affected by weather and this alone could account for annual differences in the blackbird's moult season. The bird's own history of breeding success or failure could also be a factor. Dr I. Newton (1972) found that individual finches started moulting at about the time that their last young of the year reached independence. The British Trust enquiry showed that there were reasons for variation in the timing of the moult quite independent of what A. A. Voitkevich (1966) called the external controlling factors. Dr Voitkevich, after a great deal of experimental work, suggested that the most important of these factors were light intensity and duration, acting through the anterior lobe of the pituitary to stimulate the thyroid gland.

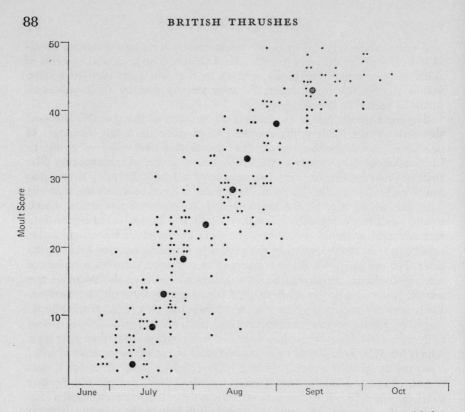

FIG. 25. Moult records of British blackbirds in 1967. See Fig. 24, page 86 for explanation of conventions. (Reproduced from *Bird Study*, Vol 16, 1969, by permission of Dr David Snow.)

In 1950 E. O. Höhn demonstrated that feathers grown during a thyroid deficiency became long and narrow and of a loose texture; he observed that there was undoubtedly a relationship between the moult and in-creased thyroid activity 'since a phase of high thyroid function preceding the moult is of widespread occurrence'. Dr Voitkevich believes that the thyroid hormones are more important in influencing moult than secretions from the gonadal system. Not all research workers agree with this view. Although accepting that thyroxin – the thyroid hormone – can increase the metabolic rate and accelerate moult they believe that the control of moult is primarily gonadal. It would seem reasonable to believe that daylength and its effect on the thyroid hormones are proximate factors in the moult of British thrushes but there are variations linked with breeding seasons and migratory range. The enquiry also revealed that there is no difference in the time of inception of blackbird moult in mainland Britain but there were some variations on offshore islands due to local ecological factors affecting the breeding season.

The moult score for the song thrush for all years when plotted against date (Fig. 24) gives a much steeper slope than that for the blackbird, due to a shorter mean duration – that of fifty days from 20 July–9 September. There are unfortunately only a few moult records for the mistle thrush but these give a somewhat tenuous indication of a long moult, perhaps of as long as one hundred days, from late May to late August or early September. Some support for the theory of a slow moult comes from the fact that in the middle of the blackbird's moult the average number of primaries in growth is 2·8; in the mistle thrush the equivalent figure is 1·9 but this was based on only seven specimens. It is clear that a great deal of work remains to be done in this particular field. Does the song thrush moult more quickly because it is more nomadic than the rather sedentary blackbird? The fieldfare and ring ouzel complete their moults between July and September and the redwing during August and September; all three, of course, are migratory species.

In four of the British thrush species – mistle thrush, song thrush, redwing and fieldfare – the sexes are basically similar in plumage but there are clear differences between male and female blackbirds and ring ouzels. We have already seen that even in the drab immature plumage of blackbirds sexual dimorphism is readily apparent. Where the sexes resemble each other the males have certain species-specific characters of voice or behaviour that must assist the females in making their ultimate choice of mate.

In September 1937 the late Colonel Richard Meinertzhagen wrote to me to draw my attention to two pure white blackbirds living in Kensington Gardens in London not far from the Long Water. During many of the years since then I have watched semi-white blackbirds near the same spot and in 1963 I directed a BBC film including a sequence showing one of the birds (Simms 1975). Albino or leucistic blackbirds are more often reported as instances of aberrant plumage than any other bird in the British Isles. I have observed about fifty in my lifetime from Aberdeenshire south to the Isles of Scilly. In twenty-five years at Dollis Hill I have known only one example of an aberrant blackbird. W. E. Glegg found that out of 201 cases of wholly or partially white birds in the British Isles 26·9% belonged to the family *Turdidae* while over two-thirds of these were blackbirds followed by a smaller proportion of song thrushes.

Albinism is the total lack of melanin pigment in the plumage, soft parts and irides and arises from a pathological condition with a genetic basis. Leucism, or paleness, is related to albinism and shows itself by an absence of pigment in the feathers combined with normal body pigmentation, producing white-marked birds with normally-coloured soft or unfeathered parts. Dilution is an overall lessening in the quality of all pigments. True albinism is congenital and acts, as far as is known, as a Mendelian recessive. Many of the aberrant blackbirds that one sees are only partially white and they can be either symmetrically – or more commonly – asymmetrically marked. A remarkably handsome and symmetrical male was photographed by G. W. Temperley while Ian D. Woodward (1961) described a male in Hertfordshire with a symmetrical gorget and eye-stripes. A male bird in my own garden in 1976 had short symmetrical wing bars and a white band across the tail.

It was suggested by J. M. Edson that a recessive gene in an isolated population may show itself more regularly than in a region of strong gene flow, hence the persistence of odd populations in some city parks. For twenty years or so partially white blackbirds were reported in areas of Hampshire and Surrey (Sage 1962) and I have known albinistic house sparrows at Dollis Hill for twenty-five years. Noble Rollin instituted a number of controlled feeding experiments to show that a deficiency of certain foods could cause blackbirds to develop white plumages and this was considered as a possible explanation of pied birds living in urban populations. The higher incidence in Russian towns was described by A. I. Ilyenko and after research into plumage aberrations in London's birds D. T. Holyoak found 1·8% of abnormal blackbirds, compared with figures of 1·2% in suburbia and 0% in the open country. It is well known that whiteness of plumage in some birds also increases with age. An adult male blackbird trapped in Lancashire on five occasions between 24 November 1950 and 1 July 1954 bore normal plumage; it was trapped again on 4 December 1955 when, after completing its moult, it carried large patches of white on the head and much of the plumage. This report by R. M. Band was then followed by a series of similar observations which showed that in progressive whitening of blackbirds the head often seemed to be the first part to lose the normal pigment. Holyoak was of the opinion that the plumage aberrations in town birds 'are more likely to be of direct genetic origin than caused by diet'. Perhaps natural selection was to some extent favouring variability in the volatile ecosystems of cities. It is unlikely that urban blackbirds would have to survive for very long on a restricted diet, but it seems clear that diet, old age, injury, perhaps disease and even shock may all have parts to play. There are also observations of birds with structurally altered white feathers while some partially white birds have also shown such defects as poor vision and deafness. Albinism in town blackbirds seems to be no great disadvantage to them but in woodlands and the countryside where predators may be commoner it could be a different story.

It is also possible for grey and fawn variants to occur among thrushes, indicating a loss of melanin. C. J. O. Harrison (1963) described grey and fawn plumages for redwings in the Berlin Museum as well as similar forms of the song thrush and dilute dark grey-brown forms of the blackbird. There are also records of cinnamon and golden brown varieties of female blackbirds, a pale buff-brown song thrush, and a grey variety of the American robin in New York. D'Urban and Matthew (1895), besides reporting a slaughter near Exeter of many pied blackbirds in the winters of 1879–80 and 1880–81, listed for the county of Devon two cream-coloured blackbirds, some white and buff-coloured mistle thrushes, partially white or cream song thrushes, all white and buff-coloured red-wings and a mottled white fieldfare. W. E. Hendy reported whitish mistle thrushes in Somerset and he knew of an albino redwing that was lodged in Taunton Museum. According to J. A. Bucknill a brown and white redwing was shot near Dulwich College. In November 1975 my daughter Amanda and I saw a fieldfare near Peterhead in Buchan with a striking all-white head. Sometimes dark varieties of thrushes can be found like the almost black fieldfare that J. E. Harting (1866) noted in *The Birds of Middlesex*.

Feather maintenance is an important part of the lives of all thrushes and birds can be seen spending part of each day in this occupation. My blackbirds in north-west London may spend up to 8% of their day preening and adjusting their feathers after flight, display, bathing or independently of these activities during 'resting' periods. Preening and oiling are important parts of daily life and it is quite possible that the use of feathers in display arose from such original actions as preening or feather and wing raising and shaking. Many of these latter movements are often well shown after thrushes have been bathing in water.

All the thrush species will bathe, lowering the front of the body and dipping the head and breast in the water. The bill is moved freely from side to side, the wings are flapped up and down and the tail lowered into the water which is then splashed over one side of the body and then over the other. It is an innate and complex affair. A song thrush which was watched by E. M. Williams in Somerset after being displaced from a bird-bath 'continued the actions of bathing, squatting on the ground, dipping its head and flapping its wings'. Blackbirds will also 'false-bathe' on grass lawns and R. B. Coleman observed a song thrush going through the motions of washing and head-ducking 'in a clump of dry ivy and butter-cup leaves' after finding the water in a pond not deep enough for proper bathing. After bathing there is always a great deal of wing flapping and feather shaking. In heavy rain I have seen blackbirds, redwings and song thrushes taking shelter in dense shrubberies or on twigs protected by branches and boughs above them, while ring ouzels may take refuge in stone walls. Occasionally it is possible to see both song thrushes and blackbirds 'bathe' in grass made sodden by dew or by light, continuous rain.

On very warm days in late summer at Dollis Hill I have watched song thrushes and blackbirds sunbathing, with birds lying prostrate on the

lawn or a flowerbed. Twice I have seen blackbirds remain in this posture
for more than ten minutes. In this situation the birds seem quite divorced
from reality and can be easily approached, which surely makes them
more vulnerable to predators. In high-intensity sunning postures both
wings and tail may be widely spread out on the ground and the mandibles
opened, so that the bird seems to have collapsed from the heat. C. W.
Teager (1967), who took a remarkable series of photographs of sunbathing
birds, watched a male blackbird during a period of forty minutes spend
26 minutes sunning itself, 8 minutes preening and 6 minutes in the shade.
Sunbathing certainly seems to stimulate preening actions. It is a fairly
common activity among herons, birds of prey, rails, doves, swallows, larks,
finches, buntings and thrushes. R. J. Kennedy described it not only as
taking place among song thrushes and blackbirds but also for the kurrichane
thrush (*T. libonyanus*), and in America for the American robin, wood thrush
(*Catharus mustelinus*), veery (*C. fuscescens*), hermit thrush (*C. guttatus*), and
olive-backed thrush (*C. ustulatus*). There is a great deal of speculation
about the role of sunbathing in birds, particularly about its function as a
response to temperature and the possibility of vitamin D irradiation. It
certainly seems that vitamin D is produced during preening activities
but Dr K. E. L. Simmons has put forward the suggestion that the increased warmth may induce parasites to move and so become more
accessible during preening. Head-scratching also seems to take place
rather commonly after birds have indulged in bouts of sunbathing.

Head-scratching movements are believed to have taxonomic significance.
They have been divided into two kinds – direct and indirect. In the former
instance a bird brings its foot straight up to the head, while in the latter
the bird first makes a positive movement by lowering one wing and then
bringing the corresponding leg over the shoulder up to the head. I have
seen indirect scratching in blackbirds, ring ouzels and song thrushes, and
Dr Simmons has records for the mistle thrush and American robin. It is
generally believed that of the two methods indirect head-scratching is the
more primitive, inherited from the birds' quadrapedal and reptilian
ancestors. This has been challenged on the grounds that the distribution
of indirect head-scratching amongst birds does not confirm this ancient
origin and that both methods may have been derived from earlier, less
sophisticated actions. Head-scratching can be set off by simple irritation
or it can be employed as an additional method of preening and oiling the
feathers of the head. Thrushes which Dr Simmons watched in the London
Zoo showed a clear sequence of bathing, drying, obtaining oil from the
preen gland on the rump by means of the bill, scratching the beak, trans-
ferring oil to the foot and then to the head. Young unfledged thrushes
often try to scratch indirectly but unsuccessfully.

Ectoparasites live on the exterior of thrushes and are the subject of the appendix. They include louse flies, fleas, chewing lice, ticks and feather mites.

One of the ways in which birds may rid themselves of ectoparasites is thought to have been the practice of 'anting' but there is no real evidence to support this theory. So far more than 200 species from more than 30 passerine families are known to 'ant'. H. Poulsen (1958) listed six species of *Turdus* engaging in this activity as well as three species of *Catharus*.

There are two main kinds of anting; 'active', whereby birds actually crush ants along the wing or tail with the bill and so apply formic acid, and 'passive' in which living ants are allowed to crawl up on to the birds' plumage. It seems to provide care and treatment for the feathers – often those rather difficult of access – from the chemical qualities of the ant fluids. Bathing, oiling and preening often follow a spell of anting. Although the process is innate, the recognition of ants as a means for anting has to be learned, but anting and preening do possess certain elements in common. Active anting has been described for blackbirds, song thrushes, mistle thrushes, redwings and ring ouzels and there are a few reports of passive anting by blackbirds, song and mistle thrushes, and redwings. W. S. Niven has described passive anting for the blackbird in which a male at Hythe, Kent, 'sank vent and belly into the moving mass of ants and spread out its wings so that the ants crept upwards through the feathers and on to its back'. In my experience blackbirds are not habitual anters and not all members of the same species of thrush seem equally attracted to or adept at the pursuit. Dr K. E. L. Simmons who has specialized in the study of this fascinating bird activity noted that the ants used by wild birds for anting in Britain included *Lasius niger* by blackbirds, song thrushes and possibly mistle thrushes, and *Lasius flavus* by blackbirds. In some interesting experiments a number of British ant species were presented to captive British birds and anting was recorded from a song thrush with the ants *Lasius niger*, *L. flavus*, *L. umbratus* and *Formica rufa* and from a mistle thrush with *F. rufa*. It would be of considerable interest to know whether *F. rufa* – the wood ant – is used in the wild in Britain. There is a wide literature on anting in British birds and references to it can be found in the full bibliography.

Finally, at the end of this review of plumage and moult among the British thrushes, some mention should be made of the fungi which are often recorded from the feathers of birds which Dr G. J. F. Pugh (1972) called 'the bird surface microhabitat'. There are two common groups of fungi – the cellulose decomposers and the keratinophilic, which bring about the decomposition of such substrates as the residues of animal remains including feathers, bone, wool and so on. Examples of the first kind have been isolated on blackbirds and song thrushes in Britain while the second in the genus *Arthrodema* were most often found on blackbirds. *A. curreyi* occurred on 30% of the blackbirds examined, on seventeen out of fifty-six song thrushes, and on one of two redwings suggesting a close link between this species and birds of the genus *Turdus*.

We have looked at many aspects of thrush plumage in this chapter since it plays a vital role in the life of the birds, both mechanically and thermally, and because there is still a great deal that is not known about it. It represents a field, as Dr Pugh suggested, 'where ornithologists, parasitologists, micrometeorologists and mycologists can profitably co-operate'.

CHAPTER 7

FOOD AND FEEDING HABITS

THRUSHES are very largely eaters of fruit or insects and other invertebrates, and this is certainly true of our six common British species. The
problem of how the interspecific differences in food selection are resolved
is both a fascinating and demanding one. To some extent competition is
avoided between the species by a different choice of habitat or the selection
of different parts of the ecosystem to exploit. The late Dr David Lack
showed that many of the closely related sympatric bird species of Europe,
if they were about the same size, generally lived in different habitats and
this kind of ecological separation ensured their satisfactory co-existence.
Where species do live alongside their close relations in the same habitat
these birds tend to show variation in body size and beak size, suggesting
their reliance on different kinds of food. There may be considerable overlap
in the diet of the thrushes, as we shall see in this chapter, but there are also
important differences.

In his New Naturalist volume, *Finches*, Dr Ian Newton showed that the
various species of finch reveal a close association between the size and
shape of their bills and the types of seedhead and the size of the seeds they
can exploit. There are also differences in the beak structure and size in
the six British thrushes. Figure 26 gives a visual indication of the average
variations between the different species. It will be seen that they fall into
two groups – blackbird, mistle thrush, ring ouzel and fieldfare with a
gradual slope downwards in size – and song thrush and redwing with
considerably shorter and finer beaks. The major ecological differences
arise from the choice and use of certain elements in the food resources,
and competition, if it takes place, will be influenced by habitat differences, the physical size and population levels of the birds, the size of
any one food crop and the availability of other foods.

There are certain obvious differences in food and feeding habits that
size will dictate. Blackbirds in my garden will take snowberries up to
1·9 cm in diameter, whereas the song thrush is incapable of taking such
large berries. Much bigger earthworms can be taken out by blackbirds
and mistle thrushes than by song thrushes because of their larger bills
and bodies and taller stance giving them greater leverage and pull back.
The kinetic properties of the bill involving the relationship of motion to
force and perhaps its internal musculature may also play a part. W. J.
Beecher (1951) has shown that adaptations such as these were largely

95

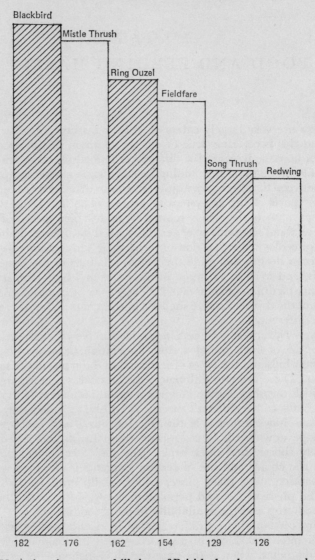

FIG. 26. Variations in average bill sizes of British thrushes, expressed as products of average maximum depth × average length in mm.

responsible for the ability of the American Icterid orioles to exploit all the available passerine food niches.

In this chapter I propose to look at all the major food resources of the

PLATE II. FIELDFARES.
Above, fieldfares often migrate by day and parties can sometimes be seen resting in trees with many individuals facing in the same direction. *Left*, a fieldfare fluffed up against the cold; the streaks and blotches on the upper breast are variable in shape, size and number.

PLATE 12. THRUSHES IN FLIGHT. *Top left*, song thrush; *right*, redwing. *Bottom left*, blackbird; *right*, fieldfare. This remarkable set of photographs of thrushes in flight was taken by Eric Hosking with high-speed flash lamps and electronic eye facing a lamp unit, ready to photograph the flying birds as they emerged from a tube.

Heads of Britain's Breeding Thrushes. *Top*, Blackbird and Mistle Thrush; *Centre*, Ring Ouzel and Fieldfare; *Bottom*, Song Thrush and Redwing

six British thrushes and then examine the dietary changes, the social behaviour and some of the aspects of food gathering and competition that have been observed. I shall start by taking a look at the animal foods first and then the vegetable material which forms part of the diet of these thrushes.

Earthworms have a most important role to play in the feeding ecology of all six species. I have watched ring ouzels in summer gathering them, sometimes with difficulty, from grassy areas within their breeding territories. The other five species of thrush find them on pasture fields, playing fields, airfields and humble garden lawns. Blackbirds will take them all the year round but in late summer and autumn fewer worms may be

Table 8. Some Important Vegetable Foods of British Thrushes

WILD FRUITS AND BERRIES	Blackbird	Song Thrush	Mistle Thrush	Ring Ouzel	Redwing	Fieldfare
Ash			●			
Birch		●				
Bird cherry	●	●	●	●		
Blackberry	●	●	●	●	●	
Buckthorn (*Rhamnus*)	●					
Crab-apple	●					●
Cowberry (*Empetrum*)				●		
Elder	●	●	●	●	●	●
Goosegrass	●					
Guelder rose	●		●			●
Hawthorn	●	●	●	●	●	●
Hip	●	●	●		●	●
Holly	●	●	●		●	●
Honeysuckle	●	●				
Ivy	●	●	●	●	●	
Juniper	●		●	●		●
Mistletoe			●			
Privet	●					
Rowan	●	●	●	●	●	●
Sloe (blackthorn)	●	●	●	●	●	●
Spindle tree	●					
Vaccinium sp.	●	●	●	●	●	●
White bryony	●					
Wild cherry	●					
Wild strawberry	●					
Yew	●	●	●	●	●	●

CULTIVATED FRUITS:
both on tree and fallen

	1	2	3	4	5	6
Apple	●	●	●		●	●
Cherry	●	●	●	●		
Cotoneaster	●	●	●		●	●
Currants	●	●	●	●		
Damson			●			
Gooseberry	●			●		
Fig	●	●				
Mulberry	●					
Pear	●	●	●		●	●
Plum	●	●	●			
Pyracantha						●
Raspberry	●	●		●		
Snowberry	●	●				
Strawberry	●	●		●		
Tomatoes	●					
Walnut	●					

ROOTS AND CEREALS

	1	2	3	4	5	6
Various plant seeds	●	●				●
Cereals	●					●
Roots, incl. Swedes and Turnips	●				●	●

available or taken out of choice. The ground is often too hard and in dry weather the worms may be far below the surface. Song thrushes regularly take worms from January to June. Blackbirds and song thrushes can often be seen standing on the grass with the head on one side as the birds peer down at the ground. Many birds that I have watched have stood in this way for ten seconds or more quite motionless. The bird will then strike quickly. It may fail to grasp the worm but in mild conditions these birds may catch a great number in a very short time – up to one or two every minute and some of the captures may be rejected or abandoned in favour of fresh ones. *Lumbricus terrestris* is the fattest and best known of the English garden earthworms; it feeds on the vegetable matter that collects on the grass and which it pulls down from the surface. It often betrays its presence by the stalks of ash or other tree leaves which protrude from its burrows. It is a key food resource for blackbirds and the commoner thrushes. Other oligochaete worms occur in lawns, including *Allolobophora longa* which is more slender, produces casts on the grass and will come to the surface if the earth is vibrated. I have already described in *Birds of Town and Suburb* how the late Dick Bagnall-Oakeley discovered that the passage and rumble of heavy sugar-beet lorries in Fenland and on the King's Lynn by-pass brought worms up to the surface where they were taken by blackbirds, song thrushes, redwings and fieldfares. The down draught from helicopter rotor blades has a similar effect. *Bimastus tenuis* occurs in leaf mould and *Eisenia foetida* in fermenting piles of organic rubbish and both are taken by blackbirds. Earthworms are often abundant in forest soils which are rich in mull humus but they are generally absent from peaty, acid soils. A great deal of blackbird 'worming' seems to take place in the mornings.

I have already mentioned how blackbirds and song thrushes will stand without moving on a lawn. They appear to be using their eyes and also listening very intently. I once watched a blackbird at a range of only two feet from a ward in the Middlesex Hospital in Mortimer Street as it looked for worms in a window box, and it certainly gave the impression of listening as well as looking. Blackbirds and other thrushes will apparently strike successfully when to our eyes no part of the worm is above ground but perhaps they glimpse the tip of the worm just inside its burrow. The characteristic cocking of the head or the peer down could well be used either to fix the prey with the eye or locate it by ear. Some interesting evidence was collected by F. Heppner (1965) into the way in which the American robin locates earthworms and perhaps his findings could apply to other members of the *Turdidae*. He used an automatic noise generator, recorded noises made by earthworms, carried out tests with artificial worm holes and made many observations in the field. He concluded that the American robin locates worms entirely by visual clues. My own field studies leave me not wholly convinced that blackbirds and song thrushes never use auditory clues.

All the six thrush species will swallow whole worms themselves but I have seen large ones intended for adult consumption or for the young being broken into small pieces or beaten, in the case of smaller worms for nestlings, into flaccid strips. Around my home in north-west London many generations of male, but rarely female, blackbirds have come to within two or three feet of me as I weeded the flowerbeds in summer to gather or receive worms to take to their young. It is a common sight to see black-birds, mistle and song thrushes feeding together on a worm-rich grassland and any competition or fighting between them for worms seems to be relatively unimportant. They normally feed together when worms are abundant and in times of shortage there is a change to other foods. All the common breeding species of thrush feeding young will drag their worm catches on the ground or wipe them from side to side, perhaps to expel surplus soil, remove the slime, or add a certain amount of grit to their nestlings' diet. In Scandinavia earthworms form an important part of the summer diet of fieldfares and redwings and both species will take them in winter from our pastures and grasslands. The toxic chemical dieldrin can be ingested by thrushes through their intake of worms and if the normal fat reserves of song thrushes are mobilized it is possible to reach a lethal level quickly – 18 ppm in the liver and 17 ppm in the brain (Jefferies and Davis 1968). Those birds which have died from other causes should show a level of only about 3 ppm.

With their efficient, multi-purpose beaks the thrushes are adept at exploiting a wide range of animal foods from just below the surface of the ground, as well as rummaging amongst loose soil and leaf litter and picking off visible insects and other invertebrates in many locations. The blackbird is the great expert at sorting out piles of leaves, moss clumps and hedgerow bottoms as well as extracting leatherjackets or cranefly larvae from below the surface – a habit it shares with the other five thrush species. For foraging in loose earth and leaf litter the blackbird has evolved a special technique. The bill is used to tip or lift leaves and bits of soil to one side while one leg comes forward to head level and scratches firmly backwards. In autumn and winter in my garden blackbirds shift large quantities of leaves every day as well as digging out moss and grass between paving stones and at the foot of my fences. They can also dig down through snow to reach hidden morsels of food.

Insects form an important part of the blackbird's diet as well as of other thrush species; these may be discovered in plants and shrubs, moving on the ground, or they can be revealed by the blackbird's own foraging technique. Indeed, whereas town and suburban blackbirds, rather like the American robin whose northward spring migration seems geared to the reappearance of earthworms after the cold winter, depend very much on worms, those living in woodland feed largely on insects, including caterpillars. In particular, the latter are widely fed to the young and their abundance seems to be related to the breeding season itself. On the other hand, in conditions of drought and dry weather, suburban blackbirds will readily resort to caterpillars. Dr David Snow found that from mid-May onwards the skin of nearly all the woodland nestling blackbirds he examined had a curious yellow tinge which he believed was derived from the pigment of the green caterpillars; the same phenomenon can be seen in nestling jays. When small caterpillars are dropping to the ground to pupate in mid-summer, blackbirds will come into woodlands from outside their breeding territories to exploit the new food resource. Song thrushes also take falling caterpillars in May and June and prefer them at this time to earthworms. Both species widely take Noctuid moth larvae and will even take the hairy caterpillars of the garden tiger *Arctia caja*.

The leaf litter animal population in woods tends to be reduced during the first two months of the year and this must to some extent control the numbers of thrushes and blackbirds feeding in woodland. In October and November I often see blackbirds in my garden assiduously searching the rose stems for aphid eggs. All six thrush species include animal foods in their diets and Table 10 lists some of the more important and regular ones. It is not intended to be complete.

Many kinds of beetles and their larvae fall prey to the six thrush species, particularly cockchafers (*Melolontha*), click beetles (*Elater*), rove beetles (*Staphylinidae*), ground beetles (*Carabus*) and weevils (*Curculionidae*). Ring ouzels will take *Orthoptera*, while caterpillars, earwigs and such members of the *Hymenoptera* as humblebees, ants, ichneumon flies, gall wasps, and sawflies figure prominently. Caddisflies (*Trichoptera*) are also taken. The two-winged flies (*Diptera*) are represented by the flowerflies, *Bibionidae* and craneflies; a single ring ouzel has been known to contain up to fifty larval craneflies. To obtain some of the heavy-bodied flying insects mistle thrushes and fieldfares may fly up like starlings high into the air in their quest for their prey and ring ouzels will chase them low over their moorland haunts. Spiders, centipedes and millipedes will also be taken to supplement the basic animal foods of worms, caterpillars and often snails.

Woodland and urban song thrushes may display differences in their feeding ecology. They do not sift through litter like blackbirds; in woods the snails most regularly eaten bury themselves in the ground while garden snails which overwinter at the bases of old walls and shrubs are more easily available. Song thrushes seem to take snails only when other sources of food are scarce, particularly caterpillars or earthworms. Dr Desmond Morris (1954) investigated the snail-eating behaviour of song thrushes and the techniques used by the birds to tackle the two snail species – the garden snail (*Helix aspersa*) and the rather variable grove or dark-lipped banded snail (*Cepaea nemoralis*). The snails are first located by a systematic search through the vegetation and then carried to a hard surface to be broken and eaten. It need not always be the same place and it is not normally close to an occupied nest site where the noise of shell-hammering might attract unwelcome predators to the area. I have seen variously sized stones and rocks used as anvils by song thrushes as well as concrete and tarmacadamed roads, the tops of brick walls, exposed tree roots and once a glass bottle. T. A. Coward also recorded in Yorkshire 'the hard stems of the sea-buckthorn'.

The snail-shell may be held by the rim of its aperture, as the song thrush flies to its anvil, and during the subsequent prolonged hammering activities. But like Dr C. Suffern (1954) I have seen the thrush holding the

Song thrush breaking snail-shell on an anvil

snail itself through the opening. The beating action is rhythmic and regular, with the bird's head held firstly to the left or right, and then the head and neck come down with considerable force. 'It is,' wrote Dr Morris, 'a combination of the lowering and turning movements that produces sufficient force to crack the snail-shell.' Generally the snail-shells are opened with the loss of just a portion of the shell and only a small proportion of shells is actually smashed to bits. The snail is thrown out and then picked up by the song thrush which sets about wiping it on the ground, either to remove pieces of shell or perhaps the slime on the snail's body. I have never seen the foot used to hold the snail and Dr Morris suggested that the song thrush does not have the 'nervous equipment' to hold things with its feet. In general, of course, a ground-feeding species needs its feet unencumbered for a quick take off if danger should threaten. Empty snail-shells are sometimes gathered and hammered but not for long.

In a study of thrush predation on the white-lipped banded snail (*Cepaea hortensis*) – a species which shows considerable variation both in its background colour and the number and thickness of the dark bands on the whorls – C. B. Goodhart (1958) found that more pink than yellow shells of this polymorphic species were gathered by thrushes in summer than in winter. This snail is a reserve food taken chiefly in cold weather or in summer after the caterpillar bloom and before the coming of the main fruit crop. Another study at Bishop's Stortford sewage farm by the College's natural history society during cold weather examined the many piles of *Cepaea* species and concluded that the less regularly marked varieties were being taken. Selective predation by the thrushes must have played some part in the polymorphism of the snail species, and many inappropriately coloured snails may be removed.

It is clear that song thrushes turn to snails at times when other kinds of food are short. The other five species will also take snails although they are not able to employ the sophisticated techniques of the song thrush. The mistle thrush is known to feed on small snails but as I pointed out in chapter 2 I have not known it to use an anvil. The blackbird is a great consumer of snails but it favours small ones and will acquire larger ones by successfully parasitizing song thrushes. Dr Desmond Morris believed that the blackbird was not equipped to hammer snails against anvils despite Yarrell's categoric statement that blackbirds obtain snails which 'are dexterously beaten against a stone to get at the soft body of the animal within', and MacGillivray's contention that the blackbird's food in winter consists principally of snails 'the shells of which it breaks by raising them in its bill, and dashing them against a stone or other hard surface'. I have never witnessed this myself; such hammering may be very unusual or perhaps the habit has been lost. I have watched blackbirds extracting snails from their shells by an untidy and slow mixture of shaking, stabbing and wiping movements, similar to those recorded by Miss Sybil Butlin (1959). However, Miss S. Vere Benson (1963) nursed a first-winter male blackbird and after giving it its liberty she then provided it with a variety of foods including earthworms, grubs, snails, soaked bread, berries and scraps. It disclosed a very special liking for large garden snails (*Helix aspersa*). Small snails of this species were swallowed whole while 'the big ones were beaten on the floor and the bodies extracted from the broken shells in the manner of Song Thrushes'. The blackbird did not use the fast-battering technique and its head was less rapidly turned about. We know little about the feeding behaviour of many of our common birds. It is interesting to note that Colonel R. Meinertzhagen observed that the blackbirds of Ushant in Brittany ate small snails so regularly in a region devoid of berries and soft fruit that the practice had excluded the song thrush from the region.

Fieldfares, redwings and ring ouzels take land snails and I have records of the first two thrushes feeding on *Cepaea* species and ring ouzels on *Clausilia* and more rarely on *Pyramidula* in limestone areas. Molluscs tend to flourish best in such regions since calcium carbonate is an important constituent of their shells. Redwings take both *Helix aspersa* and *Cepaea nemoralis* and in MacGillivray's *History of Birds* there is a description of how a redwing opens snails by 'blows of its beak on the thinner or spiral end'. An Iceland redwing in North Uist was found by J. W. Campbell (1936) to contain remains of the slippery snail (*Cochlicopa lubrica*) and of the amber snail (*Succinea* sp). It would be interesting to know how widely the genus *Turdus* avails itself in the British Isles of this kind of food.

Slugs stand rather low in human esteem due to their slimy quality and the damage that some will do in our gardens. The garden slug (*Arion hortensis*) breeds throughout most of the year and is one of our best known pests, while the netted slug (*Agriolimax reticulatus*) is the commonest British slug and when contracted has a characteristic dome-shaped body.

Both species figure in the diet of mistle thrushes, song thrushes, redwings and blackbirds. Before eating them or feeding them to their young the adult birds will generally wipe them on bare earth or on grass to remove the slime. One individual redwing in my garden spent half a minute doing this and blackbirds may remain occupied in the task for several minutes at a time. I have also seen London blackbirds removing both great pond snails (*Limnaea stagnalis*) and ramshorns (*Planorbis*) from my garden pond, and apparently song thrushes may also take these rather large freshwater molluscs. A male blackbird in Norfolk was found dead with an example of the great pond snail caught behind the spurs of its tongue and perforating its palate. Blackbirds will feed from ponds and even running water, moving quite heavy stones about and pulling up or turning leaves of aquatic plants over in their search for snails, flatworms, small frogs, tadpoles, newts and even stranded fish.

Marine molluscs are perhaps taken more widely by some of the thrush species than has been previously suspected, especially in cold weather. O. D. Hunt watched a score of song thrushes feeding on common periwinkles (*Littorina littorea*) in January 1963 along the shoreline of St John's Lake on the Cornish side of the Tamar estuary; 'they were beating the molluscs out of their shells on stones'. Some of the birds worked away on the beach while others carried the molluscs to clifftop anvils normally used for dealing with garden snails. This habit has been regularly recorded on the estuary of the Exe in Devon and was described in the County Bird Report for 1940. Following on notes in the journal *British Birds* the editors asked for further information about this habit of shoreline feeding and they received nine replies. C. J. Feare (1967) writing about the enquiry observed that the habit of thrushes feeding in the littoral zone 'does not seem to be uncommon'. Both common periwinkles and the rough winkle (*L. saxatilis*) have been found in the diets of blackbird, mistle thrush, song thrush, Hebridean song thrush and redwing. Song thrushes will also feed on dog whelks (*Thais=Nucella lapillus*) – a habit mentioned by Howard Saunders in 1899 in his *An Illustrated Manual of British Birds* – and perhaps on topshells (*Gibbula*) as well. In cold weather fieldfares can sometimes be seen exploring the beach for small marine animals. Hebridean song thrushes have been known to take small crabs and Bernard King watched song thrushes in September 1959 on St Agnes in the Isles of Scilly competing with turnstones and dunlin for the crop of sandhoppers (*Gammarus locusta*) that appeared on the wet sand and in the tide wrack. Marine worms may also form a food resource and blackbirds have been recorded taking lugworms (*Arenicola*), ribbon worms and greenish polychaete worms from the sands of the Solent and song thrushes lugworms at low tide on the Isles of Scilly.

Many of these observations illustrate the wide tastes of members of the genus *Turdus*. Mistle thrushes have also attacked sand lizards in south

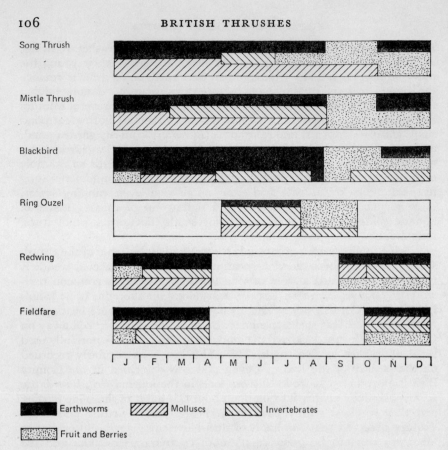

FIG. 27. Sources of food exploited by British thrushes.

Lancashire and they have also been known, according to *The Handbook of British Birds*, to kill young song thrushes, blackbirds and hedgesparrows to feed their young; slow-worms have also been taken. Song thrushes have also tried to capture slow-worms and a ring ouzel on Exmoor took a lizard to its young. Blackbirds have experimented with eggs of their own species, a dog's faeces, and even attacked and carried off shrews, including a fully grown pygmy shrew, adult house mice, fledgling house sparrows, newts, slow-worms and both common and sand lizards. Dr Desmond Morris's description of the blackbird as 'dietetically adventurous' is no overstatement!

From late summer to early winter fruit and berries form the chief food of the thrushes. About 45% of the mistle thrush's food is vegetable, about 60% of the blackbird's and the proportion for the song thrush and redwing rather smaller. Both cultivated and wild fruits or berries may figure in the late summer and autumn diet and I propose to mention the cultivated ones first, since among gardeners and smallholders these are perhaps the best known victims. In winter fallen apples have attracted all the British thrush species to my suburban garden except the ring ouzel, while fallen pears have been eaten by blackbirds, song thrushes and mistle thrushes. Blackbirds will make inroads into many cultivated fruits especially strawberries, raspberries, plums, currants, cherries, figs and even tomatoes. Both mistle and song thrushes have a strong attraction to the same kinds of fruit. Ring ouzels have been known to take cherries and gooseberries, and George Bolam, quoted by Dr David Bannerman in *The Birds of the British Isles*, condemned these mountain thrushes as 'greater thieves of fruit of all kinds than either blackbirds or thrushes'; they apparently carried out their raids in the small hours. Mistle thrushes tend to move out into the open country, the downlands and hills just as the main fruit season is coming on and they are not much of a problem to us.

Blackbirds and fieldfares are the most frequent feeders on fallen cultivated and crab-apples and at the waste heaps in commercial orchards in winter. Song thrushes are much less frequent and I have rarely seen redwings picking at the fruit. In the Venerable P. H. T. Hartley's study of wild fruits in the diet of British thrushes there were no records of redwings feeding either on crab-apples or cultivated apples. Blackbirds and fieldfares are certainly specialized apple-eaters and there is an interesting record of five thousand fieldfares finding food among apple orchards in south Warwickshire in 1962.

Orchard fruits are not the only ones to figure in the diet of British thrushes. There are the fruits of many ornamental trees and shrubs which can prove very attractive and valuable food reserves. These include figs, which are taken by blackbirds and song thrushes, cotoneasters, which provide food for the commoner species, daphnes, barberries with coral-red berries, pyracanthas and those special blackbird favourites – rowans, walnuts, snowberries and mulberries. As an undergraduate at Merton College, Oxford, I used to watch the blackbirds winging their way from all directions and over the college garden walls to visit the fruiting mulberry. Dr David Snow, studying the blackbirds of the Oxford Botanic Garden, saw them making off for Merton Garden when the fruit was ripe. Birds seem to prefer ripe fruits that are red or black while blue also rates quite high (Turcek 1963). The change in colour from dull inconspicuous tones to the full colour of ripeness is a signal to fruit-eating birds that the fruit is ready to eat. There is quite a reserve of protein in unripe fruits but these give no real selection advantage and the concentration of sugars grows with ripening at the expense of the polysaccharides. It is part of the strategy of fruits to be conspicuous, easily accessible and not sour. Young blackbirds, which will tentatively investigate many objects in an exploratory sort of way, seem to have an innate desire to peck at red and glossy berries and show a clear preference for red cherries rather than yellow ones. The presence of toxic substances in the seeds or fleshy parts of fruits would appear to be a kind of defence mechanism against birds and other animals. Birds can, however, feed on vegetable material that would cause illness or death in man or his domestic animals. It seems that each case must be looked at individually and there is still a great deal to be learned about the features which give selective value to particular foods. I have already mentioned accessibility of fruits and this is an important factor in the dispersal by birds of their seeds. Terminal bunches or single fruits are the easiest to reach. Blackbirds will crawl about and even hang loosely spread-eagled across the twigs with open wings, while song thrushes will peck, often rather ineffectively, at bobbing snowberries to remove morsels of food or more effectively at haws and yew berries. Some blackbirds will fly up and hover to take snowberries one at a time to be swallowed whole somewhere else. Mistle thrushes have been reported snatching fruits with an upward lift in the middle of a sweeping glide.

In the autumn and winter months especially the thrushes turn eagerly towards the harvest of wild fruits and berries. From Table 9 it can be seen that the song thrush is essentially the yew berry thrush (with 75·6% of the records), the blackbird the haw thrush, and the mistle thrush the yew and holly. The fieldfare and redwing are specialists on haws and have rather similar wild fruit diets; here there may be some interspecific competition with the redwing often at the losing end. The two wintering thrushes differ from the mistle and song thrushes in their low intake of yew berries and from the blackbird in their greater dependence on haws. Mistle and song thrushes show considerable similarities in their diets of wild fruits. Most fruits are eaten by thrushes at their time of ripening but holly berries, which are not highly favoured fruits, have two seasons of consumption by mistle and song thrushes and by blackbirds – from May to June and autumn to the end of the year. Table 9 also shows the catholic food tastes of the blackbird with twenty-one different fruit species appearing in 745 records, compared with only seven fruits in 531 records for the song thrush; here in part lies the success of the blackbird as a species. Although the fieldfare does not appear in the table as an eater of rowan berries I have a number of records and it should be remembered that this fruit is widely eaten in Europe. Indeed the mass occurrence of fieldfares in Finland in the winter of 1964–65 was attributed to the exceptionally good rowan crop that autumn which held back the normally migratory birds; conditions were also mild with no snow. Emigration only took place when the food supply was exhausted.

Hartley observed that blackberries are not a general food with thrushes and he reported the taking of these fruits with any frequency only in western Cornwall. Here in the early mornings blackbirds, song thrushes

Table 9. Records of Thrushes Eating Wild Fruits from Three Localities

	Combined Results					Sway. Hants.			South Wales			Berks–Oxon Borders		
	MISTLE THRUSH	FIELDFARE	SONG THRUSH	REDWING	BLACKBIRD	MISTLE THRUSH	SONG THRUSH	BLACKBIRD	MISTLE THRUSH	SONG THRUSH	BLACKBIRD	MISTLE THRUSH	SONG THRUSH	BLACKBIRD
Yew	111	—	404	1	64	58	163	17	—	—	—	41	232	39
Holly	63	3	27	12	101	1	2	3	48	11	60	12	14	27
Spindle	—	—	—	—	4	—	—	—	—	—	—	—	—	3
Blackberry	—	—	6	—	39	—	1	11	—	2	—	—	—	—
Wild strawberry	—	—	—	—	1	—	—	—	—	—	—	—	—	—
Hip	—	—	—	—	5	—	—	—	—	—	—	—	—	5
Sloe	—	—	—	—	1	—	—	—	—	—	—	—	—	—
Wild cherry	—	—	—	—	1	—	—	—	—	—	—	—	—	—
Haw	44	47	31	143	306	6	9	65	28	10	24	6	4	109
Rowan	3	—	—	1	12	—	—	—	—	—	—	—	—	5
Crab-apple	—	4	—	—	26	—	—	—	—	—	1	—	—	17
Ivy	25	—	29	7	76	—	—	—	20	6	13	1	15	24
White bryony	—	—	—	—	1	—	—	—	—	—	—	—	—	1
Walnut	—	—	—	—	1	—	—	—	—	—	—	—	—	1
Whortleberry (*Vaccinium*)	2	—	1	—	60	—	—	—	2	1	60	—	—	—
Privet	—	—	—	—	4	—	—	—	—	—	—	—	—	—
Goosegrass	—	—	—	—	1	—	—	—	—	—	—	—	—	1
Elder	2	—	33	2	37	—	—	—	2	30	34	—	2	1
Guelder rose	—	—	—	—	1	—	—	—	—	—	—	—	—	—
Honeysuckle	—	—	—	—	2	—	—	—	—	—	—	—	—	—
Gladdon (*Iris*)	—	—	—	—	2	—	—	—	—	—	—	—	—	—

Reproduced from *British Birds*, Vol. XLVII, 1954, by kind permission of the author, the Venerable P. H. T. Hartley

and robins fed regularly on blackberries and one young blackbird was seen to eat five at one feed. I have seen blackbirds taking blackberries, especially in dry seasons, on London suburban allotments. R. E. Scott kept records of passerines eating blackberries at Dungeness in Kent throughout two autumns and these included blackbird, song thrush, redwing and ring ouzel. On their migrations and summer breeding grounds ring ouzels will also feed on the fruit of *Vaccinium* and *Empetrum*, wild cherry, blackthorn, yew, ivy, elder, juniper and rowan. I have watched ring ouzels in autumn feeding on the brilliant red rowan berries

Table 10. Some Important Animal Foods of British Thrushes

Food	BLACK-BIRD	SONG THRUSH	MISTLE THRUSH	RING OUZEL	RED-WING	FIELD-FARE
Annelid worms	●	●	●	●	●	●
Cockchafers	●	●	●		●	●
Click beetles	●	●	●			●
Scarab beetles	●	●				
Weevils (*Otiorrhynchus*)	●					●
Rove beetles	●	●	●			
Wireworm beetles	●	●	●			●
Ground beetles	●		●			
Weevils (*Curculionidae*)	●	●	●			●
Orthoptera				●		
Noctuid moths	●	●		●		
„ „ larvae	●	●		●	●	
Pieris caterpillars	●	●	●			
Earwigs	●	●	●	●	●	
Humblebees (Bombus)	●	●	●	●		
Ants	●	●	●			
Ichneumons	●	●		●		
Gall wasps	●					
Sawflies	●	●				
Caddisflies	●			●		
Aphids	●					
Craneflies	●	●	●	●	●	●
Flowerflies (*Anthomyia*)	●	●	●			
Flies (*Bibionidae*)	●	●			●	
Spiders	●	●	●	●		●
Centipedes	●	●	●			
Millipedes	●	●	●			

Food	BLACK-BIRD	SONG THRUSH	MISTLE THRUSH	RING OUZEL	RED-WING	FIELD-FARE
Molluscs: Periwinkles	●	●	●		●	
Dog whelk (*Thais*)		●				
Pond snail (*Limnaea*)	●		●			
Ramshorn (*Planorbis*)			●			
Land snail (*Helix*)	●	●	●		●	
(*Cepaea*)	●	●	●		●	●
(*Clausilia*)				●		
(*Cochlicopa*)	●	●				
(*Zonitoides*)	●					
Slugs (*Agriolimax*)	●	●	●		●	
(*Arion*)	●	●	●		●	●

in the high glens of the Grampians and a London migrant at Haverstock Hill found a berry-laden rowan a welcome feeding station on his journey across the capital. The hillside homes of the ring ouzels are often dotted with shrubby evergreen junipers with their blue-black berries; these mountain thrushes will take these fruits and so also will mistle thrushes and blackbirds. In Germany the fieldfare shows such a liking for juniper berries that the bird is known as the 'Wacholderdrossel'.

In 1968 Miss Janet Kear listed the plant poisons that occur in the diet of wild birds and these included the following thrush foods: spindle (euonymine?), buckthorn (emodin), bryony (bryonin), privet (ligustrin), yew (taxine), juniper and ivy. The berries of ivy figure quite widely in the diet of British thrushes. Gilbert White, who was vastly intrigued by the migrant ring ouzels around Selborne, observed that in spring this thrush 'feeds on ivy berries, which ripen only at that season, in March and April'. Redwings will also take them and I have watched birds feeding alongside smaller numbers of blackbirds, song and mistle thrushes. In 1948 Col. B. H. Ryves found no fewer than fifty ivy berry seeds on the floor of a song thrush's nest recently evacuated by four young birds. In south Wales it was apparently a common practice for song thrushes and blackbirds to feed ivy berries to their young as an occasional change from earthworms. The undigested seeds are disgorged by the nestlings.

In bad weather blackbirds, redwings and fieldfares may turn their attention to root crops in the fields and the last species has a strong liking for turnips. Seeds and cereals may also be included in bad weather diets. In the long cold spell of 1962/63 mistle and song thrushes seem to have taken fewer strange foods than other thrush species. Visitors to bird tables included all but the redwing while all five species resorted to kitchen scraps. Redwings were seen feeding on bits of tongue, cooked peas, rich tea biscuit, cheese and 'Swoop'. Fieldfares also chose red oranges as an emergency diet. The two wintering thrushes often visit towns in cold weather. A fieldfare stayed from 20 February to 13 March 1955 in my garden in north-west London and another remained for just over three weeks in 1963 feeding on apples. In 1938 I watched a party of fieldfares strip hawthorn berries from some trees in Ladbroke Square in Kensington. Blackbirds will switch to many kinds of food, as we have seen already, but the individual that Frank Finn saw pecking at a bone in the cage of an African hawk eagle in the London Zoo was surely a little more than foolhardy!

It is clear from what I have said so far that there can be dietary changes among the British thrushes influenced by habitat, season, weather and the availability of other foods. For example, Hampshire mistle and song thrushes will eat yew berries but there were no records from the Venerable P. H. T. Hartley's survey of diets from south Wales. Bad weather may send thrushes to other parts of the country in a search for new supplies of food. The depredations on berries by the larger species may force the smaller redwings to move on or die. Besides these there are also seasonal changes and trends which can be traced for all of the thrush species. Song thrushes may eat snails early in the year and switch to earthworms particularly during the first half of the year. At the start of summer – in May and June – the collection of snails is reduced and caterpillars are widely taken, especially in woodland. In July there may be another reduction in snail-eating and worms are taken once more, but in very dry conditions, where worms are difficult to reach below the surface, the gathering of snails will continue. Then in autumn the song thrushes turn their attentions to fruits and berries.

Correspondingly, blackbirds, which take haws in mid-winter, move on to worms in January as well as small snails. Both adult insects and caterpillars are taken during the nesting season by woodland blackbirds to feed to the young, while in parks and gardens earthworms continue to be extracted and given to the nestlings. In my own garden in the summer of 1974 caterpillars formed about 10% of the nestling food; the rest was primarily earthworms. In the late summer the blackbird may not find many worms and will move on to fruit and berries and in winter will supplement its diet with hibernating invertebrates, scraps and bread. Mistle thrushes, which breed early in the year, take invertebrate foods to feed to their young and will go on collecting animal food from grassland during their late summer flocking before turning to berries and other fruits. The ring ouzel, after the nesting season, is essentially a fruit-eater and the two wintering thrushes share their varied diet of animal foods and fruits. There is an interesting report of blackbirds and song thrushes eating linseed oil putty used to repair a greenhouse at Norwich but this suggests a dietary deficiency. A blackbird has been seen eating the fallen flowers of a wild cherry and a song thrush has been reported feeding the leaves of sea-pink to a juvenile.

When groups of thrushes are feeding together aggressive encounters may take place generally between individuals of different species rather than between individuals of the same species. These attacks are usually designed either to capture items of food or to drive competitors away. I have watched blackbirds taking worms from song thrushes and redwings and also arriving to steal a newly prepared snail from an unsuspecting song thrush. In this latter instance we have an interesting example of the triumph of adaptability over specialization. A fieldfare that spent part of a winter in my garden chased all the local blackbirds up to distances of a hundred metres from its food supply. Fieldfares and mistle thrushes will dominate blackbirds, song thrushes and redwings, but do not seem to attack each other. Blackbirds will persecute redwings, song thrushes and each other, while I have seen redwings attacking only song thrushes and other redwings. Song thrushes seem to come right at the bottom of the pecking order. In 1965 P. W. Davies and Dr David Snow found that, where the food supply becomes scarce, competition does not increase 'because the thrushes change to other foods and interspecific overlap in feeding niche, at least between the Song Thrush and the Blackbird, is reduced'. In aerial chases the dominant roles may sometimes be reversed, especially between song thrushes and blackbirds. Food-fighting between different members of the family seems on the whole to be less significant than say, in the tits or crows. The thrushes, when feeding, are not themselves immune from attack by other birds, and starlings and gulls will rob mistle thrushes and blackbirds of their worms. One interesting piece of opportunism was observed in June 1967 by G. R. Gervis who saw a female blackbird 'following the trail of a Mole *Talpa europaea* which was tunnelling just under the surface of the soft water-side soil' and picking up bits of food that were exposed; it also kept other blackbirds away from this unusual feeding station.

After eating it is quite usual to see thrushes wiping their bills on the ground or on the branches and twigs of trees, especially after taking worms, snails and caterpillars. This is done with a cut-throat razor technique of stropping each side of the beak alternately on a firm object. Bills are also cleaned during the process of bathing which was described in the last chapter.

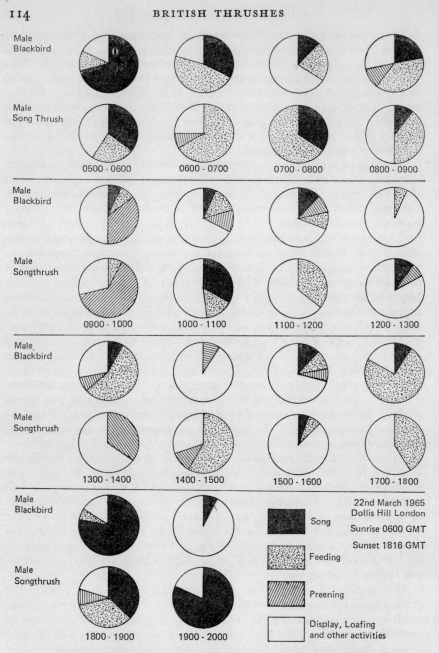

FIG. 28. Hourly activities of male blackbird and song thrush.

The frequency of feeding and drinking during the day is a difficult matter to determine. Outside the period in which young have to be fed and food-gathering goes on for most of the daylight hours, the thrushes tend to feed in short bursts, broken up by periods of rest, preening and display. To some extent the frequency of feeding will depend on the weather and the availability of food. In hard weather blackbirds will spend most of the day foraging through leaf litter and taking advantage of artificial foods. Song thrushes will desert the oakwoods in winter but the blackbird, although staying where it is, seems as I wrote in *Woodland Birds* to have 'more time for other activities than, say, the blue tit which is constantly searching for tiny items such as insect eggs'. It would also seem that the other thrushes normally find some time for 'loafing'.

I have rarely seen thrushes come to drink since they seem to obtain water for the correct metabolic function of their bodies largely from their food. All foodstuffs contain some free water and earthworms, snails and fruit with their succulent quality must supply a great deal. The temperature and humidity of the atmosphere and the activities of an individual bird play some part as well. When the birds drink they do so in a typically passerine fashion. I particularly like the description by E. W. Hendy of the mistle thrush which 'drinks delicately, sipping small dainty beakfuls; as he lifts up his head you can see his spotted throat ripple while the water trickles down'. I have seen a blackbird soak a piece of bread in water and occasionally a bird may wash a beakful of leatherjackets. Blackbirds and song thrushes have also been known to open milk bottles and drink from them. Blackbirds will also sip water lying on fallen leaves and bricks.

From this chapter it is apparent that there are ecological differences in autumn and winter between closely allied members of the thrush family. In summer there are also certain habitat and food preferences which help to prevent interspecific competition. It is very clear that the high proportion of blackbirds to mistle and song thrushes reflects the adaptability and catholic tastes of the former species which have made it the most widely known British member of the thrush family.

CHAPTER 8

BREEDING BEHAVIOUR:
THE EARLY STAGES

THE purpose of this chapter is to give a broad account of the behaviour of our breeding thrushes from the initial taking up of territories, pairing, display and song to the actual selection of nest sites. A great deal has been written already about the significance of territory in the blackbird and there is not sufficient space to reproduce all of it here. I propose to summarize this material first and then review what is known about the territorial behaviour of the other thrush species.

The basis of the system of territories among birds is a ritualized one, which avoids 'scrambles' for food and can give stability to populations of birds. Professor R. A. Hinde (1956) described territory as 'a topographically localized defended area' which is especially guarded before or during the seasons of breeding, although in some instances the defence may be continued throughout the year. There may also be some differences in territorial behaviour in a species depending on local environments. Territories may result from two distinct predispositions in their holders – an attachment to the site and generally a distinct hostility towards members of the same species and the same sex. Either predisposition can occur without the other.

The actual function of territory is to space out individuals, pairs or larger populations. Territories can be elastic in character but the more they are compressed the more they resist further compression. The exact value of the spacing out of territories is still a matter for argument but it can certainly limit the population density of a species. Density may also to some extent be regulated by newcomers avoiding previously settled areas. If these are moved on as a result of aggressive behaviour or song then their departure is the result of territorial behaviour.

In my twenty-five-year study of blackbirds at Dollis Hill in north-west London I have found the species extremely territorial by nature and the 'territories tend to have as their nuclei the traditional, often annual, breeding site'. This results in a rather static pattern of territories in the area. A pair of blackbirds has bred in a *Philadelphus* in my garden at least once in every year from 1951 to 1976. In winter the female of the pair often roosts close to the old nest. She is sometimes joined by a roosting male on odd nights in December and January and much more regularly in February or March. In one year, after using the *Philadelphus* site to raise three young, a pair built a second nest in an adjoining ash tree. When

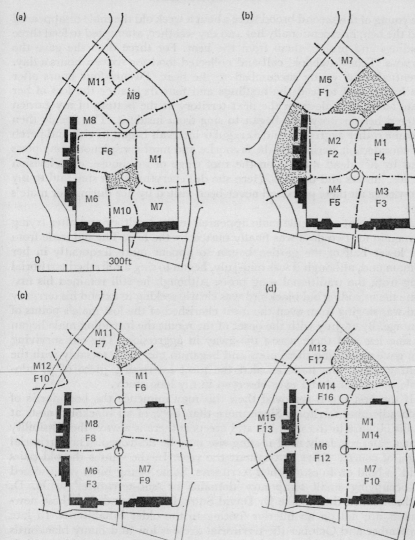

FIG. 29. Territories of song thrushes in the Oxford Botanic Garden during 1954–56: (a) winter territories of seven males and one female in February–March 1955; (b) breeding season territories of five pairs and an unmated male in 1954; (c) breeding season territories of six pairs in 1955; (d) breeding season territories of six pairs and an unmated female in 1956. The shaded areas were unoccupied. M=male, F=female; each individual has its own number. (Reproduced from *British Birds*, Vol 58, 1965, by permission of Dr David Snow.)

the young of this second brood were about a week old the male disappeared and the hen, in exceptionally hot and dry weather, attempted to feed three nestlings and protect them from the heat. For three days she gave the nervous 'Tchook-tchook' call and collected food for sixteen hours a day. Eventually the young succumbed to the heat. Twenty-four hours after she had ceased to feed the nestlings and four days after the loss of her mate an adult male from the next territory at the bottom of my garden entered her territory and began to sing from inside it. The female then became rather aggressive and at regular intervals began to visit and perch for considerable periods on the favourite and most conspicuous song posts used by her dead mate – on the roof ridge of my house, on television aerials, gutters and treetops. Here she did everything but sing and to my knowledge all these posts had never been visited by her during her mate's life!

At this point a juvenile male appeared in the territory and after trying to remain for two days was finally ousted by the hen. The old male from the lower half of the garden began to appear more frequently in her domain and, although it was mid-July, began to sing a refreshed territorial song from the traditional song posts. Although he still retained his first mate the intruding old blackbird was clearly seeking to extend his territory and was singing from even the most cherished of the lost male's points of vantage. By 25 July with the onset of the moult the intruding male began to sing less and there was a die-away in aggression. The old surviving hen gave up visiting these posts and began to mix more sociably with the visiting male. She had revealed the most interesting piece of pseudo-male behaviour that I ever observed in my long study.

If the nest site is removed then this may influence the boundaries of each adjoining territory. Since more than 80% of all blackbird nests at Dollis Hill are in trees, bushes and creepers there is always the possibility that a safe, regularly used nesting site may be destroyed. The territorial urge, of course, varies throughout the year. In the winter the old pairs tend to hold on to established territories. Some young birds will succeed in occupying small temporary domains or 'sub-territories' as R. D. Jackson called them. Like Dr David Snow I have found that these new-comers are not on an inferior footing to the older inhabitants. In late September and October the territorial drive is low and many blackbirds will feed outside their territories. I have seen small groups of blackbirds feeding close together but without giving the impression of being really social birds.

By February and March blackbirds are occupying established territories and there is a marked rise in the aggressive behaviour of both old and young birds. This activity may be delayed by adverse weather. Some of the young birds succeed in filling vacancies left by death or by squeezing themselves into a new territory between established ones; this last de-

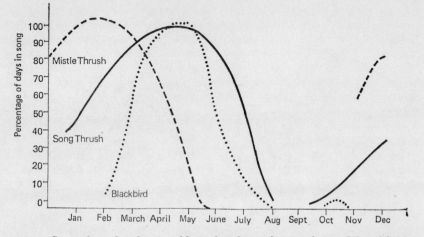

FIG. 30. Song chart for three resident thrush species, south-east Warwickshire, 1948. (Simms.)

velopment is rather unusual at Dollis Hill because of the somewhat rigid pattern of territories there. Young birds also seem to spend the early part of the day in their 'domains' and the rest of it feeding with other birds outside their territories. From spring until July the territories are defended against all other blackbirds. Then, as the moult begins, the drive starts to wither away. Autumn aggression, when the sexual drive is low, may be directed against male and female alike. Females are rather less territorial than the males but some can be very vigorous in their defence of territories. Actual defence is highest at the time when a female selects a site and builds her nest. Dr Snow (1958) pointed out that it can usually be assumed that 'if a male is seen engaging his neighbours in conflict his mate is starting or about to start a new nest'. Among young males the desire to assume territories awakens in autumn but does not reach its climax until late in the winter. Figure 31 shows the territories occupied by blackbirds over six years around my Dollis Hill home. The effect of the severe winter of 1962–63 is incidentally very clearly shown. Stability in the territories is normally assured by the survival of the established nest site and of a high proportion of old birds.

Although a nest site is vital in a territory, a suitable song post may be sufficient to attract a young male in the first instance as he tries to establish his domain. In suburbia there are forests of television aerials, chimney stacks and pots, roof tops and gutters, lamp posts, trees and shrubs to provide song posts. A male must acquire a territory before being able to obtain a mate, and attachment to this area can give positive advantages to a bird since there must be some survival value in the intimate knowledge

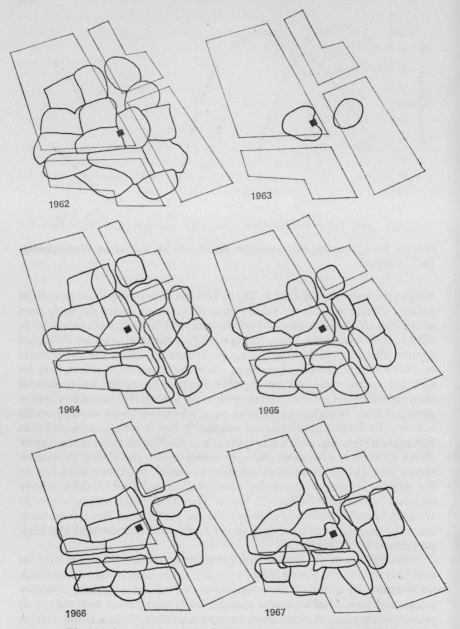

FIG. 31. Blackbird territories around the author's house, Dollis Hill, London, 1962–67. Note effect of severe winter of 1962–63.

of the topography and resources within it. We have already seen that generally females show a lower level of aggressive activity than males but there are exceptions. Among blackbirds females begin to dominate males after pairing has been completed. In the eastern robin of North America, H. Young (1951) observed that 'the males arrive first and establish these territories, but the females, once mated and established, play a large part in maintaining them and actually seem to be more influenced by territorial boundaries than do the males'. Among the blackbirds the fiercest fights between females are usually over males. The size of blackbird territories is very variable. There may be 0·089 pairs to an acre of Surrey oakwood and up to 2·771 in an overgrown garden.

Among song thrushes territories are re-established in late autumn and early winter but this process is often gradual and rather variable from year to year (Fig. 29). Many old males tend to remain in the previous season's territory and food supply may affect the reoccupation of territories. In a poor year for food the birds may not return until December, whereas in a better season territories may be defended from early November onwards. From then the song thrushes hold their territories with an increasing drive and passion except during periods of cold weather. Many thrushes will roost and feed outside their boundaries during the winter months. Both sexes in the song thrush will hold separate territories in winter but usually there is a preponderance of males. P. W. Davies and Dr D. W. Snow (1965) found in the Oxford Botanic Garden that an average 48% of the males and 80% of the females disappeared from their territories each year. It was thought that 'the disappearance of males was probably mainly due to death, whereas the disappearance of females was largely due to migration away from the area'. In woodlands song thrushes are often scarce in the winter months and territories may not be set up until just before nesting begins; these may occur at a density of some 0·1 pairs per acre while in gardens the density may be eight times as high. In Europe the territories of song thrushes are often at a greater density than those of blackbirds and in Estonia song thrushes lead the table of breeding density followed in order by redwing, blackbird and fieldfare.

The territorial behaviour of the mistle thrush is something of an enigma. The density of breeding mistle thrushes compared with that of blackbirds and song thrushes is generally low especially in the woods, parklands and gardens of Britain. On heaths and moorland mistle thrushes may outnumber song thrushes. In Ireland I often found the mistle to be the commonest thrush, occurring widely in treeless areas which suggests that its breeding density is influenced by habitat. Unlike song thrushes and blackbirds which will feed outside their territories, the mistle thrush maintains and defends the boundaries of its large territory with great vigour and passion. The mistle thrush territories that I have measured

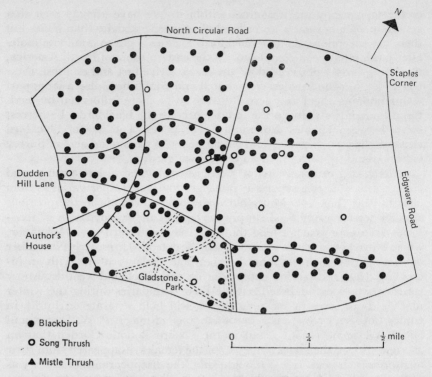

FIG. 32. The distribution of thrush nests at Dollis Hill, London, 1975. A 1928–32 estate with factories to the east where bird territories are sparse.

vary from 1½ acres in wooded parkland to several acres in woods and open country. In a Northamptonshire oakwood of about 200 acres over a period of five years I counted each year from 27 to 36 pairs of blackbirds, 8 to 12 pairs of song thrushes but never more than 2 pairs of mistle thrushes. According to the Common Birds Census densities rarely exceed 10 pairs per square kilometre while the average in 1972 for farmland was 1·9 and woodland 4·9 pairs.

Why should the behaviour patterns of the mistle thrush differ so much from those of the other common thrushes? In this particular field there is still opportunity for valuable research.

Redwings will nest in quite close proximity to each other so that one can often hear a dozen males in song at the same time; they do not actually breed in colonies. H. Tyrväinen (1969), watching in southern Finland, found that after the first broods of redwings had left the nest, the entire system of territories changed and second nests were usually built outside the territory containing the first. He discovered that even unpaired cocks also changed their territories at this time but this could have been brought about by the general shift of paired birds. Fieldfares, on the other hand, generally nest in colonies and behave in a social rather than a territorial manner. Among blackbirds the territorial behaviour secures the isolation of the nest and the protection of the mate from the attentions of rivals. Fieldfares are noisy and aggressive during the nesting season and it has been suggested that those redwings which often nest near to them may benefit from the presence of their bolder neighbours as they give notice of predators or even keep them at bay. The blackbird originated as a shy bird of woodland thickets rather than of more open woodlands and this habit may well be linked with its territorial behaviour. Ring ouzels tend to have widely distributed territories over their favoured hillsides. Singing males which I have watched in the Pennines, Cairngorms, Ireland and elsewhere always seem to be at a considerable distance from each other and the territories are quite large. In Midlothian, Roger Durman found from 12–14 first-brood nests in $1\frac{3}{4}$ miles of valley; the minimum distance apart was 160 metres.

In the family of thrushes can be found some of the most fluent or dramatic performers in the world of songbirds. Among blackbirds spring song is largely from young males establishing their territories but it seems to have no great part to play in pair formation. After all many pairs are formed in December, January and early February before song actually begins. Young males will also go on singing in gardens even after acquiring mates and it would seem that it is visual displays which play the more important part in pairing. In mid-winter in my own suburban garden pairing is achieved when aggressive behaviour between the sexes changes, often subtly, to courtship. If a resident male blackbird has lost its mate it will, like some other species, step up its output of song. The mellow song of the blackbird begins in late winter and early spring (Fig. 30) and its start is very much influenced by the weather, especially temperature levels. The birds at Dollis Hill begin to sing earlier than those in Hertfordshire or at Oxford, and I have heard blackbird song in the London area as early as mid-December. Twice in twenty-five years I have known the blackbird's territorial song to run well into August. It will increase in level during incubation, drop off as the eggs hatch, and then remain at a low but fairly constant level until July.

Figure 9 is a sonagram for a male blackbird's territorial song that I recorded at Dollis Hill in April 1957, revealing the fairly pure tone fundamental frequencies typical of this kind of song; they are confined within a range of about 1·5 kHz with not much sound above 2·5 kHz. In Figure 9 it is possible to see the sonagram of the sub-song of that same individual, revealing many impure and harsh-sounding notes both of higher and lower fundamental frequencies. This sub-song is common in the late winter among young males and adults with a low but rising sex hormone level; it has been called the 'raw material' from which full territorial song evolves. In the blackbird it flows, sometimes easily, sometimes haltingly, and it is generally audible for only a few feet. I have records of it from August to March and it is often performed in dense cover or on the ground.

The juvenile blackbird learns song phrases from the parent male and from other blackbirds in the region, but E. and I. Messmer (1956) showed that even an old bird could learn from a young one. It is clear that imitation is very largely responsible for the blackbird's full song. In early broods this may be achieved in the same season of birth but in late broods the practice will have to wait until the next singing season. In her study of the development of song in the blackbird Joan Hall-Craggs was able by her recordings to show how individuals improved their performance, confirming my own recordings of the same individual in 1956 and 1957. Counter-singing, communal and antiphonal singing as well as imitations of other birds were recorded by her and she was of the opinion that it was manipulation of material that was responsible for the song development rather than the material itself. In a letter to me in 1975 Mrs Hall-Craggs reported that 'blackbirds not only "make mistakes" in their songs (occasionally) but are also capable of recognizing the fact and correcting their errors'. It is possible that there might be some trace, even of aesthetic activity in the trial-and-error song-learning. Blackbirds will sometimes imitate other species and I made a tape recording of a male copying a song thrush at Crowland Abbey. One population of blackbirds in Essex mimicked human whistles. With the help of sonagrams E. Tretzel (1967) traced a complex whistle-motif sung by a population of blackbirds to the man who used it to summon his cat; the original imitator transposed the motif up a fifth and added ornamentation to it. In my experience some male blackbirds will sing at night. The late Commander A. W. P. Robertson (1949) described a female blackbird's sub-song as 'a soft, indeterminate flow of melody, with none of the male's characteristic pauses', and Mrs Margaret Jones heard 'typical blackbird song' from a female flying to the nest in the same situation in which a male might sing.

Figure 3 is a sonagram of the territorial song of a song thrush which was recorded by John Kirby. This individual was singing in April in Yorkshire and the purity of its tone is very clear. The sub-song from the same bird is also illustrated by a sonagram and reveals lower frequencies and a wider frequency range. To the ear the sub-song may resemble a low robin-type warbling with a curious twittering quality. The full song can be heard in most months of the year with a persistence characteristic of an isomorphic species, but it is at its richest from late winter to summer. The bird is generally rather silent in August and September. Song thrushes are very imitative and I have noted 'the song of blackbird, nightingale and great tit as well as calls of blackbird, chaffinch, jay, lapwing, mallard, curlew, stone curlew and redshank', while K. G. Spencer also noted whitethroat, snipe, redshank, oystercatcher and curlew. Song thrushes will often choose high and conspicuous song posts but I have seen birds in Ireland and Scotland in open country singing on or very close to the ground.

In March 1954 I obtained a tape recording of the full song of a mistle thrush in Kent. Figure 6 is a sonagram illustrating this bird's utterance which shows a run of characteristically pure notes in the bird's loud, repeated song phrases. From a recording of the sub-song of this same individual and the resultant sonagram it is clear that the notes become harsh and impure with a wide frequency range and a rambling quality, suggestive of an imperfectly formed full song.

In recent years in Britain we have had the opportunity to become familiar with the song of the redwing, one of the northern species now breeding further to the south. I have heard a number of territorial songs in summer from redwings in Scotland as well as occasional individuals singing at dusk or dawn in England. The opening notes are fluty in quality but the ending tends to be rather weak and indeterminate. The sonagram in Figure 15 shows an Iceland redwing's song recorded in June by the late Dr Ludwig Koch. Recognizable motifs often occur in redwing populations. Around Abisko in Sweden there were two motifs. One was an ordinary stereotyped phrase 'Trui-trui-trui' with slight variations, sung by 90% of the population, while the remainder performed 'a more melodious song with clear tones in a falling chromatic scale' (Lundevall 1952). In neighbouring Norway T. Bjorke (1974) found that there were sharp boundaries between redwing dialects although there were no physical barriers or uninhabitable zones dividing them. A few birds on the border might sing one dialect for most of the time but occasionally they indulged in the dialect of the next neighbourhood. The redwing's sub-song consists of gay, bubbling and twittering notes and often occurs in March and April. Figure 15 contains a sonagram of this delightful utterance which I recorded in March in Kent. The phrases are ill-defined with a wide frequency range.

The semi-colonial fieldfare has a feeble warbled song, interrupted by wheezes and chuckles, unlike the more precise, far-carrying notes of the other more territorial thrushes. It can, in the form of sub-song, be heard from birds at winter roosts and I have heard it in England in May. Both the poor song type and the sub-song may be given from a perch or in flight.

The ring ouzel holds quite a fair-sized territory and has an effective if simple fluting song, eminently in keeping with the wild terrain which it frequents. Figure 12 contains a sonagram made from a recording by Richard Savage of a male ring ouzel singing in June on Dartmoor. It consists of the clear piping notes, which were of two types in this individual, and a quiet song-thrush-like 'cascade' of notes. Ring ouzels may sing on the wing and are often heard at dawn and towards nightfall.

Song is very much a declaration of prospective or real occupation of a territory and so it possesses an innate aggressive value. A good deal of song may be rather functionless and desultory, especially later in the season when males may be involved with other activities, such as protection for the mate and concern with the nest. The more territorial of the thrush species may have to fight with other members of the same species and indulge in a whole series of physical postures designed to show how dominant or subservient they happen to be. The components of courtship displays can be sexual, aggressive or fear responses as well as those associated, according to R. J. Andrew, with 'alert, nesting, parental and begging behaviour'. Some aspects of courtship display among the thrushes are similar to their aggressive behaviour. In the late winter it may, in fact, be impossible to separate sexual from aggressive activity. The courtship displays are linked with pair formation when conflicting aggressive and sexual tendencies are resolved in favour of the latter. For this reason it would seem logical to describe the belligerent threat behaviour first since elements of it appear later in the activities of courtship.

Two male blackbirds in aggressive postures on boundary of territories

The blackbird's threat involves the upward stretching of the neck, the fluffing out of the feathers on the neck and nape and perhaps the rest of the body, the smoothing down of the head feathers and the raising of the beak above the horizontal. The lifting of the bill as part of an aggressive blackbird's repertoire and in reproductive fighting is a common feature of many passerine displays including both male and female courtship. It has been reported in reproductive fighting in at least 34 species and in courtship in 48 (R. J. Andrew 1961); it also occurs in the song thrush and the American robin. Lowering the bill is a feature of courtship display in the blackbird when, as in raising it, the gape may also be opened. In threat the blackbird's tail is pressed down like a half-opened fan and the wings are extended towards the ground. Sometimes the feathers on the rump are puffed out – a feature also of song thrushes and fieldfares – the tail is expanded and the high-pitched 'seee' note is introduced, indicating a raised level of aggression; eventually what Dr David Snow called 'strangled' song will reveal a very intense level of aggression. All of us who are familiar with blackbirds will have witnessed the chief features of these aggressive activities – the bouncing approach to a rival, the close pursuit through the branches, the 'bow and run' with its slow swing up of the head and back as well as the attitudes of the submissive or retreating bird – hunched with tail up and raised 'crest'. The flicking of the wings and the jerking of the tail show uncertainty and nervousness in a bird. It may even pick up twigs and other small objects.

When my local blackbirds will not break off an encounter a fight will ensue with two birds fluttering up and down to land again with bills open and tails spread before the next bout. The contestants may be males competing for territories, or male and female. At Dollis Hill there are communal displays and much fighting where several territories adjoin and contests are waged along the territorial boundaries. I have never seen a bird killed but a sick victim may be attacked by males which adopt a very malevolent look 'strangely suggestive of a reptile'.

An aggressive encounter between two song thrushes was one of the first pieces of bird behaviour that I described as a fledgling schoolboy ornithologist. It took place on 26 March 1935 when I watched two birds in the late afternoon in Ladbroke Square in London. A male had been giving his territorial song some twenty feet up in a London plane tree. A second thrush alighted in an adjoining tree, singing a low soft twittering sub-song. The first bird then switched from full to sub-song and this induced the newcomer to fly up and alight near the first singer. 'For a minute the second bird flitted from branch to branch around the singer and never more than five feet away. Then the singer fluffed out his flank feathers and dropped to the grass below. The second bird followed and the two thrushes danced round each other still twittering. Then the singer attacked the intruder and both began fiercely to beat their wings against each other and flutter several feet up into the air. The beating wings made a crisp clapping sound. Every so often both would lie horizontal on the ground and rest. Finally, the first bird alighted on the second and held it down by the breast but the latter managed to get up. Then a blackbird, who had been watching proceedings and excitedly flicking his wings, suddenly flew out calling and both song thrushes took off.' In courtship the male will run in front of the female with the head thrown back and the bill opened and the tail expanded and depressed, rather in the manner of a blackbird. B. F. Harvey in 1946 described a song thrush display in which the male circled clockwise around the female with depressed tail and head held up almost vertically and A. P. Radford noted a similar pre-copulation display near Bristol.

Forward threat posture of song thrush

The cock mistle thrush will pursue other males in the branches of trees for minutes on end in a very noisy fashion; if the pursuit is a sexual one after a female he is silent. The male can also fan the tail and spread the wings but it does not erect the rump feathers in the manner of the black-bird, song thrush and fieldfare. He will also reveal the white in his wings by flying round the female. Fluffing out the breast and flank feathers is a regular part of mistle thrush display but Dr M. F. White reported in 1971 an unusual observation in which a bird displaying in her Surrey garden trembled the feathers around the cloaca as well. There are reports of a warbling aggressive display in mistle thrushes but I have not seen it myself. Actual pairing after courtship takes place early as the bird is an early breeder.

The fieldfare has been seen to employ an aggressive display in spring in Britain in which, according to D. V. Butt (1949), a bird was seen 'to elevate its tail to an angle of ninety degrees above its back, partially spreading it, and at the same time flicking its wings and this successfully put a neighbouring fieldfare in the meadow to flight'. In the blackbird 'tail up' indicates submission but this can hardly be true of this fieldfare. In courtship the male fieldfare has a stiff-winged song flight and also a blackbird-like strut with drooping wings, the tail fanned and depressed, the rump feathers fluffed up but with the head and beak pointing towards the ground. The smaller redwing behaves rather like the song thrush, has an aggressive display and may snap its mandibles like its relation, but we remain ignorant of a great deal of its display behaviour. I have witnessed aggressive behaviour among ring ouzels in the Pennines, which resembles that of blackbirds, with the male crouching low and flying up at a rival with a lot of fluttering and occasionally the locking of claws which also happens with the commoner species. In courtship the cock ring ouzel hops or walks around the hen with head up, gorget clearly revealed, and a gentle subdued twittering issuing from his bill. In some places such as the Snake Road between Sheffield and Manchester the breeding population has been described as 'very dense' and in these circumstances display may be of more frequent occurrence than in areas where the birds are thinner on the ground. The proximity of two individuals to each other is an important factor in eliciting aggression but internal factors such as hormone levels may play an important part as well.

Male blackbird courting female

In full courtship the blackbird has a very dramatic and eye-catching display. As Dr David Snow has described it with an admirable and vivid succinctness I am pleased to quote it with his approval. 'The head, with the crown feathers partially erected and the beak open, is stretched forward; the neck feathers are compressed, and the body feathers fluffed out, especially the feathers of the rump, which form a conspicuous hump; and the tail is fanned and depressed. The displaying bird has a curiously wild, staring appearance.' On the ground this posture is enhanced by short runs and bows and some 'strangled' song. In a tree the male employs more exaggerated bowing movements, even touching the bill on the branch as in threat display. There may also be a slow-winged progress in flight from branch to branch. The whole performance bears a strong resemblance to the high-level aggressive display. In pre-copulatory behaviour the male blackbird often lowers the bill, even to the ground. There is no wing vibration in this type of display. Both blackbirds and fieldfares when committed to this display may run quite fast.

The courtship displays of blackbirds and other thrushes are linked to pair formation. In the case of established pairs they are a preliminary to copulation, inducing receptivity in the female which adopts the soliciting posture with the bill held almost vertical and the tail at the same angle like a capital 'V'. In twenty-five years of continuous study of the blackbirds at Dollis Hill I have very rarely seen copulation taking place. Courtship displays of this sort are a visible part of the bird activities of winter and spring but they are not essential to pairing. Some blackbirds and other thrushes seem able to achieve it without display. Once pairing has taken place between January and May blackbirds tend to remain together in the British Isles for life. In Europe where the population is more fluid new pairs tend to be established each year. Once the pair bond has been forged the female blackbird becomes the dominant member of the partnership.

Forty years ago it was thought that courtship feeding was not a feature of the genus *Turdus*, although it had been recognized in the related robin and a few of the warblers of the *Sylviidae*. In 1943 Major Arnold Boyd watched a mistle thrush in Cheshire flying down to another bird with food in its bill and 'it offered the food to the second bird, which accepted it and ate it, and it then mounted the back of this bird four times in fairly quick succession'. Four years later R. E. Williams described how a male mistle thrush fed a female and this food presentation was followed by copulation. About the same time there were also two records of male mistle thrushes feeding hen birds on the nest. Courtship feeding has also been recognized in the blackbird by F. Sauerbrei in 1926, and in 1956 A. Manning observed a male in Surrey picking up bread and being joined by a female which 'crouched down, head and neck vertical with the beak wide open and wings fluttering'. The male made several attempts to feed the female but without success. Two examples of males feeding females on the nest were reported from Cornwall and Devon. It would also seem to occur in redwings in Swedish Lapland where a crouching hen on the edge of a nest was watched being fed by the male bird. Courtship feeding, like 'billing', is a revival of an infantile form of behaviour and both have evolved from the activities when young birds are given food. It does not appear to be very common among the thrushes. There may be a relationship between the begging posture and the head-pushed-forward threat display. There is some evidence that male thrushes may locate food items for their mates but they do not often proffer them. I have watched both song thrushes and blackbirds behaving in this way which can also be seen when young birds are beginning to find food for themselves.

Actual breeding seasons in the British Isles are the subject of chapter 10 but it seems that the onset of breeding is timed to match the average time at which suitable weather, which permits efficient breeding to take place, comes along. The nesting period is determined by natural selection, regulated by the factors just mentioned, which provide optimal conditions of food, natural cover and breeding site, as well as proximate factors involving the bird's physiological condition and environmental changes which themselves may influence the bird's physiology. Food is obviously important but it is a complex set of proximate factors that stimulates a bird to breed and these may vary with latitude and the nature of the habitat. In higher latitudes a strong influencing factor is daylength which affects the bird's gonads while the rise in temperature may also have an effect, by triggering off an invertebrate 'bloom'.

Breeding between the different thrush species would appear to be rare. L-A. Sandstrom reported a case of interbreeding between blackbird and fieldfare and Dr K. H. Voous noted hybridization between blackbird, redwing and fieldfare. In the European breeding range there is probably some interspecific competition taking place.

In normal years – that is, without prolonged high wind, heavy rain or intense cold – the blackbirds in my garden in north-west London begin to search for nest sites towards the end of February and this is generally up to a fortnight earlier than the birds in the Hertfordshire countryside to the north. The hen blackbird generally chooses the nest site but the male will also do so on occasion. Blackbird nests can be found in a wide variety of situations but a high proportion is found in trees, bushes, hedges and bramble brakes. Of 611 nests that I found at Dollis Hill the distribution was as follows:

In trees and bushes	In creeper on walls	On pipes on walls	On ledges of fences	On stacked ladders	In sheds and buildings
497	16	15	76	3	4

Blackbirds will also exploit quite a wide range of heights and of the same 611 nests I found the height distribution as follows:

0–5 ft	5–10 ft	10–15 ft	15–20 ft	20–25 ft	25–30 ft
4	510	56	22	16	3

However, a blackbird's nest was once found in a tall sycamore in Edinburgh at a height of 30 metres. Birds will also sometimes nest on the ground, particularly among bracken, both in Europe and the British Isles. A nest in Orkney was eight feet underground in an eighteen-inch crevice. Of 204 occupied nest sites in Shetland L. S. V. and U. M. Venables found half on ledges inside buildings, 19% in stone walls, 18% in bushes and vegetation, 9% in banksides, and 4% in man-made cover such as peat and wood stacks. In Shetland buildings and stone walls take the place of hedges and shrubs. On the mainland corn stacks are sometimes used. In Stornoway, Isle of Lewis, blackbirds laid eggs on a pile of bricks, and a female in Sussex laid four eggs on the bare earth of a flowerbed. Other strange sites have included a dusty shelf in an old house – no nesting material was used – under the wing of a car and on a tractor in constant use, in the engine of a parked aircraft, and in a coil of wire netting. In New Zealand, where the blackbird was introduced about 1870, nest sites seem to be very traditional.

The song thrush is generally more conservative in its choice of nesting site, especially in towns, suburbs and parks where it is the less common of the two species. All the song thrushes at Dollis Hill have nested in hollies, elders, elms and hawthorns between 1·6 and five metres above the ground. They seem to need denser, deeper foliage than the blackbird. They like trees, including conifers, bushes, shrubs and dense hedgerows, creepers on walls and sometimes holes in buildings. Nests may be built on ledges, in banks and sometimes on the ground. In the absence of trees the Hebridean song thrush often nests on the ground among heather and bracken, on rocks and sometimes in low bushes. In Shetland I have seen nests in stone walls and along burnsides, as well as in low trees, bushes, outbuildings and among heather. The Continental song thrush is shyer and breeds less commonly near buildings. In the British Isles song thrushes have sometimes been known to use the deserted nests of blackbirds which were given a new mud lining. J. A. Bucknill reported the use of a jay's nest in Surrey and a blackbird has been known to appropriate a song thrush's nest but the practice is rather uncommon.

The bigger mistle thrush tends in my experience to choose the fork of a large tree for its nest and it can be either broad-leaved or coniferous; in the latter case the nest is often built where several branches or twigs join the bole. The nest can be at a considerable height in an oak, plane or other large tree, even a monkey puzzle (*Araucaria*), perhaps up to a height of ten metres or more. This is especially true for birds nesting in town gardens and parks, but mistle thrushes will also choose sites only a few feet above the ground – on orchard trees, bean poles, and in thorns. At Dungeness nests have been built in low clumps of elders and hollies. In treeless areas these thrushes have also been known to nest in holes in walls and on the ground (especially in Ireland), in rock recesses, on the ledges of quarries, and, according to T. A. Coward, 'on rocks only a few feet above high-water mark'.

The ring ouzel tends to choose nest sites in its mountain home where the moorland drops down to a stream and in a heather or *Vaccinium*-covered bank. The site may be quite difficult to find and many that I located in the northern Pennines were hidden by an overhanging bank or roof of vegetation or a little vertical earth 'cliff', along the course of a beck. One nest in Derbyshire was under a small waterfall in a site reminiscent of that used by dippers. According to Dr J. J. M. Flegg and David Glue (1975) who investigated the British Trust for Ornithology's Nest Record Cards for the ring ouzel, there is one apparent characteristic – 'the location of a nest in or near a disruptive feature in an otherwise fairly uniform habitat, e.g., a rocky cleft or outcrop breaking the grassy flanks of a hillside'. From the Record Cards the two authors classified the sites: 28% occurred in open heather, on grass slopes or banks, 12% on crags, 22% in gullies and the largest group – 39% – in man-made structures. Twenty nests were reported in potholes or mineshafts between 2·6 and five metres below ground and also in quarries and buildings. Only three nests were recorded in trees more than one metre above the ground, while F. McIntosh saw one nest 3·1 m up in a tree. In Yorkshire nests have been observed in firs and in Derbyshire in an alder. The Alpine ring ouzel, although sometimes breeding among rocks and on stony ground, regularly builds its nest in spruces and firs. In Scandinavia many ring ouzels also nest in spruces and birches up to heights of three metres or so. Some British nests are on the ground on sheep walks with a bare earth bank behind. Of the 408 pairs represented on the Nest Record Cards 82% were to be found between 250 and 580 metres above sea level with extremes also as low as 33–66 metres above sea level in Sutherland and Caernarvon and as high as 1250 metres in the Cairngorm Mountains. Not all the nests are, in my experience, difficult to find, especially those that are built in stone walls. George Bolam, quoted by Dr David Bannerman (1954), came across a bird sitting on eggs 'on the turf-wall in the inside of a shooting hut'. It is interesting to note that W. S. M. D'Urban and M. A. Matthew in 1895 reported ring ouzels nesting in Devon on the sides of 'turf-tyes' – pits from which turf was dug for fuel. W. Robson (1975) found a nest in a deserted farmhouse 'as high as it could be on the exposed beam at the apex of one of the bedrooms', another nest was seen in the wall of a game-keeper's garden, a third in the spouting of a house and another in a crashed aircraft.

Redwings in Europe usually build their nests near to or actually on the ground, but those of the latter kind are often a feature late in the season when they are better concealed. A typical site is in the fork of a birch tree a foot or so above the ground, on a tree stump, among the roots of a fallen tree, on a log, or in a low juniper. In Swedish Lapland from 1964–69 O. Arheimer (1973) found that almost 50% of redwing nests were on the ground but there were none at all in 1970, the absence being attributed to an abundance of lemmings. Many of the nests are very difficult to find. Nests are sometimes built in Europe quite close to a high-water mark near the sea while other less usual sites include walls, under bridges, in outbuildings, on window sills, among rocks (like the ring ouzel,) in peat mosses and in piles of drying fish heads. The Iceland redwing is the characteristic bird of the island's birchwoods – it is the Icelanders' thrush. It nests in the city of Reykjavik just as the Continental redwing breeds in Bergen and other Scandinavian towns. Ground nests are common among Iceland redwings and the birds show great discretion and skill in creating the impression that their nests are in patches of ground cover other than where they actually are.

A redwing's nest was built in Sutherland in 1933 'in a red-currant bush against the garden wall of the Lodge' of an estate and another was seen in recent years against the wall of a hotel garden in Scotland. In 1966 E. G. Holt described another redwing's nest in Sutherland nearly one metre up in a rhododendron which formed part of the understory of a mixed birch and conifer wood. In a State forest in Ross-shire where I heard redwings singing in 1971 the birds tended to fall silent early in May and from this point they proved rather elusive. In the same county F. and E. Bartlett in 1974 noted first redwing song on 14 April but this was spasmodic until 22 April. From then on until 2 May the song was heard all day. After this date the birds fell silent and although this may not always be typical behaviour it suggests that song may well end several days before laying begins. Although Ross-shire nests may be built in tangles of spruce branches, I have found redwings building in evergreen shrubs around large isolated houses. Other sites include birch trees and a beech hedge, earthbanks and in the roots of wind-felled trees.

The fieldfare is a colonial nester but it is not unusual to find redwings nesting close by. Birchwoods are favourite breeding areas but in some regions there is a preference for conifers and other evergreens. Alder and mixed woods near marshes and other open ground are often favoured. Single nests become more frequent as the forest gradually gives way to scrub and open, more rocky terrain. Fieldfares will nest in many situations but there seems to be some preference for the forks of birch trees or close up against the boles of pines and spruces; there is generally one nest to a tree. In tall trees nests may be as high as 13 metres but the majority are usually within the 1·6 to 5 metres range. Nests in Europe may also be in hollow trees, low shrubs such as sallow and birch, among boulders and rocks and even on steep cliffs. Ground nests also occur and birds will build in empty houses, on scaffolding, wood piles and in gardens and town streets, like those in Christiansund, Bergen and Trondheim in Norway.

The pair that bred in Orkney in the summer of 1967 nested some 1·6 metres up in a small bushy elder in a little shrub-lined valley with a small burn. A nest in Shetland in 1968 was on the bank of a dried-up stream. In northern Britain nests have been recorded in grass and heather on the ground by a stream or ditch, and up to 8 metres in conifers as well as oak and sycamore. Nest sites like those of the redwing are often in the vicinity of water. Too few isolated pairs are yet nesting in Britain to reveal other strong preferences. The future of this species as a breeding bird in Britain, like that of the redwing, will be of great interest. The nesting is part of those dynamic changes in bird communities that take place over the years and which have increasingly brought other typically Scandinavian breeding bird species to Britain.

Among the thrushes competition for nest sites tends to be reduced by differences in habitat preference, by social living or by a territorial system. Competition for breeding places is well marked in densely packed colonial nesters such as seabirds. The actual competition for nest sites is often fiercest among birds with rather specialist requirements. With the thrushes breeding in Britain the birds are not sociable and the holding of territories reduces the competition for nest sites. Should the territorial system break down, through death or emigration caused by severe weather, as happened at Dollis Hill among my blackbirds in the winter of 1962–63, then nest building may be 'spasmodic, uncertain in its choice of site and often interfered with by territorial fights'. Blackbirds, song thrushes and mistle thrushes may share the same habitats with little interspecific competition for nest sites but I have on occasion witnessed territorial conflicts between blackbirds and song thrushes. I could not subscribe to the belief that there are, in Eliot Howard's words, 'incessant quarrels'. As we have already seen, there are often slight differences in choice of actual sites. Mistle thrushes seem to favour forks and boughs, often rather high up. Song thrushes like the dense cover provided by thick hedges, shrubs and evergreens at a lower level and blackbirds are able to make do with many situations. The less common of the British breeding thrush species all reveal habitat and site preferences which help to separate them when selecting places in which to build their nests.

There is some evidence, however, that at lower levels where ring ouzels overlap with blackbirds the former may have been ousted by the latter through interspecific competition. In the Pentland Hills Roger Durman has found little aggression between ring ouzels and blackbirds but he observed a considerable amount of aggressive behaviour between ring ouzels and mistle thrushes, which nest on the ground and have adapted their requirements to the particular habitat. We know that the Scottish mistle thrush population has increased during a period when ring ouzels were on the decline. We do not know, however, whether these changes are related.

CHAPTER 9

BREEDING BEHAVIOUR:
NESTS AND YOUNG

So far I have traced the breeding history of Britain's six thrush species through the acquisition of territories, song, display and pairing up to the selection of the nest site itself. In the present chapter I propose to review the breeding behaviour as it proceeds from the construction of the nest through incubation to the post-fledging dispersal of the young. This examination will also embrace the size and variation in clutches, numbers of broods and other aspects of behaviour during the breeding cycle.

Basically all the nests of the British thrushes are similar in construction, being made of grasses, twigs, leaves or other similar material, strengthened with earth, clay or mud. Only the nest of the British song thrush normally has a smooth lining formed from rotten wood or dung mixed with saliva. The nest of the Hebridean song thrush usually has a grass lining. It is the custom for the hen to build the nest with occasional help from her mate but in the case of the ring ouzel both sexes generally take part. I have watched male blackbirds and mistle thrushes bringing in material. The first nests of the season may be built in a somewhat leisurely fashion, a song thrush taking twenty-four days to build, a mistle thrush more than a fortnight and I have watched a blackbird take up to sixteen days to complete her nest. Such slow building may reflect the rather gradual rise in the hormone level in the birds. Late nests are often put together quickly and show signs of 'jerry-building'. There is evidence to suggest that the first actual nest building is associated with wet, damp weather and in wet years the breeding itself may go on longer than in dry seasons. At Dollis Hill 1958 was a year of that kind.

The blackbird's nest is generally the best known of those built by the British thrushes. It is a substantial cup formed from dry grasses, roots, stalks, moss, even plastic, paper, string and similar materials, and cemented together on the inside of the cup with mud or damp leaves. This structure is then lined with more mud and finally given a soft inner lining of dry grasses. A Hampshire blackbird nest was lined with feathers but this is very unusual. I always find it a very charming sight to watch a hen black-bird moving around in the nest, shaping it with her breast and working the materials into a firm rounded fabric. She will also pull loose grasses and twigs down towards her and place them firmly in the nest with her bill. About 10% of the females that have bred in my garden have flown into the site with materials and have called with the 'Tchook-tchook' alarm; the remainder have been shyer and absolutely silent.

After a first successful use the nest may be refurbished and I have known one to be used for four successful broods in the same season. There are several records of the same nest being used by blackbirds for two years in succession while R. F. Bawtree reported that a nest was used six times in three successive seasons. An even more remarkable case of usage was quoted by J. Lord and D. J. Munns in 1970; a nest built on a high shelf in a shed was used twice a year from 1953 to 1956, held three broods in 1957 and finally had a new nest built alongside it in 1958! Some blackbird nests are quite large. A pair nesting in a wigwam-shaped stack of old smooth hop poles about four metres long found that their nest material slipped downwards. Before stability was finally achieved the nest reached a height of 13 cm, surmounted by a normal cup. F. S. Mitchell in 1885 reported a nest, built in an old lime quarry, which slipped down under its own weight, until a pile 0.6 metres long and 12.5 cm wide had formed. An Essex blackbird was completing its nest when a hedgesparrow built inside it but this was removed by the blackbird and two young were successfully reared.

The nest of the song thrush is very similar to that of the blackbird in construction but it normally has a characteristically smooth lining of wood pulp or dung; it may be used several times. In dry seasons this hard lining may be missing and even the mud strengthening; the cup is then made soft with twigs or grasses – a practice regularly adopted by the Hebridean song thrush. The larger and rather solid nest of the mistle thrush is also solidified with earth or mud and provided with a grass lining. It is decorated sometimes with lichens, sprigs of leaves, wool, feathers and plastic bags, and I have also seen bits of cloth, string and newspaper used by birds in many areas. Fieldfares build similar nests to those of the mistle thrush with a mud-supported lining of withered grass and this classic design has been used in the British Isles. In Europe the nests of several seasons may be found in one tree and these may be repaired and used again, and new ones built on the remains of old.

Redwings' nests are smaller and flatter but are also built of similar materials, strengthened with mud, and occasionally decorated on the outside with bits of lichen and moss. Nests in Ross-shire have been built of birch twigs, moss and wool and 'lined with brittle earthy material', while one was adapted from a song thrush's nest and given a grassy lining. A similar thrush-type nest is built by the ring ouzel, often from coarse moorland grasses, heather twigs and mud, but it too receives a soft lining of dead grasses. Z. Bochénski (1968) used similarities and slight differences in nest structure to reveal certain phylogenetic relationships in the genus *Turdus*.

There are quite a few instances of multiple nest building among the

Table 11. Some Vital Breeding Statistics for British Thrushes

	Mistle Thrush	Hebridean Song Thrush	British Song Thrush	Blackbird	Ring Ouzel	Iceland Redwing	European Redwing	Fieldfare
NEST: Strengthened with mud or earth	•	•	•	•	•	•	•	•
NEST: Grass lining	•			•	•	•	•	•
EGG SIZE: Average in mm	31·2 × 22·3	29·1 × 20·8	27·6 × 20·9	29·4 × 21·5	30·4 × 21·5	26·0 × 19·4	25·8 × 19·2	28·8 × 20·9
EGG COLOUR: See key below	WB	BS	BS	BB	BB	BS	BS	BB
CLUTCH SIZE: Average	4	4	3–5	3–5	4	4–6	5–6	5–6
INCUBATION BY MALE=M AND FEMALE=F	F		F:(M?)	F	F:M	F:M	F:(M?)	F:M
INCUBATION PERIOD (in days)	13–14	c. 14	13–14	13–14	13–14	14–15	13	13–14
FLEDGING PERIOD (in days)	14–16	c. 14	13–14	13–14	12–14	11–14	12–14	14
NUMBER OF CLUTCHES	2	1 (occ. 2)	2–3	2–3	often 2	1 (occ. 2)	2	1 (occ. 2)

Figures based on those in *The Handbook of British Birds*, published information from Havlin (1963), Snow (1958, 1969), Tyrväinen (1969) and Simms (unpublished).

Egg Colour Key: BB = Greenish-blue ground with red-brown blotches
     BS = Greenish-blue ground speckled or dotted with brown
     WB = Creamy or whitish with brown speckles

thrushes. These seemed to have arisen as a result of a breakdown in the birds' ability to orientate when they became confused by the presence of a number of exactly similar sites. For example, five mistle thrush nests were found in 1968 at Bradwell nuclear power station in Essex built on top of identical iron and concrete pillars, 2·6 metres in height and some seven metres apart. The pillars were topped with ceramic insulators in a block about 70 metres by 27 metres. Only one pair of mistle thrushes was seen. A similar situation confronted a pair of blackbirds in Shetland which were duped by piles of evenly stacked lobster pots, each an exact duplicate of the other, into building two complete nests and one unlined nest in a shed near Loch Spiggie. Ladders hanging on walls can also be confusing to blackbirds and song thrushes. A. R. Lucas reported six song thrush nests being built by the same bird in April 1946 between the rungs of a ladder; four eggs were laid in one nest and two in another but no young birds hatched out. A. M. Hemmingsen (1956) described three cases of multiple nest building by the blackbird in Denmark with two series of five nests and even one of eight nests. Other confusing sites for birds include rafters in barns, beams and roof gutterings whose uniformity along their lengths seems to cause disorientation. This need not be the only explanation for multiple nests. The practice may occur when a bird has a highly developed breeding urge and G. F. Mees's observations of three simultaneously constructed song thrush nests in Holland would appear to support this possibility.

In the genus *Turdus* most species lay rather similar eggs although there are two chief variations and several minor ones. The song thrush is obviously a member of the genus, although it is unique and differs from its congeners in laying blue eggs with black or more rarely red-brown spots, or even unspotted varieties. In taxonomy the colour of eggs is unreliable and can be, as Dr David Lack pointed out, 'misleading as an indication of affinity'. Of the four common thrush species breeding in the British Isles the mistle thrush, which often favours more open situations, may differ from the others in laying creamy, tawny or pale greenish-blue eggs, with sienna-brown blotches. Sometimes the markings are absent. Blackbird eggs tend to have a bluish-green ground and may be freckled with brownish-red markings which can form zones on the shells. A clear blue ground colour is occasionally reported and the freckles may be missing. *The Handbook* mentions that a 'rare erythristic variety is white with red-brown spots'. The eggs of the fieldfare are rather variable, sometimes resembling blackbirds' eggs, while others are paler blue, heavily blotched with brown or even unmarked. According to Dr David Bannerman (1954), in many clutches of fieldfare eggs one is 'less heavily marked, and therefore more striking than the remainder'. Redwings lay considerably smaller eggs and their greenish ground is usually very finely and evenly marked with reddish brown. Uncommon varieties include eggs with ground colours of buff or pale cream. The ground colour of ring ouzels' eggs is bluish green, sparsely but often boldly marked with dark red-brown; eggs are sometimes immaculate. The average size of the eggs of all six thrush species can be found in Table 11. Normal clutch size is also shown in the same table.

The normal clutch size of all six British thrush species lies within the limits of three to six. The rate at which birds reproduce is potentially the highest within the birds' capabilities in the habitats in which they live. This suggests that each species raises as many birds as can be reared during that time of the year when there is enough food to support the young. Correspondingly each species will also lay that number of eggs which will on average result in the biggest numbers of survivors in each brood. In passerine birds the limit is set by the increased mortality in large broods due to the lack of food. Many bird species show adaptive modification of their clutch size according to particular conditions. It is possible, however, to indicate five significant factors that influence the size of clutches among the thrushes. These are the season, the weather, the nature of the habitat, the geographical situation, and certain individual differences in birds due to age, disease and other causes. Blackbirds and song thrushes in Britain usually produce clutches of from three to five eggs but there is a marked variation throughout the breeding season. At the beginning the clutch is from three to four while five eggs are not to be expected before late April. As the breeding season moves forward clutches of five will increase in number and three will decrease. Then after the middle of May the clutch size begins to fall. Clutches of two are not common and may have been the result of loss before the clutch was examined. The number of clutches of six eggs is even smaller. The blackbird's mean clutch size starts below 3·5 eggs, reaches a peak of 4·56 and then falls quite sharply. In the song thrush the mean clutch size shows a steadier pattern, beginning at 3·8 in March, rising gradually to a shallower peak at 4·48 at the end of April and early May; it then falls but not to as low a level as that of the blackbird.

The curve for the mean clutch size of the mistle thrush resembles that for the song thrush but it is 0·25 eggs lower and does not reveal the steep seasonal change of the blackbird's curve. Mistle thrushes also seem to lay more clutches of four than the other two species. For the redwing H. Tyrväinen found in Finland that the average clutch size increased from 4·9 in early May to 5·5 in late May; by the middle of June it had fallen to 4·6. Most of the larger clutches were found to be repeats. The fieldfare generally has one brood and two are more occasional – a similar situation to that of the Iceland redwing. The fieldfare usually lays five or six eggs but there are records of three, four, seven and eight. From some 79 clutches of the ring ouzel the mean clutch size in Britain was 4·1 eggs.

Although the pattern of clutches over several seasons may seem fairly

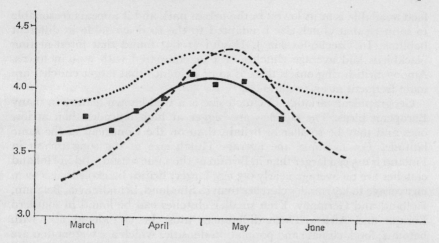

FIG. 33. Seasonal variation in mean clutch-size of mistle thrush (squares and solid line), song thrush (dotted line) and blackbird (broken line) in Britain. (Reproduced from *Bird Study*, Vol. 16, 1969, by permission of Dr David Snow.)

regular, there can be quite different pictures in individual years. The seasonal rise and fall, with its peak in the breeding season when conditions are best for rearing young birds, is almost entirely adaptive. Support for this belief was obtained by Dr David Snow when he found that the average weight of nestling blackbirds was higher in the middle than at the start or the end of the breeding season. It would therefore seem that the peak coincides with optimal conditions brought about by a combination of daylength, local weather conditions and the highest availability of food. Severe weather and drought at the time of laying can reduce the clutch size since sufficient food is needed by the hen 'for the task of producing a number of eggs on successive days'. If the weather is warm and fine, clutch size may be above average in March and April. The late Dr David Lack suggested that weather conditions could 'mislead' birds and cause them to produce a clutch which was really adapted to the season for which such weather was characteristic. For example, in the warm April of 1961 the average song thrush clutch of eggs rose to 4·4 – well above the four-year mean of 4·16 found by Dr Snow. The tendency for the clutch sizes of thrushes to vary in a parallel fashion in different years can be correlated with annual differences in temperature.

The third factor working on clutch size is that of habitat. In city parks blackbirds appear to lay the smallest clutches. Then there is a slight proportional increase for birds living in gardens, on farmland and in woodland, where the clutches are regularly larger. It would seem that the food available is at its lowest in the urban park and it appears reasonable to suppose that clutch size is adapted to the food available in different habitats. In Czechoslovakia J. Havlin (1963) found that forest-nesting blackbirds laid average clutches of 4·14 compared with 3·94 in towns. Among British ring ouzels there is some evidence that larger clutches are more frequent at lower altitudes.

Geographical variation in clutch size is a well-known feature in many European birds. The clutches are bigger at high latitudes than at low ones and may be smaller in Britain than on the Continent at the same latitude. For example, the average clutch size of the song thrush in Finland is 0·5 egg larger than in Britain at the same season, and in Holland clutches are on average nearly 0·3 egg larger. British blackbirds also seem on average to lay smaller clutches than in Shetland, Scandinavia, Belgium, Holland and Germany. Even smaller clutches can be found in southern Europe and Africa. These differences must be considered also with habitats, food, climate and population densities which are factors that are interwoven with that of geography. Yet it would seem likely that longer days and a richer insect life would permit larger clutches to be laid, and that the number of eggs is very finely adapted to the parents' ability to raise their young. There can also be individual sources of variation among thrushes according to age since older birds tend to lay larger clutches than new, first-year and less experienced females.

The eggs of blackbirds are laid each day, often in the morning, and the same appears to be true for the song thrush. Actual incubation periods can be difficult to assess but often the calculation is made from the date on which the last egg of the clutch was laid until the date on which the last young hatched. There can, however, be a delay of a day or two after the clutch is complete and before regular incubation begins. In the blackbird incubation is carried out by the female and generally starts before the clutch is complete; it lasts from 13–14 days. By the time she has completed the clutch she will spend all the night and most of the day on the eggs. The eggs hatch in the order in which they were laid over a period generally shorter than 48 hours. With the song thrush the interval between eggs may not be 24 hours and with the redwing the eggs are laid at intervals of under 24 hours. With the latter species incubation starts before the clutch is complete. In Finland the period seems to be about 12 to 13 days while the Iceland redwing appears to take rather longer. Both these species reflect the general pattern of behaviour in thrushes at this stage of the breeding cycle. Incubation is by the female alone in the mistle thrush, blackbird, and apparently the European redwing and British song thrush, although there have been suggestions that the males of the last two species may participate. Male Iceland redwings may relieve the hen in the early stages. Among fieldfares there seems to be the possibility of occasional sharing of duties but in the ring ouzel there is a slightly more even division of labour and I have seen both sexes on eggs. From 101 Nest Record Cards of the British Trust for Ornithology for the ring ouzel there were 93 for hens incubating, 5 for cocks and 3 for both birds, suggesting that dual incubation is not quite as frequent as some earlier authorities had claimed. Incubation periods for all six species of thrush are very close to each other.

Similarly there is quite a close correlation in the fledging periods which average out at about 13 to 14 days, but both incubation and fledging periods may be slightly longer early in the nesting season. 123 Nest Record Cards for the blackbird showed that the incubation period, measured as a whole from the laying of the last egg to the date of the hatching of the last young 'averaged 13·7 days for March nests, 13·1 days for May and 12·7 days for June' (Snow 1958). Nestling blackbirds weigh about 6 gm on hatching and grow to about 70 gm when they leave the nest. The average weight of nestlings at eight days old was found to vary with the time of year, brood size and habitat; the middle part of the breeding season and woodland were factors in providing optimal conditions for blackbirds. The young from large broods are also generally heavier than those from small broods. Broods are also larger in woodland but 4·8 nestlings per pair survive to eight days old in London compared with 4·2 in rural habitats. Later two juveniles per pair are reared in London compared with 1·7 outside. This means that about 14% more nestlings and 18% more juveniles are produced in the urban environment than in the country.

In the song thrush the brood size in June averages 3·77 with an average clutch size of 4·76. Whereas the clutch size appears to be somewhat greater in southern than in northern England, the average brood size seems to follow a reverse pattern. On average 71% of song thrush eggs hatch and 78% of the hatched young leave the nest; 55% of the eggs laid therefore produce fledged young (Silva 1949). For the mistle thrush the mean family size for the whole season is 3·32 – or 86% of the mean clutch size – but it also reveals a seasonal trend similar to that for the song thrush. Each breeding pair raises on average some 2·6 to 3·3 young per year with a higher nesting success in March than later in the season. The ring ouzel has an overall mean clutch size of 4·1 eggs and a brood size of 3·6 young. H. Tyrväinen (1969) has written very fully about the breeding biology of the redwing.

The number of broods in the thrushes is somewhat variable but those rearing an occasional second brood include the Iceland redwing, fieldfare and Hebridean song thrush. Ring ouzels quite often and European redwings and mistle thrushes regularly have two broods. The British song thrush and the blackbird average from two to three. At Dollis Hill two blackbird broods a year are regular and three not uncommon. In 1958 a pair of blackbirds built on top of a partially completed house sparrow's nest on a rain-pipe beneath the gutter of a neighbour's house and success-fully raised four broods in the same nest. 'At one stage the male of this pair was simultaneously feeding the fledged young of the third brood and the newly hatched nestlings of the fourth' (Simms 1962). Four broods in a year have also been reported from Kenton in Middlesex, where a pair reared their young in a nest in a similar situation to mine. Of the few other records of four broods some were all reared in the same nest, others in separate ones. H. Mayer-Gross and Dr C. M. Perrins reported in 1962 a blackbird pair rearing five broods in the same season. Such a high number of families will depend on the weather, an early start to breeding, continuing success and opportunity for late nesting.

As we have seen earlier in this book, all the nestling thrushes with their initial naked beginning and subsequent long whitish or yellowish down and yellow gapes bear a considerable family resemblance to each other. The growth of the feathers may be broadly associated with weight but this cannot be categorically stated for all the species. Primaries and secondaries begin to appear from their sheaths at about seven or eight days. A nestling blackbird under 40 grams in weight at about eight days old is almost sure to die. In all the thrush species with which we are concerned the young birds in the nest are fed by both parents, and the faecal sacs swallowed or removed. Woodland blackbirds tend to feed their young chiefly on cater-pillars while suburban and garden birds concentrate on earthworms. It may be that in very dry spells these sources may be reduced and I have observations of birds in suburban gardens collecting slugs and bread for their young. Young song thrushes are often fed on worms, snails, slugs, insect larvae and some vegetable material while nestling mistle thrushes besides receiving a similar animal diet may occasionally be given the young of other birds. In Swedish Lapland young redwings are fed on earthworms and adult insects between 1600 hours and 0900 but many more insects and grubs from 0900 to 1600.

In an interesting study of the diurnal rhythm of thrushes when feeding their young, J. Keskpaik in Estonia found that the order of starting forag-ing for food for the young was headed by the redwing, then the blackbird and finally the song thrush. There were three main peaks of feeding in the day when the young were three days old or less, and four peaks from the fifth day onwards. The highest feeding rate came at the last peak. The redwing also brooded its young more than the other two species. Further research by Keskpaik enabled him to monitor the oxygen consumption of the nestlings of song thrush, blackbird and redwing from the third to the tenth day after hatching. By observing the daily increments in oxygen intake he identified three age phases. During the first four days a high level of consumption with a peak on the fourth day reflected the maximum growth rate. Then followed a fairly even rate of oxygen consumption until the sixth day, apart from the blackbird whose greatest daily incre-

PLATE 13.
WINTER ACTIVITIES.
Above, fieldfare in act of
swallowing berry. *Centre*,
fieldfares are very much
attracted by fallen apples in
the autumn and winter.
Below, redwings feeding on
cotoneaster berries in winter
quarters.

PLATE 14. BATHING ACTIVITIES. *Above left*, a blackbird sun-bathing with tail fully spread and wings extended; bare dry ground close to cover is often favoured; *right*, a juvenile robin sun-bathing in high intensity posture. *Below*, a hen blackbird bathing and using her wings to splash water over herself.

ment was reached in this period. After the seventh day the rate was the same in all three species.

Adults may occasionally desert nests, and eggs may be taken by various predators such as crows, magpies, jays, owls, grey squirrels, marauding boys and so on. Some nestlings may die in the nest and adult thrushes will often remove them if they are under nine days old; after that they are too heavy to be shifted and have to remain. Crows, squirrels and cats will also remove nestlings.

Table 12. Some Predators on Thrush Species

	MISTLE THRUSH	SONG THRUSH	BLACK-BIRD	RING OUZEL	RED-WING	FIELD-FARE
Peregrine	●	●	●	●	●	●
Hobby		●	●			
Merlin	●	●	●	●	●	●
Kestrel		●	●			●
Buzzard	●	●	●	●		●
Montagu's Harrier		●			●	
Hen Harrier		●	●	●		
Sparrowhawk	●	●	●	●	●	●
Kite					●	
Honey Buzzard		●				
Little Owl	●	●	●			
Long-eared Owl	●	●	●			
Short-eared Owl		●	●			
Tawny Owl	●	●	●			
Barn Owl		●	●			
Hooded/ Carrion Crow	●	●	●	●	●	●
Jackdaw	●	●	●			
Rook	●	●	●			
Magpie	●	●	●			
Jay	●	●	●			
Heron			●			
Gulls	●	●			●	●

The behaviour of the adult thrushes during incubation and the fledging period can vary between the species and also between different individuals. For example, in the woodlands blackbirds may leave their nests silently or with a soft alarm and then remain concealed until the danger has passed. Others I have watched remain much longer and then leave the nest with the sharper 'Tchook-tchook' alarm call. In gardens and parks many birds are very tame and will sit tight so that it is possible to approach them to within a few feet and even touch them with the hand. Some fluff themselves up into a gentle threat posture and snap the mandibles together. Such tame birds seem to remain essentially confiding even with an increasing amount of disturbance around them. On the other hand there are instances of blackbirds 'mobbing' human intruders and even striking them with wings or claws. The mistle thrush, although shy and wary at other times, is justly renowned for its fearless defence of its nest against birds of prey, crows and even human intruders. I have also known them to attack foxes, dogs and cats. Song thrushes tend to slip quietly off their nests but some will fly only a short distance, snap their bills and even fluff out their feathers, fan their tails and lower their heads. Redwings sit more closely than fieldfares when incubating but if the incubation is quite well advanced the birds will flutter up, snap their mandibles and call loudly. G. K. Yeates found that the breeding Iceland redwing 'When really roused, he stooped at us with loud scolding – a furious bold bird'. Fieldfares show a remarkable pugnacity in their colonies often driving away crows and birds of prey by combined and noisy assaults. R. K. Furrer (1975) has described how mobbing fieldfares with chicks use systematic defaecation as an effective deterrent against predators. This remarkable behaviour seems to be increasing in fieldfare colonies in central Europe. Ring ouzels are also very bold in their defence of the nest and will harry crows and buzzards and even buffet the human intruder.

Some of the thrush species will also apparently on occasion employ distraction displays to lure intruders away from the nest – a habit commonly used by many wading birds. This 'injury-feigning' has been described for the blackbird on a number of occasions. Dr Geoffrey Beven watched a male fly down in front of a cat and flutter 'as if injured, just above the ground' and this behaviour has also been reported in the face of human intruders as well. E. M. Cawkell described a song thrush that 'stumbled along dragging its half-open wings'. Henry Seebohm recorded a ring ouzel 'reeling and tumbling on the ground' and E. P. Butterfield, according to The Handbook, mentioned 'fluttering a few yards in a lazy sort of fashion' but I have never seen this distraction display and I think it must be rather unusual in ring ouzels. This kind of display is especially associated with ground-nesting birds.

There is also a number of instances of aberrant or atypical behaviour among breeding thrushes. Firstly, there are a few instances of hybridization. Secondly, there are cases of unusual breeding behaviour. Blackbird and song thrush have been known to incubate eggs in the same nest; two female blackbirds shared the same nest and a male blackbird was observed rearing young song thrushes. In 1958 in Northumberland a female blackbird incubated and a song thrush reared a combined brood, and a male blackbird in Cumberland fed some fully feathered young song thrushes in their nest. There are also a few interesting examples of thrush species feeding the young of other species. Blackbirds have been observed feeding broods of blue tits, hedgesparrows and bullfinches besides those of song thrushes. Conversely, robins have been seen tending nestling song thrushes and blackbirds. In some instances the normal route of one species to its nest passed close to the nest of another species and the first became confused and could well have fed either brood.

When young thrushes leave their nests they are scarcely able to fly and tend to keep to cover in the territorial species, less so in the social. The fledgling blackbird is chubby and with a characteristically short tail. It sits motionless in thick cover and cheeps quietly at first – a sound which becomes a sharp 'Tchick' or 'Tchick-uck' which enables the hard-working parents to locate their young. Then the call changes to a sharp slurred phrase with the first note shriller and higher than the second. There is some evidence that each parent blackbird cares for certain of the young only and observations that I carried out in my own garden in the summer of 1975 bear this out. About a week after fledging the young blackbirds begin to experiment with foods and food-objects, and I have seen aggressive postures adopted between fledglings at seven days after leaving the nest. They will begin to make trial flicking movements among leaf-litter at about ten days. The first week out of the nest is passed by my garden blackbirds from four to seven metres up in dense shrubs and here their survival rate is very good. They become more vulnerable as they start to emerge from cover and begin to feed themselves on the ground. Soon they are able to fly well and they are then not taken so regularly by cats and other ground predators. Young blackbirds are dependent on their parents, especially the male if the female nests again, for about three weeks and will often show a curious mixture of juvenile and adult actions. They may continue to beg for food on occasion but they also begin to sing inward types of song. One day the young are about in the garden and then, after preliminary inspections of the regions beyond their parents' territory, they are gone. The dispersal is sudden. These brown-spotted young blackbirds are tolerated by strange adults but they soon begin to show both social and aggressive tendencies. We do not know how long the young birds of one family stay with each other but Dr Snow has suggested that they may associate with each other as late as mid-winter. With birds colour-ringed in north-west London I could not establish such a continuing relationship beyond early autumn. They may, of course, meet at night solely for roosting purposes.

Juvenile mistle thrushes are fed for about two weeks after leaving the nest. Later, young birds begin to form flocks, usually from late July onwards, and may start to move south or west, since ringed nestlings have been recovered in Ireland and northern and western France. Song thrushes are secretive and their young slip away almost unnoticed; nestlings ringed in Britain have moved west to Ireland or south to Europe. Nestling blackbirds ringed in Britain have been recovered in Ireland or on the Continent but the species shows a marked tendency to breed where it has been reared. I. Werth (1947) showed that 93% of British blackbirds ringed as nestlings and recovered in later breeding seasons were within five miles of their birthplace. Fledgling ring ouzels often move away from a first nest fairly soon after fledging and within a few days may have travelled up to a mile from the nest site where they can be fed by both parents. With second broods I have found a tendency for young birds to remain longer in the area of the nest and Roger Durman found that in a second brood of ring ouzels in Midlothian fledglings were 'being fed in the immediate locality of the nest twelve days after fledging'. Then young birds begin to move away from the breeding grounds in August. They can be found quite often joining up with other parties to explore the bracken on the hill slopes or the downs for berries. Fieldfares and redwings may remain socially in flocks and migrate together.

CHAPTER 10

BREEDING SEASONS

THE period of the year during which birds of a species breed seems to be resolved by natural selection which operates, firstly, through complex proximate factors involving both the physiology and the habitat that ensure that the birds are ready to breed, and, secondly, through ultimate factors including food, cover and breeding sites which tend to favour nesting more at one time of the year than another. In this chapter I propose to review these factors that determine the breeding seasons of the British thrushes and also to examine some of the likenesses and dissimilarities that occur in the group. There is, of course, a considerable difference between European and, say, tropical birds, since the former breed during one period of the year which in the British Isles chiefly embraces the months from April to June. The food available to the birds is at its peak of abundance in late spring and summer, reflecting the movement of the sun to the north and a great increase in the region's vegetation.

Our members of the genus *Turdus* tend to start laying in March and April with the mistle thrush leading the way, followed shortly by the song thrush and then the blackbird. It is interesting to note that song thrushes in Lapland, far to the north, start laying in the middle of June. In Britain individual birds may breed earlier in gardens than in near-by broad-leaved woodland, perhaps due to the differences in timing in the food supplies for the breeding females, and perhaps in suburbia to a difference in temperature. Generally length of daylight and temperature are part of the direct influence of climate affecting the natural gonad cycle of birds but 'more important still are the biological changes in each species that accompany the physical changes' (Simms 1971). By displaying variations in their clutch size throughout the breeding season the thrushes reflect the relative difficulty of finding food at various times. Blackbirds will lay earliest in very mild springs and small early broods can be lost if the weather pattern changes, but actual breeding success and survival after fledging do not vary a great deal with the date of the onset of breeding. Dr C. M. Perrins believes that blackbirds probably 'are breeding as early as practicable for raising young'. J. Havlin (1962) found a slightly higher survival of blackbirds in first broods than in later ones. It also seems that older females tend to lay earlier than females breeding for the first time. This is certainly true of blackbirds, as Dr David Snow has observed, and it may be a general rule among birds.

The breeding season itself of mistle thrush, song thrush and blackbird in

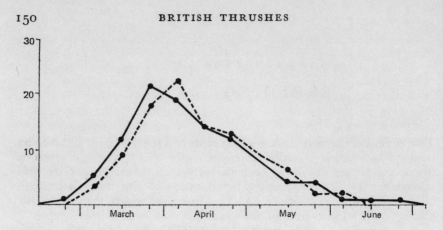

FIG. 34. Breeding season (first egg dates) of British mistle thrushes. Solid line =
south of Britain, broken line = north of Britain. (Reproduced from *Bird Study*,
Vol 16, 1969, by permission of Dr David Snow.)

Britain tends to last in some years from late March to May or June and
occasionally beyond this. That for the mistle thrush is the shortest and
that for the song thrush the longest in duration. The ring ouzel breeds
between early April and early July. In Scandinavia the fieldfare's breeding
season lasts from May to July and in Europe most redwing eggs are laid
between late May and July. In Scotland redwings seem to lay in May or
June while the Iceland race breeds between mid-May and July.

At Dollis Hill blackbirds nesting in the gardens there lay their first
eggs towards the end of March and their last normally in May and June.
Occasionally birds will start earlier than this and the season can last
beyond June. Each nesting follows the previous one very closely and
between two and three nesting attempts are common. Four or five are
exceptional and such a number depends on either an early start or a late
finish to the breeding season – or both. M. T. Myres (1955) analysed the
Nest Record Cards of the British Trust for Ornithology for 9500 nesting
blackbirds, song thrushes and mistle thrushes – a formidable task! He
found that there were peaks giving high abundance in April and a tailing
off in May and June. The positions of the rather sharp peaks were not
caused by observers but the relative heights of the peaks were unnatural
due perhaps to the early season ardour of observers.

The geographical distribution of the cards was also uneven but the
scheme did provide information which could only have been obtained by
co-operative reporting. It did not reveal, for example, how many nesting
attempts a mistle thrush pair might make in the course of the breeding
season. It was clear, however, that a burst of early blackbird and song
thrush layings in mid-March might ensue some five days after a rise in

the mean temperature to about 4·5°C. This indicated that the onset of breeding may vary each year according to the weather and this I have confirmed at Dollis Hill. As we have seen, old female blackbirds are stimulated to lay earlier than young birds. Some young hens are late being paired while the older birds have spent much of the winter in the company of their mates. This suggests that social behaviour may, in addition to such proximate factors as temperature and light, have some influence on the time of breeding. Bad weather including snow or drought can affect the start of nesting. Habitat conditions can also play a part since it is clear that blackbirds start to sing and begin their breeding season later in a woodland environment than in that provided by towns and suburbs. This seems also to be true for song thrushes and robins. Birds in suburban or garden settings tend to remain near their territories, which provide them with good food resources, both natural and artificial, and perhaps the enhanced conditions of temperature and light are important. The Nest Record Cards for the blackbird in 1954 showed that the first main peak of breeding was between five and ten days later in the woodland populations than in those of gardens and suburbs.

The gap between nesting attempts in blackbirds can vary considerably. Continuing bad weather may have an effect but in normal conditions the interval is usually between four and ten days. R. Berndt reported an instance of eggs being laid in a second, new nest while nestlings were still in the old one. Dr Snow found that 'Young females, with a mean interval of 10·6 days, took on average a little longer to start their new clutches than old females, whose mean was 7·5 days'. Because they bred later and to some extent finished earlier the young birds managed fewer clutches than the old hens. At Oxford the respective averages were 2·3 to 3·1. The date when the last blackbird clutch is laid may be influenced by the history and timing of previous clutches. In 1958 wet weather prolonged the nesting season at Dollis Hill and there is evidence that very dry conditions will tend to terminate it. It is perhaps the weather at the start of the breeding season rather than the food supply which is the more important determining factor in the start of nesting. Garden blackbirds feed earthworms to their young in the spring and then switch in summer to larval insects such as caterpillars but this supply begins to dwindle by early July. At this time worms may also be difficult to obtain as the lawns and flowerbeds harden in the sun. In the broad-leaved woodlands caterpillars are the staple diet of the young blackbirds, and under the trees the leaf litter will remain moist enough to support plenty of invertebrates even in periods of considerable drought.

Between 1904 and 1946 A. Whitaker recorded every thrush nest that he found in Yorkshire during more than forty years' residence in the same area. Although there was some bias in Whitaker's figures, Dr David Lack (1950) published a list of the number of clutches started in each weekly period. From six clutches begun in the week 18–24 March the total rose to 77 in the first week of April, to 138 between 8–14 April and then reached a peak of 184 in the following week; the number then steadily declined to 40 in early June and finally to 3 in the first week of July. The peak for the blackbird could be compared with peaks for the song thrush of 185 in the second week of April and 42 for the mistle thrush in the first week of that month. Thus the peaks were not far removed in time and followed in successive weeks starting with the mistle thrush and ending with the blackbird. There are often three or four peaks of laying during a season. The three common species of thrush may coincide in the peaks and troughs of their egg-laying activity, reflecting a more or less equal response to environmental conditions, such as low temperatures and wet and dry conditions (Fig. 35). There does appear to be some difference on occasion in the way in which the three common species may react to these factors with the song thrush, for example, being quicker in its response to improving conditions than the blackbird.

Breeding in blackbirds and song thrushes starts earlier in the south than in the north of the country; in Shetland the blackbird's nesting season has been moved on by a month or more. Shetland blackbirds come into song about two months later than in southern England but they

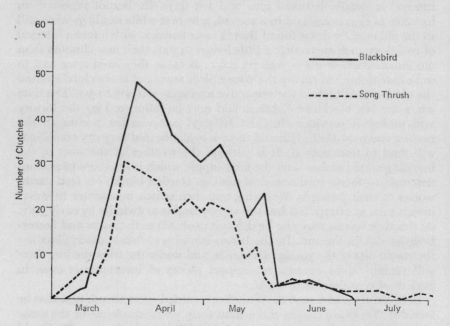

FIG. 35. How commencement dates of clutches of blackbird and song thrush in the south of England may compare in the same year. (After Myres, 1955.)

cease about the same time. In New Zealand, where the blackbird was introduced, the breeding season lasts usually from late August to December; here in an environment often similar to that of Britain the bird has easily adapted itself to the different seasons of the southern hemisphere (Gurr 1954).

Occasionally blackbirds and song thrushes will continue their breeding activities much later than is normal. This occurred, for example, in the winter of 1953–54. It was very warm at the end of the year and particularly so from the middle of November onwards. In thirteen reported blackbird nests ten clutches were begun in the second half of November or the first half of December. One in Roxburghshire was laid about 31 December. The clutch size was not abnormally low and in the reported nests hatching took place in three of them and young actually fledged in January from one of them. In the winter of 1956–57 blackbirds were breeding both in December and January while nests of song thrush and mistle thrush were located in February 1957. The evidence suggested that during this mild spring temperature was acting directly on the birds and not through such secondary factors as the green burgeoning of the leaves. In 1960 the breeding season of blackbirds was extended for up to a month beyond its usual time; it was associated with a period of high rainfall and below average July sunshine. The incidence of late breeding among blackbirds was higher in the north-east, while in the south and west and in the region of the River Thames song thrush nests predominated. Low sunshine levels and long damp conditions led to an extension of blackbird and song thrush nesting in the summer of 1958 in north-west London.

The breeding season of the song thrush is the longest for the three common species. The bird starts laying earlier than the blackbird and goes on longer and this is also true for birds that were introduced to New Zealand. This would suggest that the song thrush is able to respond to a lower threshold of favourable environmental conditions than the blackbird. The species also seems to have fewer partial nesting failures than the blackbird, and H. Mayer-Gross (1964) thought that this might well be due to song thrushes relying on snails as a reserve of food in dry conditions. Snails enabled the song thrush not only to go on breeding longer but also permitted it to sustain its clutch size towards the end of the nesting season more effectively than the blackbird. Miss E. T. Silva, after analysing 282 Nest Record Cards for the song thrush in the southern part of England, found that 1·4% of clutches were completed in July and August. Arthur Whitaker, whose figures I quoted earlier in this chapter, recorded a 2% rate of July nestings for the song thrush. During the late nesting of 1960 the period of wet weather, which only marginally affected blackbirds, was sufficiently long to stimulate song thrushes to nest again. Song thrushes bred as late as December in 1953 and young hatched in five nests and fledged from three. Other species such as robins, starlings and house sparrows were also reported nesting and showing similar tendencies to those of the song thrush to react to environmental conditions. In the Outer Isles the Hebridean song thrush breeds in May and June.

It is clear that a rise in temperature in autumn of only a few degrees could lead to a number of British bird species breeding in this period, assuming that their present physiological adaptations remained unaltered. It would seem less likely as a regular feature when one considers that such a practice might draw too heavily on a bird's physical reserves which are necessary for its survival through the moult and the winter as well as its breeding efficiency in the following year. Such a protracted breeding season could thus lead to losses among the adult thrushes that would not be adequately compensated for by the low survival rate of the autumn-bred young. Dr Snow has pointed out that there is no regular breeding in autumn in the southern parts of Europe where temperatures are higher than those in Britain.

The length of the mistle thrush's breeding season is shorter than that of both blackbird and song thrush (Fig. 34). Birds may begin to nest in southern Britain – south, that is, of a line from the Humber to the Mersey – as early as February. In 1961, for example, there were records of nests with eggs in February but with the main peak of laying falling between 2 and 11 March. Correspondingly in late years there are not many clutches laid before the end of March. In many years the main peak in southern Britain falls in the period 22–31 March, while in the north it tends to be later – between 1 and 10 April. W. H. Payn has described the occurrence of a mistle thrush's nest near Beccles as early as 20 January and another near Flatford as late as 23 November. The end of the breeding season is also slightly later in the north than the south. The average pair of mistle thrushes makes fewer nesting attempts than the average black-bird pair but it seems that the mistle thrush is to some extent less affected by severe weather. S. G. Cummings observed a pair of mistle thrushes whose nest in March was filled with snow before the lining had been added. When the snow had melted and drained away the mistle thrushes continued building but were held up again by snow. By 8 April the birds had not only completed the nest but a bird was sitting, hidden behind a wall of snow piled up on the edge of the nest.

The fourth of the regular breeding thrushes of Britain is the summer visiting ring ouzel and as a migrant it has some limits set on the start of its breeding season. The figures from the Nest Record Card system have certain built-in biases and these include the reporting of nests by watchers whose chief concern was to put rings on the young. This does not preclude some analysis, as Dr J. J. M. Flegg and David Glue (1975) proved in their paper on ring ouzels in *Bird Study*. Figure 36 shows the breeding season of the ring ouzel as revealed by the number of first egg-laying dates in 'quarter month' periods. As there are few first egg dates available com-

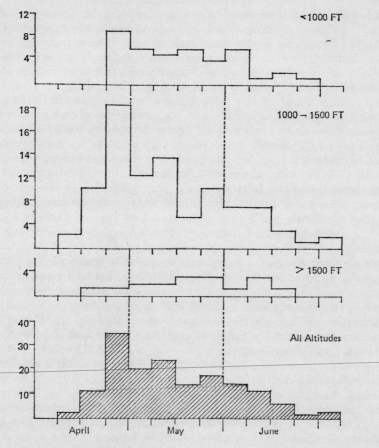

FIG. 36. The breeding season of the ring ouzel as shown by the number of first-egg laying dates in 'quarter month' periods. The first-egg laying dates are displayed in three altitudinal divisions and summed in the fourth histogram. (Reproduced from *Bird Study*, Vol 22, 1975, by permission of Dr J. J. M. Flegg and David Glue.)

pared with hatching dates (with an accuracy of ± 2 or 3 days) the latter have been used to estimate first egg dates and to illustrate the range of the breeding season, after a subtraction of 14 days for the length of the incubation period. It seems from the figures that laying may be somewhat later at 500 metres than below this height. The records indicated a clear laying peak at the end of April and early May, reflecting the situation that I found among ring ouzels in the northern Pennines. There was also a lesser peak in late May and early June; this seemed to suggest that not as many pairs are double brooded as was once thought. Some birds come late to the breeding grounds. I have known birds in Westmorland arrive from late March up to the third week of April. The picture can also be complicated by the laying of replacement clutches. The ring ouzel is a difficult and challenging bird to study and we still need to know more about its life history and breeding biology. The incubation period has been given at 8 and 12 days, while figures that I gathered in the Pennines in the 1940s gave 12 to 14 days, and Roger Durman gives figures of from 13 to 14 days, which suggest that a figure of 8 must be too low. Four nests that I have studied gave figures of 12, 13, 13 and 14 for fledging. In the west of Norway laying sometimes begins in April but is most widespread in the middle of May. In the north of Scandinavia and on the high fjelds ring ouzels lay in late May and early June, while the Alpine race of the mountain ranges of central and southern Europe may lay in the first week of May while snow is still on the ground. Many pairs of *Turdus a. alpestris* do not breed, however, before late May and laying may continue into July.

In southern Norway redwings are occasionally found nesting as early as 15 and 19 April but these might well be birds that had remained in the country for the winter. Generally in the southern half of Norway most redwings lay in early May, and nestlings have been found as late as early August; second broods are not uncommon. In southern Finland the breeding season seems to last from early May to the end of June. As you travel further north, the season is later, and in Arctic Norway first clutches of eggs are not normally laid before the end of May while fresh clutches can go on to the end of June and even the middle of July. At Abisko in Sweden the dates of first eggs fall somewhere between 19 May and 1 June and, for a second brood, between 18 and 23 June. Here the redwings, which nest near or actually on the ground, are dependent each year upon the time at which the snow cover melts. In Iceland *Turdus iliacus coburni* breeds from mid-May to July. For those redwings that breed in Scotland the nesting season appears to last from about mid-May through June.

In Poland the fieldfare begins breeding in April – the month in which many thrushes tend to start in central Europe. In Germany and Switzerland the eggs are laid from late April but more regularly in May and June. Fieldfares in southern Norway lay at the beginning of May while they tend to be a fortnight later near Trondheim. In the far north fieldfares lay, unless it is a very cold spring, towards the end of May or early in June. Two clutches seem to be common at Abisko. In Finmark eggs may not be laid until July. British breeding fieldfares seem to nest primarily in June and July. Newly hatched young were seen in Shetland on 14 July while nesting in Orkney has occurred in July and August.

The breeding seasons of Britain's thrushes appear to be determined by natural selection and coincide in each species with the time of the year when young in a region can be reared with the greatest success. The most important ultimate factor involved is the food for young birds and these resources are dependent upon conditions which ensure the availability of this food in sufficient quantities. However, breeding may be brought to a close, even before the apparent diminution of food supplies, by certain modifying factors, such as the heavy pressure on adults due to the food needed to see them through their annual moult and on the young birds which, after leaving the nest, should find sufficient food available for them to survive. In migratory species both old and young birds need to build up their reserves of strength before setting off on their travels. The proximate factors, such as daylength and perhaps temperature, provide a timing device so that the breeding seasons ensure that on average the young thrushes hatch out at a time when there is enough food for them to be raised as successfully as possible.

FLOCKING, ROOSTING AND OTHER WINTER ACTIVITIES

THE main purpose of this chapter is to consider the activities of those thrushes which occur in the British Isles during the winter months. These include social and territorial activity, roosting behaviour, pair formation, feeding, voice, and sex and age ratios where these can be determined. Since the sexes of some thrush species are superficially alike and it may sometimes be difficult to determine the age of birds, there are inevitable gaps in our knowledge as well as sources of possible error in the data acquired. Nevertheless, I would like to review some of the broad fields of research which have shed light on the winter behaviour and activities of British thrushes. At the time of migration the summer-visiting ring ouzel is generally gregarious by nature and in its winter quarters small flocks will forage socially for food.

In the winter months and on migration it is impossible to regard redwings and fieldfares as other than social animals, since we find them travelling, foraging, feeding and roosting together in loose assemblies. Towards the end of the winter there may be signs of aggressive display and sub-song, but their flocking together is very much part of their way of life. In open country the flocks are often composed of both species, but smaller flocks of single species occur on migration and quite often in suburbia. I have seen many large mixed parties on farmland, and, although both fieldfares and redwings will visit woods, I have never seen the former in the kind of low scrub and bushes in woodland which the latter often favour. At Dollis Hill, where redwings are now wintering regularly in a park but fieldfares are much less common, the flocks are never mixed.

From the late summer into early winter mistle thrushes tend to gather and travel in family parties or even larger aggregations in which individuals maintain an open kind of bond with each other. Flocks will move about under the influence of both weather and food supply, but they do not mass in compact groups and individual mistle thrushes will leave the open assembly in a rather random manner. By mid-winter the early breeding mistle thrush is becoming concerned with territorial and court-ship activities and the congregations begin to break up.

It is not unusual for song thrushes and blackbirds to migrate separately and in small flocks, and this is their behaviour over my part of suburban London, the Midlands and a number of other locations in Britain where I have seen birds on the move. In winter the blackbirds at Dollis Hill tend to keep to their established territories and, although they may feed and roost in the proximity of other blackbirds, they do not give the impression of being really gregarious by nature. After the moult the territorial drive among blackbirds is not very high; even in autumn when some boundary contests may be taking place I have counted parties of from three to thirty-six blackbirds feeding under oak trees in Gladstone Park or elms on some near-by grassland. A few immigrants will also come in for a short time and mix with the residents as they feed outside their territories. Young blackbirds may also take up small domains or sub-territories during the winter, but their impetus towards a fuller territorial drive does not seem to arrive until February or March. Sometimes, when young black-birds are feeding together, a warm autumn day may release aggressive tendencies in them and sharp aerial chases may ensue. It is in the spring that most new pairs are actually formed.

The song thrush is not a social bird outside the seasons of migration but it is possible to see very open, fortuitous gatherings with other thrushes particularly on playing fields, golf courses and other areas of grassland, especially when there is a rich supply of food. It is unusual to observe more than a score in this situation and a dozen is a much more likely number.

A number of counts have been made in various parts of the British Isles of the proportion of male to female blackbirds, especially by L. S. V. and U. Venables, J. H. Phillips and L. A. Batten. Male blackbirds tend to be more sedentary than females. There are also some differences in the migratory habits of male and female birds particularly in the northern part of their breeding range. There may be a difference also in the timing of migration, and it is also possible that more male than female black-birds come to spend the winter in Britain. Dr R. Drost in 1935 showed that females were commoner than males as migrants at Heligoland in the proportion of 3:2 in autumn and 2:1 in spring. Counts made in the British Isles revealed a preponderance of male birds present in the winter months. In the West Midlands C. D. T. Minton reported that 'no systematic month-to-month variation took place, the percentage of males usually being between 67% and 73%, i.e., more than twice as many males as females'.

From work carried out in Cambridgeshire in the winter of 1960–61 by J. H. Phillips and C. J. Mead it seems that among the adult blackbirds mist-netted in winter there was very approximately a 1:1 sex ratio but there was a disparity among young birds. Of first-winter birds more than 70% were male; this figure can be compared with W. D. Campbell's 63% of males in 99 first-winter birds obtained by bat-fowling. There was no significant alteration of the total male to female ratio throughout the winter.

In a large thrush roost by the Brent Reservoir Leo Batten caught a

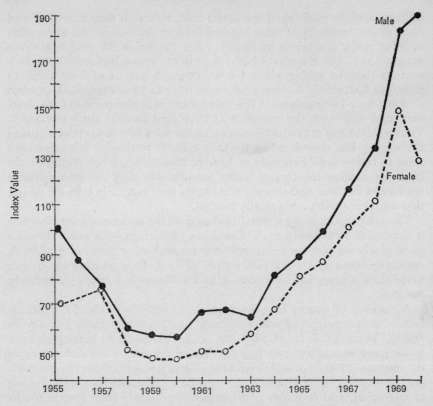

FIG. 37. Population indices of male and female blackbirds for southern England. Male index of 100=1966. (Supplied by L. A. Batten.)

total of 1392 males and 973 females between September 1966 and August 1967, giving a male percentage of 58·86 ± 1·0. When the winter months from September to February were considered by themselves the percentage rose to 59·1 ± 1·2. For a similar period Dr David Snow found a 58·34% of males in 1714 blackbirds living in Oxford. The closeness of these figures suggests that the sex ratio is a real one and raises the questions of whether more males are born or whether there is a higher mortality among the females.

From the point of view of age many first-year blackbirds move from surrounding areas to feed in such favourable areas as parks, and in this way they temporarily swell the population in regions which they do not normally occupy. The birds may then move back into their chosen breeding grounds, and these movements among first-winter birds are

PLATE 15. ADAPTABILITY. *Above*, a male blackbird at its nest in a roll of wire netting. *Below*, a robin's nest in a boot, but the species will also use old kettles and tins.

PLATE 16. JUVENILE PLUMAGES. *Above left*, a newly fledged blackbird without tail, with developing wing feathers and some down feathers attached; *right*, a recently fledged song thrush with undeveloped tail and primaries. *Below left*, a fieldfare just out of the nest and with some down feathers still attached; *right*, a juvenile robin approaching first winter moult.

regular at Dollis Hill. I have observed them in Rugby and at Oxford where Dr Snow also found a high proportion of young males in winter in the Oxford University Parks. J. H. Phillips has described how at Fulbourn Fen in Cambridgeshire out of 201 blackbirds mist-netted in the winter of 1960–61, there were 33 adult males, 35 adult females, 86 first-winter males, 41 first-winter females and 6 of uncertain age. An observed increase in the ratio of adult to first-winter males during the period might have been due to two possible causes – an outward movement of young birds or an influx of adults. There was a similar trend at the Brent roost and Batten has suggested that young birds may be easier to catch than old ones because of their lack of experience. This feature persists until December after which the ratio becomes more 'realistic'.

Batten's research has also shown a change in the sex ratio among blackbirds with increasing age. He found a higher proportion of males in the older age groups and this suggested perhaps a higher mortality among females. However, Dr David Lack (1954) showed that the average annual mortality rate among blackbirds ringed in Britain in winter was 46% for males and 50% for females and Dr J. C. Coulson found 'no significant difference between the mortality rates of adult male and female Black-birds'. After the first December of life the mortality of first-year blackbirds appears to be the same as for adults. More study is required to discover whether the ringing of birds at roosts may reflect a differential attendance rate at them.

Although work has been done on the sex and age ratios of blackbirds, less is known about the other species of thrush. Out of 63 redwings caught and ringed at Fulbourn Fen near Cambridge the age ratio of adult to first-winter birds was 1:5 and of 51 fieldfares trapped at the same place the ratio was 1:2. The samples, however, were not large enough for any firm deductions. Of 47 fieldfares which were sexed at Fulbourn 34 were females and 13 males. 169 song thrushes were caught at Coton near by and only 10% were retraps. These thrushes obviously move around in the winter.

Most of the work on the sex and age ratios of blackbirds was carried out at the birds' roosts and all five of the wintering thrush species can be found at night in trees or shrubs. I have found mistle thrushes roosting together, often in coniferous trees, through the autumn until December when they divide up again. They will also roost in evergreens, high hedges and bushes and even in dense bramble brakes or creepers. In Europe mistle thrushes have been known to spend the night in creepers on trees and, very appropriately, in clumps of mistletoe. They can be very noisy going to roost, giving their harsh churring rattles and rapid 'Tuc-tuc' notes. Inside the roost individual birds seem to stay at least 0·65 m from each other. The largest mistle thrush roost I have seen in Britain consisted of about two dozen birds, and I have watched up to fifty flying into a roost in France. After the middle of winter birds start to roost individually or in pairs, and an interesting site for a single bird was on the window sill of a house in Derby.

The fieldfare also favours pines and other conifers at night as well as evergreens, tall hedgerows and thorns, and I have located roosts in young plantations as well as dense woodland. It is not unusual for birds to spend the night on ploughlands, stubble, grassland and marshes; I have disturbed birds on heathery moors in the Pennines as I walked over the fells in the dark. About three hundred birds roosted in willows and hawthorns in Staffordshire and this is a fairly common number for a roost. However, about a thousand roosted in conifers at Hanchurch in the same county, and A. J. Harthan reported a roost of redwings and fieldfares – both species often roost together – in scrub woodland with some 15,000 to 20,000 birds of which about 60% were fieldfares. Where both winter-visiting thrushes share a roost, the fieldfares tend to spend the night at somewhat higher levels.

Redwing roosts are often in thick shrubberies, evergreens such as yew, holly, laurel and rhododendron, thorns, plantations, coverts and dense hedgerows. My suburban birds in north-west London will spend the night in the canopies of oak trees. Redwings have been seen coming to roost in a clump of hawthorns at Corsham Lake in Wiltshire and then flying down into an adjoining bed of *Phragmites* reeds. This habit is also known from Cambridgeshire and C. J. Mead suggested that it usually only occurs when the reeds and roosting bushes are situated close to each other. In one redwing roost which I studied the birds used to arrive in the evening in twos and threes, giving the soft 'see-ip' call until between fifty and a hundred birds were present. The air then became full of harsh 'Chittuck' notes. Many roosts will contain several hundred birds but in the Midlands totals may reach several thousand. Birds ringed in Stafford-shire roosts have been recovered as far away as Cittanova in Italy and in the Ukraine.

In south Warwickshire I have traced redwings flying up to thirteen km to a roost. W. R. Philipson, who studied a redwing roost in Northumber-land, reported flight lines to it up to nineteen km in length; these latter birds moved across country in small numbers and 'on the way to roost these parties will halt frequently, usually joining other redwings in the fields or in the trees, and from there they leave in the same surreptitious manner'. Their morning departures are also rather secretive and only become noticeable when unusually large numbers of birds are involved. I have sometimes heard redwings singing in the night from the heart of a roost. C. A. Norris and I heard one in a Staffordshire roost in December 1951. I noted in *Voices of the Wild* that 'there arose without warning from the dark mass of the bushes several clear, fluty notes repeated three or perhaps four times'.

In contrast to the socially roosting fieldfares and redwings, song thrushes which often choose bushes and shrubs for the night may roost singly, in small discrete groups or on occasion intermingled with blackbirds and other thrushes. In the thrush roost by the Brent Reservoir song thrushes are outnumbered by blackbirds eight to one. Song thrushes often indulge, as we have already seen, in local winter movements, either remaining broadly in the region all the year round or even leaving the district for the winter. Some birds move to the coast and roost near the shore: I have disturbed song thrushes roosting in coastal sand dunes in Northumberland and Aberdeenshire. The Hebridean song thrush has been found roosting among heather, in low scrub and even in stacks of peat.

The almost ubiquitous blackbird will roost in a wide range of situations but it seems to favour shrubberies, bushes, dense thorn thickets, plantations and hedgerows. The roost can be shared with other species of thrush. In winter I find small numbers of male and female blackbirds roosting singly and then being joined by or joining their mates in the winter or early spring. In my own garden for the last few winters a female has roosted in a *Philadelphus* bush sometimes within twelve inches or so of the preceding year's nest and never further from it than three feet. In the winter of 1975–76, from mid-September until early April – a female was present in this situation on 195 nights. She was missing on two nights of exceptionally high wind when a near gale whipped the whole bush about in an alarming manner; in October and December she was joined on two separate occasions by a male. In the winter of 1976–77 she was missing on eight nights out of 216 and her absence on a calm evening invariably meant that a storm was due later in the night. On most of these nights the male roosted in a dense honeysuckle at my front door and in the company of his mate and of three or four other blackbirds but on twelve he spent the night in an elder some ten feet from the *Philadelphus*. Some males occupy their winter roosts during the breeding season and others roost close to the nest site. Many roosting places hold from one or two to a dozen birds. Some suburban gardens may have no suitable roosting site and blackbirds which feed and even hold territories in them may have to spend the night elsewhere. On the Continent many large blackbird roosts arise because of this reason. Moulting birds will also choose to stay away from a traditional communal roost and local conditions of fog may prevent birds setting off in the evening to reach it.

I have records of country roosts holding several hundred birds. More than 250 were seen flying to a roost at Kenwood in Middlesex and a roost of from 200 to 300 birds was reported at Ruislip. The largest suburban roost at Dollis Hill held about fifty birds and was situated in an old thick hawthorn hedge; other roosts in the region have been in high privet hedges, almonds, ornamental shrubs, Virginia creeper and ivy. But all these roosts are small compared to one on 9·7 quiet hectares of woodland and scrub at the Brent Reservoir in north-west London. This draws some of the birds that live on the northern part of Dollis Hill but not, as far as I have been able to tell, from my own immediate neighbourhood. There may be up to two thousand blackbirds coming to this roost with smaller numbers of song thrushes, redwings and fieldfares in many, if not all, years.

Leo Batten has made an intensive study of this roost where he has ringed over six thousand blackbirds and I am very grateful to him for allowing me to review some of the research that he has been able to carry out on the banks of the Brent Reservoir. What now follows is basically a synopsis of his original work. The catchment area for the roost occupied some 200 hectares of gardens and the highest numbers of birds were recorded in October and November. There were few adults during the period of moult from late July to September, as one might expect, but juveniles could be found using the roost during this time. When I joined Leo Batten at the roost in August 1975 the juveniles were arriving considerably earlier than the adults. In the summer territory-holding males continue to use the roost. Out of a mammoth total of 6500 blackbirds ringed about 290 were recorded again locally. Only one in fifty moved more than 25 km from the roost and most recoveries were within five km. Only two were found abroad – one at Malmö in Sweden and a second bird at Lavardac in France. This indicates a mainly sedentary population. It has been known for some time that the blackbird as a British species has a marked tendency to breed where it is reared. Werth (1947) pointed out that 72% of recoveries of blackbirds in summer were in the places where they were reared and that just under 50% remained all through the year.

Leo Batten carried out a considerable amount of research into the functions and advantages of a communal roost such as the woodland and scrub in Brent provided. He was interested in the theory that communal roosts may assist with the conservation of energy in the autumn and winter months. There were no important differences in temperature and humidity inside the roost but there was an average 73% reduction in wind speed through it. Blackbirds select the thickest and most sheltered bushes for roosting and the reduction in wind speed there compared with outside was measured on two sensitive anemometers. As the chilling effect of wind is a very important factor in heat loss, Batten tried to quantify the effects of the reduction in the wind on the metabolism of roosting blackbirds. Birds were roosted singly at night in cages made from wood and net. It was found that, when there was wind and the temperature was close to freezing, among birds in the most favourable sites the weight reduction was only about 60% of that lost by birds in more open or exposed situations. The saving only amounted to about 15% in calm conditions. Since blackbirds maintain a distance of several feet from each other in the roost, they cannot warm each other in the way that perhaps starlings are able to do. However, birds were also artificially roosted in large cages at different densities. With two birds per ten cubic feet the average weight loss per hour was about 0·38 gm but when there were six birds in the same space the loss rose to 0·54 gm. When there was one bird to only one cubic foot of space the hourly loss was measured at 0·7 gm. At a high roosting density the restlessness and unsociability of the blackbirds had resulted in a serious change in their weights. Dispersal in the roost might make it more difficult for predators to locate birds and alarm notes given by individual birds not threatened by a predator might distract a cat or tawny owl from its intended victim. It was concluded that the value of the communal roosting habit was primarily as a protection from predators and there was no evidence that the habit in suburban blackbirds at all fitted the proposition that it was a device for passing on information about food sources. In Brent there are rich reserves of food dispersed so widely that there is no special value in knowing the location of one particular source.

Suburban blackbirds appear to have enough reserves of fat to ensure their survival through the night but woodland blackbirds in some country areas reveal considerably lower weights during periods of cold weather. Birds caught at the Brent roost in cold winters averaged 125 gm while blackbirds trapped at Northwood Hill in Kent averaged only 92 gm. The body weights of thrushes may be influenced by proximate temperature and perhaps also by daylength. Blackbirds show a marked increase in their body weights in autumn and early winter; then after a peak in December and January there is a steady decline which may be accelerated by the onset of cold weather. The initial rise in weight would appear to be an insurance against bad conditions in winter and the subsequent drop a preparation for the forthcoming breeding season. Some of the rise in autumn may be due to an increase in water content in the developing feathers. The weights of juveniles were found by Batten to be negatively correlated with sunshine and low weights in late summer could perhaps be attributed to a drying of the ground and the resulting retreat of such food resources as earthworms.

The autumn and winter evenings are often made noisy by the metallic clamour of blackbirds going to roost. Dawn too is often punctuated by sharp ringing 'Chink-chink' or 'Mik-mik' notes. The actual degree and intensity of calling is often greatest where favourable roost sites attract newcomers from outside the region and these are often harassed by the resident birds until they finally accept the strangers in their midst. It seems very likely that local weather conditions may also be reflected in the vocal activities of blackbirds going to roost, and some of the other thrushes as well. M. K. Colquhoun after carrying out watches over sixty winter evenings found that a wind force of about 5 mph cut down the

total of blackbird calls to one-third that on a calm day, while one of
15 mph or over inhibited all calling. Falls in temperature can also have a
damping effect.

The winter activities of our thrushes range widely throughout the day.
The gathering of food is, of course, a vital and time-consuming pursuit.
Many blackbirds will remain in the woodlands throughout the winter
and only leave at the onset of very bad weather. On the other hand song
thrushes may only stay in woodland while fruits are especially abundant.
Food sources are important in the winter and will often lead to local
observations of birds like that of 250 mistle thrushes on yews, 1500 fieldfares on apples and so on. As we have seen in chapter 7, there are ecological differences in autumn between the closely-allied thrush species, and
there are often considerable movements of birds where food supplies,
unlike those of towns and suburbs, are scattered and varied. During the
winter months birds may have to search very carefully and persistently
for what insect and invertebrate foods still remain. In January and
February, as Dr Geoffrey Beven has shown in the classic investigation of
Bookham Common, there is a drop in the leaf litter population of animals
which must affect the number of ground-feeding birds in a wood.

In *Woodland Birds* I described how I watched 'a male blackbird in
February searching for invertebrate food and employing in one and a
quarter minutes 52 sideways strokes of its bill: in this time it picked up
only four small items which it swallowed'. Tits may have to spend up to
90% of a nine-hour winter day feeding and generally the smaller the
species the longer the time required each day for gathering food. Observations I have made show that the commoner thrushes spend up to
55% of a winter day engaged on feeding activities but if the temperature
falls to freezing or below, and there is food available, they can spend up
to 80% feeding. On a January day in 1963 a fieldfare was engaged for
seven hours in eating apples that I had put out in the garden. Blackbirds
seem to take part in dawn feeding, even more than the early rising robin,
but very little in the evening. Their feeding hours in winter, according to
John Lees, have maxima close together, one and a half hours on either
side of midday but they will have taken 55% of their food before solar
noon. I agree with this conclusion but find two peaks after noon at Dollis
Hill in March (Fig. 28).

From my own observations I find that song thrushes in winter tend to
start feeding later than blackbirds with an earlier maximum in the
morning but a similar one in the afternoon. What few records I have of
the mistle thrush seem to suggest a feeding pattern rather like that of the
song thrush. After watching redwings on a Warwickshire farm and in my
local suburban park I find that their feeding on the grasslands or football
pitches begins quite early and is maintained throughout most of the day.
Where the ground is heavy, compacted and rather difficult to penetrate

either from above or below, a great deal of searching is needed to extract or gather the food items. In these circumstances redwings may start to feed in woodland where the ground is easier to work.

Although much of a winter's day has to be spent in the vital quest for food, there is also time for other activities as well. The clearly declaimed notes of song thrushes in full territorial song can be heard in most months of the year with August and September – the time of moult – the most silent months. Song thrushes reoccupying their territories in early winter are dependent in their timing on the food available in that particular year. J. P. Burkitt has shown that the dawn chorus of song thrushes in Ulster in February anticipated dawn by about forty minutes and it got earlier until by late May it was eighty-four minutes before. Birds will also sing later into the darkness. From the autumn into winter song thrushes will sing strongly in the morning, but in 1961, after a silence in January, they sang then only in the afternoon and evening until the third week of February. Early in the year blackbirds often start to sing quite late in the day and then they extend the singing period into the afternoon. By March blackbirds will even begin their dawn song before the song thrush which is an early starter. However, quite a number of factors may influence the degree of winter song – the age and sexual maturity of birds, degree of competition and the weather. In early April 1976 I was working on a *World About Us* television film for the BBC with Michael Salisbury of the Corporation's Natural History Unit. We were filming the dawn chorus at Westbury-on-Trym and it was interesting to see how slight changes of wind and temperature could almost totally inhibit song thrushes while blackbirds went on singing almost unaffected. The song thrushes at Dollis Hill seemed to be less influenced by these changes, but I do not know why. Young male blackbirds will begin to take up territories in autumn and their persistence can often be correlated with locally rich sources of food such as fruit. They may indulge in display and subdued song from September to March but the full territorial song does not usually start before January or February.

During the first fifteen days of December 1959 in southern England there was only spasmodic bird song. Then on the sixteenth and seventeenth came a remarkable outburst, dominated by song thrushes, but with a rich chorus of hedgesparrows, wrens, starlings, house sparrows and even a woodpigeon. During the month I kept records of maximum day and minimum night temperatures before correlating the output of bird song with these temperatures. It was interesting to note that the difference between the day and night temperatures from 1 to 15 December varied between 2 and 14°F. On the 16th of the month there was a difference of 17°F and on the 17th some 19°F. The two great outbursts of song occurred on warmer days with the temperatures between 52°F and 54°F in th daytime, following cold nights with minima of 34°F. By artificially raising the temperature in winter research workers have induced many song thrushes to sing prematurely.

It is possible to witness instances of display and other less common activity in the winter months. In December a young male blackbird defending a territory has been known to throw a laurel leaf in the air while a song thrush in autumn has been seen picking a petal from a scarlet geranium and dancing up and down with it. Around some of their scattered drinking and feeding places blackbirds will often gather and indulge in chases, flights and what Averil Morley described as 'a kind of tourney'. Such communal displays, not observed or reported on by all observers, seem to take place between early winter and spring with a peak in the latter period. Both sexes may be involved and there are sometimes rather stylized and aggressive encounters; these seem to be triggered off by a highly assertive condition in birds meeting for some other purpose and the behaviour is then continued through habituation. Female blackbirds will sometimes gather nest material in autumn, especially in mild weather, without actually starting to build.

Besides the activities involved with feeding, roosting, occasional song and perhaps some display the thrushes also have to find time to drink, bathe, preen and rest. In mild weather the birds may manage very well but both song thrush and redwing are sensitive to hard winters. The former may undertake partial migrations and visits to pasture lands and the latter hard-weather movements and entry into towns to offset the effects of very cold weather. Blackbirds and mistle thrushes are hardier and the former will enter the woodlands in winter. Redwings and field-fares are also highly nomadic by nature, shifting their winter quarters from season to season and even from day to day. Mistle thrushes survived the phenomenally severe winter of 1962–63, either by emigrating or entering urban areas but they suffered badly in Hampshire and Dorset (Ash 1964). We shall look in more detail at the effects of hard winters in the next chapter but there are some aspects that I would like to discuss here.

The exceptional weather in the winter of 1962–63, unlike the previous cold spells in 1955 and 1961–62, had an appreciable and quite long-lasting effect on the numbers of blackbirds living at Dollis Hill. With the coming of frosts from 20 December 1962 growing numbers of blackbirds started to come and feed regularly on the apples that I put out for them. On 27 December a number of different species of hard-weather migrants started to cross the area and two days later small numbers of redwings and fieldfares began for the first time to frequent gardens in the district. In the first ten days of January 1963 temperatures in many places were as low as −12°c. By 7 January the number of blackbirds in the area had dropped dramatically and the last resident male within a radius of 200 yards of my house disappeared on 9 January. This exodus coincided with the heaviest and most widespread hard-weather passage of the whole winter (Dobinson and Richards 1964), and the worst amount of wind chill – the dry convective cooling power of the atmosphere. From 9 January until 20 February there were no blackbirds at all in my district and only half a dozen within half a mile of my house, instead of the usual 350–400. Fieldfares and redwings still came to feed in my garden but roosted elsewhere. I did not find a single dead blackbird and, despite artificial feeding and the provision of water in many gardens, it was clear that a mass evacuation of blackbirds had taken place.

The blackbirds started to come back in late February and early March. They returned singly and the male that appeared in my garden was unmated until the second week of March. Before this he sang very loudly from song posts quite different from those used by males in previous years. Once I saw him in his unmated condition 'with humped back, fanned tail, fluffed out body-feathers and raised crest in full sexual display to an object on a snow-free concrete path in the garden. He bowed, ran forward, bowed again: this continued for a quarter of an hour until at last he mounted, attempted coition for some ten seconds, dropped down and finally flew off. I went out at once to find that the substitute for the female was, in fact, a particularly black lump of coal some two inches long and one inch wide.' An inanimate surrogate of this kind was quite beyond my experience. Later some 86 or 87 pairs of blackbirds were established compared with 192 in the previous year. Many territories were left empty or remained only partially occupied. New territories were having to be established and newcomers to the area were behaving like autumn migrants or subordinate birds. It was clear that some catastrophe had overtaken most of the Dollis Hill population – perhaps to the west or south of England, or even on the Continent since blackbirds suffered very badly in Brittany, or possibly even because a highly sedentary urban population had lost the ability to 'home'. The result was a complete breakdown in the old and traditional territorial pattern and in the spring of 1964 when 244 singing males were counted the whole system of territories was in a state of flux.

It was reflected by an unprecedented brilliance and volume of song, fierce and unrelenting display and aggressive encounters, and by spasmodic and irregular nest building. The breeding success that year was low. This I attributed to the disturbance resulting from competition among the birds and the building of nests in 'hopeless' situations by new birds unfamiliar with their newly acquired territories and traditional nest sites. That same winter of 1962–63 forced the mistle thrushes away from Dollis Hill and the song thrush population fell from between six and eight pairs to two. Departures and emigrations of both these thrush species were reported in England in that winter with returning birds arriving back in early March.

During one spell of cold weather in 1938 I watched redwings and fieldfares feeding on haws in London, while in 1940 both kinds of thrush entered many towns and villages attracted by kitchen scraps and other kinds of food. In 1955 and 1963 fieldfares arrived in my own suburban garden and fed with a few redwings. In recent years redwings have wintered in suburban London and in the winter of 1975–76 I watched at least a score feeding unconcernedly within a few feet of unobservant commuters walking towards Kilburn Bakerloo station. Having entered London only in severe weather, redwings have now chosen to spend the whole of the winter in suburban parks. It is the dynamic nature and ability to adapt in the group of thrushes which make them so interesting and challenging to the ornithologist. In the next chapter I shall look at some of the complicated factors that may influence thrush populations.

CHAPTER 12

MORTALITY AND POPULATION DYNAMICS

I ARRIVE at this chapter in the book with more than slight trepidation. Although there have been some research and much observation published on the complex subject of population dynamics, there has also been a great deal of subjective speculation, much of it extremely logical but often without any firm evidence to support it. It is not difficult to put forward correlations of certain events and some observers have done this prematurely without tests by experiment to confirm the relationships or re-examining 'models'. In research of this kind there are many uncontrolled factors. Some may have different effects at different times and the general techniques and methods employed in population studies may be too crude and inaccurate to measure them. Dr Adam Watson in a stimulating paper in *British Birds* set out positively 'to sharpen constructive criticism' of papers on population dynamics in birds. The present author feels that he can only indicate in this chapter some of the recent trends in studies into thrush populations in the British Isles.

Some of the basic difficulties that confront research are those which are associated with all assumptions and suppositions. There are many ways of tackling population problems and their validity would seem to depend on a steady period of successful testing and trial. My long-term study of the thrush populations at Dollis Hill has served continually to remind me that individual birds may show differences in behaviour from other members of the species – in nervousness, vociferousness, adventurousness, shyness of man and so on. These may be passed on to their offspring or affect their neighbours directly or their own chances of survival in any competition for food or nest site and in their breeding success. Within the wider network of population dynamics and the basic concepts of behaviour, predators, weather and qualitative changes in the habitat, these individual variations need to be recognized. The great web of natural processes still remains too complex and subtle for us to comprehend in its entirety and so we are forced – as yet – to think only upon simplified lines.

G. C. Varley and G. R. Gradwell (1968) have described a method for analysing key factors in the winter moth. Its purpose was to discover which stages in time can account for variations in the population – to diagnose where, if at all, in the life cycle there is a mortality which is the main component of the fluctuations in numbers over succeeding generations. A model such as this is used to test observations and confirm that the study is being correctly organized. There can, of course, be more complicated models, involving more steps than key factor analysis, where complex relationships, systems analysis and energy flows come more within the scope of the computer than the unaided human mind. Nevertheless, research techniques have made great strides in recent years but there is a very long way to go.

In general, primary causes can often be difficult to isolate. For example, a song thrush may die because it was taken by a sparrowhawk or cat, struck by a car, or it may have died from a bacterial infection or from starvation. If it was originally a subordinate bird which had failed to establish a territory and thus not obtained enough food, then its lack of success in territorial competition could have been a primary cause in its death; it was too slow, too weak and without resistance. Birds can die through predation, accident, disease and lack of food. Causal factors are notoriously difficult to isolate and test experimentally. Only through a wide range of population monitoring schemes will it perhaps be possible to judge the increasingly subjective information now being collected. In most of the theories about bird populations it is probable that there is no one all-embracing answer but there may well be elements in many, if not all of them, that contain part of the truth. Set against these rather general introductory remarks I now propose to review the main causes of mortality in thrushes in Britain and to examine some of the research into their populations.

I have already mentioned predation as one of the causes of death in thrushes. Among bird predators peregrines, merlins and sparrowhawks have been known to take adults of all six British thrush species while buzzards have been recorded preying on at least five. Hobbies, kestrels, hen and Montagu's harriers, and even kites and honey buzzards have taken thrushes on occasion. Out of a total of 213 birds identified at Wytham near Oxford as the prey of tawny owls H. N. Southern (1954) found the remains of fourteen blackbirds, nine song thrushes and a single mistle thrush. Tawny owls may be regular visitors to thrush roosts. David Glue examined 109 bird skulls from barn owl pellets collected in southern England and found a song thrush, a blackbird and two unidentified thrushes. The commonest thrushes are also regularly taken by little, long-eared and short-eared owls. Members of the crow family will take many young thrushes as well as eggs and sick or injured adults. Carrion crows systematically search for nests and will visit certain productive areas many times through the breeding season. Sick and wounded birds are also taken and P. Hope Jones (1962) reported that in Anglesey in January 1962 'Doubtless many dead and dying Fieldfares were eaten by the abundant Carrion Crows'. Hooded crows will raid ring ouzel nests and in Swedish Lapland it was found that one-third of the redwing nests destroyed were the work of this species of crow. Rooks and jackdaws, magpies (increasingly in the suburbs), and jays will also take the eggs and young of the common thrush species. I have found that in many woodlands song thrushes and blackbirds suffer very much from the attentions of jays and this predation together with the effects of disturbance and perhaps other factors may result in only 41% of hatching in blackbird nests and 36% in song thrushes, as shown by the national averages calculated by Dr David Snow. An interesting predator among birds is the heron which has been recorded swallowing a female blackbird.

In suburban areas cats, rats and grey squirrels often prove to be important mammalian predators on the common thrushes. As the result of sample counts over 26 years at Dollis Hill I estimated that in 1951 'there was one cat to every five households, in 1961 one to every twelve, and in 1971 one to every eight'. My local feline predators have taken both adult and young blackbirds and song thrushes and an adult mistle thrush. Dr J. C. Coulson (1961) found from the ringing recoveries of blackbirds that one in ten had been killed by a cat. It is interesting that he also discovered that the proportion of young blackbirds which was killed was not higher than that amongst adults. In north-west London Leo Batten has observed that cats were the second most common cause of death. In more open country cats are replaced as predators by our native carnivores and adders. Ring ouzels have been seen attacking adders near their nests and Max Wenner took a photograph of a young ring ouzel being mesmerized by an adder. E. W. Hendy once examined an adder which was in the act of swallowing a nestling; he did not name the species but found 'the nestling's head and shoulders were covered with saliva, and drawn out from the rest of the body'.

Various kinds of disease may be responsible for mortality among thrushes and the causes may be either immediate or predisposing. A bird's resistance to disease may be reduced by a drop in food reserves or by a change in temperature. Persistent wet or cold weather can affect the lungs of nestlings and result in chilling which may lead to death. Disease can be caused by pathogenic organisms such as bacteria, viruses and fungi or by protozoan or metazoan parasites which become out of balance with their hosts. Birds may also be poisoned, starved or meet their deaths by accident. The role of disease itself in influencing the populations of wild birds is still not fully understood but it is generally believed that numbers are largely controlled by food supply and that predation or disease have only a secondary part to play. Yet lack of food and disease can be linked together. Dr J. S. Ash (1957) has shown 'that diseased, injured or heavily parasitized birds are the first to die during severe weather when food is scarce'.

Bacterial, mycotic and viral infections all occur in wild birds and the thrushes are no exception. Tuberculosis, caused by the avian strain of

Mycobacterium tuberculosis, has been identified in blackbirds. Pasteurellosis is a common pathogen in wild birds, with an organism which causes lesions in various parts of the body, and it has been reported in black-birds and song thrushes. Infections with Salmonella organisms are common in poultry, but at least ten blackbirds in some Edinburgh gardens died in January 1967 from *Salmonella hessarok* first isolated in 1953 in Iran. Although there are some one thousand different species of Salmonella it is *S. typhimurium* which is the most regular cause of Salmonellosis in animals, but it is not common in the general population of wild birds. Intermediate in nature between the Salmonellae and *Escerichia coli* are the paracolon organisms which cause enlargement of the liver and spleen; acute paracolon infection has been diagnosed in a blackbird. Coryza, which is an infection of the upper respiratory tract, not uncommon in birds, has also been reported in blackbirds. The virus infection pox, which is fairly common in house sparrows, has not often been observed in thrushes. Aspergillosis is a mycotic infection in birds, especially waterfowl, caused by inhaling mould spores from decaying vegetable material and this has been recorded in blackbirds. Alopecia, which is usually reported in blackbirds and occasionally in song thrushes, with a loss of feathers from the dorsal part of the neck, the shoulders and under each wing, often is accompanied by skin irritation and sometimes a heavy burden of ectoparasites. Death in blackbirds and song thrushes has also resulted from ruptured organs such as the spleen and pancreas and from pneumonia following trauma, while redwings have been found suffering from haemorrhagic enteritis and entero-hepatitis. Thrushes have been recorded with tumours subsequent to injuries, while egg peritonitis, brought about perhaps by injury to the abdominal wall or disturbance at the nest, has been described in the blackbird by A. R. Jennings (1959).

Birds can be hosts to a very large number of internal parasites, known as endoparasites, to distinguish them from external, or ectoparasites. There is an account of these in the appendix.

In the past thrushes have suffered quite badly from the effects of poisons including phosphorous rodenticides and some slug baits. In 1962 J. W. Macdonald found that 40% of the birds of all species sent for examination to the Veterinary Laboratory of the Ministry of Agriculture, Fisheries and Food had died from poisoning, compared with 25% from parasites. These included song thrushes and blackbirds. Toxic chemicals were widely used in the 1960s in the British Isles and at that time the Second Report of the Joint Committee of the British Trust for Ornithology and the Royal Society for the Protection of Birds on Toxic Chemicals, in collaboration with the Game Research Association, reported thrushes, especially song thrushes and blackbirds, as figuring high on the casualty lists. It remarked: 'These birds are animal and vegetable eaters (worms, molluscs, insects, spiders, fruit, berries and seeds). Whilst it is possible that some of the thrushes died from eating dressed seed, it appears to us more probable that they were killed indirectly by eating insects which had accumulated poison.' In subsequent analyses blackbirds and song thrushes were found to contain mercury, which was often used in dual-purpose seed dressings and was generally absent from sprays, and organic chlorine. A song thrush found dead in central London in June 1962 contained BHC, dieldrin and an unidentified compound but no mercury; these poisons could have originated in private or public gardens. By 1963 garden birds such as blackbird and song thrush began to head the list of the number of bodies sent to the Joint Committee for examination. From 1962–66 voluntary bans were introduced on the use of dieldrin and other persistent organo-chlorine insecticides as seed dressings and there were signs of an improvement in bird populations but the use continued in some places and must have had a detrimental effect locally.

Bird populations can also be affected by adverse weather conditions. The Common Birds Census has shown how the song thrush population was reduced by a half after the winter of 1962–63 and there were considerable local decreases in mistle thrushes. After the earlier bad winters of 1940 and 1947 fieldfares did not suffer as badly as redwings but mistle thrushes were more badly affected in the second of those two winters. Blackbirds managed very well in both winters except in the south-west and Cardigan where their numbers were more reduced than those of song thrushes. In the appalling winter of 1962–63 many mistle thrushes departed from Britain but there was nevertheless a large reduction in breeding strength; according to the Common Birds Census numbers were not made up until 1968. In that same period song thrushes and fieldfares also moved out of Britain in some numbers but large mortality figures were returned for redwings. Blackbirds appear to have withstood the cold spell of 1962–63 fairly well and in more than half of the regions the species seems to have been unaffected. However, the Nest Record Cards suggested a bigger reduction than that revealed by the questionnaires returned from 261 different parts of Great Britain. At Dollis Hill the cold spell of January 1962 had little or no effect on the population of blackbirds but, as we have seen, it was otherwise in 1963.

Very many birds died in the early part of 1963. Dr J. S. Ash (1964) found that mistle thrushes suffered badly in Hampshire and Dorset; they lost from 24–45% of their normal weight with an average around 33%. In a small sample females seemed to have lost more weight than males. Some song thrushes lost relatively less weight perhaps being more vulnerable to the onset of cold itself; they were more severely affected early in the cold spell than blackbirds were but they moved away. Most corpses were found on the coast. Amongst blackbirds Dr Ash found the heaviest mortality in 'adult males in open country (perhaps territory-holding residents)'. Many of the surviving blackbirds could be found close to

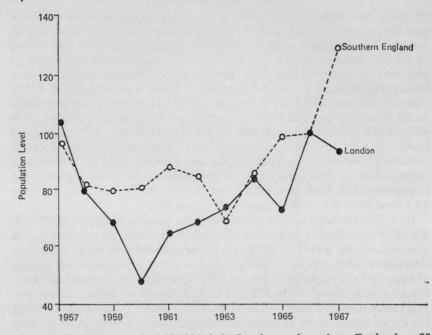

FIG. 38. Population level of blackbirds in London and southern England. 1966 index=100. (Supplied by L. A. Batten.)

human habitations. Redwings, like mistle thrushes, seem capable of surviving a greater weight loss than song thrushes with an average around 54% but over a narrower weight range. In contrast, blackbirds were rather like song thrushes, with a loss of 34% in fifteen males and 31% in twelve females. Some individual blackbirds were able to sustain quite high weights.

Where a reasonable food supply is assured, the weights of wintering birds tend to rise with a fall in temperature and this has been shown to be true for reed buntings, American tree sparrows and slate-coloured juncos. Where there is a severe shortage of food, weights, as we have seen, may go down. S-A. Bengtson (1970) estimated that the number of redwings breeding in Iceland was halved in 1963 after severe mortality in their British wintering quarters during a time of cold weather and acute food shortage.

The Common Birds Census has disclosed those bird species which can be most badly affected by cold weather in winter, requiring perhaps several years to make up the losses. Birds are not perhaps the most precise indicators of broad climatic changes which may themselves show variation with increasing altitude. Kenneth Williamson pointed out in 1975 'One cannot but wish that the CBC and Nest Records Schemes were better equipped to comment on such situations as and when they arise'. High mean temperatures can affect the amount of insects and seeds available to birds and mild winters can ensure both a high survival rate and increased breeding in the ensuing summers. Drought in the summer, especially of the kind that we experienced in Britain in the summer of 1976, can lead to increased mortality. In urban and suburban regions blackbirds, living in an artificially heated environment, show a high rate of winter survival and better recruitment than blackbirds in the open country.

Thrushes are also liable to die from a number of other causes – from becoming fatally entangled in netting put out to protect fruit, from being shot, from injuries from collisions and accidents and from trauma arising from such impacts. In his long study of blackbirds in north-west London Leo Batten found that the greatest single cause of death was traffic, followed by predation by cats and various misadventures. He has kindly allowed me to quote the following list of British casualties from his unpublished manuscript on blackbird population dynamics (Fig. 39): 'Killed striking door, window and various stationary objects, including a boy's leg; flying into power cables and telephone wires; drowned in bucket of creosote, rainwater tub and cattle trough; strangled in own nesting material and fork of branch in roost site; caught on a branch due to cotton on feet; trapped in tar, rat trap, cold frame, greenhouses, garage and fishing line; hit by golf ball and hail stones; dashed against tree by strong wind and caught in storm.' Some birds may die in territorial fights, others down chimneys. Van Steenbergen in 1971 suggested that the higher mortality among Belgian blackbirds compared with those in Britain was probably due to a higher hunting pressure. Certainly many European blackbirds and other thrushes are taken for food amongst the millions of songbirds annually trapped, netted, limed or shot on the continent of Europe.

The Road Deaths Enquiry from 1960–61, reflecting the study of bird casualties on 76 stretches of road, revealed a mortality cost of 767 blackbirds, 461 song thrushes, 29 mistle thrushes, 4 fieldfares and 4 redwings. During that same period a watch was also kept on a two-mile stretch of the A 6003 Kettering to Uppingham road and here the deaths were reported of 69 blackbirds, 35 song thrushes, 3 mistle thrushes and a redwing. In an unusual experiment all the nestlings of all species being reared in nests in hedgerows and buildings to a depth of one hundred feet on each side of a Wiltshire road were ringed; the casualties, recovered with their identity rings, showed that traffic killed about one-tenth of all the blackbirds and song thrushes marked in this way. Many thrushes on migration have been reported dead after flying into lighthouses and those

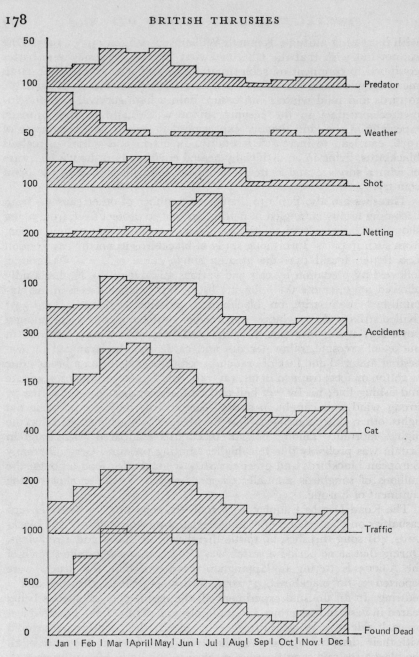

FIG. 39. Seasonal distribution of some causes of blackbird mortality. (Supplied by L. A. Batten.)

whose columns were subsequently floodlit showed a marked drop in deaths. I have sometimes counted scores of redwing corpses beneath unlit lighthouse columns. Blackbirds, song thrushes and fieldfares also die in this way. We have already seen that blackbirds are sometimes killed by flying into power cables and it is interesting to note that a joint RSPB-CEGB survey made between 1964 and 1970 at Dungeness reported more than a thousand birds of 74 different species killed in this manner. Most of the casualties were gulls flying to and from their roosts but there were also many night migrants including 61 song thrushes, 55 redwings, 52 blackbirds, 38 fieldfares, 5 ring ouzels and 2 mistle thrushes.

These accidents are only part of the drain that can be put upon migrating thrushes moving between their breeding grounds and winter quarters. W. H. Payn (1962) described how one October more than six hundred redwings were found dead on the beach between Gorleston and Gunton. Each year the weather patterns vary and the migrational drain on the thrush species must reveal annual differences. It is difficult to assess how great the real losses may be from this cause.

One of the fundamental problems in bird population dynamics is to try to discover what it is that brings about the apparent stability of populations. It would seem that disease, bad weather on migration, predation and food shortage may have some effect. There is considerable evidence that the last factor – food scarcity – may have a significant role to play. It may be that all the factors interact with 'disease and starvation increasing the liability to predation, predation reducing the proportion of diseased prey in the population and allowing a more effective use of food and other resources' (Lack 1964). It was once thought that the stability of populations was achieved by an animal's reproductive rate being adjusted to its mortality rate but it now seems that the former is as high as the species can attain in the particular habitat in which it lives. So a bird raises as many broods as it can when there is sufficient food to support the young and lays that number of eggs which could produce, on average, the largest number of survivors. Amongst passerine birds the clutch size is influenced by the higher mortality in bigger broods because of the shortage of food. Dr David Lack showed that, while the ultimate factor in controlling the average clutch size in a species was natural selection, there could also be adaptive variations in the size according to the year, season and habitat.

Mortality in passerine birds is rather high with generally less than half of the eggs laid producing fledged and flying young; a further loss takes place before these are able to live independently of the adults which reared them. Amongst adult birds mortality is also high, ranging in certain passerines from 40%–60%, with many more birds dying in the breeding season in urban situations than at any other time. Since a number of studies have been undertaken into the population dynamics of blackbirds I propose to look at them first. However, before doing this, I would like to make some reference to the use of ringing returns and the Nest Record Card scheme which have been employed by various workers in their examination of bird populations. Ringing returns have been used to calculate the expectation of life and mortality rates, while Nest Record Cards have been studied for status changes and a guide to populations. There are many biases built into the information and this has tended to deter research workers from using the totals that the Nest Records provide. It is not desirable, for example, to compare the totals of one species of bird with the grand total of all species since much of the ringing work or nest reporting is done in areas of high bird density or variety, which may not reflect the relative abundance of species over larger geographic areas. There have also been changes in the practice and technique of ringing birds and recording nests, all providing additional sources of bias. Some alterations in habitats may also have led to rises and falls in the absolute total of all birds, but this cannot readily be determined.

Nevertheless, despite a tendency for what H. B. Ginn pointed out in 1969 as 'an optimistic picture to emerge from the totals', the totals of birds marked and of Nest Record Cards may point to changes of status and to the relative changes between different species. In assessing populations the totals of birds ringed or nests recorded are probably of most use where the numbers of birds are small enough to limit the totals. The presence of biases has been examined by Ginn (1969). He was able to show by a direct comparison between the totals of pulli (young birds up to the flying stage) that were ringed and the Nest Record Cards for the song thrush and blackbird that severe winters in Britain have tended to reduce the totals of the former more than those of the latter. The pattern of recovery was sufficiently variable to indicate that there was probably some subtle factor preventing the song thrush from regaining the dominance that it once unquestionably had; in the early part of this century the song thrush was, according to Charles Dixon, 'the commonest thrush' in outer London. John Parslow (1973) observed that 'Even allowing for the fact that the Blackbird has increased, there can be little doubt that the numbers of Song Thrushes have declined appreciably'. The use of ringing and Nest Cards for direct comparison is confined to pairs of species with similar habitats, breeding seasons, clutch sizes and so on, whose nests can be located in the same kind of proportion as they actually occur in the population.

From 1951–76 the total number of pairs of blackbirds breeding at least once each year within a study area of 546 acres around my home at Dollis Hill varied between 160 and 212, with the exception of 1963 when the total dropped dramatically to 86 pairs. In every year it seemed probable that a high proportion of old birds survived from one breeding season to the next; this would prove a stabilizing factor in the pattern of

Table 13. Breeding Densities of Blackbirds in Britain and Europe (Pairs per acre)

Overgrown garden, south Wales	2·771
Botanic Garden, Oxford (1954)	2·660
Botanic Garden, Oxford (1955)	2·160
Botanic Garden, Oxford (1953)	1·830
Scrub/woodland, Brent, London	1·538
London suburb, Brent Reservoir	1·125
Park in Frankfurt	1·051
City park, Zurich	1·051
Allotments, Brent Reservoir	1·024
Dublin suburb	0·724
Berlin suburb	0·724
Oxford University Parks (1954–56)	0·485
Oxford University Parks (1953)	0·442
Ladbroke Square Garden, London	0·428
Dollis Hill, London (1961)	0·354
Small gardens, urban area, Zurich	0·323
Surrey oakwood, upper limit	0·283
Garden city, Zurich	0·242
Farmland, Oxfordshire	0·161
Augsburg Zoo	0·161
Town and gardens, Oederan, Germany	0·161
Borghese Garden, Rome	0·161
Oakwood, Northamptonshire	0·150
Oak/hornbeam wood, Germany	0·123
Surrey oakwood, lower limit	0·089
Urban area, few gardens, Zurich	0·082
Swiss orchards and fields	0·082
German pine plantation	0·082
Mixed woods, Finland	0·082
Mixed woods, Switzerland	0·040
Suburban farmland, Brent, London	0·040
Willow swamp, Brent Reservoir	0·040
Broad-leaved groves, Finland	0·032
Broad-leaved meadow-like woods, Finland	0·020
Spruce and mixed coniferous wood, Finland	0·016
Open country, Shetland	0·004

Compiled mainly from Snow (1958), Simms (1971) and Batten (1972)

territories and only in 1963 and 1964 was the traditional pattern disturbed. Coulson (1961) showed that the annual mortality of adult blackbirds could vary between such limits as 34% in 1953–54 and 69% in 1938–39. Colour ringing experiments that I carried out at Dollis Hill in the early 1950s showed that about 65% of adult blackbirds survived to the next breeding season. The replacement rate per pair to the next year's breeding population in order to recoup its losses needed to be about 0·7 young; this was a similar figure obtained by Snow (1958) for the years 1953–55 in the Oxford Botanic Garden. In fact, Dr Snow found that a higher proportion than this survived to the next breeding season – about 1·7 young per pair – (compared with 1·9 at Dollis Hill) – from an average of 4·1 young per pair actually fledged. This indicated that one local Oxford blackbird population was 'consistently over-producing'. This production of more young birds than was needed to make up for the losses in a rather dense population, both at Dollis Hill and Oxford, leads to keen competition for territorial space. I believe that my own blackbird population is very much limited by territorial behaviour. Leo Batten came to the same conclusion after finding that the territorial section of the blackbird population remained stable, but the total population, as calculated from ringing recoveries, and the proportion of young to old birds in the population each March continued to rise after 1966. He claimed that this suggests 'that territorial behaviour imposes a limiting effect on Blackbird populations by only allowing a proportion of the population to breed'. I shall return to this 'floating population' in the country later in the present chapter. After studying blackbirds in a Swiss urban park J-P. Ribaut (1964) concluded that the main limiting factor on population was not shortage of food or the effect of predators but a high level of territorial activity due to high density which resulted in a low breeding success. My own observations for Dollis Hill show that in 1964 'the breeding success was low and this was largely attributable to the disturbance resulting from competition among the local birds' (Simms 1965); this followed the influx after the bad winter of 1962–63, of a large number of male blackbirds, far in excess of the previous territorial strength, which replaced the 'lost' population. There is evidence, albeit less strong, to show that territorial behaviour may have had some effect in the other years as well.

Blackbirds are now a very highly successful breeding species in many European urban and suburban areas after moving out from their original woodland home. They are now at higher densities in gardens and parks than in rural habitats. For example, in Britain, the breeding density in oakwoods may be only one-tenth that of gardens. Parkland is not so well populated as gardens, and farmland supports a population about one-twentieth that of the best gardens. British gardens tend to be more densely populated than many Continental ones due to the presence of more luxuriant cover. J. Havlin (1963) determined the breeding density of blackbirds in the middle of Brno in Czechoslovakia at nearly four times the average for rural woodland, and in a city park in Zurich W. Epprecht (1946) calculated the density at 260 pairs per square kilometre whereas there were only 20 pairs in an equal area of Swiss orchards and fields.

Blackbirds have therefore adapted very successfully to their new urban or suburban habitats. Leo Batten has made a special study of the population

Table 14. Population Parameters of Blackbirds

Parameter	Average values 1960–68 London Suburban		Rural : Southern England	
Adult mortality	41·8%	±1·0%	34·9%	±0·5%
Recruitment	44·5%	±1·8%	39·1%	±1·0%
Nestling survival	19·6%	±4·0%	19·9%	±3·5%
Juvenile survival	47·1%	±7·8%	49·6%	±5·2%
Number of nesting attempts per pair	2·87	±0·16	2·76	±0·08
Weighted mean clutch size	3·77	±0·12	3·90	±0·04
Number of eggs incubated per pair	10·97	±0·57	10·72	±0·26
Weighted mean family size	3·04	±0·11	3·15	±0·05
Weighted mean success rate	39·46	±2·17%	30·40	±1·11%
Average number of nestlings surviving to 8 days per pair per year	4·78	±1·10	4·21	±0·40
Average number of nestlings fledged per pair per year	3·46	±0·26	2·61	±0·13
Average number of juveniles per pair per year	1·98	±0·13	1·69	±0·05

Reproduced from *Bird Study*, Vol. 20, 1973, by permission of L. A. Batten

dynamics of London's suburban blackbirds and he found that the annual average mortality rate was higher in London than it was for birds living in rural districts. This finding was at variance with the researches of Ribaut (1964) in Switzerland and Erz (1963) in Germany. About 42% of London's blackbirds die each year compared to a figure of 35% for rural birds. From December to January adult survival – concerning all birds from the previous year since after 1 January first-year mortality resembles adult – is higher, but this is compensated for by increased mortality during the rest of the year. There was no real difference between the average mortality for the sexes and estimates of mortality, derived from retraps and from recoveries from the same population, agreed rather well. Since the London population level has not apparently declined Batten suggested that there must be a higher recruitment rate. Such recruitment might arise from a high survival rate among nestlings or juveniles, or more birds being reared each year than in rural habitats. Batten (1973) found 'virtually no difference between the two habitats in the survival of nestlings, although there is an indication that subsequent survival of juveniles is slightly lower in London'. Twenty per cent of the nestlings which live for eight days will survive to breed in the following year in both town and country, but, whereas 50% of the juveniles which are still alive after the first month will live to the next breeding season in

Table 15.

METHODS USED TO CALCULATE THE POPULATION PARAMETERS

Adult mortality

This statistic is obtained from the following formula:

$$\frac{\text{Number of birds dying in year x that were ringed before year x}}{\text{Number of birds dying in year x and in all subsequent years that were ringed before}}$$
year x

The mortality year running from 1 April to 31 March was adopted in these calculations so as to include the whole winter's mortality in one year. In later years it is necessary to make an allowance for those birds still to be recovered. This number is assessed by calculating the proportion of birds which should be recovered each year based on the average annual mortality of earlier years. In view of this it was considered at the time of writing advisable to calculate mortality rates up to 1967–68 only, even though the data were available to March 1970. This meant that only 5·1% and 6·7% of the data for London and the rest of southern England respectively were provisional.

Juvenile and nestling survival to first breeding season

This parameter can be calculated by extracting from the schedules the total number of post-juvenile birds, juveniles and nestlings ringed between 1 April and 31 July and expressing the number of recoveries from each of these age groups after the next 1 April as a percentage of the number ringed. The percentage of adults recovered can be related to the survival of adults already calculated by the method mentioned above. The percentage of juveniles and nestlings recovered can therefore be related to a survival rate in the following way:

$$\text{Nestling survival} = \frac{\text{Percentage nestlings recovered} \times \text{adult survival}}{\text{Percentage adults recovered}}$$

All recoveries made by the ringer were rejected for each age group as these may bias the result. Nestlings for example are more likely to be recovered by the ringer than the other two age groups.

Productivity

Using the following formula a ratio of adults to nestlings or adults to juveniles is obtained for the breeding season depending on whether the nestling or juvenile survival figure is used.

$$\frac{\% \text{ Ad } \male \text{ in March}}{\substack{\text{Ad survival from} \\ \text{previous breeding} \\ \text{season.}}} \quad : \quad \frac{\% \text{ 1Y } \male \text{ in March}}{\substack{\text{Nestling survival} \\ \text{from previous} \\ \text{breeding season.}}}$$

Productivity per pair is obtained simply by halving the adult value in the calculated ratio.

Calculation of a population index from adult mortality and recruitment

One year is selected as datum year, and the population level is arbitrarily fixed at 100 for that year. Population levels for all other years are expressed relative to the datum year, which is in this case 1966. To calculate the index the following formula is used:

Index $(I+1) \times Ad$ $\male$ % in March = Index $1 \times Ad$ Survival, where Index I is value of index in year I.
Reproduced from *Bird Study*, Vol. 20, by permission of L. A. Batten

rural habitats, 47% will do so in London. One of the reasons for the success of the blackbird population in London would seem to be its ability to increase productivity in the suburban environment.

Batten calculated from nestling, juvenile and adult survival rates and recruitment rates in the succeeding March that about 14% more nestlings per pair survive to an age of eight days in London and nearly 18% more juveniles are produced than in rural habitats. These findings seem to be confirmed from the Nest Record Cards. Productivity per unit area is about three times greater in London than in rural habitats.

From examining ringing recoveries Coulson (1961) found an average value of 3·9 young fledged per pair which is close to Snow's average of 4·1 at Oxford. One should point out that the average age of nestlings used in the ringing analysis is slightly lower than that for nestlings from the Nest Records. Coulson assumed a constant population level to calculate his estimates of the number of young fledged from the ringing data whereas Batten's estimates for the number of fledged young from ringing data were made using the actual population values.

There are problems in assessing productivity in a multi-brooded species like the blackbird and there are additional biases in the data due to an increased difficulty in finding nests in thicker foliage and a decreased effort in seeking out nests as the season progresses. In Czechoslovakia Havlin (1963) found an average of 4·3 young blackbirds being reared per pair in forests but only 4·1 in towns. London blackbirds have both a lower weighted mean clutch size (derived from dividing the average number of eggs incubated by the average number of nesting attempts per pair) and family size than rurally based birds, although the average number of eggs laid is roughly the same in both environments. On average the town blackbirds make some 2·87 nesting attempts each year and those in the rural habitats 2·76. The increased productivity would seem to be due to a lower mortality in the nest combined with a slightly higher number of clutches on average per pair. The higher success rate in suburban gardens compared to that found in pieces of suburban wood or scrub would seem to be due to increased predation in the latter habitats.

Both the blackbird and the song thrush share similar habitats and Dr Snow (1955) made some interesting comparisons between the nesting success of the two species. Of all the nests that were begun a great proportion of those of blackbirds successfully reached the hatching and fledging stages for the young. Of these nests which reached hatching without mishap the song thrush 'consistently hatches a higher percentage of its eggs than the blackbird'. It also fledges proportionally more young from its successful nests, relative to the initial clutch size, than the blackbird. In fact, the song thrush undergoes a greater *total* loss but less *partial* loss, perhaps due to its smaller size, more retiring nature and dislike of disturbance. Yet these adverse factors are also balanced by a stronger tendency to incubate eggs and an ability to find food later in the season, which enable it to produce on average more young from each successful nest than the blackbird and to keep its higher level of achievement going throughout the season. D. I. M. Wallace (1974) examined some 1500 pairs of blackbirds and 518 pairs of song thrushes breeding or attempting to breed in Regent's Park in London between 1959 and 1968 and found that productivity in the blackbird was lower than that in the song thrush.

It is interesting to speculate about a marked decrease in annual mortality in the blackbird since 1951. Some fluctuations could be attributed to cold winters but other factors must have been at work, including perhaps higher winter temperatures and artificial feeding. The effect on the number of blackbirds would depend on the recruitment rate over the same period. If this had remained relatively unaltered at a level which maintained the population, then the total would have gone up by about 70% between 1951 and 1961. There was no evidence of such a rise which suggested that the level of recruitment has fallen and thus the level of numbers has been kept steady. On the other hand it may be that increased juvenile mortality or the absorption of surplus males by more marginal habitats may have been having an effect. At high population levels there tends to be a higher proportion of males and it would seem that there is therefore a floating population of blackbirds able to occupy territories as they become available.

In this respect an experiment in Hampshire conducted by Peter Edwards of ICI is of especial interest. Birds on a farm were mist-netted for retention to see how soon afterwards vacant territories would be reoccupied. It was estimated that there were twelve blackbird territories but seventeen cocks and twelve hens were captured. Three of the newly vacant territories were filled between one and two days later, six territories were occupied at four days and nine at six days and that last figure was sustained for the next sixty days. Four male and five female song thrushes were caught in five suspected territories but there was no evidence of return before nine days; two territories were occupied between nine and twenty-four days and one more was established between thirty and sixty days. The pattern for the two species was very different and the experiment seemed to confirm that there was a floating population of blackbirds.

A similar phenomenon was shown by another experiment in America in which 81% of 148 males of certain territorial species in 40 acres of spruce/fir forest were killed. Numbers were then kept down to this new level but to achieve this it was necessary to shoot 455 new birds that had settled, including twice as many males as were present before the experiment began. In the following year 79% of 154 pairs were shot and to hold this level 528 new settlers were killed. This gory experiment showed that the presence of settled birds was deterring others from coming in; the effect was density-limiting. Batten believed that the apparent differences since 1966 between the ringing and Common Birds Census indices suggest that there may be a variable number of non-territorial males in the populations not only of London but also southern England. Dr J. R. Krebs (1976) removed territorial resident great tits from a wood near Oxford and new pairs appeared rapidly, some coming from territories outside the wood while others appeared to be non-territorial 'floaters'. The new arrivals came in only hours and so must have been monitoring the wood. This may also be happening with blackbirds and perhaps other thrushes. Dr Krebs thought that the monitoring might be accomplished by listening to the songs of the territorial residents. Blackbirds and song thrushes have, as we have already seen, quite large song repertoires which could make individual recognition easier, and direct the 'keep-out' signals to particular intruders; these could have evolved through sexual selection or be nothing more than anti-habituation devices to ensure that 'familiarity does not breed contempt'. Perhaps in the case of blackbird and other thrush songs there is no simple answer.

It is possible for a number of factors to influence bird numbers and the evidence that density-dependent factors are important is impressive. When populations are reduced some other factor may become less severe so that recovery may take place. It is not easy to assess the effects of food shortages and it may be a series of limiting factors that determine numbers which may be held down because food is short or nest sites have been occupied to the limit. I have come to the conclusion that at Dollis Hill it is the availability of nest sites and the associated territorial behaviour which puts a limit on the blackbird population. Other factors appear to be at work with the song thrushes in that region.

An important prerequisite in any study of population dynamics is that the population under investigation should be a closed one, since bird movements into and out of an area could appreciably affect the general conclusions. For most practical purposes London afforded a blackbird population of this kind. Since there can be some quite large standard errors in the figures arrived at from ringing data, especially over juvenile and nestling survival rates, these have to be treated with some caution. Nevertheless, the findings shed a very interesting light on the population dynamics of London's suburban blackbirds.

With the mistle thrush, which takes up quite large domains in the breeding season, numbers seem to be controlled to quite a high degree by sensitive and highly aggressive behaviour on the boundaries of territories. My suburban population of mistle thrushes has almost invariably consisted of one pair with a second pair present in only five out of twenty-six years. After family flocking in the late summer the new birds of the year disperse. The stability at Dollis Hill is matched by Regent's Park where Wallace (1974) found no change in the summer population of the mistle thrush between 1961 and 1965. After the entry of this species into parks and gardens in Britain, western and central Europe numbers seem to have remained fairly constant with occasional checks by hard winters although this species will also move away from areas during bad weather and return later. Young birds may disperse widely in Britain, and ringed nestlings have been recovered in northern and western France. Adults too may move south to the Continent or west to Ireland. It seems that some young mistle thrushes in areas of low density may have to travel considerable distances to find vacant territories.

Table 16. Breeding Densities of Song Thrushes in Britain (Pairs per acre)

North Oxford gardens	0·800
Botanic Garden, Oxford (1954–56)	0·800
Ladbroke Square Garden, London	0·280
Marley Wood, Oxfordshire	0·100
Surrey oakwood	0·100
Scrub and woodland, Brent Reservoir, London	0·098
Regent's Park, London	0·065
Badby Wood, Northants	0·055
Allotments, north-west London	0·039
Suburban estate, Brent	0·028
Suburban estate, Dollis Hill	0·025
Warwickshire farm	0·015
Middlesex farm	0·013

Compiled mainly from Snow (1958), Simms (1971, 1975 and unpub.), Batten (1972) and G. Beven (1963). Population changes in a Surrey oakwood during fifteen years, *Brit. Birds,* 56:307–323 and D. I. M. Wallace (1961), The birds of Regent's Park and Primrose Hill, 1959. *Lond. Bird Rept.* 24:81–107.

In their territories song thrushes will drive off intruders unless inundated by large numbers of males visiting a specially rich fruit crop. Young song thrushes disperse much more widely than young blackbirds. New territories are seldom established close to their birthplace and so with such a fluid population it is difficult to study the dynamics in the way that research has been carried out with blackbirds. Females also tend to be more migratory than males. Dr David Lack (1943) calculated the average annual mortality rate for British song thrushes as 52%. The pattern of the song thrush's life – its subordination to other thrush species, its lack of need for and involvement in food-fighting, its different feeding ecology in various habitats, its territorial behaviour – shows many characteristic thrush-like features but the amount of movement in song thrush populations makes it difficult to trace population changes. What is clear is that there has been an appreciable decline in numbers, perhaps to some extent due to recurring cold winters, and in most habitats the blackbird outnumbers the song thrush and this disparity has been increasing in the last few years.

Among song thrushes it is the need for breeding that gives their territories their main significance but there still remain many unanswered questions. At Dollis Hill, in many oakwoods that I have studied, in conifer plantations, in open treeless regions, in London's Royal Parks the territories are clearly marked by song and often defended by fierce combats which may serve to deter intruders. From 1951–76 the song thrush population within half a mile of my home in north-west London has risen from 6–8 breeding pairs (1951–62) to 15 pairs in 1971 and 1974, but the total fell back slightly in 1975 and 1976 to 12–13 pairs. I have not been able to explain this increase which was to some extent paralleled by the Common Bird Census index for song thrushes on farmland but not in woodland, where there was a decline after 1969. There has been a similar rise at Dollis Hill in the population of breeding robins; again there is a national parallel on farmland but not in woodland. There may be lower mortality or an improvement in the habitat but I have not been able to identify this improvement. Over 546 acres at Dollis Hill the density of breeding song thrushes varied between 0·014 and 0·025 pairs to the acre. In Badby Wood – a pedunculate oakwood in Northamptonshire – I found a breeding density between 0·04 and 0·06 pairs to the acre. A density of 0·1 pairs per acre was determined in a Surrey oakwood and in Marley Wood at Wytham near Oxford; this was higher than in Finnish coniferous woodland but slightly lower than in Slovakian spruce forests. The Common Birds Census reported 5–20 pairs per square kilometre on British farmland and up to 120 pairs in woodland with an average of 27·1.

Redwings are not sociable in their breeding habits and are territorial by nature, although nests are sometimes closer to each other than one would expect and many singing males are often audible in quite a small area. In Finland redwings can be found at their highest breeding density in rich broad-leaved forests with a thick understory and some well-developed trees. The breeding success varies from year to year with an average 50% survival from egg-laying to leaving the nest. The commonest clutch size of five eggs corresponds, according to Tyrväinen (1969), to the largest number of young that the adults can feed. Redwings may suffer losses on their migratory journeys and in their winter quarters and we have already seen how the breeding population of Iceland redwings was halved after the bad winter of 1962–63 in the British Isles. Birds will move to avoid the worse effects of cold weather but nevertheless mortality

Table 17. Revised Index of Thrush Populations on Farmland and Woodland 1962–75

	1962	1963	1964	1965	1966	1967	1968	1969	1970	1971	1972	1973	1974	1975	1976
FARMLAND															
Mistle Thrush	130	32	56	95	100	113	138	139	111	115	123	118	143	135	136
Song Thrush	112	48	81	100	100	121	137	128	121	121	128	116	126	128	110
Blackbird	69	57	90	101	100	103	108	110	105	104	104	99	104	100	97
WOODLAND															
Mistle Thrush	—	—	—	95	100	101	114	102	102	99	115	111	113	134	132
Song Thrush	—	—	81	91	100	97	101	103	90	92	91	84	86	79	73
Blackbird	—	—	80	91	100	97	101	105	98	101	108	97	108	109	106

Index from the Common Birds Census, compiled and up-dated by L. A. Batten. (Based on papers by Batten, L. A., and Marchant, J. H. in *Bird Study* (1976, 1977)) (Calculated from a standard of 100 in 1966) can be very high. Like wintering fieldfares, redwings will also make for the coast but both species of thrush may be decimated in a cold period if the snow lies long and deep and the frost is unrelenting. Fieldfares are very colonial breeders and their density and populations are not subject to territorial limitations like those of some of the other thrushes.

A stable population of birds can be achieved only by strong checks or regulations on numbers. Some species may live side by side but occupy different ecological niches although their habitats overlap. Each thrush may reveal different characteristics of abundance, behavioural plasticity and distribution. The blackbird has been particularly well studied since its community is often a local, closed resident one. The relative abundance and distribution of some thrushes may be due to environmental preferences as well as factors arising from natural selection. There may be interaction between a number of factors and the separation or isolation of these and an examination of the way in which they are interwoven is one of the more recent matters for scientific enquiry. Attempts to unravel the threads may be made more difficult by such biotic factors as our felling of trees, replacement of woodlands with hedgerows and the subsequent removal of the latter, establishing agricultural land, employing toxic chemicals on crops, building towns and suburbs, creating gardens and parks with a variety of habitats and perhaps reafforesting regions which go on to develop only a restricted diversity of living things. When we interfere with or even break the chains which bind together our natural or semi-natural communities of animals, we may make them more unstable, perhaps more vulnerable to disease and insect pests. For blackbirds we have created more favourable environments by ringing our towns with bushy, grassy and flower-bedecked suburbs.

Table 18. Some Ring Ouzel Breeding Statistics

Year	First Arrivals	Main Arrival	Breeding Started	Mean Clutch Size	Mean Brood Size
1941	8 April	14 April	23 April	4·17 (6)	3·4
1942	6 April	11 April	25 April	3·60 (5)	3·1
1943	11 April	16 April	26 April	3·80 (5)	3·2

The figures in brackets represent the number of clutches recorded. The site was about 330 metres above sea level in the northern Pennines. Incubation in two cases lasted fourteen days; the others were not accurately measured.

Birds, of course, may live on three different levels – those for the individual, for the population and for the community. In the study of population dynamics it is generally recognized that the relative importance of density-dependence and heterogeneity, as shown by the varying nature of habitats and animal types, can differ in a range of species and situation. The problems are very complex and difficult to resolve but a better understanding of them will help us to sustain and improve the habitats for birds. The true *Turdus* thrushes – the most highly developed of the subfamily of the *Turdinae* – have shown remarkable powers of recovery and colonization, features of a successful group of birds.

CHAPTER 13

MIGRATIONS AND HARD-WEATHER MOVEMENTS

It is primarily with what may be called typical migration that the first and larger part of this chapter is concerned. Migration in its true sense has a distinctive regularity, a purposive character and a definite quality of direction which bring about the normally complete evacuation of one region in favour of another. There is therefore a real transfer of a breeding population from its area of summer distribution to another which is occupied in the winter. Migration is a seasonal movement with what Sir Landsborough Thomson called 'a shift in what may be called the centre of gravity of the population'. In the latter part of the chapter I will consider irruptions, such as those revealed sometimes by fieldfares, and the movements initiated by the onset of hard weather, but these two kinds of movement lack the basic annual rhythm inherent in true migration.

It has sometimes been argued that the migrations of some European birds arose from various fluctuations during the Pleistocene Period. At the height of the glaciation much of Europe was covered by ice or tundra and could support only a few breeding bird species. Migrants whose summer homes were on the tundra would have to fly over the great belts of taiga and deciduous forest to reach a more open terrain with a Mediterranean vegetation. At that time their winter quarters in North Africa and the Middle East might well have been less arid and more congenial than they are now as well as much closer to their summer haunts. These regular journeys are much more likely to have arisen from a need to locate new sources of food 'than that the birds have a long-held memory of the quiet settled period of the Pliocene and are seeking to regain their favoured feeding-grounds'.

In any case, the origins of the migration of a single species must be bound up with its evolution, previous range and the influence over the centuries of such factors as climate and ecology. Migration is obviously related to climatic conditions since it is a pattern of behaviour adapted to seasonal alterations in the environment. If a bird species can survive better if it leaves for the winter, because the food resources in the nesting area have become insufficient to support that population, then this is clearly the ultimate controlling factor, but not necessarily the one which triggers off the migratory movement itself. The breeding seasons of the thrushes are primarily an adaptation to the seasonal and optimal supply of food and migration must be related to this as well. Birds will react to proximate stimuli such as their own physiology through changes in the hormonal balance as well as local weather conditions and perhaps social stimuli. The innate drive to migrate from the breeding site can prove to be a very strong one but it can also vary within a population according to sex or age.

The British thrushes present a varied and interesting series of migratory patterns and behaviour. The ring ouzel is our only primarily summer visitor but it is also a passage migrant and a few have even been known to remain throughout the winter. The mistle thrush and blackbird are residents, migrant breeders and also passage and winter visitors. The song thrush is a resident breeding bird, a migrant breeder, a passage and winter visitor. The fieldfare can now be described as an increasing casual breeder as well as a winter visitor and passage migrant. The redwing is perhaps either a resident or migrant breeder in small numbers, and a winter and passage visitor. Much of what we now know about the migrations of European thrushes of the genus *Turdus* has been gathered from recoveries of ringed birds which permit the comparison of movements in closely related species, from direct observations such as I have carried out for many years, by radar studies, and from physiological research. Thrush migrations are often spectacular, easy to observe and some can equally well be seen inland in Britain as on the coast. Fieldfares and redwings can provide many stirring sights because of the size of their movements, but I have also watched blackbirds, song thrushes and mistle thrushes in smaller groups. Ring ouzels tend to be more secretive and are most likely to be spotted when pausing to feed on rowans in some favoured place but I have occasionally seen small parties on the move in the south-west of England.

The ring ouzel is a total migrant throughout the greater part of its breeding distribution in Europe but the number of recoveries of ringed birds is not large. The southern population tends to winter on lower ground in the breeding range but birds from further north move south to spend the winter chiefly in the region of the Mediterranean. The recoveries of ring ouzels bred in Britain, Norway and Switzerland come mainly from southern France with a few from Spain, Africa and the Balkans. In spring ring ouzels arrive in south-west England and Ireland from the second week of March through to the beginning of May. Passage has been reported in south-east England from March to mid-May as well as in the Scottish islands and Denmark (Ashmole 1962).

Using the daily logs from seven bird observatories Roger Durman analysed the reports of ring ouzels recorded there. He has very kindly allowed me to summarize his general findings which at the time of writing he is preparing for publication. He found that in the last ten days of March significant numbers of ring ouzels could be seen at Portland Bill and to a lesser degree on Lundy and at the Calf of Man. During April large passages took place at the west coast observatories and Spurn with peaks in the middle of the month, but birds were rather scarce at Dungeness and Gibraltar Point. The small peak at Dungeness in late April and early May suggested it involved a population different from those on the west coast and at Spurn. By early May the passage at Portland Bill and Lundy is no longer in evidence but it can still be traced at Dungeness for the first few days of the month. Ring ouzels continue to travel through Spurn and the Calf of Man and there is also a heavy May passage on Fair Isle probably involving Scandinavian migrants (Williamson 1952). In 1951 most of the records during the first three weeks of May were on the east coast when the prevailing winds were from the west and some of the movements seem to have been the result of migrational drift from the Continent, involving birds which were moving to Scandinavia from central Europe, having come from the south-east. Later movements in the spring at Fair Isle represented the outward passage of drift migrants. Displaced ring ouzels showed a tendency to delay their onward migration in a favourable area until a change in the weather provided them with a stimulus to continue the journey.

In autumn ring ouzels in the British Isles begin to abandon their breeding grounds in August. Durman has reported significant passages at Spurn, Lundy and Portland Bill in late September; in October the larger movements are on the east coast with some occurring at Dungeness as well. Birds reported early in the month are probably British birds leaving Britain while the mid-October passages seem to involve ring ouzels from Scandinavia. Figure 41 gives some ring ouzel recoveries. Some birds may be drifted westwards while over the North Sea, together perhaps with fieldfares or redwings. The autumn passage of ring ouzels is reported annually from a number of counties – from single birds to groups of a dozen or more.

The mistle thrush is both sedentary and migratory with birds from the most northerly part of the range travelling south to spend the winter in more temperate areas. Allowing for the biases inherent in ringing recoveries, there is quite a strong suggestion that part of the juvenile population of mistle thrushes in northern England has a strong migratory tendency while other birds stay fairly close to their places of birth (Snow 1969) (Fig. 40). Of thirteen first-winter recoveries of mistle thrushes seven were from France, one from a spot one hundred miles east of the place of birth and five within ten miles of or actually at the birthplace. First-winter birds seem to take a fairly strict southerly route on their way to France but older birds seem to migrate more to the west. Perhaps half or even a larger proportion of British mistle thrushes appears to be sedentary. Scottish mistle thrushes appear to stay highly migratory throughout their lives but more recoveries are needed before it is possible to confirm this absolutely.

Migratory mistle thrushes from Sweden, Holland and Belgium move

Table 19. Patterns of Primaries and Tail Feathers in Six British Thrushes

Species	Primaries	Tail Feathers
Mistle Thrush	1st 8–15 mm shorter than primary coverts, 3rd and 4th longest, 2nd 4–8 shorter, 5th 3–7 shorter, 6th 15–22 shorter. Also 3rd to 5th clearly and 6th slightly emarginated outer web.	Outermost feathers some 5 mm shorter than rest.
Song Thrush	1st 6–13 mm shorter than primary coverts (in juvenile and first winter 1st primary usually longer than in adults), 3rd longest, 4th generally as long but sometimes from 1–3 shorter, 2nd and 5th shorter but often not equal, 6th 12–18 shorter; 3rd to 5th emarginated outer webs.	Outermost feathers some 3–5 mm shorter than rest.
Blackbird	1st 3–7 mm shorter than primary coverts (occasionally as long), 4th and 5th longest but 5th sometimes 1–2 shorter, 3rd sometimes as long but normally 1–3 shorter, 6th 4–7 shorter, 2nd 11–16 shorter, usually between 6th and 7th, sometimes equal to but rarely shorter than 7th; 3rd to 6th emarginated webs.	Outermost feathers 6–10 shorter than remainder.
Ring Ouzel	1st 11–17 mm shorter than primary coverts, 3rd longest, 4th may be as long but usually 1–2 shorter, 2nd 4–8 shorter, 5th 5–9 shorter, 6th 18–22 shorter; 3rd to 5th emarginated outer webs.	Outermost feathers 6–10 shorter than rest.
Redwing	1st 8–14 mm shorter than primary coverts, 3rd and 4th longest (4th infrequently 1 mm shorter), 2nd 3–6 shorter, 5th 5–7 shorter, 6th 15–19 shorter; 3rd to 5th emarginated outer webs.	Outermost feathers only slightly shorter than rest.
Fieldfare	1st about half primary coverts, 3rd longest, 4th sometimes equal usually 1–2 mm shorter, 2nd 5–10 shorter, 5th 5–10 shorter, 6th 20–25 shorter; 3rd to 5th emarginated outer webs.	Outermost feathers about 5 mm shorter than remainder.

south-west in the autumn reaching winter quarters in western France or, less typically, even eastern Spain. Swedish birds appear to 'leap-frog' the Dutch and Belgian populations to achieve a somewhat longer migratory journey. British migrants appear to favour western France, birds from

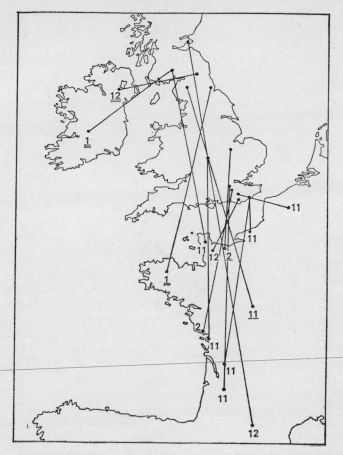

FIG. 40. Overseas recoveries of British-born mistle thrushes. Numerals indicate month of recovery; those not underlined were in the same calendar year as the year of birth. Those underlined once were in the following calendar year etc. (Reproduced from *Bird Study*, Vol 16, 1969, by permission of Dr David Snow.)

Germany central France and the most easterly recovery in southern France was that of a bird ringed in Czechoslovakia. Despite the lack of ringing recoveries there is observational evidence of immigration of mistle thrushes from the Continent in the autumn with a corresponding return in spring. Birds have been seen at lighthouse lanterns. At Fair Isle the mistle thrush was 'always in very small numbers' (Williamson 1965) and in East Anglia the autumn movements of mistle thrushes described in the past as 'considerable' were thought by N. F. Ticehurst to be birds which had come from northern Britain. In Ireland 'a large immigration is

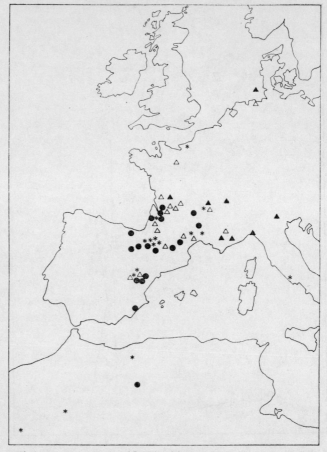

● Known or assumed to be of British origin.

△ Recovered in same migration period as ringing (assumed Continental origin).

▲ Recovered in subsequent migration period after ringing (assumed
   Continental origin).

* No assumption made as to area of origin.

FIG. 41. Foreign recoveries of ring ouzels ringed in Britain. (Reproduced from *Bird Study*, Vol 23, 1976, by permission of Roger Durman.)

noticeable on all coasts in September, October and November' (Ruttledge 1966). I have watched small numbers moving internally inside Britain – over Rugby, along the 'Cotswold corridor' that I discovered in 1948, and over Dollis Hill. The most unusual internal movement that I have come

across was observed by E. E. Huntley who watched 280 flying west on
12 September 1954 at Limpsfield Common in Surrey.

Most song thrushes from the north and east of their European range
migrate in autumn while the western populations appear to hold a large
number of permanent residents. In the British Isles both sub-species,
Turdus philomelos clarkei and *T. p. hebridensis*, are basically sedentary but
British-ringed examples of the former have been recovered in France
(e.g., Basses Pyrénées, Vendée, Gironde), Portugal, Spain and the Balearic
Islands, and of the latter in England and North Africa. British birds also
have been recovered in Ireland. As a partial migrant in the British Isles
about 48% of adult song thrushes and 64% of juveniles migrate (Lack
1943). Nearly all Fenno-Scandian and German song thrushes and those
from further east migrate in autumn, while in the Low Countries as well
as the British Isles about half the population remains. There is a general
tendency to move south-west in the autumn. Many Scandinavian birds
winter further south than those from north-west Germany, Holland and
Belgium with the northern population 'leap-frogging' the more southerly
in the manner of the mistle thrush. Migrants that winter furthest east in
Europe appear to come from the more eastern populations and furthest
west from the more western. There also seems to be a tendency for the
song thrushes living most to the north to migrate furthest to the south.
M. J. Ashmole (1962) has shown that around the North Sea song thrushes
from Holland move WSW into England in autumn, while birds from
southern Britain move west and from northern Britain WSW to SSW into
Ireland. Scandinavian song thrushes move south-west into France and
Spain crossing over the westward passage of Dutch birds but, according
to Ashmole, 'some pass through the British Isles either under conditions
of drift or, in the S.E., on the fringe of a broad movement'. A song thrush
ringed at 61° 54'N, in Norway in August 1968 was recovered in Co. Leix
in Eire in the following month and another marked as a juvenile at
58° 34'N in Sweden was found in a subsequent winter at Winchelsea in
Sussex.

Most song thrushes in Fenno-Scandia leave their breeding areas about
mid-September to October. There are movements through southern
France in October and November and in Cyprus in October. The main
immigration to Britain begins in the last week of September and continues
into early October. Many movements are at night and I have observed
heavy passages around the old Dungeness Lighthouse in Kent – for
example, on the night of 8–9 October 1957. The passage of Continental
birds has been traced along many parts of the east and south-east coasts.
Michael Barry (1960), who was on a light vessel in the Wash in the
autumn of 1956, described birds flying SSW/S usually in overcast conditions with or without rain, particularly song thrushes, blackbirds and
redwings. Their arrival times often suggest diurnal emigration from

Scandinavia and D. F. Owen (1953) reported thrushes passing the Kentish Knock light vessel at times that also indicated a daylight departure from the Continent.

In autumn song thrushes pass over Dollis Hill in daylight and twice I have counted more than a hundred on a morning – on 24 September 1973 and 7 October 1975 – but visible migration of this species inland is uncommon. I have seen small movements in October along the Cotswolds and a few other scattered localities. After a heavy fall of migrants at night scores may appear on factory lawns and parks in north-west London. Richard Perry (1946) has also described how on Holy Island after a south-east gale early in October the area became 'alive with Song Thrushes, who rose in scores from every bit of cover, even from links and sand-hills'. I sometimes hear migrant song thrushes calling at night in March or October as they pass overhead. Spring movements reach their peak in southern France in late March and the winter visitors vacate the British Isles about the same time.

Except in the extreme north of their breeding range a proportion of blackbirds in all the European populations is sedentary throughout the winter. After analysing recoveries of British blackbirds, Dr David Lack showed that a fraction of the British-reared total went to Ireland for the winter, the proportion being greater in Scotland and the Borders than in the southern half of England. A subsequent analysis was devised by Dr Snow (1966a); it was not able to cast further light on the biological significance of partial migration but it revealed a number of interesting features. A proportion of first-year birds in southern England migrates in a north-westerly direction without actually leaving the country and 'this direction is also taken by the few north British birds which migrate to a distance without crossing the sea'. Some blackbirds from the extreme south of the country migrate west, however, or a little south of west, in their first winter without emigrating, while others may travel south across the English Channel to northern or western France (Fig. 43). In late winter the direction tends to be more south-westerly and the migratory journey longer. Some Scottish blackbirds in their first winter migrate to Ireland in a south-westerly direction while birds from the north of England take a route just south of west (Fig. 43). The early dispersal of juvenile blackbirds appears to be unorientated but by September movement is chiefly in a westerly direction. Young birds which have dispersed to a distance in late summer also migrate westwards in the autumn.

Weimann (1938) described from ringing data how many Continental blackbirds, which migrate in their first winter, become sedentary in subsequent winters but Dr Snow was able to show that the tendency to migrate did not change appreciably with age. This presents an interesting problem since in many partial migrants young birds show greater migratory tendencies than old birds. Old established blackbirds should be able to

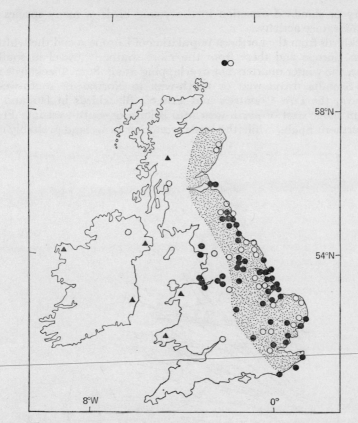

FIG. 42. Winter quarters of Swedish and Finnish blackbirds in the British Isles. Hatched area and triangles=Swedish birds (based on Goodacre 1959). Dots= ringing localities of blackbirds subsequently recovered in Finland. Open circles= recovery localities of blackbirds ringed in Finland. (Reproduced from *Bird Study*, Vol 22, 1975, by permission of Robert Spencer.)

live and survive better in winter on the familiar breeding site than young birds could do. We know already that in northern Europe more female than male blackbirds migrate since the latter are more aggressive and thus perhaps better able to survive on the nesting site. What little evidence does exist suggests that there is no appreciable difference in migratory behaviour in British blackbirds between the sexes in relation to westward movements to Ireland. What does emerge is a complex double pattern of innate preferred directions – west to Ireland or south to France – and more experiment will be necessary to evaluate the behaviour of any one blackbird in any year. We need to know much more about the normal primary or standard direction in the young birds of many species that show migratory activity.

Blackbirds from the northern population of Europe spend the winter in western Europe and those from the more southerly travel to southern Europe, the winter quarters not overlapping at all. Some blackbirds from Fenno-Scandia travel west or north-west to Norway or south-west to Denmark, the Low Countries and France. Blackbirds in Holland and Belgium move west or north-west into Britain or south-west into France and northern Spain, while the birds wintering in Iceland probably come

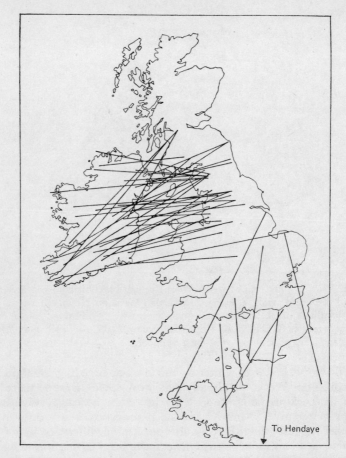

To Hendaye

FIG. 43. Overseas recoveries in their first winter of blackbirds born in Great Britain. The lines join the places of ringing and of recovery, but are not intended to indicate the route taken. (Reproduced from *Bird Study*, Vol 13, 1966, by permission of Dr David Snow.)

FIG. 44. Distant recoveries of British-born blackbirds in their second and later winters. In the case of recoveries within the country, arrowheads indicate the places of recovery. The north Scottish bird was recovered at Carolinensiel, Ost Friesland, Germany. (Reproduced from *Bird Study*, Vol 13, 1966, by permission of Dr David Snow.)

from Scandinavia. In autumn blackbirds come to the British Isles from Scandinavia on a broad front with Norwegian birds most common in winter in Scotland but less so in northern England. The birds in southern England are mainly from Sweden or even further south. Since there appears to be a rise in the number of blackbirds of Swedish or Danish origin in January and February in Britain it seems likely that the birds which moved west in autumn push on later across the North Sea; an analysis by H. Rendahl (1960) gives support to this theory. Polish blackbirds travel south into Europe where they may be joined by Czech birds;

blackbirds from Hungary have been recovered in Corsica and central Italy. There is no evidence of 'leap-frog' migration but birds from different populations certainly cross each other's tracks in the autumn.

Between 1958 and 1975 one hundred and eleven British-ringed blackbirds were recovered in Finland (Spencer 1975) (Fig. 42) and this change in the recovery pattern – presumably birds from Finland had occurred in Britain before but had not been trapped in Finland in the pre-mist-net era – was thought to reflect the growing colonization of that country by birds from Sweden or possibly Estonia.

Most blackbirds arriving on the east coast of England are on their normal migration routes, not 'drifted' as perhaps are Scandinavian song thrushes. The main immigration from Europe seems to take place in late October and early November (Davis 1964). As blackbirds travel at night I sometimes hear their calls overhead and have seen them attracted to lighthouse lanterns, but it is generally by finding the hedgerows and fields full of tired migrants that one knows that an immigration has occurred. I have also seen small visible movements in September and October along the 'Cotswold corridor', and over Dollis Hill where the immigrants – up to 45 at a time – betray their presence by a higher flight pattern and clear 'Tseerk' calls. These migrants seem to stay only a short while; Batten (1972) has pointed out that, although nationally one in eleven blackbird recoveries refer to Continental birds, he has had only two foreign returns of the more than 6000 blackbirds he has ringed at the Brent Reservoir.

On the east coast of England I have seen parties of blackbirds coming ashore, sometimes with a light south-easterly breeze, and arriving from a little east of north. Migrants have been seen alighting on the sea and taking off again. At Fair Isle the autumn passage may begin in late September but it normally lasts from early October to early November with perhaps 2000 birds at the peak. Blackbirds ringed on the island in autumn have been recovered in their breeding range in Norway and Sweden. In early November 1955 2000 blackbirds were reported on the road down the Spurn Head peninsula and birds were seen in good numbers flying by day past the Kentish Knock light vessel (Owen 1953). November movements of considerable size were reported at Monk's House in Northumberland and at Cley in Norfolk where there was also a December immigration; these late influxes could perhaps be linked with the mild weather during the autumn particularly as four blackbirds ringed in Fair Isle, Lincolnshire, and at Cley were recovered in the first week of November still in Scandinavia (Davis 1954). Blackbirds arriving on the northern part of the east coast generally come from more northerly breeding grounds than those making more southerly landfalls. Heavy movements are sometimes observed on the Irish coast.

In spring the foreign winter immigrants tend to leave rather unnoticed. Small arrivals have been recorded however at Fair Isle from

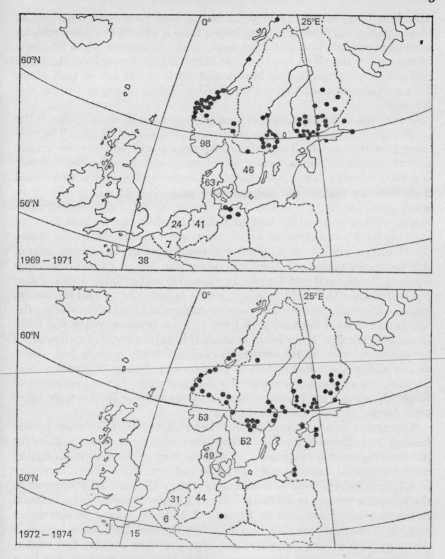

FIG. 45. Recoveries abroad of blackbirds ringed in the British Isles. Only the more distant ones are plotted individually. (Reproduced from *Bird Study*, Vol 22, 1975, by permission of Robert Spencer.)

March to June, usually up to 50 birds but 2000 have been reported. At Dungeness in 1957 spring passage lasted from 4 March to 2 May with an average of ten individuals on most days. At the Eddystone Light W. Eagle Clarke (1912) described blackbirds as occurring 'in spring from the latter half of February, throughout March and April and as late as 10th May'. Figure 45 gives the recoveries abroad of blackbirds ringed in Britain and Ireland.

One of the more interesting aspects of migration in the thrushes is the great variety of movements demonstrated by different species. The redwing is a thrush which reveals most curious and often very erratic migratory habits. Throughout most of its breeding range the redwing is a total migrant. The populations of Continental redwings that breed from Norway east to the Baltic States and Finland winter chiefly in south-west Norway, the British Isles, France, Spain, Italy, the Mediterranean region and further east to Bulgaria, while the Iceland redwing seems to have a rather restricted winter range – in some Icelandic towns, the Hebrides, north-west Scotland and some parts of the extreme west of the European mainland. However, there can be an expected overlap between Continental and Iceland birds in central Scotland, Holland and parts of France (Ashmole 1962). There is apparently no real separation between the more western and eastern European populations during the winter and most of the European birds migrate between WSW and SSW in autumn but in a 'fanned-out' manner (Holgerson 1953). In an analysis by Rendahl (1960) of the recoveries of ringed birds in their first winter and of adults it was found that, in the case of redwings originating from Sweden, the most extreme reports for east and west – in the south-west of England, north-west France, Portugal and southern Italy – were all of adult birds.

The rather erratic migratory behaviour of redwings is shown by the finding of individual birds in subsequent winters in entirely different places. This could be explained by drift on migration, movement during hard weather or 'an unusually nomadic instinct'. Birds ringed in winter in Gloucestershire, Worcestershire and Cornwall were all recovered in the following winters in northern Italy and a Lincolnshire bird was found two and a half years later in Cyprus. A redwing ringed in November 1974 in Nuneaton was shot in December 1975 in Iran. However, it is necessary to point out that some redwings ringed in autumn and winter, for example in Belgium, were recovered in that same country in a later year. There is no evidence that a population, or part of one, follows the same direction in any one year and two birds ringed in Norway during the breeding season were recovered in November, one in Italy and the other in Belgium. Drifted birds may, of course, redetermine their passage route.

Some of the movements of the Iceland redwing 'may take place in two steps, culminating in an overseas flight from southern Greenland' (Williamson 1958). The greater body size with an allometric increase in the length of wings and tail of this north-western population over the Continental could have arisen as a result of the selection pressure brought about by a long forced migration across the sea. If the Iceland redwing is subject to downwind drift in anticyclonic weather, then, in order to reach their wintering grounds, birds may have to cross the Denmark Strait, follow the east coast of Greenland and then make a fast but long Atlantic flight.

Redwings are typically night migrants and their soft contact calls can be heard above the open country and the roar of city traffic. When I was living in Rugby I noted 106 calls in just over an hour of one October night and I counted more than 2000 between 18.30 and 23.10 GMT over Dollis Hill in October 1958. The peak of these nocturnal calls is sometimes reached however between 02.00 and 04.00 hours GMT. If the weather becomes overcast redwings are often attracted to the lanterns of light-houses, and after such disorientation may appear around the street lamps in towns. One October I watched hundreds around the lamp standards on the sea-front at Hastings.

Redwings can often be seen making landfall in the early morning on the south and east coasts of Britain especially at a time of easterly winds. I have witnessed early morning arrivals of this kind in Kent, Essex, Suffolk, Norfolk, Lincolnshire, Northumberland, and along the eastern Scottish coast. Birds may drop down to rest in trees, sand dunes and saltings before beginning to preen and then hop slowly around on the ground in their search for food. One of the greatest 'falls' I have ever seen occurred on the morning of 26 October 1976 near Cruden Bay in Aberdeenshire. At 08.10 GMT I became aware of parties of redwings coming in from the sea at heights between 260 and 330 metres. There had been rain and high winds in the period immediately before the 26th although strong passage had taken place on 23 October. On 26 October there was an overcast and a light to moderate easterly wind. By 08.15 redwings were also coming in at lower heights from 33 to 70 metres. A small stream runs eastward down a narrow wooded valley towards the sea and here there is a narrow strip of sycamores, horse chestnuts and wych elms. Soon red-wings began to cascade out of the sky pouring like a torrent of dark liquid into the bare canopies of the trees. Thousands of redwings were making their landfall. With them were small numbers of fieldfares, song thrushes and blackbirds, a few starlings and twenty ring ouzels. Also associated with this fall were a hundred robins, one or two blackcaps, some goldcrests and an Arctic redpoll. For four hours redwings were coming down into the little valley or moving further inland and the immediate countryside was alive with redwings. Many thousands must have arrived and by 10.00 hours some of the birds were down on the grass between the trees.

In the afternoon my wife, daughter and I made a survey drive of the area. Between 13.00 and 15.00 we found a coastal strip of Aberdeenshire some 24 kilometres long and 8 km wide between the Hill of Mormond and Ellon where every field, hedgerow, copse, wood and tree was alive with redwings perched or feeding. The total number in this strip was beyond computation or estimate – it was a staggering sight. On the following morning there was a small fall of blackbirds and goldcrests but no other thrush species were involved.

Often these early morning movements will continue across land. I counted 3000 streaming inland during the last week of September in north Norfolk. In October 1975 I witnessed a broad front movement of redwings involving 15,000 birds between Darlington and the Cheviot Hills. Then on 23 October 1976 a transect between 08.00 and 12.15 made by car revealed a broad front movement of many redwings between Jedburgh and Forfar – a front of some 160 kilometres. Redwings that I see in autumn flying over Dollis Hill – perhaps a thousand in a morning – are travelling north-north-west and may well have set off from the Continent that same morning since the flying time is only between two and three hours.

Many autumn migrants may be both nocturnal and diurnal. Redwings often cross London in the early morning and I have seen diurnal passages along the Cotswolds, over Birmingham, Rugby, Dunstable, the Pass of Ryvoan near Aviemore and many other places.

Continental redwings begin to migrate towards the end of September with the greatest movements in October and early November. Arctic birds have already moved into the lowlands in late August and early September. During the winter bad-weather movements can happen at almost any time. In spring the redwings begin to depart from the British Isles between the middle of March and the middle of April; birds may occur at Fair Isle to mid-May and even as late as 18 June. Figure 47 shows recoveries of redwings.

The sixth species of thrush – the fieldfare – leaves the most northerly parts of its range for the winter, but there is some overlap between the southern part of its breeding distribution and its winter quarters. It seems likely that those birds that spend the winter in southern Norway or Sweden are local breeding birds or birds from further north but not east, since very few fieldfares ringed in the distant east have been recovered in Norway later than November (Ashmole 1962). In October numbers of fieldfares, mainly young birds, from Sweden and less often from Finland move west into Norway. By November most recoveries are to the south of Scandinavia with fieldfares from Finland being recovered mainly through Belgium, France and northern Italy, from Sweden in Norway and France, and from Norway in Belgium and France. By December those birds which have moved into Norway have travelled south even into

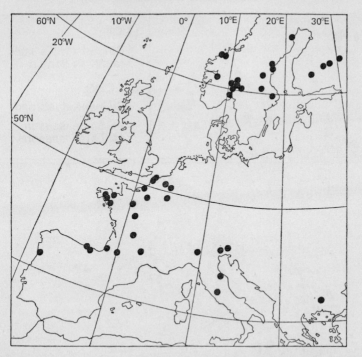

FIG. 46. Foreign recoveries of fieldfares. (Reproduced with slight amendment from *British Birds*, Ringing Supplement 1965, by permission of Robert Spencer.)

central Europe. Norwegian and Swedish fieldfares in January are found chiefly in Belgium, northern and south-western France while birds from Norway reach Iberia and from Finland northern Italy. Fair Isle Bird Observatory has often reported large arrivals in December or early January apparently unrelated to hard weather. In February there is a steep rise in the number of Norwegian fieldfares found in the British Isles but this increase may be associated with severe weather conditions. There are many recoveries too of Norwegian birds in Britain in March. In winter there seems to be no great separation of birds from the three Fenno-Scandian populations but it is possible that some regions are used more in the same month of some years than in others. Figure 46 gives some foreign recoveries of fieldfares.

Fieldfares leave their northern breeding grounds in late September or early October. Autumn passage has been noted in Denmark and at Heligoland in the second half of October. Large numbers of fieldfares occur at Fair Isle in October and many big immigrations into the British Isles take place in that month and much of November. Birds also move

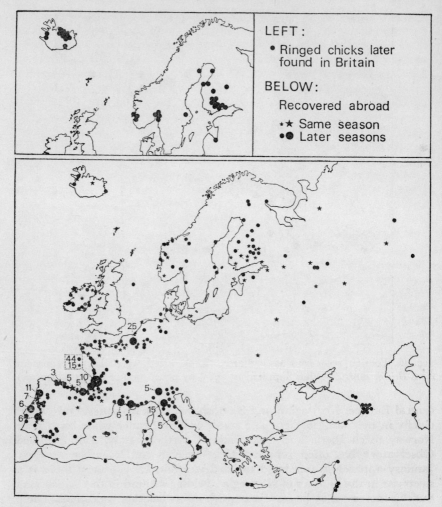

FIG. 47. Recoveries of redwings. The top map shows the ringing places of nestling redwings later recovered in Britain and Ireland. The large map below shows where redwings ringed in winter and on passage through Britain have travelled. Those marked by stars in France and Iberia (and one in Greece) have moved further during the season in which they were ringed. The spread of recoveries through Russia shows how far some of the redwings which reach us for the winter will travel. The records along the Mediterranean, and in Turkey and Georgia, indicate that birds which have come here in one winter may spend a subsequent one far away. The records in Ireland are of English ringed birds which were probably forced westwards by cold weather. (Reproduced from *Bird Ringing*, Guide Number 16, by C. J. Mead with the permission of the British Trust for Ornithology.)

into Ireland in November and December and considerable movements can be traced along the west coast of Scotland. Eagle Clarke (1912) described this migratory stream of fieldfares which can be observed in the Inner Hebrides 'but extends as far to the west as St Kilda, the Flannan and the Monach groups, and comes under observation at the rock stations of Skerryvore and Dhu Hearteach. The Outer Hebridean branch of this stream reaches the north coast of Ireland, whence numbers of the birds proceed inland to winter quarters.' In the spring passage birds reach the south coast of England from late March, and movements of these and British winter visitors will go on until May. Allowing for the biases in ringing returns it does seem likely that fieldfares from a single breeding population may be recovered from a wide area of Europe, reflecting the nomadic behaviour of this thrush species. In some 'invasion' years visitors to France may come from as far away as 91°E.

Gunnar Svärdson (1957) has described how every three or four winters Sweden is invaded by 'a mass of fieldfares' which sometimes remain to breed in the following summer. These irruptions, which are unlike migration, being irregular in both space and time, can often be found in northern forest birds which are also specialist feeders. The trees and shrubs upon which they depend are irregular in their crop production of fruit. The fieldfare prefers berries which often show fluctuations in production. Climatic extremes, food specialization and irregular fruit crops can together bring about an imbalance between the population of birds and the level of their food resources. Good weather in the flowering season also means a good breeding season and the resultant berry crop helps fieldfares to survive the winter. In the following autumn when the trees and shrubs are 'resting' the crop is low but the bird population is high and so the irregular migrants – the irruptive species – fly to new regions in their search for food.

I have sometimes observed fieldfares at lighthouse lanterns in the autumn together with redwings and other thrushes. Kenneth Williamson (1965) watched migrant redwings and fieldfares being held in the revolving beams of the Skadan Light on Fair Isle; 'the hundreds of fieldfares looked strangely beautiful as the glare caught the shining white undersides of their wings'. The birds on Fair Isle were calling but I do not hear their chuckling notes at night over Dollis Hill and London in the way that I listen to redwing calls. I have witnessed fieldfare arrivals in the early morning on the east coast of Britain and sometimes in the afternoon as well. Every autumn I see fieldfares passing over Dollis Hill; the numbers are often small 'but the strongest passages were of 2500 flying west-north-west over a period of 100 minutes on 26 October 1966 and of 1050 flying north-west in November 1961' (Simms 1975). In November 1959 Leo Batten reported more than a thousand flying over the Brent Reservoir in north-west London. Migrating fieldfares which I watched over my home in October 1955 were part of a much larger broad-front movement which was also witnessed at the same time in Essex, Kent and Surrey.

I have many inland records of fieldfares on the move in autumn and, less often, in the spring. Some have been broad-front movements across wide tracts of countryside while others have been funnelled into narrow passes or defiles such as Ryvoan, which links Rothiemurchus and Abernethy Forests, below the Cairngorms. Here is a description of a watch I carried out at Ryvoan in 1953, from *Voices of the Wild* (1957). 'On the morning of 10 October I went out once more to watch the nearby pass for migrants. In the space of half an hour I counted more than fifty greylag geese flying at a good height above the valley; at a lower height appeared hundreds of redwings and smaller numbers of fieldfares, skylarks and meadowpipits all flying from the same direction. It seemed clear that all these passage birds were arriving on the Moray Firth and following the valley of the Spey south-west. The migrants then probably fanned out across Abernethy Forest and entered Glenmore by the pass. The passage lasted on 10 October until four and a half hours after dawn.' Similarly I have studied the movements in October through a pass in Switzerland above Lake Geneva and these involved fieldfares and also redwings, blackbirds, song and mistle thrushes (Simms 1960).

Thus all the six thrush species migrate in autumn almost certainly on a broad front to regions that lie to the south and west of their summer breeding ranges. Most recoveries in winter of the migratory thrushes are from the British Isles, Belgium, France, Spain and Italy and the islands of the Mediterranean. All the species, with perhaps the exception of the ring ouzel, are partial migrants; in some parts of the range some birds migrate and others do not. On the other hand the northern ring ouzel and European robin can be regarded as fully migratory. The wintering areas of the six species overlap to a considerable extent but some populations only overlap with other species for part of the year. Song thrushes from south Sweden, where redwings do not normally nest, can be found in winter with redwings in France and Spain. All six thrush species can be found wintering together in south-west France and northern Spain, and throughout a great part of southern Europe four or five species can be found together. On the other hand, populations of different thrush species which nest in the same region may find quite different winter quarters, with Swedish blackbirds coming to the British Isles for the winter but Swedish mistle and song thrushes making for southern France or Spain. Redwings and fieldfares have such different winter ranges from their areas of summer distribution that they are not faced with the prospect of competing with resident individuals of their own species, but in some parts of Europe northern migrants may be in competition during the winter with residents that, in fact, breed there. In the south and west of Europe the populations of blackbirds and thrushes are less migratory and immigrants in winter of these species could well outnumber those of the resident population that leave in autumn. Westerly movements of field-fares and blackbirds into Norway may be a similar device for exploiting the berry crop like the movements of fieldfares into Sweden. Elsewhere in Europe it seems that the most suitable regions for wintering are exploited, allowing for the occupation of both optimal and more crowded habitats and marginal ones where the population pressure is lower. Winter com-petition for food during prolonged spells of cold weather can be severe and it is interesting to speculate on the thrush foods in the drier parts of their southern winter range which support so many birds in the winter. Nevertheless, migration takes place as birds are given a better chance of survival and in cold weather this could mean moving into inhabited areas leading to competition with birds already present in the towns and cities. Since different nesting populations of song thrush, blackbird and perhaps the mistle thrush gather in different winter areas, it is probable that they are adapted to different habitats throughout Europe, and, since the field-fare and redwing appear to be less separated in winter, the individuals of the two species must be adapted to a greater series of habitats. Blackbirds have been extending their range due perhaps to a better survival in winter consequent upon the improvement in the climate and the coloniz-ation of more built-up areas, and these changing factors may well influence some of the blackbird migrations in north-west Europe.

That bird migration is closely linked with weather has been established for a long time but it is only in the last twenty years or so that detailed research has been undertaken into the correlation of bird movements with those of air masses and the relevant weather charts. And even so, there is still no total agreement about the factors which bring the greatest influence to bear on migration itself. Good weather such as exists during anticyclonic conditions – with an area of high atmospheric pressure with the wind circu-lating clockwise in the northern hemisphere – is often likely to initiate a migratory movement among birds that are physiologically ready to make the journey. A low or falling temperature in autumn and a high tem-perature in spring may also play a part. A major factor also seems to be wind which can order and shape bird movements in the British Isles and over its encircling seas. Many great broad-front falls of migrants on the east coast of Britain have taken place in anticyclonic weather with light or moderate easterly winds, but the most spectacular are likely to be those of young birds still moving and dispersing in a random way after the breeding season. At Fair Isle the most remarkable falls of migrants in both autumn and spring occurred with winds in the easterly quarter. 'Rushes' often take place when migration has been held up for several days by the weather which then improves and releases the birds.

The autumn passage of redwings at Fair Isle, which was studied in detail by Williamson (1958), showed that migration, both on the island

and the east coast of Britain, most often took place with easterly and south-easterly weather in the North Sea. Such weather could be anticyclonic or the result of frontal developments associated with low pressure areas. Other Continental species such as blackbirds, song thrushes and fieldfares often arrived in conditions similar to those that favoured the redwings. The largest broad-front arrivals of Continental redwings were associated with anticyclonic weather over Scandinavia which generated an easterly airflow over the North Sea, but smaller movements may occur with high pressure over Scandinavia and low pressure developments providing prefrontal easterly winds to the North Sea. The Continental redwing depends very much on calm, light winds and clear skies which appear with cols and anticyclonic conditions. Iceland redwings often appear at Fair Isle with cyclonic westerly or north-westerly weather and perhaps also with anticyclonic developments over the north-east Atlantic with a following wind (Fig. 48).

FIG. 48. Immigrations of redwings to the British Isles.
Anticyclonic drift with E to SE winds bringing Continental redwings to northern isles from Scandinavia. October 1954. A=anticyclone. (Redrawn from Williamson, 1958.)
Cyclonic drift with W to NW winds bringing Iceland redwings to northern Britain. October 1956. A=anticyclone; C=cyclone. (Redrawn from Williamson, 1958.)

A north-westerly or westerly air stream across London seems to be an important factor in inducing visible migrations of redwings and fieldfares over the city and its suburbs. Strong winds that appear in low pressure systems may inhibit movements or bring about an excessive amount of drift particularly in nocturnal migrants like the thrushes. Migrational drift with a following wind can displace birds from coastal leading lines on whose view and recognition migrants may depend. Birds that use guidelines or landmarks are able to adjust for the effect of wind but night migrants and those travelling over the sea or above cloud may be subjected to lateral drift by the wind. Birds leaving the Continent in good weather may fly into rain and overcast skies and be borne on easterly or south-easterly winds which carry them westwards to the British Isles. There might also be a downwind movement rather than a lateral deflection. Radar has provided no firm evidence, although it is possible that 'down-wind directional drift' can take place below radar range.

Two Swedish research workers, T. Alerstom and S-G. Petterson (1976), tracked redwings by radar and found that the birds stayed on course overland, presumably by means of landmarks, but over the sea with crosswinds they had problems. They suggested that when a bird ap-proaches the sea from the land it looks along its flight-path and observes the waves which are orientated by the wind. The redwing then steers in such a way that the surface of the sea keeps on looking the same. In this way the bird's track is corrected to some extent for wind drift, but the birds were unable to allow for friction at the sea surface that twisted the wave direction through an angle of about fourteen degrees. The waves are therefore not accurate indicators of wind direction and so the birds make errors in flight. The two scientists predicted just how much redwings will be drifted off course for a particular direction and speed of wind. The plotting was carried out over comparatively short stretches of the Baltic and it would be interesting to know what happens on the longer sea crossings from Norway or Iceland to Britain.

Norwegian thrushes which are drifted westward over the North Sea by easterly winds in autumn may alter their course in the daylight hours from their nocturnal direction of SSW to SSE; this takes place in the early part of the morning perhaps as a response to the sight of the sea and the awareness of their westward drift. They appear to return to a SSW heading after making the land (Lack 1962), although their initial correction of some 45 degrees to the east is not always fully effective. Dr Lack reported that 'usually all migrants travelling over the sea eventually changed to a SSE heading, and since it seems unlikely that all the birds in all these movements were adults, the behaviour in question presumably occurs both in adults and juveniles migrating for the first time'. This type of behaviour was not observed during any SSW immigrations towards Norfolk of Scandinavian chats, warblers and flycatchers arriving in late August and September with easterly winds. If juveniles in general in their first autumn were unable to correct for drift, then this could explain why so many British rarities are juveniles in their first autumn. M. T. Myres (1964) described the increase 'in density of radar responses at, or just before dawn', over a wide area of the sea around Shetland and it was

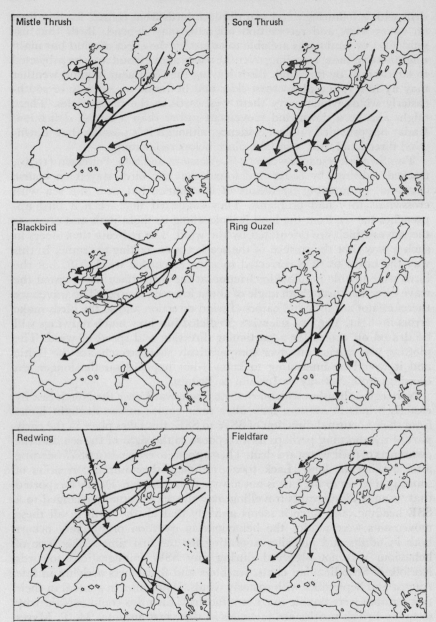

FIG. 49. Directions of six migrant thrush species in autumn.

thought reasonably certain that the birds involved, which demonstrated a dawn ascent and a subsequent reorientation, were mainly redwings, fieldfares and blackbirds. These two phenomena of ascent and reorientation, have also been recorded over the north Atlantic Ocean between the Outer Hebrides and Faeroes (Lee 1963), over the northern North Sea off eastern Scotland, and over the southern North Sea off Norfolk. It has been suggested that the south-eastward reorientation in the air of thrushes is an adaptation which permits members of a population which find themselves over the eastern Atlantic to regain the western seaboard of Europe. The behaviour itself can on average bring birds, which are out of sight of land at dawn, to land in the minimum time. Dawn ascents and reorientation do not appear to be a feature of Scandinavian thrush arrivals in the spring. Radar observations in Norfolk (Lack 1969) revealed that winter visitors such as blackbirds depart in March and April almost due east with light winds, but north of east when the wind had a southerly component, and somewhat south of east with a north-easterly component. In spring passerines setting out east seem more ready to leave in strong crosswinds than in the autumn.

Reversed migrations may occur in both spring and autumn, set off over the land by winds which are opposite to the normal direction of the migratory flight for the season in question. Small passage movements have been traced eastwards from East Anglia in October with westerly winds. Evidence for these reversed movements, which I have also watched in skylarks, is provided in thrushes by some of the ringing returns. A blackbird which was ringed on 6 November 1954 in Yorkshire was recovered four days later in Germany, a second ringed in October 1959 on Fair Isle was found in Norway ten days later, and a third, also ringed on Fair Isle at the same time, was recovered two days afterwards in Norway. Four blackbirds which were marked in the autumn in Heligoland were found again a few days later in Norway. Some of these birds may have gone back to their place of departure after being drifted off course. Reversed migrations can take place both by day and night, but if the birds use the sun or stars just as a compass they should have no real problem (Sauer 1961). Reversed migration of thrushes has been observed in spring at Ottenby at the south point of Öland, and Svärdson (1953) attributed these movements especially to falling temperatures.

The commoner passerine winter visitors and passage migrants to the British Isles travel chiefly below 1660 m., but they tend to fly higher in spring than in autumn and higher by night than by day. The technique of radar plotting finally made a true assessment of the heights at which birds were migrating a practical possibility. In late October and November Dr David Lack tracked early morning south-westward arrivals of night migrants from Scandinavia in East Anglia by radar. The echoes were typical of passerines of medium size and the commonest species were thought to be redwings, fieldfares and perhaps blackbirds. During these movements many birds were to be found at heights up to 2330 m., with a few from 2660–3330 m. and one at 3700 m. – all of birds that had presumably left Scandinavia around dawn. Blackbirds from Holland were at a lower height – at or below some 1000 m. above the sea. One would not expect migrants to climb to greater heights than necessary for a safe journey, since the ascent means an expenditure of energy, the higher altitudes a loss in efficiency together with the adverse effects of higher wind speeds and lower temperatures. Autumn migrants build up a reserve of fat and the migratory pattern of sustained nocturnal flights alternating with diurnal bouts of feeding must put a severe strain on the birds' metabolisms. Those thrushes which fly and are drifted over the sea may need time to build up their energy stores during what Kenneth Williamson called a recuperative 'off-passage' period.

Radar films have clearly shown some of the hard-weather movements that thrushes may undertake in the middle of the winter. Many of these cold-weather passages are set in motion by the tracking of a cold front, perhaps with snow storms, which pushes the birds in front of it. If the weather deteriorates in northern Britain birds may move to the south-west and Ireland, but when, as in the winter of 1962–63, snow-free areas of refuge are not available then random movements are likely to follow. When the south and south-west of the country are still open then one may witness the kind of movement that brought an invasion of fieldfares to Warwickshire in 1962 after leaving the cold countryside of the north. Ringing records showed that there was a massive movement of song thrushes into south-western England during the first three weeks of January 1963, accompanied by smaller hard-weather passages into Ireland and France. In the rest of January and in February there were far fewer recoveries in south-west England but many more in Brittany. In the same period of 1964 there was only one recovery of a song thrush in France (Fig. 50). Mistle thrushes will move in advance of cold weather and British-ringed birds were found in 1963 in France. Redwings are great hard-weather migrants and in that same year birds left Britain for Spain and Ireland, while one bird was recovered on board a ship in the middle of the Atlantic.

I have many observations of redwings taking part in hard-weather movements in the winter. Birds passed in January 1960, for example, at the rate of 600 an hour over the BBC Television Centre in west London and I have notes of movements over Dollis Hill not only in that month but also in December and February. On a January day in 1962 redwings and fieldfares were travelling with nearly 5000 skylarks over my home, while in January 1963 Leo Batten observed some 1600 fieldfares and 700 redwings flying west over the Brent Reservoir.

Blackbirds suffered quite heavy mortality during the cold weather of

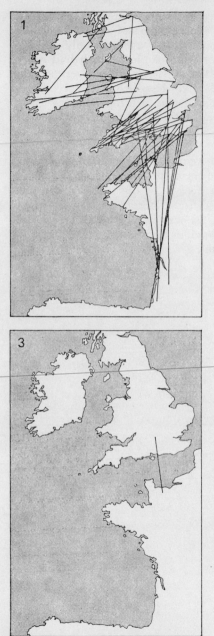

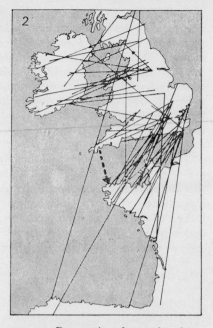

FIG. 50. Recoveries of song thrushes (at 160km or more from the point of ringing) to show the movement into south-western England during 1st–21st January 1963 (map 1), the switch to north-western France during 22nd January–28th February 1963 (map 2) and the almost total lack of movement in January and February 1964 (map 3). All the movements in January and February 1963 were to the south and west, apart from a few to the north-west (marked by small arrow heads on map 2); the dotted line on map 2 indicates what seems a more likely route for the song thrushes to have taken in evacuating south-west Britain than is suggested by the recovery lines. (Reproduced from *British Birds*, Ringing Supplement 1964, by permission of Robert Spencer.)

1962–63; the severest weather occurred between 16 and 25 January and
was marked by a large increase in the numbers of ringed blackbirds
recovered. Robert Spencer (1964) reported that 'Whereas only one-third
of Song Thrush recoveries in January were of birds which had moved
less than three miles, nearly two-thirds of all Blackbird recoveries in that
month were "local"'. However, as I have described elsewhere (Simms
1965), my local blackbird population at Dollis Hill moved away during
the greatest period of convective cooling. Other cold-weather movements
undoubtedly occurred in 1962–63 and must account for some of the
recoveries in France.

The typical migrations and the hard-weather movements of the thrushes
are often complex and varied. It is clear from my previous remarks in
this chapter that there is still a great deal to be discovered about these
movements, about the interaction between different species and populations of the same species, and about the way in which natural selection
continues to modify the migratory behaviour and patterns exemplified by
each of the European species of thrush.

CHAPTER 14

BRITAIN'S VAGRANT THRUSHES

From time to time the British Isles are visited by rare thrushes from the Palaearctic, Holarctic or Nearctic Regions. They have occurred chiefly in autumn, either as juveniles drifted off course by the wind or perhaps as adults on an accidental 'reversed migration'. The occurrences of different species range from just one to almost three dozen and the sight of any of the eleven species to which this chapter is devoted would be a highlight in any ornithologist's day. Although the following account of these rare vagrants cannot hope to be comprehensive, I hope to give some indications of the appearance, behaviour, world distribution and occurrence in the British Isles of the species involved. There are five species of the genus *Turdus*, four of *Catharus* and one each of *Zoothera* and *Monticola*.

THE EYE-BROWED THRUSH

The first of the *Turdus* species is the eye-browed thrush (*Turdus obscurus*), which is slightly smaller than a redwing with a somewhat variable grey upper breast and rusty or orange-buff lower breast and flanks. The upper parts are olive-brown, the crown is greyish, and there is a clear white stripe above the eye as well as a whitish patch stretching from the eye to the chin. The bird closely resembles the redwing in the shade of the upper parts but the lack of streaks on the breast and flanks is enough to distinguish it from the commoner bird. The call of British birds has been described as a soft 'Tchuck' and 'similar to that of a redwing, but rather more liquid and less rasping'. Various authors have reported on the call notes used by migrants; these include, according to Parslow (1968), 'a peculiar *che-e* on being disturbed' (Caldwell and Caldwell 1931), 'a thin pipit-like *zip-zip*' (Smythies 1940) and the 'voice chuckling, and a harsh *seee*' (Yamashina 1961). I have never heard a tape recording of the eye-browed thrush's song.

The bird breeds in Siberia and eastern Asia from the Yenisei and Lake Baikal to the Sea of Okhotsk south to Amurland with isolated populations in Sakhalin and the central Kurile Islands and in Japan. The breeding grounds lie mainly between 69°N and 45°N with some as far south as 35°N (Fig. 51). The species is migratory and winters in Burma, southern China and Taiwan south to the Malay Peninsula, the Philippines and Indonesia. The eye-browed thrush occurs through the boreal forest region of central and eastern Siberia arriving there during the second half of

May and in the north-west in early June. It is a characteristic bird of the
taiga, especially fir and larch woods, where it builds a nest rather like
that of the fieldfare. Southward movements take place in September and
on migration eye-browed thrushes can be found in eastern Asia, Japan and
Taiwan, frequenting wooded, hilly country often above 1000 m. and
feeding on worms, grubs and insects.

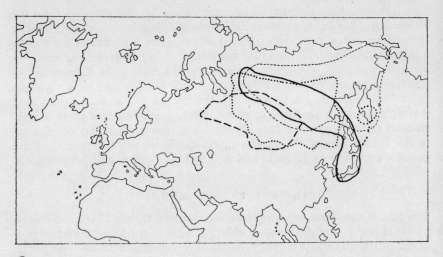

Siberian Thrush   Black Throated and   Eye-Browed Thrush   Dusky Thrush
                   Red Throated
                   Thrush

FIG. 51. The breeding range of four vagrant British thrushes. (After G. P.
Dementiev and H. A. Gladkov, 1954, *The Birds of the Soviet Union*, Moscow;
Voous, 1960, and Holgerson, 1953.)

Despite its extreme easterly range the eye-browed thrush has been
recorded in Italy, southern France, Germany, Holland and Belgium and
an immature bird was reported in Scandinavia in 1961. It seems to
resemble the northern race *eunomus* – the dusky thrush – of *Turdus naumanni*
in its wanderings. It was not, however, until 1964 that the species was
first identified in Britain when no less than three eye-browed thrushes
were reported in different parts of the country: one in a garden at
Oundle in Northamptonshire on 5 October; one on North Rona in the
Outer Hebrides on 16 October, and a third on St Agnes in the Isles of
Scilly on 5 December. The Northamptonshire bird was seen feeding with
newly arrived song thrushes on yew berries as well as drinking and bathing
at a pool. The Hebridean and St Agnes vagrants were observed pecking
amongst damp grass. Both the North Rona and Oundle birds had pale

tips to the greater wing-coverts, which H. Seebohm and R. B. Sharpe (1902) regarded as being characteristic of immatures but this feature may be retained by adults.

BLACK-THROATED THRUSH

This thrush is about the size of the ring ouzel but looks and behaves rather like a fieldfare. It is a central Palaearctic species formed of two geographical groups which are very different in appearance. There is a western lowland group *Turdus ruficollis atrogularis* – the black-throated thrush – and a more easterly mountain group *Turdus r. ruficollis* – the red-throated thrush. The former breeds from eastern Russia to the Yenisei, the Tunguska and northern Altai, while the eastern form can be found in south-central Siberia and northern Mongolia and unlike the black-throated form bears a brick-red throat (Fig. 51). According to Voous (1960), the two groups appear to hybridize freely where they overlap in an altitudinal zone of from 2100–2330 m. The two forms seem to have arisen in ecologically distinct regions perhaps during the vagaries of the Pleistocene Period. As they also share some environments with fieldfares, there may be considerable interspecific competition.

The male black-throated thrush is a striking bird with a black throat and upper breast – partly fringed with white in winter – grey-brown upper parts and off-white underparts. The female has a whitish throat with dark streaks and the upper portion of the breast very closely streaked or spotted with black; she also differs from the female of the red-throated form in not having chestnut in the tail. In flight the underwing shows up a rusty or rufous buff. Immature birds resemble females but young males approach adults in their colouring. The bill is dark brown but the basal two-thirds of the lower mandible are often a striking orange yellow.

The ordinary call, according to *The Handbook of British Birds*, has been described as resembling the alarm chuckle of the blackbird; there is also a redwing-like call. The alarm call on the breeding ground has been described by H. L. Popham (*The Handbook*) as 'Chit, chit, *cheet*'. and the song as a few whistled notes, bearing some resemblance to those of the song thrush and varied but not repeated. A male present on Fair Isle was not heard to call.

The black-throated thrush is a bird of the edges and open parts of coniferous woodland especially fir and less often pine, of some broad-leaved woods and also buckthorn scrub. Birds migrate from these breeding grounds to Iraq, Iran, Baluchistan and northern India and perhaps Arabia, where they can normally be found in regions of damp groves and cultivated areas including paddyfields. It seems that some birds will remain in the breeding area. The food appears to consist largely of worms, insects and berries such as those of Viburnum and hawthorn but it will adopt a largely insectivorous diet in India.

This thrush is a vagrant westwards across Europe to Norway, France, Italy and the British Isles. The first British records were in Sussex in December 1868, and Perthshire in February 1879. An adult male was seen on Fair Isle from December 1957 to January 1958, while the first female was recorded at Tolob in Shetland on 5 and 6 October 1974. An immature was present at Holkham in Norfolk from 21 to 24 October 1975. A black-throated thrush was located at Coltishall in Norfolk in February 1976 and was trapped and ringed there on 13 March (*Brit. Birds* 69:231,280). The male is a comparatively easy bird to identify with its large black bib contrasting with the whiteness of the breast and body. The bird often elevates its tail on alighting rather like a blackbird. The Fair Isle bird explored the short turf of the sheep grazings in the manner of a blackbird. When approached, according to Peter Davis (1958), the bird 'would stop, raise its head and stare intently often for some minutes . . . The usual manner of retreat was by running and it would only fly when hard pressed or too restricted by obstacles.' The bird also kept to itself except for the company on one occasion of two redwings. Recent unconfirmed reports involve birds in Shetland in 1974, the Isles of Scilly in 1975 and one in Co. Durham in January 1976.

It is interesting to note that the occurrences in the British Isles have been chiefly in the middle of winter but we have seen that some individuals stay on their breeding grounds in central Russia; these might be influenced by cold weather to move their quarters. It seems strange that more examples of these birds with a westerly range do not appear more often in the British Isles and since the males are so conspicuous they can hardly be overlooked; females are another question, of course.

THE DUSKY THRUSH

The dusky thrush *Turdus naumanni eunomus* of the eastern Palaearctic resembles Naumann's thrush *T. n. naumanni* which replaces it southwards in eastern Siberia. Both thrushes may be treated as sub-species but they may also appear in the literature as full species – *Turdus eunomus* and *Turdus naumanni*. Some individuals appear to be intermediate in appearance and since interbreeding seems probable the two forms are likely to be conspecific. Naumann's thrush has a lot of chestnut on the tail as well as a chestnut breast and flanks, whereas the dusky thrush has blackish markings on the breast, perhaps in crescentic bands, and also on the flanks and tail. There is a conspicuous whitish eye-stripe. There are quite broad chestnut areas on the rump and the upper and lower surfaces of the wings. Females and young birds in the autumn are duller and browner than the dark-backed males and have less chestnut on the wing.

PLATE 17. ABNORMAL PLUMAGES. *Above*, an albino female blackbird with a normally marked male at a nest on top of a tool-bag in a shed in Ayr. *Below*, an oddly marked blackbird at a nest on a ledge above petrol pumps in a busy garage in Kilmarnock.

PLATE 18. VAGRANT BRIT-
ISH THRUSHES. *Above*, the
black-throated thrush from
Central Asia present at Coltishall in Norfolk in March
1976. *Centre*, an American
robin showing the white
markings around the eye
and white chin with black
streaks. *Below*, grey-cheeked
thrush, another American
vagrant, photographed on
the Isles of Scilly.

The dusky thrush breeds across the northern half of the range from the Taz, Yenisei and Lake Baikal to Kamchatka (Fig. 51), and winters from India across to China and Japan. It is a breeding bird of forests, thinly wooded regions, broad-leaved scrub and coppice but in winter it frequents open grasslands with few trees. Its diet, from what little is known, resembles that of the black-throated thrush. The breeding season on the Amur lasts from the second week of May to the middle of June. The nests may be in small trees standing alone, quite close to the ground, and sometimes on it.

The call which was recorded on tape in Japan by Reiji Nakatsubo (Palmér and Boswall 1972) appears to be a thickish, fruity and slightly rasping 'Tchick-tchick' or 'Tchuck-tchuck'. A male in first-winter plumage in Co. Durham in December had a rare call described by B. J. Coates (1960) as 'Blackbird-like but less deep – a clucking note uttered only in flight either singly or up to three times in succession. A wheezy note, reminiscent of a starling (*Sturnus vulgaris*), was also heard in flight.'

The dusky thrush is a rare vagrant to the British Isles. It has also turned up in a number of European countries including Norway, France and Italy. The first British record was of a bird near Gunthorpe in Nottinghamshire on 13 October 1905. A male in first-winter plumage remained at Hartlepool in Durham from 12 December 1959 to 20 February 1960. A first-winter female was present on Fair Isle from 18 October to 21 October 1961 during which time it was trapped. A bird of this species was probably seen on Fair Isle by G. Stout on 7 October 1937. The fourth British record was of a bird at Whalsay in Shetland on 24 September 1968.

The bird watched and mist-netted at Hartlepool frequented a school playing field near the sea. Its food was almost exclusively earthworms but it also took bread. It bore two clear breast bands and its behaviour was very much like that of a fieldfare with an upright stance, the holding up of the bill at an angle of 20 degrees and an occasional cocking of the tail on landing. It was thought that it had been brought in by the easterly gales which prevailed during the week before the bird was first located.

A dusky thrush was reported at Firth in Shetland from 7–13 November 1975; if accepted this will be the first record since 1968 (*Brit. Birds* 69:160).

THE SIBERIAN THRUSH

The breeding range of the typical race of the Siberian thrush *Turdus s. sibiricus* extends over Siberia and eastern Asia from the Yenisei and Lake Baikal to the Sea of Okhotsk, Amurland and Sakhalin; breeding birds in Japan are separated as the race *T. s. davisoni* and the males lack all or nearly all the white on the belly and outer tail coverts that can be found in the mainland race. The breeding distribution lies between 69°N and 35°N (Fig. 51). In winter birds move south to eastern India through Burma, Thailand and Indo-China to Malaysia and Indonesia.

The male Siberian thrush is slate-black in colour with a brilliantly clear white eye-stripe and a white centre to the belly. The female has olive-brown upper parts, a more buff-coloured eye-stripe and whitish buff underparts rather heavily barred with rows of close spots. When flying both sexes reveal a conspicuous white band across the undersides of the wings which helps to distinguish them from the dusky or black-throated thrushes. A full description of a male can be found in *Brit. Birds* 47:21–25. The call appears to be 'a gruff squawk when suddenly flushed at close quarters and a short "zit", very much like that of a Song Thrush (*Turdus philomelos*) but softer and perhaps purer' (Andrew, Nelder and Hawkes 1955). The song on the breeding ground in Japan consists of short fluted phrases which degenerate or die away into a high scratchy twitter.

A male of this species was trapped on the Isle of May in Fife on 2 October 1954 after being first observed on the preceding day; it had left the island by 7 October. The race of this bird was not determined. The bird proved to be a typical thrush in build, stance and behaviour. It most closely resembled a blackbird and tended to keep to cover although it was not shy. The Siberian thrush arrived during a brief spell of south-easterly wind and drizzle and only a small arrival of redwings and other passerines coincided with its appearance. This example of the Siberian thrush was that of a bird new to the British list but there had been previous suggestions of earlier occurrences in the British Isles including a bird said to have been shot in Surrey during the winter of 1860–61 and another reputed to have been picked up in the Isle of Wight in the winter of 1874. Other examples have been obtained in Germany, Belgium, Holland, Italy, Hungary, Norway, France and Bulgaria. A male occured in Hampshire, Dec. 1976.

THE AMERICAN ROBIN

This Nearctic species is the last of the genus *Turdus* to appear in this chapter and it is one of the more frequent trans-Atlantic passerine vagrants although it does not appear annually. The American robin is a very handsome bird indeed – rather like an improved blackbird with a uniformly brick-red breast, dark greyish head and back, bold white streaks around the eyes, a white chin streaked with black and white-tipped outer tail feathers. The sexes are rather similar but the male's head is darker, and the female is somewhat duller with a paler breast and back. The first winter plumage is similar to the winter plumages of the adults but the colours are duller and more veiled.

The American robin breeds throughout most of North America from Alaska, Mackenzie, Quebec and Labrador south to northern Mexico

between 69°N and 17°N. Most birds travel southwards in the autumn to
spend the winter in the milder climate of the middle Atlantic and Gulf
States but some may remain as far north as Quebec and Maine. Northern
populations may winter from southern British Columbia, Illinois and
Virginia south as far as Mexico and Guatemala with occasional stragglers
turning up in Cuba and Bermuda. Birds which I saw arriving in north-
east Canada appeared soon after the temperature rose above freezing
and the snow melted. There are several races of the American robin. The
eastern robin *Turdus m. migratorius* breeds from the tree limit in Canada
south to Kansas, Illinois, Ohio, Pennsylvania and New Jersey and winters
in the southern United States north to the Ohio Valley and the north-
east coast. The southern robin *Turdus m. achrusterus* breeds from Maryland
and south Illinois to western South Carolina, northern Georgia, central
Alabama and northern Mississippi. The black-backed robin *Turdus m.
nigrideus* breeds in Newfoundland, Labrador and northern Quebec.
There are also western races. Some of the earlier British vagrants were
recorded as *Turdus m. migratorius*. Some birds leave the southern states in
spring as late as April while early spring arrivals may range from late
February in Pennsylvania to late March in North Dakota and Alberta
and even May in Yukon and Alaska. Autumn departures also vary from
early September in Alaska to mid-November in Washington D.C.

The American robin is very much a bird of woodlands, thickets,
villages, towns and gardens and is now the most familiar native bird of
American suburbia. I have seen nests in the United States and Canada
in barns, garages and outhouses and the bird reminded me very much of
the European blackbird to which it is so closely related. About 60% of
the American robin's food is vegetable, including wild fruits, while the
rest is made up especially from beetles and caterpillars with flies, bugs,
grasshoppers, spiders, earthworms, sowbugs and snails playing a smaller
part. The birds have a short straight run on the ground with a quick gait
and when looking for worms will cast their heads on one side like a song
thrush. The American robin is a nervous and I found rather restless bird
but very bouncy, assertive and attractive. It has an upright stance with
head held up and with wing tips lowered or flicking and the tail sometimes
pumped up and down like that of a blackbird. In flight it has a straight
back and expanded breast and a characteristic short beat of the wing
which I think is helpful in identification. I found the song very easy to
fix in the memory – two- to ten-second bursts of rounded, repeated notes
'Tchurri-tchooee-tchooee-tchurri-tchooee'. This rendering of a song that
I heard in New Brunswick is similar to Arthur Cleveland Bent's description 'Cheerily, cheery' with phrases of two or three syllables regularly
given at a rate of about two phrases per second. There is a variety of
different calls – Bent listed ten notes – including 'sssp' – a faint hiss often
given when a bird starts away in flight and before going to roost. I also

heard a blackbird-like 'Wik-wik-wik', a soft 'Whut-whut' and a high
'Tchit-tchit-tchit'.

American robins have been reported as vagrants in Europe, for example, in Germany, France, Belgium, Austria, Czechoslovakia, Yugoslavia and the British Isles. Between 1876 and 1894 there were five birds
reported in the British Isles and two more between 1927 and 1937. These
were not regarded as very acceptable records since there were fears that
the birds might have escaped from captivity and attempts had, in fact,
been made to release birds in Surrey about 1910. Except for two records
in the spring these occurrences took place between September and
December – a pattern that was to match the later, more acceptable
records. The first generally accepted occurrence was on Lundy in Devon
in October and November 1952 but by 1967 there were twelve records in
all involving thirteen birds: Devon (Oct.–Nov. 1952; Oct. 1955; Nov.
1962); Wexford (Dec. 1954); Kerry (Jan. 1955; Jan. 1965); Orkney
(May 1961); Isles of Scilly (two, Dec. 1963); Dorset (Jan.–Mar. 1966);
Surrey (Feb.–Mar. 1966); Kirkcudbright (May 1966) and Shetland
(Nov. 1967). The Co. Kerry bird in January 1965 apparently made a
brief stop on a trawler. There have been reports at the time of writing
of a bird present on St Kilda in 1975 which was confirmed (*Brit. Birds*
69:345) and another in the same year in Hampshire (*Brit. Birds* 68:348;
69:160). A bird was present on St Agnes, 17–30 October 1976.

Some birds that arrive in the British Isles may be storm-driven by
westerly winds while on their southward migration but some may have
had ship-assisted passage as well. Alan Durand (1961) has described how
he saw an American robin on board the RMS *Queen Elizabeth* in April
1961 some 700 miles out from New York and it was seen about for four
days. It is interesting to note that there is a two-way traffic since Durand
(1972) reported fieldfares, song thrushes and redwings flying parallel
with the RMS *Queen Mary* due south of Ireland on her way to New York.

THE GREY-CHEEKED THRUSH

The breeding range of this Holarctic species extends from north-eastern
Siberia (from the lower Kolyma to Anadyr and the Chukotski Peninsula)
into the northern parts of North America from Alaska and British
Columbia across to Labrador, Newfoundland, Nova Scotia and the
north-eastern states between approximately 68°N and 42°N. *Catharus
minimus bicknelli*, sometimes known as Bicknell's thrush, is a montane form
and breeds in Nova Scotia, southern Quebec and the mountains of
northern New England south to the Catskills: I found this thrush in thick
evergreens at over 1000 m. in the Catskill Mountains. The often larger
C. m. minimus – the northern grey-cheeked thrush – can be found breeding
throughout the rest of the range in Canada and north-eastern Siberia,

wintering in Central and South America. There is often an overlap in size between the two races and it is rather dangerous to try and separate them in the field. In winter Bicknell's thrush has been found on the island of Hispaniola; it has a predilection for animal foods but becomes frugivorous in autumn.

The grey-cheeked is a small thrush with a greyish-brown back and to some extent it resembles the olive-backed thrush of North America, but it has grey cheeks, an inconspicuous whitish ring around the eye and less warm markings on the throat and breast and its back is greyer in colour. Both species are smaller than a song thrush and have darker backs; they are greyish white underneath where the song thrush is a warmer buff in tone and has blotches. The northern grey-cheeked thrush is a shy bird of willow and birch scrub and dwarf spruce up to the tree limit. Migrants can be seen wherever there is cover – in forests and woods, in conifer plantations, in scrub along streams, and even in gardens and city parks.

The weak, rather thin song is inferior to those of the wood and hermit thrushes and it can sometimes be heard from spring migrants. On the breeding ground the song is fuller and a little richer. It may open with some quiet clucking sounds and a slurring note 'Wee-oh' which are then followed by two or three high-pitched staccato notes resembling 'Chee-chee' mixed up with almost inaudible cymbal-like tones (Gillespie 1927). The Bicknell's thrushes I heard in song had a thin, scratchy but quite wild-sounding delivery of several notes starting with clucks and a thin 'Weech-eech-oo' and followed by slurred-down phrases with a clear break in the middle. Bent (1964) described the complete song of Bicknell's thrush as 'Chook-chook, wee-o, wee-o, wee-o-ti-t-ter-ee'. There may be some regional differences. The grey-cheeked thrush has a harsh scolding note and some short call notes – 'Whet, chuck, pheu or fee-a' (Bent); the last note has been described also as a high-pitched 'Quee-a'. The most characteristic note of Bicknell's thrush is a harsh, penetrating slurred whistle, piercing in alarm and descending to a quiet 'Pe-irt' when the bird is curious or slightly nervous. The adults also have a low 'Chook-chook' and a rolling 'Crr-rr-rr'.

The first grey-cheeked thrush to be reported in the British Isles was on Fair Isle on 5 October 1953 – a bird with a marked buffish tone to its breast. It was a first-winter bird with white spots on the tips of the greater coverts. A larva of the American tick *Haemophysalis leporis-palustris*, which spends its adult life on snow-shoe hares, and was a first record for Britain, was found attached to the bird's chin (Williamson 1954). This bird could not be separated subspecifically. Another bird was trapped, again on Fair Isle, on 29 October 1958 – the third European record with the first at Elba in Italy in 1901. Birds have also occurred on Bardsey Island, Caernarvonshire, on 10 October 1961 (a first-winter bird identified by Dr Charles Vaurie as a specimen of *C. m. bicknelli* (Clafton 1963), and

again in October 1968 and October 1971 – this last, the third record for
the island was the eighth British record. The fourth British record was
that of a bird on St Kilda in October 1965 which may have been of the
northern race. The fifth record was of a bird in Morayshire found in
November 1965 dying under a gorse bush at the RNAS Station at Lossie-
mouth; it was a first-winter male very probably of the northern race. A
grey-cheeked thrush was also recorded from Horden in Co. Durham on
17 October 1968. It has been suggested that the arrival of many small
American land birds in the British Isles coincides with gales or strong
westerly winds on the south side of large Atlantic lows (Williamson and
Ferguson-Lees 1960) but single records may be difficult to link with
meteorological conditions if the actual date of arrival of American
individual vagrants is not known. Birds have also appeared in Iceland
and Germany. Three occured on the Isles of Scilly and one in Cornwall
in 1976.

THE OLIVE-BACKED THRUSH (SWAINSON'S THRUSH)

There are two eastern forms of this North American thrush *Catharus
ustulatus*. The two races of this Nearctic species range as breeding birds
over most of the wooded areas of Alaska, the Canadian Zone and Newfoundland south to California and the Sierra Nevada, Utah, Colorado,
northern Michigan, northern New England and the mountains of
Pennsylvania and West Virginia. The olive-backed, or Swainson's, thrush
C. u. swainsoni breeds throughout the northern and eastern parts of this
range south to British Columbia and the north-eastern United States. The
typical race *C. u. ustulatus* – the russet-backed thrush – breeds from south-
eastern Alaska and coastal British Columbia to southern California while
the western olive-backed thrush *C. u. almae* breeds in the Rocky Mountains.
In winter *C. u. swainsoni* travels to South America and ranges from
Colombia east to Brazil, Bolivia and Argentina and west to Peru and
northern Ecuador. *C. u. ustulatus* appears to winter north to central
Mexico and south to Guatemala.

This small American thrush is a uniform olive-brown or grey-brown on
the upper parts, paler below and carries black spots on the upper breast
and the sides of the throat. The side of the head, the throat and upper
breast are washed with buff and the bird has a distinctive pale ochraceous
buff eye-ring. To separate the olive-backed thrush from the grey-headed
or Bicknell's it is necessary to see the buff cheeks quite clearly and the
conspicuous orbital ring. The uniform greyish or olive – not rufous –
upper parts separate *Catharus ustulatus* and the grey-cheeked thrush from
the more rufous-headed and olive-tailed wood thrush and the more
olive-headed and rufous-tailed hermit thrush. The olive-backed thrush
has a blackish bill and pale brown legs. In flight it looks rather like a small

song thrush but at rest it seems tubby and compact and in size nearer to a robin. It is primarily an animal feeder, taking especially beetles, flies, ants, wasps and bugs, but it will also feed on small wild soft-skinned fruits.

The song of the olive-backed thrush is fine and arresting but not of the first American rank. It is long and sustained, sweet and musical and reminds me in part of the mellow notes of the European blackbird, especially an island bird. Each phrase is different and a call note – "Whit' or a high piping call may be incorporated in the performance. Bent (1964) quotes a description of the song from Aretas A. Saunders: 'There is a somewhat windy quality about it, as though the bird was saying 'Whao-whayo-whiyo-wheya-wheeya'' '. I found its tones and rising phrases very pleasing to listen to but not as satisfying as the songs of the hermit and wood thrush. The song of the russet-backed thrush is very similar and is characterized by the same rising pitch. The call note of the russet-back is a soft, liquid 'What' or 'Whoit' 'sounding much like the drip of water into a barrel' (Grinnell and Storer 1924); there are also an abrupt burred call 'Chee-ur-r' and a single whistle, louder and higher. Notes of the olive-backed thrush include a high 'Whit', or 'Pip' and a piping note like that of a spring peeper *Hyla crucifer*. A bird in Eire gave 'a short, mono-syllabic, high, quiet "Zeet" ' (Sharrock *et al.*, 1973) and I noted an American bird giving a sharp alarm 'Tchut'.

In north New England and eastern Canada the olive-backed thrush is a bird of the low, wet areas of spruce and fir forests where it is very common. It may also occur in drier upland coniferous woods and even mixed forests. The nests in New England are generally in spruces or balsam firs.

The first record of the olive-backed thrush in the British Isles was that of a bird found dead at the Blackrock Lighthouse, Co. Mayo, on 26 May 1956. The skin was sent to America where it was critically examined and referred to the race *C. u. swainsoni* (Ruttledge 1966). The first British record was of an individual trapped on the island of Skokholm, Pembroke-shire, which was present from 14–19 October 1967. In the following year another was discovered on Cape Clear Island, Co. Cork on 14 October and it was seen again on 16 October 1968; it fed largely on blackberries. The races of these last two occurrences were not determined. Other vagrants have turned up in Iceland, France, Belgium, Germany, Austria and Italy. One was reported at Sandwich Bay, Kent, 27 October 1976.

THE HERMIT THRUSH

On 2 June 1975 a hermit thrush *Catharus guttatus* was identified on Fair Isle (*Brit. Birds* 68:254, 435; 69:345). There are several races. The eastern hermit thrush breeds in the mixed evergreen-hardwood forests from northern Manitoba and southern Quebec south to central Minnesota,

Michigan and Virginia; it winters throughout the southern United States to Ohio and even southern New England. I found it very common in the hammocks and swamps of Florida. Its song is pure and flute-like, composed of phrases of different pitches, each preceded by a long and diagnostic key note. The calls are a low 'Chuck', 'Quirk' or 'Quoit', a scolding 'Tuk-tuk-tuk' and a harsh 'Pay'. The hermit thrush has a characteristic habit of cocking and then slowly lowering its tail.

In his description of a remarkable fall of American land birds on board RMS *Mauretania* in October 1962 Alan Durand described how he saw a hermit thrush for two days when the ship was between 632 and 1460 kms out from New York en route for Southampton; it 'liked the safety net over the First-class Swimming pool'. The hermit thrush has been reported as an accidental vagrant to Germany and Iceland.

THE VEERY

This small American thrush *Catharus fuscescens* was a species new to Britain and Europe when one was trapped on 6 October 1970 at Porth-gwarra in Cornwall. The eastern veery breeds from the Gulf of St Lawrence west to northern Oregon and British Columbia, south to Georgia, Ohio, Utah and Nevada and north to Alberta, Saskatchewan, Manitoba, south Ontario and Quebec. For the winter the bird migrates through the southern United States to South America – Colombia, Brazil and Guyana with many gathering in the Mato Grosso. This is the least spotted of the *Catharus* genus. It is uniformly tawny, cinnamon or yellowish brown above with such indistinct spots on the breast that this feature may look clear at a distance. The Cornish bird had some streaking on the upper breast separated from uniform whitish below.

The veery makes its summer home in shady woods with a thick under-story and moist conditions, perhaps even a wooded swamp with pines, elms and red maples. The bird has a dignified reserve and travels rather silently on its migratory journeys. It feeds a great deal on the forest floor, thrusting about with its bill in the leaf litter looking for insects. Veeries move with 'long, springing frog-like jumps'. The song has been described as a liquid breezy whistle going downwards – 'Whree-u,whree-u,whree-u, whree-u' – four or five phrases with a downward inflection from which the veery gets its name. The commonest call note is a smooth whistled 'Hee-oo' or 'Wheew' (Bent 1964) or 'View' as I recorded in my own notes. There are also a low guttural 'Whuck' of danger or alarm and a long loud fluctuating 'Ka-a-a-a-a'.

The Cornish veery was described by E. M. P. Allsopp (1972) as 'a dumpy bird noticeably smaller than a Song Thrush *Turdus philomelos* but larger than a Robin, with rich warm brown upperparts and rather long, thin legs for its size, but with no supercilium or orbital ring'. It was seen feeding on elderberries and it sometimes flicked its wings and tail.

WHITE'S THRUSH

This straggler to the British Isles is a Palaearctic, Oriental and Australasian species with its breeding distribution between 64°N and 43°S. The range stretches as far west as western Siberia and eastern Russia but the main breeding region is from the Yenisei south to Lake Baikal, north to the middle Tunguska and eastwards to Manchuria, Korea and Japan. Other populations occur from the Himalayan massif to Burma and Indo-China, in India, Sri Lanka and Malaysia through Indonesia to Australia and Tasmania (Fig. 52).

White's thrush *Zoothera dauma aurea* – with fourteen tail feathers – breeds throughout the main Palaearctic range of the species except Japan,

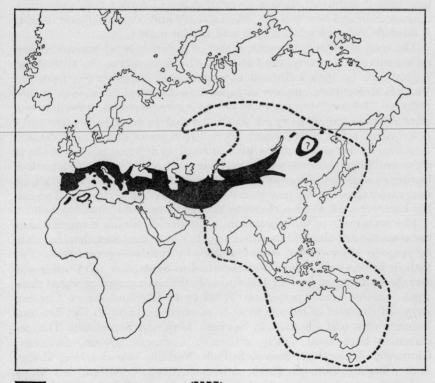

Breeding range of Rock Thrush ⌐ ⌐ ⌐ Possible range of White's Thrush (All races)

FIG. 52. Ranges of rock thrush and White's thrush.

Assuriland and Korea; the occurrences in the British Isles are likely to be of this race although this has not been determined in all instances. There are several allied races including the larger *Z. d. amami* with twelve tail feathers which can be found in the Ryukyu Islands, *T. d. dauma* in the Himalayas which also has only twelve tail feathers and is smaller than White's thrush, and *T. d. horsfieldi* which lives in Java and Lombok and has fourteen tail feathers and is much smaller. The Palaearctic populations winter in India, Burma, southern China, Indo-China, Thailand, Taiwan and the Philippines.

White's thrush is as large as a mistle thrush but it can be recognized by its rich golden-brown, not greyish, plumage and the crescentic black tips to the feathers on the head and both the upper and the under parts. Its flight is undulating and the bold black and white bands under the wings are very distinctive. The sexes are similar. White's thrush does not hop but runs and is very much a bird of the ground zone; it will fly up into trees if disturbed. It is a lover of dense fir forests with very thick undergrowth and here it is shy, often solitary and feeds chiefly on insects. A Norfolk bird took small beetles and fibrous matter.

The song of White's thrush is a sort of melancholy whistle and a low rather squeaky warbling; the former has been likened to the note of the pygmy owl. In 1956 I listened to a recording of the species from the Victoria Recording Company of Japan and described the note as 'a thin plaintive "Tcheeee" but pure and of varying frequencies and swelling to a climax before fading away'. I was interested to read Jeffery Boswall's description (1964), after he had listened to a set of discs called *Japanese Bird Songs*; 'a drawn-out, pure whistle uttered, at different pitches, at about six second intervals; each whistle starts imperceptibly, comes to a peak of loudness and slowly dies away'. It would seem that this piping is, in fact, its song rather than the call note as it has been described in the past. The call has been reported to be a churring similar to that of a mistle thrush.

The occurrence of White's thrush in the British Isles as a vagrant does not seem to have changed its pattern greatly over the years, despite better coverage by observers and more searching for rarities in recent years. The 35th in Britain and Ireland was recorded in September 1973 – this was also the sixth record for Fair Isle and only the sixth record accepted since 1958. Another was reported on Whalsay in Shetland on 11 October 1975. Of the total of records most have occurred between October and January with odd instances in 'spring', May and September. The occurrences have been widely scattered: Cornwall, Devon, Somerset, Gloucester, Hampshire, Sussex, Suffolk, Norfolk, Warwickshire, Shropshire, Cheshire, Berwick, Perth, Aberdeen, Cork, Longford, and Mayo with the most records from Yorkshire, Durham and Fair Isle. Birds have also been noted in Norway, Iceland, France and Sardinia. One was seen in Yorkshire in December 1976.

THE ROCK THRUSH

This attractive bird is a Palaearctic species in the genus *Monticola* which itself is also Oriental and Ethiopian. The rock thrush *Monticola saxatilis* breeds in north-west Africa and from the Iberian Peninsula through southern Europe north to Switzerland, southern Poland and southern Russia, east through Asia Minor and the Caucasus to Iran, Afghanistan and Baluchistan and north to the Altai, Mongolia, Lake Baikal and China (Fig. 52). Its breeding range lies between 56°N and 28°N. Its original distribution in Europe was once wider than it is at present and birds formerly nested locally in southern Germany; however, the rock thrush seems to be increasing in Switzerland. The winter quarters are on the savannahs in Africa from west Africa to the Sudan and Somalia south to southern Tanzania. I have seen birds on their breeding ground in Spain, southern France, the Alps and the Balkans and wintering in the Sudan and east Africa. The relationship of the rock thrush to some of the African species in the same genus is not clear.

The male rock thrush in summer is one of the most striking of all European birds with a pale slate-blue head, neck and upper back, white lower back and rump, dark wings and chestnut-orange or rufous-chestnut underparts and tail. Immature males have no white on the back and look rather mottled. In winter the colours of the adult male are somewhat veiled by buffish fringes to the feathers above and whitish below. The female is a mottled dark brown above, sometimes with a trace of white on the back and a rufous buff underneath with dark crescentic marks. In all plumages the short orange or chestnut tail is diagnostic and distinguishes this species from the blue rock thrush with which it may share its breeding habitat. The rock thrush is rather shy and retiring on the nesting ground but is much less so in its winter quarters.

This plump species about the size of a song thrush is very much a bird of the ground, progressing with long hops, but it will also perch on rocks, buildings, trees and even telegraph wires. When perched it assumes an upright manner, suggestive of a chat, but it will sometimes adopt a more crouching attitude. The rock thrush has a characteristic tail action in which the tail is raised or allowed to swing from the body. It flies low and elegantly to seek cover behind rocks or hill slopes. In the breeding season it is a bird of high sunny and rocky terrain or ruins with perhaps a few trees (more than can usually be found in the blue rock thrush's habitat) and often at a height of from 1000–2660 m. in southern Europe, but in some areas it can be found at lower levels. In the Alps and the Caucasus the rock thrush occurs up to 2430 m., in the High Atlas of Morocco to 3200 m. and in Afghanistan as high as 3830 m. (Voous 1960). It is essentially a feeder on insects of all kinds, spiders, snails, worms, lizards and occasionally berries, especially the cherries *Prunus cerasus* (morello) and *P. avium* (wild cherry).

My description of the song is 'a very clear, true, fluting warble given occasionally in a short display flight but generally heard from a rock or perch or similar song post'. I find the song wavy in form, chat-like, wild and sometimes containing a scratchy note or two among the fluent mellow phrases. To me it is more varied, shorter and more staccato than the song of the blue rock thrush. The call is a rather subdued 'Tchak-tchak' and *The Handbook* gives a high-pitched 'Fid' described by G. Niethammer which I have not heard. The adults apparently call 'Soop' while waiting to feed the young (Beven 1969). The bird may fan its bright tail in the display flight but it may also sing in ordinary flight. A soft warbling utterance has been recorded in Kenya.

The first accepted British record of the rock thrush is that of a bird at Therfield in Hertfordshire on 19 May 1843. Since then some ten others have been accepted on the British and Irish list with nine occurrences in May and June and two in October and November. The full list at the time of writing is: Hertford (May 1843); Orkney (two, May 1910); Shetland (November 1931, October 1936, June 1970); Kent (June 1933); Outer Hebrides (June 1962); Devon (May 1963); Norfolk (May 1969); Co. Louth (first Irish record, 20–21 May 1974). The species has appeared in a number of European countries as a vagrant including Belgium, Holland, Germany and Sweden.

An example of the blue rock thrush (*Monticola solitarius*) was present from 29 August to 6 September 1966 on North Ronaldsay in Orkney. Although this could have been the first British record of this rather sedentary thrush from southern Europe, Asia and north-west Africa, numbers have been imported as cage-birds and the British Records Committee of the BOU regarded this record as suspect on those grounds (*Brit. Birds* 60:324).

CHAPTER 15

THE SMALL CHAT-LIKE THRUSHES
OF THE BRITISH ISLES

FROM the outset it was intended that this volume should demonstrate almost exclusively the natural history and ecology of Britain's six true thrush species. However, for the sake of completeness it seems desirable to make some comments, albeit in a shortened form, about their smaller relations – the chat-like thrushes. This chapter is designed to review briefly the distribution and behaviour of the seven common species of chat-like thrushes in the family *Turdidae* and to make some reference to the ten other scarce or extremely rare members of this group. As we have already seen in chapter 1, the chat-like thrushes are small birds with more slender legs, weaker and less far-carrying songs, and more varied plumages and patterns of behaviour than the true thrushes. Some are rather simply coloured like the robin and nightingale, which are primarily birds of damp woodland. The redstart is strikingly handsome – a bird of forest and heathland, while the chats and wheatears tend towards black, white and brown and live in rocky and open country habitats. The group is very diverse and reveals a wide range of evolutionary developments and end-lines.

I propose to deal firstly with the distribution, habitats and reproduction of the seven common species in a systematic way and to follow this major section with a discussion of some of the broader aspects of their natural history such as moult, breeding season, migrations and so on. The rare visitors and vagrants will be described rather briefly at the end of the chapter.

THE ROBIN

It seems appropriate to start with Britain's national bird – the robin (*Erithacus rubecula*). It is a western Palaearctic bird, occurring in the boreal, temperate and Mediterranean climatic zones. The British race *E. r. melophilus* is a familiar and much loved inhabitant of many British woods and gardens, yet the Continental race *E. r. rubecula* is shyer and more retiring, living in deep woods, both broad-leaved and coniferous. The robin breeds in the Azores, Madeira, the Canary Islands and north-west Africa and then eastwards from Spain, Portugal, France and the British Isles across Europe to western Siberia and northern Iran, and northwards to Fenno-Scandia (Fig. 53). The range seems to lie between

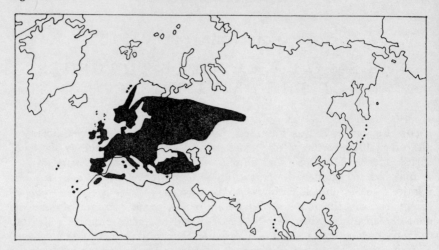

FIG. 53. Breeding distribution of the robin.

68° and 28°N, or between the July isotherms of 55°F in the north and 72°F
in the south. In the British Isles the robin has been recorded from 93%
of the 10 km squares in *The Atlas of Breeding Birds in Britain and Ireland*.
It is very widely distributed, nesting on many islands but not Shetland.
There seems to have been very little change in either its range or numbers
in the British Isles over the last one hundred years.

In Britain the robin was originally a denizen of broad-leaved high
forest but its possible early association with woodcutters and their forest
clearings may have preadapted the species to the colonization of farm
hedgerows, parks and gardens. It is a bird of both deciduous and coniferous woods and I have recorded it in woods of birch, pedunculate and
sessile oak, ash, beech, alder carrs, hazel scrub and in mature pinewoods
and conifer plantations as well as coppices, scrub and similar ecotones.
When I added up all the contacts for nearly three hundred different
woods that I censused in the British Isles I found it to be the third commonest species after the chaffinch and wren. Robins are common in all
but the most highly developed parts of towns but at Dollis Hill only
winter territories were maintained in the 1928–32 estate until 1961; after
that nesting became regular. Densities of breeding robins can vary
enormously according to the nature of the habitat ranging from 10 pairs
per square kilometre in Scots pine to more than 300 in a similar area of
planted English estate garden.

The British race is basically sedentary but some from the south-east
of Britain may emigrate to south-west France and Iberia, while others
from northern Britain may cross over to Ireland. Continental robins often

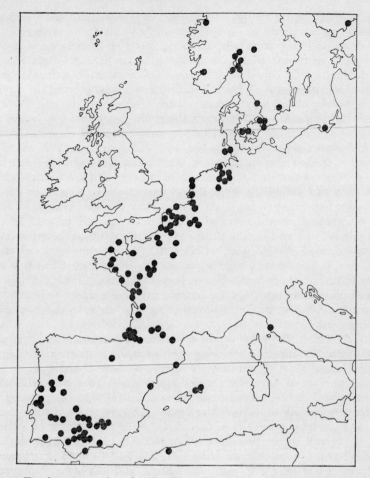

FIG. 54. Foreign recoveries of 118 robins. (Reproduced with slight amendment from *British Birds*, Report on Bird Ringing for 1968, by permission of Robert Spencer.)

arrive in numbers on the east coast; some may remain while others continue south to France and Spain. Figure 54 gives the foreign recoveries of 118 robins.

The robin is very much a bird of thick undergrowth. It can be very secretive both during the moult in late summer and when visiting the nest, which is often very difficult to find. At other times it appears to be the most confiding of our garden birds, perching on spade or fork handles and watching our activities in the garden with a beady eye. I have seen robins sunbathing on the ground in very exposed situations. Territories are taken up in August towards the end of the moult by birds of either sex, which will sing from within them, but the females have usually ceded theirs from late December onwards. After that the territories are shared. The late Dr David Lack's classic *Life of the Robin* and subsequent papers in scientific journals have described in absorbing detail the ecology and life history of this very attractive little bird.

With its comparatively large eyes the robin can feed early in the day and in poor conditions of light, taking insects such as earwigs, beetles, moths, the larvae of many *Lepidoptera*, ants, gall-insects and flies as well as centipedes, spiders and earthworms. Robins have favourite perches and in my garden use certain fence posts, garden canes and low branches from which they can survey the ground and dart down to collect an item of food before returning to the same perch. They will also take small fruit, such as currants, raspberries and blackberries, as well as wild berries. The robin is lively and alert in its movements, hopping on the ground and pausing in a stiff upright position often flicking its wings and tail at the same time. It can be very aggressive towards its own kind but it is rare for one robin to kill another. The red breast plays a significant part in the bird's displays and posturings. In courtship the male feeds the female and this activity can last, in fact, from nest-building right to the end of the breeding season.

With the robin the possession of a territory is psychologically essential for nesting and competitions among robins for one may stimulate aggression and more song. The robin's song has a sweet-sharp quality with warbled phrases of long clear notes and various runs and trills. The autumn song is thinner, more plaintive and wistful. The song period is a long one and young birds have the innate capacity to learn the songs of their parents. I have sometimes heard birds singing in the dark close to street lights and there are even records of birds feeding in the dark by artificial light. I have described the sub-song elsewhere as 'a low, sweet introspective warbling with many high notes' and it is often employed in display.

Robins breed from late March or early April in Britain, even occasionally in winter, and indeed there are records for every month of the year. Few common birds choose such a wide range of nesting sites from hollows in banks and holes in trees or stumps to creepers on walls, hedgerows, cavities in walls, abandoned kettles, tins and saucepans, peg bags and rolls of wire, trucks and aircraft, and even an unmade bed in the city of Birmingham from which a brood was successfully raised! The nest itself is a rather bulky construction of dead leaves – perhaps two or three hundred – grasses and mosses, even nylon cord, and plastic strips from bags have been used in my own garden. The lining is often provided by hair or a few feathers. Normally the hen bird builds but a male in France

PLATE 19. ROCK THRUSH. *Above*, a male rock thrush with caterpillar. *Below*, a female rock thrush with her strikingly barred underparts. Both sexes have a bright orange tail. The rock thrush is a Palaearctic bird breeding in north-west Africa, Iberia and southern Europe across Asia and wintering in Africa. These photographs were taken in Hungary. The few British records are scattered from Devon to Shetland.

PLATE 20. ROBIN AND NIGHTINGALE. *Above*, a robin in characteristically upright stance on the ground. *Below*, a nightingale at the nest showing some resemblance to the softer plumaged robin but it is slightly larger and more elegantly proportioned.

was reported taking material into a nestbox. I have often seen a male pick up a leaf, and drop it; it was then taken by the hen to the nest. When the nest is built on the ground it is sometimes embellished with an approach tunnel formed from grasses or leaves. Nests can be built up to 2 metres above the ground, occasionally even 3 metres, and there is one record of a nest 13 metres up in a tree.

In England and Wales the clutch size increases from early March until early June after which it declines. It rises from 4·7 eggs to 5·15 in May and falls to 4·9 in June. Seasonal variations seem to be rather more marked on the continent of Europe than in England. The average clutch size shows variation also in different parts of the robin's range increasing from south to north. The figure rises from 4·2 in North Africa to 4·9 in Iberia, 5·9 in northern France and Germany, and 6·3 in Scandinavia. The clutch size also increases from west to east, standing at 5·1 in England and Wales and rising to 5·7 in Holland, 5·9 in Germany and 6·0 in Galicia. In the robin clutch size appears to vary with the daylength and with the season. The limit to clutch size is determined by the increased mortality in large broods due to shortage of food. While natural selection may be the ultimate factor there can be various adaptive modifications brought about by particular conditions. According to Dr Lack, the number of young fledged from a robin's nest was on average 0·76 smaller than the average clutch size. Some 57% of the eggs in completed clutches produce fledglings – a figure intermediate between those for typical open-nesting birds and typical hole-nesting species. Robins suffer very badly in winters marked by periods of very cold weather.

Robins' eggs are white and blotched and spotted with reddish marks; a few may be unspotted, white or bluish-white. The hen incubates the eggs during which time the cock feeds her. David Lack showed that nest-building takes about four days, laying five days, incubation thirteen days and fledging is accomplished in about twelve. The young become independent in another three weeks. Occasionally robins may build a second nest before the departure of the first brood. There are generally two and sometimes three broods.

The robin shares its habitat with other thrush species but does not seem to compete with them, taking perhaps smaller items of food and capturing faster moving ones. The robin feeds mainly on the ground and in this respect it resembles the nightingale, but it does not demand the dense ground cover that the other bird seems to need. There has been considerable discussion as to whether the separation of the robins (*Erithacus*) and nightingale (*Luscinia*) on a generic basis is a valid one.

The sombrely-coloured nightingale (*Luscinia megarhynchos*) is a European faunal type found in the south-western Palaearctic, favouring particularly the temperate, Mediterranean and steppe climatic zones. The distinction between this bird and the very similar thrush nightingale (*Luscinia luscinia*) whose plumage, song and choice of habitats resemble those of the common bird, was probably achieved, according to Dr K. H. Voous (1960), by geographical isolation during the last glacial period. The nightingale can be found breeding from north-west Africa, Iberia and the British Isles east to Denmark (where it is occasional), Germany, Poland, the Balkans and south-west Russia and then from the Crimea, Caucasus, Asia Minor, Syria and Iraq to the borders of Sinkiang, northern Afghanistan and eastern Iran (Fig. 55). It breeds between 55°N and 30°N with its distribution limits between the July isotherms of 62°F in the north and 86°F in the south. *L. m. megarhynchos* breeds in north-west Africa and Europe east to south-west Russia, the Caucasus and Asia Minor. There are allied forms in, for example, Turkestan and Iran. The nightingale winters in tropical Africa from Nigeria across to Kenya and Tanzania.

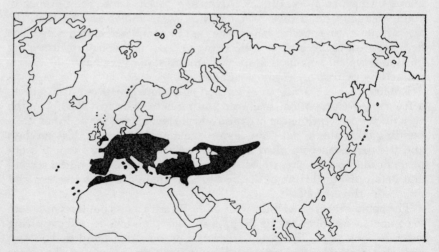

FIG. 55. Breeding distribution of the nightingale.

The nightingale is a summer visitor to Britain south of a line from Yorkshire across to south Wales and Devon. There are perhaps some 10,000 pairs in all but there has been some decline in numbers since about 1950. Concentration is often quite high in south-eastern England but the bird is more local west and north to Devon, Monmouth, Hereford,

Shropshire, south Yorkshire and Lincolnshire. It is a vagrant to Scotland and Ireland where birds have sometimes been reported in song. The first British record of the pale race from south-central Asia *L. m. hafizi* was obtained on Fair Isle in October 1971.

In Britain the species is most often found in pedunculate oakwoods and beechwoods, hazel coppices especially with standard oaks, thorn scrub, deep hedgerows and sometimes gardens. In *Woodland Birds* in this series I wrote that nightingales bred, in my experience, '*usually* not more than 400 feet above sea level' but after a broadcast which I made in the Radio 4 programme *The Living World* I received five letters from listeners who had heard a nightingale in song at about 500 feet above sea level in Surrey and Hertfordshire, at 600 feet in Kent and Gloucestershire and at 700 feet near Cheltenham. I still believe that height and possibly summer temperatures play their part in determining the distribution in England and Wales of the nightingale.

In woodland the nightingale favours broad-leaved trees, after arriving probably during the Atlantic Phase, and with a good shrub layer, shade and a rich humus. I have found the bird most numerous in extensive thorn scrub and spinneys in south Warwickshire, the mixed broad-leaved woods of Breckland, Surrey commons, Suffolk lanesides and yew and oakwoods in Sussex. On the fringes of its range in Britain nightingales are often to be found in the river valleys. On the Continent the bird can often be found in gardens and hedges and I have heard birds singing in the Greek forum in Athens and near the Vatican in Rome.

In the nightingale's habitat the ground zone under the shrub layer is generally rich in brambles, wild roses, nettles and umbellifers, growing in rather damp situations. It is not a bird of rocky ground but it can be found up to 1330 m. in the Alps and nearly 2000 m. in southern Europe. It is decreasing in some parts of Europe because conifers have been planted on the site of felled deciduous forests. In England coppices, generally of chestnut, hazel or hornbeam, can be very attractive to birds such as the nightingale and garden warbler which demand a good shrub layer. Peter Stuttard and Kenneth Williamson (1971) concluded after an extensive survey that 'a coppice-with-standards management, with rotational cutting at intervals of 12–25 years (depending upon the tree species) provides the most satisfactory habitat for Nightingales in this situation'. Birds will disappear for a time while a wood recovers from the effects of coppicing while overgrown, untended coppice forms a thick canopy which shades out the ground flora. A rich ground zone seems to be a regular feature of nightingale habitats. The loss of hedgerows and small copses must have adversely affected nightingale numbers in Britain.

The nightingale's magnificent song can be heard in the daylight hours and at night but it is most frequent at dusk and during the early part of the night and again at dawn. In English woodlands the bird tends to sing from dense cover whereas in Provence, for example, I have seen birds singing from rooftops and telegraph poles. The song is one of remarkable quality with long, high, plaintive notes, fast, slurred *jugs*, quick, clean jumps of pitch and hard metallic trills. The bird only sings from mid-April to mid-June. The alarm notes are harsh and grating with a jay-like quality and the call is a high chaffinch-like '*Hweet*'. The display of the nightingale involves a spreading of the rufous tail and the fluttering of the wings.

The nest is hard to find being tucked away in a dark place perhaps among nettles or ivy and it is usually on or close to the ground. Nests have been recorded at heights of four or five feet and even on top of a wooden paling fence. Domed nests may also occur. The hen is responsible for the construction. There are generally four or five eggs in a clutch; they are olive-green or brown due to the superimposition of thick brown speckles on a blue ground. Zoned markings sometimes occur and even eggs of a light blue colour. They are very difficult to see in the nest among the oak leaves, hairs and grasses used in its construction. Most birds start to nest in May in England and the hen incubates the eggs for from 13 to 14 days. Fledging takes from 11 to 12 days. The young look rather like young robins with rufous tails. The species is single brooded.

The nightingale is a very terrestrial bird and feeds mainly on the ground searching for worms, beetles, the larvae of *Lepidoptera*, the pupae of ants, flies and spiders. In the autumn birds will also take fruits such as those of elders and many kinds of berry. Its behaviour is suggestive of that of a large robin with the constant cocking of its head on one side, its large eye, erect carriage and manner of flight but it is more elegant, more 'deliberate' in its actions and much more secretive.

THE REDSTART

The redstart (*Phoenicurus phoenicurus*) is distributed throughout the western and central Palaearctic and in similar climatic zones to those of the nightingale – temperate, Mediterranean and steppe. Breeding takes place from north-west Africa, the British Isles, Spain, Portugal and France eastwards across much of Europe except in the far north, some regions around the Mediterranean and south-west Russia. The range then extends across Siberia to the western shore of Lake Baikal, south to the Kirghiz Steppes and Altai and also through Asia Minor and the Middle East to Iran and possibly north-west Afghanistan (Fig. 56). Such a range lies between 71°N and 30°N, or the July isotherms of 50° and 75°F. *P. p. phoenicurus* breeds throughout most of this range except for the Crimea, Caucasus, Asia Minor, Iran and some other regions. In eastern Asia the redstart may be replaced by *P. auroreus* – the Daurian redstart. Redstarts winter in southern Arabia and from Ethiopia and Kenya across to west

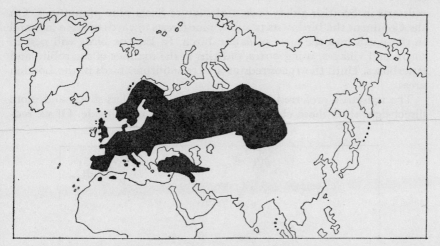

FIG. 56. Breeding distribution of the redstart.

Africa. In October 1975 an adult male of the handsome race *P. p. samamisicus*, or Ehrenburg's redstart, from south Russia to Iran, was found at Heacham in Norfolk, and another in Fife in September 1976.

Redstarts are recognizable at all ages by their orange-chestnut tails which quiver up and down in a way different from that of the other chats. The extremely handsome male has a black face and throat, orange breast and flanks, grey upper parts and white forehead. The female is paler on the back with a buffish-orange underside which separates her from the female black redstart. Female redstarts may sometimes show partial male characteristics of plumage.

The redstart is a fairly numerous summer visitor to Britain, with perhaps over 50,000 birds, and was recorded breeding in 75% of the 10 km squares in the *Atlas*. There has been somewhat of a decrease recently due perhaps to the failure of the rains in the Sahel to the south of the western Sahara Desert. It breeds only erratically in Ireland although there is no shortage of suitable habitats; I have discovered birds in sessile oak and beechwoods in Co. Wicklow. The redstart may have first evolved in pine-clad heath but today in Britain the species predominantly favours open-canopy broad-leaved woods or forest with both open space and a good shrub layer, heaths and moors with scattered trees, riverbanks with pollarded willows, well-timbered parklands, old gardens and orchards. I have found redstarts most commonly in Britain's sessile oakwoods, northern ashwoods, English beech and Scottish birch. It is less fond of English pedunculate oakwoods and was seventh in my list of relative abundance for the old Caledonian Forest in Speyside. I have also seen

redstarts in Scottish alderwoods and mature Scots pine plantations. On
the Continent the bird nests in sub-alpine forests towards the tree line and
in the north into the zone of Arctic birch. In Europe birds will nest in
towns and villages, using boxes, old tins in the manner of the robin, and
letterboxes. Until the 1920s redstarts were suburban birds in the London
area.

The redstart's preferred habitat seems to require less shade and more
direct light than those chosen by the robin and nightingale. Of six red-

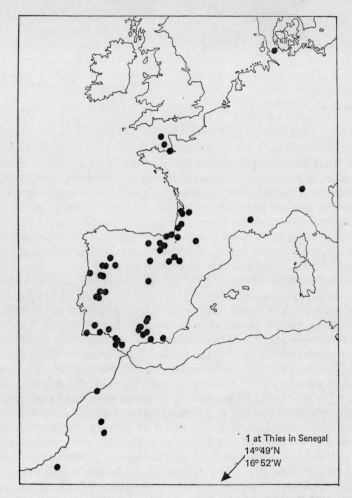

1 at Thies in Senegal
14°49′N
16° 52′W

FIG. 57. Foreign recoveries of redstarts. (Reproduced with slight amendment
from *British Birds*, Ringing Supplement 1964, by permission of Robert Spencer.)

start territories that I located in a 200-acre oakwood in Northampton-shire four were on the very edge of the wood and the other two in a wide clearing in the middle. The male's flycatching technique, his need for wide views around his song posts and his remarkable display flights seem to require plenty of space for them to be fulfilled. Active and very restless, the redstart in its flight, stance and movements bears some resemblance to the robin.

The food consists mainly of insects and in this respect is little different in kind from that of the robin and nightingale. There must be some dif-ference, however, between the diet of birds living in the Caledonian Forest, the hill country of Yorkshire or a Midland oakwood. John Buxton pointed out in his monograph *The Redstart* (1950) that the hen bird feeds chiefly on the ground whereas the cock spends much of his time catching insects in flight; 'the difference of habit may be described by likening the hen's method to that of a pipit, and the cock's to a flycatcher's, though the hen does occasionally catch flying insects'. Caterpillars, sawflies, aphids, ants, earwigs, grasshoppers, woodlice and very small snails may be taken as well as berries and fruits; chicks have been fed with white currants.

The territorial song of the redstart is a mechanical but quite pleasing run of warbled notes with rather a weak ending. Some individuals have longer and better songs, opening their performances with pure robin-like and swallow-style notes but still tending to collapse into a 'half-told tale'. The redstart is strongly imitative and Buxton noted mimicry of at least thirteen different species of bird. The alarm is a scolding 'Hwee-tuc-tue' and the call a Phylloscopid-like 'Hweet'. The male redstart employs a most striking display flight and an elaborate ritual of raised wings and fanned tail. He chooses the nest site and indicates his choice with the help of his white patch and fiery tail. In some woods there may be com-petition from other hole-nesting birds such as nuthatches, tits and pied flycatchers.

The nest is often built in a hole in a tree and the work is carried out by the hen. Some nests are high up but others may be built on the ground with an approach tunnel. Nest boxes and woodpecker holes may be utilized and in hilly country many nests are in stone walls. The nest is a somewhat untidy construction of grasses, bark strips, moss, roots and fibres and is lined with hair or feathers. There are normally six eggs laid in Britain – more in northern Europe – and these are a delicate pale blue, occasionally lightly freckled with reddish brown. Nesting begins generally in the middle of May and the cock bird falls silent for a week or so before resuming his song. The hen normally incubates the eggs for from 12 to 14 days; those records of males seen incubating may refer to females with some plumage similarities to males, and this is not so uncommon. The young are fed by both sexes and remain in the nest for about 14 or 15 days. The redstart is frequently double-brooded.

There are some eleven species of *Phoenicurus* redstart in the world. Apart from the common and black redstarts they are exclusively birds of the mountains and even these two species show some predilection for hilly country. All employ the remarkable and unique quivering up and down of the tail which is different from that of the other chats but is paralleled to some extent by the actions of the rock thrush. In Britain the redstart is only likely to be confused with the black redstart but in summer, when the former is with us, the male of this latter species is a much blacker bird and lacks the white frontal band.

THE BLACK REDSTART

The black redstart (*Phoenicurus ochruros*) is classified, like the rock and blue rock thrushes, as a palaeo-xeromontane type – an original member of the fauna of the low arid hill slopes of the southern Palaearctic Region but which also spread, after the Ice Age, on to the dry sunny slopes of the high mountains. The species is also marginally Oriental. It can be found in the boreal, temperate, Mediterranean, steppe and desert climatic zones and on mountains. The black redstart breeds over a wide area – in north-west Africa and from the Iberian Peninsula, France, England and southern Scandinavia east across Europe and into the Caucasus, Asia Minor, Iran, Afghanistan to Baluchistan, Kashmir and the Himalayan range and thence as far east as the mountains of western China and as far north as those of Mongolia (Fig. 58). Through most of Europe from the North Sea to Russia and south to the Mediterranean the breeding race is *P. o. gibraltariensis* and it also occurs in Morocco. In the British Isles it is a summer breeding species, a winter visitor and a visitor on passage. The black redstart winters chiefly in the southern parts of its breeding range, in Africa north of the Sahara to Somalia, Arabia, Iraq, southern Iran and as far as India and Burma. Small numbers winter often in coastal areas of southern and south-west England, south Wales and Ireland. I have regularly seen birds in winter on the shores of the Isles of Scilly.

In north-west Europe and the British Isles the black redstart is very much an urban breeding bird. Apart from a few isolated records firm breeding began in Britain in 1923 on the coastal cliffs of Sussex and some-what erratically elsewhere in south-eastern England. London was first colonized in 1926, and, after the wartime blitzes resulted in many untended bomb sites appearing on the scene, for the next ten years between fifteen and thirty pairs were recorded every year. It was thought that as the bomb sites were redeveloped the population of breeding black redstarts was going down but B. S. Meadows (1970) showed, after a survey of the London area, that the principal breeding sites had become concentrated along the River Thames and the River Lea, where there was heavy industry, and on more outlying industrial sites. In 1973 there was a total

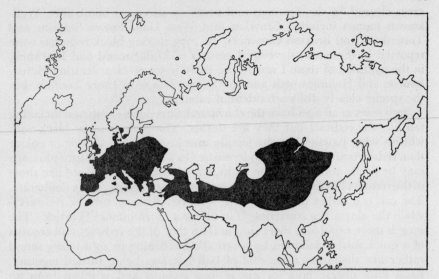

FIG. 58. Breeding distribution of the black redstart.

of 63 breeding pairs and 90 territories all south of a line from Flamborough Head to the Severn Estuary, and there was a similar total in 1974. There is a well-established breeding population now which has averaged some thirty pairs over the last thirty years and whose total has probably never been higher than one hundred pairs even in a good year. This species is afforded special protection.

Outside the British Isles the black redstart can be found nesting on warm, rocky slopes with clefts and gullies, steep rock faces from sea level to 2870 m. in the Alps and 5330 m. in the Himalayas. It will also select house roofs, large stone buildings, ruins, walls, marshalling yards and towers. I have seen birds singing on the Louvre in Paris, the Palais des Papes in Avignon, the Prado in Madrid and a large abbey in northern Spain, on the Duomo in Milan, the Temple of Apollo in Corinth and cattle sheds high in the Alps. The habitat is different from that of the redstart but the two species apparently occur together among rocks in southern Italy. Since the middle of the last century the black redstart has extended its breeding range in Europe perhaps in the wake of cultivation and town development.

In Britain birds will nest on seacliffs but industrial complexes appear to be the most favoured habitat. A survey of birds nesting near London from 1964–69 showed that some twenty pairs occurred at power stations, eighteen pairs at gasworks, eleven pairs at other industrial sites including railway sidings, timberyards and riverside warehouses, nine pairs on areas cleared for development and seven on surviving bomb sites. Well-known hauns included Croydon and West Ham Power Stations and Tottenham and Beckton Gasworks. In 1973 singing black redstarts were reported in the newly developed centres of Maidenhead and Bracknell, in the tradition of those I saw in the early 1950s on Broadcasting House, Bourne and Hollingsworth and the Senate House in Inner London, but the species clearly dislikes residential suburbs.

Both sexes at all ages have the characteristic reddish rump and flickering tail like the redstart but they are darker. The male is sooty black with whitish wing patches but the female and juveniles are deeper in colour than redstarts and have grey underparts. Cock birds in immature plumage may be fertile and breed. The flight, stance and behaviour are like those of the redstart but some individuals seem to be less restive, more deliberate. The call is a rather plaintive 'Tsip' – shorter than that of the redstart – while the alarm is a stuttering 'Tic-tic' or a more intense 'Tititick'. The song is more rapid and more simple than that of the redstart and consists of a quick warble followed by a remarkable hissing or spluttering sound rather like that from a handful of ball bearings being rattled together. Each song phrase lasts for about four seconds and is given from an exposed song post such as a rocky outcrop, wall, pediment top, tree or tall flagpole. Males sometimes sing on the wing and I have heard song regularly at night in Europe.

The Continental diet is chiefly formed from insects which may be caught on the ground or captured in the air. Beetles, flies and butterflies, spiders, centipedes and berries are widely taken. In London the food consists of beetles, ants, aphids, caterpillars, moths and butterflies, and flies, often non-biting midges. Birds have been known to take the seeds of *Compositae* and also perhaps crustaceans both freshwater and marine.

The nest is often built on a ledge or in a rock crevice or wall, especially where bricks may be missing, in a ruin or a cave. Nests in Europe are often under bridges, in holes in the ground, in outbuildings, farm sheds and under rafters. As many as three pairs have been known to share the same shed in Switzerland. The hen normally builds alone and puts together a loose mass of dry grass, moss and fibres which is then lined with a few feathers or hair. The four to six eggs are a glossy white with a bluish tinge or very slight spotting with brown. Nesting takes place from early April but the actual time is governed by the altitude. The hen incubates the eggs and in the case of nine clutches laid in Dover the period was always from 13 to 14 days and the fledging period from 16 to 17 days. Two broods are regular and three not uncommon.

The black redstart shows a close affinity in manner and actions to the redstart but it spends more time on the ground hopping and running frequently, and it is much more a bird of the open spaces. It will also hover in the air like a redstart. The black redstart has a courtship flight

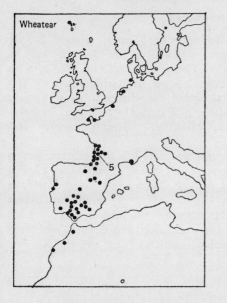

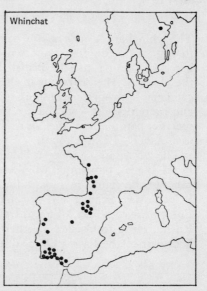

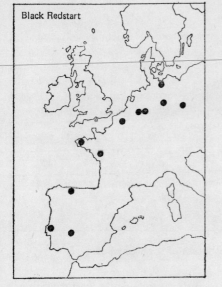

FIG. 59. Foreign recoveries of wheatear, whinchat and black redstart. (Reproduced with slight amendment from *British Birds*, Report on Bird Ringing for 1966, by permission of Robert Spencer.)

and may indulge in aerial chases and a performance described by Dr J. G. Harrison and quoted in Bannerman and Lodge (1954) as 'not unlike a male greenfinch's butterfly flight'.

252

THE WHINCHAT

The whinchat (*Saxicola rubetra*) and the stonechat (*Saxicola torquata*) belong to a genus containing some ten species but these are the only two to breed in Europe and the British Isles. The genus shows an affinity with the *Oenanthe* wheatears but it also reveals some similarities with the fly-catchers. Both species are short-tailed birds – the whinchat being slimmer and more upright – and have a number of features in common. In inter-specific competition the stonechat, however, shows 'pugnacity and dominance' (Phillips 1970).

The whinchat is a western Palaearctic bird and, like the redstart, occurs in the boreal, temperate, Mediterranean and steppe climatic zones but it can also be found in mountainous regions. Whinchats breed from the British Isles, France and northern Iberia, Italy and Sicily east across Europe through Asia Minor to Iran, north to Fenno-Scandia and northern Russia, south to Corsica, northern Italy and northern Greece, and from here east to the Rivers Ob and Yenisei, south to Altai and the Kirghiz

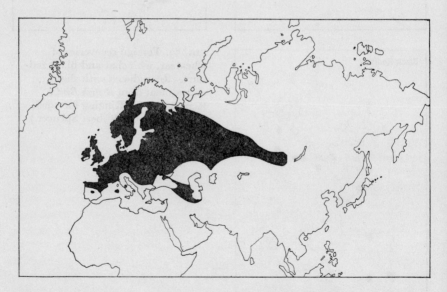

FIG. 60. Breeding distribution of the whinchat.

Steppes (Fig. 60). There has been a push eastwards in western Siberia with the growth of agriculture and the development of roads and railways. The whinchat's breeding range lies between 69°N and 34°N, or the July isotherms of 55° and 75°F. Whinchats spend the winter in tropical Africa south to Cameroun, Zaire and Rhodesia, and I have seen birds in Uganda,

Kenya and Tanzania. A few individuals have been known to winter in the British Isles.

Whinchats have declined in the British Isles in the last half-century perhaps as a result of loss of habitat, the cutting of grass verges and other more subtle factors; a slight recovery has taken place in the last twenty-five years or so with afforestation since young conifer plantations have a special attraction. In Britain today the whinchat is an uncommon upland bird of the north and west but in Ireland the greatest numbers are apparently in the central lowlands. It is uncommon or rare in many counties of south-east England, and despite a recent spread, is still absent from some Irish counties.

The ideal habitat appears to be one of tussocky grass with one-metre-high song or look-out posts. It may be on heathland, often with gorse, on swampy marshland and rough grassland up to 500 metres above sea level, uncultivated and waste ground, grassy verges along railway embankments and roadsides generally with low bushes or fences, brackeny slopes and young forestry plantations. I have seen males holding territories in Caledonian pines, in birches in Glen Feshie, in oaks in Sunart, a small mixed wood with grass on the Isle of Skye, and thicket plantations in many parts of Wales, the Borders and Scotland. In the London area whinchats have nested on rubbish dumps, gravel pits, sewage works and by reservoirs; birds also bred at Elstree Airfield in 1964 and at Hornchurch in 1969.

Whinchats, with their prominent eye-stripes and white patches at the base of the tail which are present in both sexes, are rather slight birds, hopping on the ground and bobbing and flicking their tails and wings. They are fond of perching on fence posts, strands of wire, telegraph wires, bushes and low plants and are very much birds of the open, like the stone-chat. Neither is a bird of cover. The common call is a sharp, scolding 'Tic-tic', sometimes 'Tu-tic-tic', not quite as hard or pebble-like as that of the stonechat, and occasionally running into a sequence 'Tic-tic-wee-tick-tuk'. There are also churring and clicking notes.

The song is a rather brief metallic but pleasant, sometimes sweet, warble and 'consisting of short phrases with considerable intervals between them: tee-tse . . . tee-tse-see-i . . . tee-tse-see-i' (North and Simms 1958). Both the sweet quality and intermittent nature of the delivery are suggestive of the robin and the wheatear's harsh notes are missing. Sometimes an individual may suggest stonechat, redstart or even whitethroat in its notes and phrasing. The song period lasts from April to June and the bird sings from low points of vantage, occasionally as high as seven metres, sometimes on the ground and even on the wing. The song travels quite a distance and on a very still evening in Rothiemurchus Forest I have heard a bird at a range of 83 metres. The male is reported to have a tree pipit-like display flight but I have never observed this. However, it may employ another form of display in which the bird sings to the hen with his tail fanned out, his head held back and his wings a-quiver, revealing the white patches on wings and tail. The female is paler than the male with smaller wing patches and she lacks his dark cheeks. She will solicit for food from the male with tail up and wings flicking even when she already has food in her bill for the nestlings!

The whinchat is an insectivorous bird taking beetles, dipterous flies, the larvae of many species, earwigs, as well as worms, spiders and occasionally small molluscs. Dr K. H. Voous points out that the whinchat takes 'mainly flower-visiting insects, most of them being caught on the flowers of umbelliferous plants'. The whinchat seems to take most of its insect food on plants and grasses while the stonechat feeds more on the ground. I have watched both breeding and migrant birds occasionally hawking for and hunting insects in the air.

The hen whinchat can sometimes be seen dropping into the probable nest site at the time the choice is being made but the final selection may be made by the male. The nest is built on the ground among high grasses and plants, in mowing grass, on commons, and perhaps at the foot of bushes on a hill slope. It is built by the hen with the male in attendance and is made from dry grass and moss with a lining of bents and hair. There are perhaps five or more often six eggs of a deep greenish blue, occasionally unmarked but usually freckled and dotted with pale or rusty brown. Large clutches – twelve has been described – are probably the result of a second set of eggs being laid above a previously deserted clutch. The hen incubates alone for thirteen days and the young fledge in the same amount of time. Whinchats are often double-brooded in England but not invariably so.

At the end of the last century the whinchat was regarded as a common, even abundant bird of roadsides, rough cultivated land and waste ground. There is no evidence that upland populations have altered significantly in recent years and the decreases have been primarily in the lowlands. Increases due to afforestation are most marked in south-west and northern England, Wales and south-west Scotland but the whinchat still remains an uncommon species.

THE STONECHAT

The male stonechat (*Saxicola torquata*) is a striking and for me rather appealing bird with its black head and throat, broad white half collar and narrow white stripe on the wing, white rump and rich chestnut underparts. The female and juveniles are streaked on the back, lack the white on the neck or rump, and bear some resemblance to dull-looking whinchats without eye-stripes or white at the sides of the tail. The stonechat is a Palaearctic chat but its distribution is discontinuous in the Region, and broken also in the Ethiopian Region; it is marginally Oriental. It can be found in the boreal, temperate, Mediterranean, steppe and desert climatic zones and in mountainous regions as well. The stonechat breeds throughout much of Eurasia from the British Isles, Portugal, Spain, France east across Europe, north to Denmark, southern Poland and Russia through Asia Minor, the Caucasus, Iraq and Iran. There is a big gap in northern and eastern Europe and western Asia and then the species reappears from northern and eastern Russia, the Kirghiz Steppes and Turkestan across Asia to Japan, north to the lower reaches of the Rivers Ob, Yenisei and Lena, south to Baluchistan, the Himalayas and Burma. It can be found as well in north-west Africa and much of that continent to the south of the Sahara Desert, in the Comoro Islands and the Malagasy Republic (Fig. 61). Its range thus lies approximately between the extremes of 70°N and 35°s. Western populations are rather sedentary or only partially migratory (Fig. 62) while the eastern ones migrate to north-east Africa, Arabia, India and parts of south-east Asia.

S. t. hibernans breeds in the British Isles, north-west France and the coast of Portugal. It is replaced by the Continental stonechat *S. t. rubicola* in Europe, while the paler and browner eastern race *S. t. maura* or *stejnegeri*,

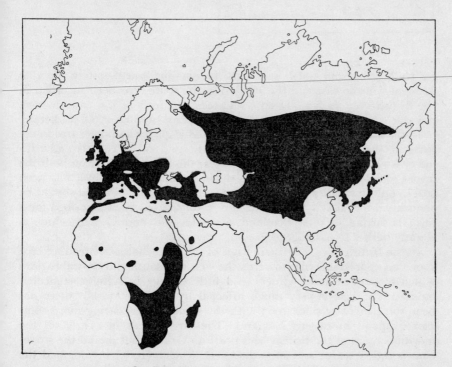

FIG. 61. Breeding distribution of the stonechat.

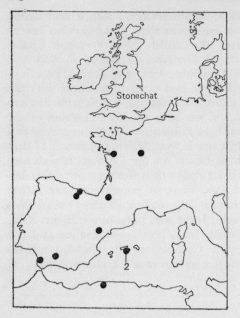

FIG. 62. Foreign recoveries of stonechats. (Reproduced from *British Birds*, Report on Bird Ringing for 1961, Ringing Supplement 1962, by permission of Robert Spencer.)

which breeds from north and east Russia and north-eastern Iran to Mongolia in the east and the Punjab in the south, has been recorded in the British Isles. In fact, by 1976 eighteen examples of the eastern race, popularly known as the Siberian stonechat, had been reported in Britain.

In the male *S. t. maura* the upper parts have longer and paler tips to the feathers, the underparts are paler and the underwing coverts and axillaries are black with narrow white edges; the female is paler on both the upper and lower parts than the British breeding race. Doubt has been cast upon the validity of *S. t. hibernans* suggesting that *hibernans* should be a synonym for *rubicola*, while a race *S. t. theresae* has been described for a form occurring in west Scotland, west Ireland and Ushant which is slightly darker in plumage.

In the British Isles the distribution of the stonechat as a breeding bird shows an appreciable bias towards the west and south and coastal regions which experience mild winters and little change in suitable stonechat habitat. The bird is very much affected by bad winters but there has been some increase since 1963 with the stonechat appearing more commonly inland in eastern England. The bird breeds in nearly all the maritime areas of the British Isles north to Orkney but inland the stonechat is rather scarce and sporadic. J. D. Magee (1965) investigated the reasons for a general decline and reached the conclusion that it was

PLATE 21. VAGRANT CHAT-LIKE THRUSHES. *Above*, a rufous bushchat at the nest. It is a rare vagrant from the Mediterranean and western Asia, intermediate between the thrushes and warblers, and regularly cocks and fans its long graduated tail. *Below*, the thrush nightingale, or sprosser, breeds from Denmark and southern Sweden east to Siberia and is a rare visitor to the east of Britain.

PLATE 22. ROBIN-LIKE CHATS. *Above left*, the male redstart shows a white forehead and black throat; *right*, the male black redstart. Redstarts are robin-like birds of woodlands or rocky terrain. *Below*, this male red-spotted blue-throat in Finland is another slim robin-like bird which is a regular passage migrant to the east coast of England.

attributable, in part, to the effects of severe weather but more importantly
to habitat change and disturbance.

In the British Isles the stonechat favours rough, coastal land with a
mixture of gorse, heather or bracken and short, often cropped grass.
E. D. H. Johnson (1971) after his study of stonechats in Jersey pointed
out that a stonechat's territory 'must contain certain essential topographical features, the most important of which is a regular scattering of
lightly constructed perches up to 1·5 metres in height'. These are desirable
since the bird feeds by dropping on to an insect from above. In one territory
on the edge of a buzzard's regular plucking station, which I studied on
the island of Rathlin, there were almost a dozen regularly used plant
stems or sprays that provided perches. In winter the dried stems of
umbellifers and other plants remain uncleared on waste, unused ground
and these are employed for exactly the same reason. On the Continent
there are similar perches in vineyards and among the maquis and in
North Africa among the palmetto scrub. Stonechats will also perch on
posts and telegraph wires using them as long-distance look-outs. Territories
also appear to include clefts or gullies, banks, rocky outcrops and undu-
lations and other topographical features to which the bird's evasive flight
is especially adapted. Inland heaths and commons are colonized but not
to the extent they once were; W. H. Hudson in 1900 described a walk
along the South Downs when pipits, linnets and stonechats were common.
One new and important habitat is that of young forestry plantations
under ten years old with a ground zone of heather. If the ground zone is
mainly one of grass then the whinchat is the more common of the two
species, just as it is in more agricultural habitats. In the Alps stonechats
occur up to 1330 metres but they also live up to 3830 metres in the
Himalayas and 5000 metres or more in parts of Tibet and western China.
Although a bird of alpine meadows and sub-alpine vegetational zones the
stonechat, according to Dr Voous, also appears in parts of Europe and Asia
on farmlands, 'notably in fields of corn and maize'. It is clear that in Asia
the stonechat makes use of a much wider range of potential habitats than
in Britain.

Many British coastal territories are continuously occupied and the
winter territories seem to be usually an extension of the breeding area
(Parrinder and Parrinder 1945; Johnson 1961). On the Ayrshire coast
J. S. Phillips (1967) found four which 'appeared to be purely winter
territories'.

The stonechat is an attractive bird as it sits bravely on one of its low
exposed perches, hovers motionless above the ground with trailing legs as
it searches for insects or indulges in courtship display, drops swiftly down
to the ground like a stone or flits away to sweep up on to an alternative
perch. Ants figure quite largely in a diet which also includes small beetles
and their larvae, *Lepidoptera* and dipterous flies and their larvae, sand-

hoppers, spiders and worms. Seeds are also sometimes taken including those of crucifers and, in Jersey, spindle tree (*Euonymus*). Young birds are fed on a variety of larvae, which are mashed up on a stone or road surface, including many caterpillars, some moths and the larvae of glow-worms. A stonechat has been seen to hover over water in a search for fish fry and I have seen a bird on allotments at Dollis Hill near my home picking mosquito larvae off the surface of a water tank used for irrigation. As a species it is rarely seen in towns.

In his long and important study of stonechats in Jersey, where he ringed nearly one thousand birds, E. D. H. Johnson (1971) found that the birds paired after the assumption of the first winter plumage and remained paired throughout the winter. Stonechats will, however, change mates in spring and autumn while some males engage in polygamous relationships with two or more females. The hen bird relies on her dull coloration for concealment but the male uses his striking plumage patterns to court the hen and defend his territory from rivals as well. In courtship display the male will hover above the female or perch in front of her and display the white patches in his plumage, raising and lowering the tail while fanning and shutting it at the same time. In the face of an intruder a male may hover in the air going up and down as if on a string and in one displace-ment activity it collapsed on the ground as if it were injured.

The usual note is a sharp, pebble-like 'Tsac-tsac' or 'Tsek-tsek' while a plaintive 'Hweet' or 'Whee' with some resemblance to the calls of the wheatear but higher in pitch may be added, producing a run 'Whee-tsac-tsac'. Excited chacking calls are used in courtship accompanying the display of the white neck, rump and wings. There are also a clicking whinchat-like note and some clear drawn-out notes used in the summer. The song is rather variable and suggests the quality of the hedgesparrow but it is higher, thinner and less rich or 'fruity' to my ear than the song of the whinchat. It is typically a simple and irregular repetition of double notes given from an elevated perch or an occasional song flight in which the male hovers some thirty or forty feet above the ground, rising and falling. Song may begin in the middle of March but I have also heard it in late February, while in Jersey it can start as early as the first week of that month.

While the male sings the female chooses the nest site which is quite often on a north-facing slope in a clump of grass, in ground litter at the bottom of a bush, or sometimes in the fork of a gorse bush up to two feet above the ground. The nest is nearly always well hidden and is usually reached by a tunnel or a vertical shaft in the grass; a convenient perch is often close by. The nest is bulky and untidy and the hen makes little effort to weave the material together; she builds in the early morning, collecting dried grass and bents and lining the rough cup with hair or feathers. Some birds have used pine needles, dead thistles, bracken, broom seed pods, heather, gorse and wool while stonechats in Jersey have gathered strips of rag, upholstery stuffing and rabbit fur. There are normally from five to six eggs, paler than those of the whinchat, with a ground colour shading from pale blue to greenish blue with chestnut or reddish-brown markings and spots, often in a definite band or zone. Laying occurs in the early morning and incubation lasts for fourteen days. While she is sitting the hen may be fed by her mate. In Jersey hatching success was 81%. Both adults help to feed the young which are in the nest for from twelve to sixteen days. After the young have left the nest they may be fed by both parents for four or five days after which the hen starts to build the nest for the second brood; the male then cares for the fledged young. Again in Jersey fledging success was 79% and breeding success 64%. There are generally two broods and in some parts of the country three are regular, so that the rather sedentary populations of Britain and the Channel Islands seem to do rather better than populations on the Continent. Fourth broods were recorded in the Channel Islands in 1956 and 1958. The breeding season can be quite a long one stretching from the middle of March to late August.

THE WHEATEAR

The wheatear (*Oenanthe oenanthe*) is the last of the seven better-known chat-like thrushes that occur in the British Isles. It is a Holarctic bird with a foot also in the Ethiopian Region as well. It can be found in the tundra, boreal, temperate, Mediterranean, steppe and desert climatic zones. The wheatear breeds throughout Europe and most of Asia (except the east and south). It can be found north to the Arctic Ocean, south to north-west Africa, Asia Minor, Iran and Afghanistan, east to Mongolia, northern Manchuria and the Chukot Range. In the New World its range includes northern Alaska, the Yukon and the Pribilof Islands, north-

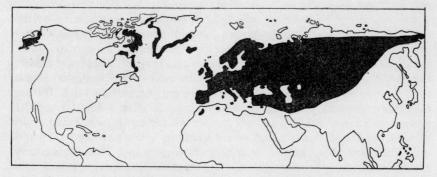

FIG. 63. Breeding distribution of the wheatear.

eastern Canada from Quebec and Labrador to Baffin Island, Ellesmere Island and Greenland (Fig. 63). The range thus lies between 78°N and 26°N, or the July isotherms of approximately 37°F and 90°F. The wheatear probably reached Greenland and Canada by way of the Faeroe Islands and Iceland after the last glacial period but it also reached America from the west across the Bering Strait. A recent extension of range in north Greenland and on Baffin Island has been attributed to the rise in mean summer temperatures in that region. There appears to be some inter-specific competition with the black-eared wheatear (*O. hispanica*) in the Mediterranean area and the isabelline wheatear (*O. isabellina*) in central Asia. The wintering area is chiefly in the African savannah country from Senegal to Nigeria, Zaire and Zambia and also east to Iran, Mesopotamia and perhaps north-west India.

O. o. oenanthe, the European wheatear, breeds throughout Eurasia (but not in Iceland, the Faeroes and Jan Mayen), and in Alaska and the Yukon.

O. o. leucorrhoa, sometimes a larger, more rufous or buff bird, the Green-land wheatear, breeds in north-eastern Canada, Greenland, Jan Mayen, Iceland and the Faeroes, but the last three island populations are some-what intermediate in form. This bird is a passage migrant to the British Isles.

The European wheatear can be found in a wide variety of more remote upland and open country habitats and less regularly in lowland regions chiefly where sheep or rabbits graze the turf on heath or chalk downland. Rocks, screes and stone walls, even roadside verges are regular breeding sites in the higher lands of the north and west in Britain. Coastal shingle and island clifftops may also be selected. Breeding may occur in Britain from sea level up to 1200 metres. Outside Britain wheatears can be found on alpine meadows, rocky tundra, high mountain screes, in cultivated areas and, according to Dr K. H. Voous, 'in central Europe frequently the ruins of towns bombed during the Second World War'. In Alaska they can be found especially on mountains and barren hill tops.

The wheatear is a bird in which both sexes have conspicuous white rumps and sides to their tails. In breeding plumage the male has a blue-grey back, broad white eye-stripe, black ear patches and wings and buffish underparts. In autumn the bird is browner and more resembles the female but the browns and buffs of the autumn plumages vary, I find, very much with the quality of the light. Wheatears are dapper, restless birds, flitting over open ground, perching on low eminences after a flight near the ground and in east Africa I have seen them sitting on the whitening skulls of wildebeest and Grant's and other gazelles. They bow and bob and wave their fanned-out tails on their lowly vantage points. They remain very much terrestrial birds and, although low perches are favoured, I have seen European and Greenland wheatears perch in bushes and trees, while in the far north of Europe the former have been known to perch quite frequently on the tops of tall pine trees.

The summer visiting wheatear has shown a marked decrease as a breeding species in England south of Yorkshire and Lancashire. This decline has been attributed to the growth of cultivation, the afforestation of the more marginal land which wheatears like, and the alterations to and deterioration of the habitat resulting from the disappearance of the rabbit. A glance at the *Atlas* map shows that the bird's present distribution is largely concentrated in the west and north of the British Isles. There has also been a decrease in inland areas in Ireland. As a rule male wheatears arrive before the females and establish territories by singing and a vigorous defence of the area. On Skokholm Peter Conder (1956) found that wheatear territories ranged in size from 1·2 to 8·1 acres, with an average of 4·6, but ten pairs per square kilometre seem to be the average density elsewhere. Territories tend to be larger in flat, open country than in broken terrain where rocks, ridges and banks afford clear visual limits to territories. European wheatears may behave territorially in their winter quarters (Smith 1971).

The species is largely insectivorous taking many kinds of beetle and dipterous fly, humblebees, ants, moths and their larvae, grasshoppers, small land snails, centipedes and spiders. Vegetable food does not appear to have been regularly recorded apart from a few small seeds of grasses and other plants. In Alaska a European wheatear was reported as taking unidentified bulblets which formed 96% of its food content, while others fed on grass seeds and those of *Saxifraga*.

The ordinary note of the wheatear is a deep harsh 'Chak-chak', alternating with a high 'Wheet' as in 'Chak-wheet' and 'Wheet-chak-chak'. The song is generally superior to those of the other chats with even a suggestion of skylark or warbler. It contains both modulated warbles and harsh chatters and is pleasing and spasmodic with short phrases and intervals. Much of it consists of a whitethroat-like warbling in short snatches with harsh chattering discords. It may be delivered from stones, clods, fences or walls and in a little fluttering song flight, which Edmund Selous likened to 'a little lyric frenzy', with the bird rising and gliding down again with spread tail.

Wheatears can often be seen hovering. Various accounts have suggested that it is simply to spy out food, others that it forms a dancing display since its tempo is similar to that of Khachaturian's Sabre Dance with the bird jerking itself sideways and back as 'if caught on a piece of cotton' (Pettit and Butt 1950). A kestrel-type of hovering also takes place from three to five metres above the ground and exceptionally up to ten metres without the bird changing its position. The bird could be looking for food or potential or real predators, or indulging in sexual display or just 'exuberance, or just doing it for no apparent reason.' With his extensive knowledge of the behaviour of the wheatear Peter Conder (1954) believes that 'hovering was really used for observing' and that it is an incidental part of any sexual or courtship display.

Territories are important to wheatears in establishing pairs, maintaining them and setting up a breeding area and ensuring an adequate supply of food. The nest is usually in a dark place in rocky cracks, among stones, in scree slopes, and in many kinds of natural and artificial hole. On downland rabbit holes are frequently used; in Scotland and the islands I have seen nests in stone walls and stacks of peat. On the Continent old bee-eater holes are sometimes commandeered. Drain pipes, tins, kettles and even exploded shell cases may be taken over, and on the shingle at Dungeness I have seen nests under iron sheets and in specially provided ammunition boxes sunk in the gravel.

The female wheatear makes the final choice as to the site. Both birds will co-operate in nest-building with the female doing most of the work. The nest itself is rather loosely built of grasses or moss and is lined with grass, hair, feathers, bits of wool or vegetable down. There are usually six eggs in a European clutch, sometimes five and occasionally seven. They are a uniform, delicate pale glossy blue and only rarely showing some red-brown specklings or spots. Incubation, which lasts about fourteen days, is chiefly carried out by the hen. In the British Isles eggs can be found from mid- or late April or early May but principally in the latter month. In Germany the period is later – in late May and June – and in Norway late June. The young are fed by both parents and leave the nest when they are about fifteen days old. Lowland birds generally have two broods but birds breeding in the north of Britain or high up on mountains normally have only one.

Ecology and Feeding Behaviour

In this middle part of the chapter I propose to discuss some of the broader ecological and behavioural aspects of the seven species of chat-like thrush whose range and life histories I have just reviewed.

It is interesting to note that the wheatear enjoys the widest distribution of the seven throughout the world, followed by the stonechat; these two species, with the black redstart, also occur in more climatic zones than do the other four. Robin and nightingale are restricted to the fewest number of zones. In the British Isles the wheatear is a bird of uplands and coastal shingle and the black redstart of rocks, cliffs, towns and industrial sites. The stonechat favours rough moorland or coasts with gorse or heather while the whinchat, although sharing some habitats with the stonechat, tends to select tussocky marginal grassland. Robin, nightingale and redstart are birds of woodland; the first two species need thick undergrowth and the third space and light among the trees.

Table 20. Ecology and Breeding of Britain's Chat-like Thrushes

Species	Climatic zone	Feeding behaviour	Status	Habitat demands	Breeding season	Height of nest (feet)	Incubation period (days)	Fledging period (days)	Number of broods
ROBIN	BMT	Terrestrial, arboreal (Autumn)	REIPW	Thick undergrowth and cover	Late March–early July	0–10	13 Hen only	12–13	2–3
NIGHTINGALE	MTS	Terrestrial, arboreal	E	Thick undergrowth and cover	From early May	0–5	13–14 Hen only	11–12	1
REDSTART	BMST	Arboreal, aerial	EP	Trees, space and light	Mid-May to late June	3–30	12–14 Hen chiefly	14–15	2
BLACK REDSTART	BDMST	Terrestrial, aerial	REPW	Rocks, cliffs, towns, industrial sites	From early April	3–30	13–14 Hen only	16–17	2–3
WHINCHAT	BMST	Vegetal	EP	Tussocky grassland with low perches	From mid or late May	0–2	13 Hen only	13	1–2
STONECHAT	BDMST	Terrestrial	RE	Moorland, coast with heather, gorse and some grass	From late March or April to late July	0–2	14 Hen chiefly	12–16	2–3
WHEATEAR	BDMSTTu	Terrestrial	EP	Uplands, moors, coastal shingle	From April/May to early July	0	14 Hen chiefly	15	1–2

Climatic Zone Key: B = Boreal
D = Desert
M = Mediterranean
S = Steppe
T = Temperate
Tu = Tundra

Status Key: R = Resident
E = Emigrant
I = Immigrant
P = Passage migrant
W = Winter visitor

The essentially terrestrial feeders are the wheatear and stonechat, while other partially terrestrial feeders like the black redstart will feed on flying insects and both the robin and nightingale will take autumn fruits and berries. The whinchat is a vegetal feeder taking insects from plants and flower-heads while the redstart is both an arboreal and aerial feeder. The seven species show general affinities in territorial activity and songs, although the nightingale and robin reveal the finest and most elaborate utterances and the stonechat the weakest. There are also resemblances in their diets, loose nest constructions and choice of materials and in their general breeding biology – in their eggs, incubation behaviour and fledging periods.

Moult

The moult of the robin appears to last about fifty days with the mean date of onset in the first half of July (Snow 1969). Stonechats seem to have a moulting period of about the same length, starting in the second half of July. Wheatears observed on Fair Isle completed their moult over seven to eight weeks (Williamson 1957) beginning in early July. Whinchats may show a similar pattern to that of the wheatear. There are not many moult records for the redstart but those that exist suggest a duration of about forty days beginning in early July. With the black redstart the evidence available indicates that the moult is later than that of the common redstart. The migration period in autumn corresponds in most species with the time of ending of the moult which indicates perhaps that the adults (or amongst partial migrants, the migrating birds) depart soon after the moult is over. There is a general tendency in the thrushes and chats and some other species for long-distance migrants, under some pressure to start their journeys, to moult more quickly than resident species.

The Migrations of the British Chat-like Thrushes

Among the chat-like thrushes are individual species whose status in the British Isles can vary enormously. The nightingale is a migrant breeder, the redstart, wheatear and whinchat migrant breeders and birds of passage, the stonechat a resident and migrant breeder and a scarce visitor, while the robin and black redstart occur as resident and migrant breeders, winter visitors and passage migrants.

The breeding population of the robin is largely resident but a proportion of the birds from south-east England, including many females, moves to the Continent, travelling south-east to northern France and then south-south-west to south-western France and Iberia. Scottish robins either fly a long way south inside Britain or take shorter journeys around the mountain ranges. Some robins in southern England may also cross the country from west to east or vice versa. It is possible too that some birds from the north of Britain cross over to Ireland for the winter. Some Continental robins winter in their homelands but others fly to Iran, Egypt and parts of North Africa. From September to November and March to May winter visitors and passage migrants occur on the east and south coasts of Britain and periodic and sometimes quite large falls of birds occur. For example, in October 1951 546 were trapped at Spurn, part perhaps of a simultaneous immigration on a front of some 400 km; this fall was almost certainly initiated by an anticyclone which moved across Russia and then turned towards Scandinavia. The resulting easterly winds carried the birds to Britain. In October 1976 in anticyclonic weather with a light easterly wind, which brought thousands of redwings to a small valley at Cruden Bay in Aberdeenshire, I counted more than a hundred robins much involved in aggressive behaviour towards each other. This is a phenomenon one also sees among densely packed migrant wheatears. A frontal system moving north produced another large fall along the North Sea coast on 14 and 15 October 1966. The robin is essentially a night migrant stopping to feed and rest but fit, healthy birds seem to dominate the weaker ones, forcing them to move out of hospitable areas (Szuch-Olech 1965). In spring migrating robins are in a greater hurry, as one might expect, than during the autumn passage.

Outside its summer breeding range the nightingale is a very scarce vagrant indeed. Summer residents generally arrive in England from tropical Africa in the second week of April but birds may continue to come until the third week of May. The males arrive before the females. The movement across Africa seems to be on a broad front crossing the Sahara on both journeys. Less is known about the autumn movements but birds begin to vacate their breeding grounds in late July and actual departure may go on until mid-September.

The redstart winters in Africa and Arabia and the passage in Britain generally lasts from late March to the middle of June with return occurring between July and early November. The migration can best be witnessed on the east and south coasts with the arrival of British birds in April and occasional heavy falls of Continental birds in August and September. The main movement across Europe in spring is to the north-east with a main thrust through France, Holland and north-west Germany to western Scandinavia. The British Isles 'receive only the wash of the main movement, thrown off along its flank' (Southern 1939). The migration of the redstart over Europe lasts from about 15 March in the Pyrenees, southern Italy and north-east Africa to 15 May at the Arctic Circle. In 61 days 3200 km are covered in the west and 4000 in the east, both spring and migrants spreading fast across the Russian steppes. The average rate of spread varies from 53 km per day in the west to 66 in the east. Males tend to precede the females by from 6 to 17 days and at Fair Isle on 7 May there were 200 males to only one female; later in the month the proportion is more evenly balanced. Birds are scarcer on the west coast of Britain and in Ireland. Redstarts ringed in Germany, Denmark and Sweden have been recovered in Britain. A remarkable fall of migrants occurred in East Anglia on 3 September 1965 (Davis 1966) when a high pressure area was centred over Scandinavia. Numbers estimated at Walberswick were 15,000, at Minsmere 7000 and at Southwold 1000. At Cromer in 1965 redstarts were seen flying around the street lights. This remarkable immigration of redstarts also involved thousands of wheatears and hundreds of whinchats. Redstarts quite often appear in towns on migration and I see odd birds in autumn at Dollis Hill. In autumn all the redstart populations including those in the south and east of Europe seem to fly southwest, unlike the black redstarts which appear to have a different pattern.

The majority of black redstarts in Europe migrate along westerly routes to France, Spain and Africa in a similar manner to that of the redstart but recoveries of ringed birds suggest that a smaller group of birds from central Europe migrates south-east. In Britain some black redstarts may overwinter – I have seen birds in December in the south-west of England and on the Isles of Scilly, but most are migrant breeders from April to September. As a bird of passage the black redstart occurs most regularly on the east and south coasts of Britain north to Yorkshire. North of that and on the west coast the bird is less frequent. At Fair Isle the bird was described as annual in spring and occurring almost every year in the autumn. The spring passage lies between March and May and the autumn between late August and November. In Scotland passage birds may be seen on islands besides the Fair Isle and in Ireland on the south and east coasts.

Early arrivals of whinchats from tropical Africa may take place in March but most arrive in April and remain until September. A few birds have even been known to winter. In some years the main weight of the arrivals falls on the south-east coast of England but at other times it may spread along the whole of the south coast. There are also passage migrants moving through from April to May and even June, and from mid-July to early October. The most spectacular movements are those reported on the south and east coasts of Britain in August and September. Whinchats often occur as the result of autumn wind-drift all along the east coast. In early September 1956 there were 500 on Fair Isle and 1500 at Walberswick in Suffolk in early September 1965. Migrants can often be seen inland and in the London area are more numerous in autumn than in spring. I see occasional birds on suburban allotments, railway banks, sewage farms and reservoir slopes. Whinchats ringed in Sweden and on Heligoland have been recovered in Britain while a British-ringed bird was taken in Sweden. Other recoveries of British-ringed birds in France, Spain, Portugal and Algeria indicate the route taken to the African continent.

The spring migration of stonechats through Jersey is a rare event but some birds do occur and betray their origin by their hunger, restlessness and an especially advanced state of plumage (Johnson 1971). The spring passage of birds is also exceptional along the western seaboard of France. That the Iberian Peninsula is the chief wintering quarters of western European stonechats was demonstrated in 1965 by Van Hecke. The western populations of the stonechat, unlike the eastern, are mainly resident and only partially migratory. Some British-ringed stonechats may spend the winter abroad from France and Belgium south to Spain and North Africa. In inland districts the bird may be only a summer resident moving for the winter to the coast or to the Continent. There is some evidence of passage movements by northern and island birds along the west and east coasts of Britain. The bird is rare on passage in towns but it may occur on allotments, waste ground, and similar habitats in suburbia. As we have seen already, the Siberian stonechat is a scarce vagrant, while Continental stonechats move on to the Mediterranean, even as far as Morocco, Algeria and Tunisia, but do not seem to enter the British Isles.

The last of our group of seven small thrushes is a spectacular migrant – the wheatear. It breeds throughout most of Eurasia as well as Alaska and the Yukon, while the Greenland wheatear breeds in Canada, Greenland and some of the more northern isles. Nearly all populations, including the one that colonized Alaska, migrate towards winter quarters in Africa. The birds from Canada and Greenland strike out across the Atlantic on a prodigious journey to follow the coast of western Europe across to tropical Africa, returning in spring to follow a long and demanding northern route where ice and snow persist and food is in short supply. In Eurasia the autumn journey seems to be south-westerly with birds from Alaska making their way across eastern and southern Asia. British summer residents arrive from the second week of March to the middle of April. The waves of wheatears move up at a rate perhaps of 960 km in five days, sometimes aided by an area of high pressure, light winds and rising temperatures. Birds often arrive at the south-western Bird Observatories before they reach the most southerly on the east coast. Wheatears following the Atlantic seaboard seem to move up before those that have embarked on a more trans-continental route. Passage migration lasts from March to June and wheatears from Greenland and Iceland regularly pass through the British Isles especially in the coastal regions of the north and west. At Fair Isle wheatears arrive to breed in March and early April while Greenland or Iceland birds normally first appear in the third week of April with the main passage in early May, lasting in some years to the middle of June. Summer residents begin to move south in July with overland passage continuing until late October. A wheatear ringed in Wales was recovered 43 hours later 936 km away in France.

Continental birds sometimes arrive in considerable numbers on the east coast of Britain, e.g. 8000 at Walberswick and 4000 at Minsmere in September 1965. Greenland wheatears 'often travel round depressions to the British Isles' (Williamson 1965). Autumn falls of wheatears have occurred in Inner London in daylight although the species also travels at night. The range of variation in the size, plumage and perching idiosyncracies among wheatears makes the identification of Greenland birds somewhat difficult. However, the more distant the origin of wheatears the bigger and heavier they are and the Greenland race may be half as big again as wheatears breeding in Britain. I have seen long-winged, long-tailed birds of the Greenland race in a number of places in Britain, from Dungeness to Shetland and including birds at Midland reservoirs and on farmland and one that I watched in Kensington Gardens in London on 2 May 1951. Birds ringed in Greenland and Iceland have been recovered in Britain. Wheatears marked in Britain have been found again in Holland, the Faeroe Islands, France, Spain, Portugal and north-west Africa (Fig. 59). Certain Greenland birds ringed on Fair Isle have been recovered in France and Spain. The selection process during the migration period may well favour members of this race which, as we have seen, has to undergo a most demanding crossing of both sea and uninviting terrain.

Breeding Seasons

The robin has been known to nest in every month of the year but the main weight of its breeding effort falls between late March and early July with two, sometimes three broods. The nightingale's breeding season starts in early or mid-May and the species is single-brooded. Redstarts breed from early or mid-May as well and go on until late June and often raise two broods. Altitude can affect the nesting time of the black redstart but in Britain breeding often starts in early April and two broods are frequent and three not uncommon. The whinchat's breeding season begins in the middle of May with most birds nesting from late May onwards; two broods may be reared. Stonechats start breeding in late March or early April and continue until July; two broods are normal and three not unknown. The breeding season for the wheatear lasts from mid-April or early May into July and the species is often double-brooded.

Vagrants and Passage Migrants

There are ten species of chat-like thrush which have occurred in the British Isles, half of these being, in fact, different species of *Oenanthe* wheatear. Over the years the journal *British Birds* has listed their occurrences and sometimes described their natural history, so I do not intend to provide exhaustive accounts of them here. However, I shall present a brief review of each of the ten species.

The first is the **rufous bush robin** or **bush chat** (*Cercotrichas galactotes*), which is intermediate in form between the thrushes and warblers with a long rufous, black-tipped tail which is often cocked, jerked and fanned. The western race has the whole of the upper parts rufous in colour but the eastern bird *C. g. syriacus* is grey-brown on the back and with a rufous rump and tail. The songs that I have heard in Spain and the Balkans are broken and rather lark-like, sometimes loud, sometimes quiet. The call is a sharp 'Tec-tec'. The bush robin feeds in scrub, vineyards, olive groves and, as I have found in Spain, regularly in prickly pears. It also can be seen on the ground, standing rather upright and high on its pinkish grey legs. It has a very attractive butterfly-like display flight. The species is Palaearctic, Ethiopian and marginally Oriental. Rufous bush robins breed in Iberia, Africa south to the borders of Senegal, Nigeria, Chad, Sudan, Ethiopia and Somalia and east from the Balkans and Asia Minor to the Caucasus, Iraq, Iran, Pakistan and Kazakhstan. The species spends the winter in the southern part of its range and in east Africa south to Kenya and Uganda. Up to 1972 there were eight records in south coast counties of Ireland and England – Cork (two), Wexford, Devon (three), Sussex and Kent, and two on the English east coast. Autumn records from September to October are typical and there was only one spring record – that in Cork in April 1968.

The **thrush nightingale** (*Luscinia luscinia*), or sprosser as it is sometimes called, can only be separated from the nightingale at close quarters when it can be seen to be darker brown in colour with a mottled breast and white centre to the throat and a less chestnut tail and rump. The song is more powerful than the nightingale's with pure bell-like notes, a regular trisyllabic phrase 'Chiddy-ock' (Orr 1976), but it lacks the crescendos of the former bird. The calls are a sharper, higher 'Wheet' or 'Whit', a loud 'Tack', and a low croak often accompanied by jerking of the tail. Both nightingales form a western Palaearctic species group each distinct in the biological sense and probably separated during the last glacial period. There is no record of hybridization in the wild. The thrush nightingale breeds in the boreal, temperate and steppe climatic zones from Finland, Sweden, Denmark and Germany through Poland east to south-central Siberia. After 1940 the species extended its breeding range north in Scandinavia. The thrush nightingale is a summer visitor to damp forests and thickets and winters in tropical east Africa in dense scrub. It is a rare vagrant to Britain where, up to the end of 1975, there were 28 records with 24 in spring and 4 in the autumn. Before 1965 there were only three accepted records and the recent increase could be either a real one or just a reflection of an increase in observers and efficient trapping techniques. Most records have occurred at Fair Isle and all have been in the east of Britain, except for the September 1976 record on Bardsey, Gwynedd.

Our third species in this group is the **bluethroat** (*Luscinia svecica*) and it is unique in that besides being a scarce migrant to Britain it apparently bred in Scotland in 1968 when a female was seen and a nest found in the Moray Basin in Inverness-shire (*British Birds* 61:524–5). The blue-throat is a Palaearctic and marginally Nearctic species, breeding across Eurasia from Scandinavia to the Chukotski Peninsula and western Alaska, south to central Spain where I have seen the bird in the Sierra de Guadarrama, France, Germany, Yugoslavia, southern Russia, the Caucasus, Kashmir, China, Mongolia and the Sea of Okhotsk. On its southern range there are a number of isolated breeding places due perhaps to the effects of the Ice Age. The bluethroat winters in the region of the Mediterranean, North Africa south to Nigeria and the Sudan, the Middle East, India and south-east Asia. *L. s. svecica* breeds across the northern part of the range north of 60°N from Fenno-Scandia to Alaska; it is known as the red-spotted bluethroat. *L. s. cyanecula* – the white-spotted form – nests throughout the European range east to western Russia but not in Fenno-Scandia. The bluethroat is a shy bird which breeds in swampy woods, more marshy than those of the thrush nightingale, and in sub-alpine scrub. The chief calls are a nightingale-like 'Hweet' or 'Seep', a hard 'Chat-chat' and a croaking 'Turrc-turrc'. The song is rich, loud, and sweet with liquid trilling phrases, hissing sounds and bell-like notes. In the Arctic it dominates the northern tundras, swamps and scrub. The bluethroat is a robin-like bird but it is more upright in its bearing and has a jaunty, flirting black and chestnut tail and a pale eye-stripe. Between 1958 and 1967 at least 600 bluethroats were recorded in Britain and Ireland with *L. s. svecica* predominating. Four-fifths of the records were in autumn and one-fifth in spring (Sharrock 1976). In autumn birds occur regularly in small numbers along the east coast from Kent to Shetland with September the peak month but in spring bluethroats are vagrants to Britain. In Norfolk I have found the bluethroat a great skulker, hiding away in suaeda bushes until flushed perhaps by young and over-enthusiastic birdwatchers.

Larger than the bluethroat and with longer legs is the **Siberian ruby-throat** (*Luscinia calliope*); this is a species in which the male has a bright red throat and white stripes above and below the eye. Its actions are very bluethroat-like. This is a discontinuously eastern Palaearctic bird to be found in the boreal climatic zone and mountain areas. It is a bird of the taiga, breeding in dank, dark coniferous forests from the Urals east to Kamchatka, Sakhalin and Hokkaido with an isolated population in north-western China. A bird was present on Fair Isle from 9–11 October 1975. This is the only record and at the time of writing is under scrutiny before admission to the British list. There are old records for France and Italy. The closely related Himalayan rubythroat (*L. pectoralis*) is imported as a cagebird and a Siberian blue robin (*L. cyane*) was trapped on Sark on 27 October 1975. A second *L. calliope* was reported in Lincolnshire in 1977.

Another remarkably attractive bird is the **red-flanked bluetail** (*Tarsiger cyanurus*) in which the male looks like a bright blue redstart with chestnut flanks and a blue tail. The female is olive-brown with reddish flanks and blue only on the tail. This bird resembles to some extent the robin and redstart, having the shape of the former and the flight and stance on the ground of the latter. It also behaves to some extent like a tit, a flycatcher and a warbler – a truly intriguing bird! The breeding range is wide, stretching across the taiga of Siberia, the mountain forests of Mongolia, Kamchatka, Sakhalin, the northern islands of Japan and a few isolated spots in the coniferous mountain forests of central Asia. Birds have moved westwards into Finland in recent years. Northern populations move south to south-east Asia from Assam to China and Taiwan for the winter; some populations are sedentary, but the species is chiefly migratory. The calls are a sharp, high 'Tic-tic' and a guttural 'Kerr'. The song is loud and usually from a treetop – 'Tetee-teeleeee-tetete'. By 1976 7 had been reported in Great Britain – Lincoln (Sept. 1903), Shetland (Oct. 1947), Kent (Oct. 1956), Northumberland (Oct. 1960), Shetland (June 1971) Isle of May, Fife (Oct. 1975), Fifeness, Fife (Oct. 1976).

The last part of this chapter will be devoted to the five species of wheatear which complete the list of chat-like vagrants to Britain. The first of these is the **isabelline wheatear** (*Oenanthe isabellina*) – a pale, sandy, rather long-legged, upright and heavy-headed wheatear in which the sexes are alike and both resemble a large pale female Greenland wheatear without the dark ear coverts. The calls are a chirp and an unchat-like loud whistle. It is a bird of the arid eastern Palaearctic and Oriental Regions, breeding from southern Greece, south-east Russia, Asia Minor, the Middle East and Arabia across central Asia to Lake Baikal, Manchuria, Mongolia, the Himalayas and perhaps north-west India. The isabelline wheatear winters in the southern parts of the range and south to India, Iran and Iraq, Arabia and Africa south to Zaire and Mali; I have seen it on arid land in Kenya in late December. The first record in Britain was of a bird at Allonby in Cumberland on 11 November 1887. A second record of a bird on St Mary's in the Isles of Scilly on 1 November 1971 is still being scrutinized.

The **desert wheatear** (*Oenanthe deserti*) has an almost completely black tail. The male bears some resemblance to the black-throated form of the black-eared wheatear (*Oenanthe hispanica*) but it carries more white on the wings and with the black on the wings also joining the black on the throat. This is a Palaearctic and marginally Ethiopian species breeding across North Africa, the Middle East and Asia from the Caspian to Mongolia. *O. d. homochroa* nests in North Africa west of the River Nile, *O. d. deserti* from Egypt east of the Nile through Arabia and the Middle East, and *O. d. atrogularis* from the southern parts of the Caucasus to Mongolia and Gobi. The desert wheatear is a restless little bird, rather silent, but it is said to have a plaintive hoarse whistle. A December bird in Co. Durham and a July bird in Essex both produced a subdued harsh 'Tchuk'. By 1972 there were eighteen records in eastern Britain from Hampshire to Shetland and single records in Cornwall and Clackmannan. Most of the records were in October and November. All three races have been recognized in Britain but in some cases the actual race was not determined. The desert wheatear is both sedentary and migratory with populations from Asia moving south to India and north-east Africa.

The **black-eared wheatear** (*Oenanthe hispanica*) is slightly smaller and more slender than the wheatear and is a bird of the south-western Palaearctic. *O. h. hispanica* breeds in north-west Africa, Iberia, southern France, Italy (except the south), and Yugoslavia. The male is a striking creamy buff colour with black cheeks, wings and centre to the tail; it is a bird I have observed in Provence, in northern and central Spain and especially along the Portuguese frontier. *O. h. melanoleuca* breeds from southern Italy, southern Yugoslavia and the Balkans east to Iran. The males are dimorphic with black marks through the eye and whitish throats, or with the whole throat black. The present species is 'the ecological substitute of the Wheatear in the Mediterranean lowlands, the rocky mountain areas being inhabited by the Wheatear' (Voous 1960). The black-eared wheatear is a bird of rocky lowlands and dry stony plains, limestone hills, screes and heathlands. It is a summer visitor wintering on the African savannahs and Sahara south from Senegal to Ethiopia. The bird has a rasping alarm and a plaintive whistle. By 1975 there were 31 records of this wheatear species in Britain and Ireland including birds of both races. Overshooting males are not infrequent with three in 1975 – a repeat of three occurrences in the previous year. The records are chiefly in April and May and from late August to early October with birds showing a westerly bias in their distribution. H. C. Holme and I saw a male of the black-throated form in Regent's Park in Inner London on 23 April 1951.

The ecological replacement of the black-eared wheatear to the east is the **pied wheatear** (*Oenanthe pleschanka*) and the two species form a Palaearctic species group whose members were probably separated only recently. The black back of the male distinguishes the pied wheatear from the black-throated phase of the eastern black-eared wheatear (*O. h. melanoleuca*). It also needs to be separated from the mourning wheatear or chat (*O. lugens*), the red-rumped wheatear (*O. moesta*) and the hooded wheatear (*O. monacha*) – all black-throated and black-backed Palaearctic birds of North Africa and the Middle East. Females are difficult to identify (Ash and Rooke 1956). The song resembles that of the black-eared wheatear and the call is a harsh wheatear-like 'Zack-zack'. The pied wheatear breeds from Cyprus, Bulgaria, Rumania and southern Russia eastwards across southern Siberia, central Asia, Iran and Afghanistan as far as the

PLATE 23. CHATS. *Above left*, the male stonechat has a black head and white neck patch; *right*, the female stonechat is duller and streaked on the head. *Below left*, both sexes of whinchat have white eye-stripes but this male shows the dark cheek; *right*, female whinchat. Whinchats are less plump and upright than stonechats.

PLATE 24. WHEATEARS. *Above left*, the male wheatear can be distinguished from all other wheatears by its head pattern; *right*, the browner female wheatear. *Centre left*, a male black-eared wheatear – a rare vagrant to Britain; *right*, the desert wheatear is another rare visitor and breeds from North Africa across to Mongolia. *Below right*, the black wheatear is a large wheatear from the western Mediterranean with a handful of records for Britain.

Himalayas, Lake Baikal, Mongolia and China. The wintering quarters are in Arabia, north-east and east Africa south to Tanzania. It is a bird of open stony country, bushy hillsides and some cultivated areas. There are four British records all in late autumn at the time of writing: Fife (19 October 1909), Orkney (1 November 1916), Dorset (17-19 October 1954) and Skokholm (27 October 1968).

The last of the wheatears on the British and Irish list is the **black wheatear** (*Oenanthe leucura*). It is a large thrush-like wheatear – all black in the male and brownish-black in the female – with a white rump and outer tail feathers. This is a Palaearctic species of the steppe and Mediterranean climatic zones. It breeds in Iberia, south-eastern France, north-west Italy, and in north-west Africa from Rio de Oro and Morocco east to Libya with this latter race sometimes separated as *O. l. syenitica*. It is a bird of cliffs and ravines and in Spain I found it to be a bird of bare rock slopes at quite high altitudes. The call is 'Pee' or 'Pee-pee-pee'. There are five British and Irish records mainly from August to October: Shetland (September 1912 and October 1953), Cheshire (August 1943), Kent (October 1954) and Donegal (June 1964).

PARASITES

ECTOPARASITES, which live on the exterior of a bird's body in the plumage, occur very widely in passerines, and the true thrushes have no special immunity from them. They can be conveniently divided into bird-keds or louse flies (*Hippoboscidae*), fleas (*Siphonaptera*) and chewing lice (*Mallophaga*) among the insects, and ticks and feather mites among the arachnids. There are also nest parasites. Anyone who has handled black-birds and other thrushes will be aware of the way in which some mallophaga, particularly of the genus *Menacanthus*, are ready to desert the host's body because of the disturbance. A bird may be parasitized by several species of mallophaga each adapted to different micro-environments on the body of the host. Each order of birds may hold parasites of a genus or even genera peculiar to it and they can provide useful evidence of the relationships between birds.

Mallophaga feed on feathers, blood and tissue fluids and are very food specific. For example, *Philopterus turdi* establishes itself on the nape, back of the neck and sometimes the throat of blackbirds and will breed only on these feathers. Up to 40% of blackbirds may carry this louse. Temperature is also important to this species of louse which thrives on blackbird feathers at 37·5°C and favours a humidity of about 80% (Ash 1960). Blackbirds can also carry two species of *Brüelia* (*B. merulensis* and *B. marginata*) and nearly 40% of birds are infected with the first. There are also species of *Myrsidea*, and *Ricinus* besides *Menacanthus* which can be found on black-birds. The *Brüelia* species on the *Turdidae* seem to favour the breast, lower back and rump feathers with occasional resting places among the tail and secondary feathers. *Ricinus* occurs on the lower breast and *Menacanthus* on the throat. Mallophaga are, in fact, regular on all the species of thrush. It is possible that the various stages of development in the life cycle of mallophaga require somewhat different conditions which may be the explanation of why it is so difficult to breed them artificially. A healthy bird usually keeps its mallophaga burden in check by preening but the lice are themselves rejected as food. The rate of infestation by mallophaga seems to be higher on male rather than female birds but no explanation has been advanced to account for this difference.

Other external parasites include mites, ticks and fleas. Nestling black-birds often carry a high population of the flea *Dasypsyllus gallinulae*. Dipterous flies of the genus *Protocalliphora* lay their eggs in birds' nests and the emergent larvae become ectoparasites on the nestling birds, feeding on their blood. Flies of one species, *Protocalliphora azurea*, have been bred successfully from the nests of blackbirds and song thrushes (Owen and Ash 1955), but hole-nesting species seem to be more adversely affected than those using open sites. In Britain another fly, *Neottiophillum praeustum*, has similar habits to *Protocalliphora* but it seems to be more local in its distribution. It has been found in the nests of both song thrushes and blackbirds and from the nest of a mistle thrush in Cumbria. The presence of these blood-sucking larvae is likely to have an effect on the weights of nestling thrushes.

With most internal parasites, known as endoparasites, there is no direct transmission of infection between members of the host species as occurs in the infections which I described in chapter 12. Generally the parasite has to spend some time developing outside the bird host before the parasite can infect another; inside the host it reveals a number of recognizable stages of development. It is very much the bird's habitat and the nature of its food which affect the incidence of various endoparasites. Heavy infestations of endoparasites can bring about a severe loss of condition and even death. There is a subtle balance between the condition of the host and the number of parasites and the factors which maintain this equilibrium are not fully understood. Should a bird already burdened by many endoparasites be attacked by some other disease or be faced with an acute shortage of food, then its chances of survival may be greatly reduced.

The main categories of endoparasite are the unicellular *Protozoa*, *Nematoda* (round worms), *Cestoda* (tapeworms) *Acanthocephala* (thorny-headed worms), and *Trematoda* (flukes). The Protozoa include coccidia, trypanosomes and malarial organisms. In Great Britain the coccidia are the most important genus, living as microscopic animals in the cells of the intestines of poultry and many wild birds. Coccidiosis has been recognized in blackbirds and nestling song thrushes. Thrushes and blackbirds may also carry blood organisms of the *Haemoproteus* genus which are passed on by blood-sucking flies.

Nematodes or round worms are a common endoparasite on thrushes. *Porrocaecum ensicaudatum*, which is common in many passerine birds, as well as certain species of *Capillaria* have been regularly found in the mistle and song thrush, blackbird, redwing and fieldfare. I once watched a female blackbird in the Champs-Élysées in Paris void a pile of Nematode worms at least two inches high. Heavy infections could prove fatal. One of the important Nematode parasites is the gapeworm *Syngamus trachea* which has been discovered in the lining of the windpipe of blackbirds. Filarial worms live as adults in various organs but their larvae occur in the blood and have been isolated in blackbirds and other thrush species in the British Isles. Thorny-headed worms are small and equipped with a retractable proboscis with which they can affix themselves to the tissues of the bowel walls. *Polymorphus boschadis* has been found in mistle thrushes, blackbirds, fieldfares and redwings, and *Prosthrorhynchus transversus* in blackbirds, song thrushes and an Iceland redwing.

Certain groups of birds seem to have their own particular fauna of Cestodes or tapeworms. *Railletina* occurs in thrushes and has been isolated in the mistle thrush, fieldfare and redwing; *Hymenolepis* (with intermediate hosts) in fieldfares and blackbirds; *Anomotaenia* in blackbirds, song thrushes and Iceland redwing, and *Choanotaenia* in blackbirds and fieldfares. The Cestode *Dilepis undula* has been recognized in blackbirds, mistle and song thrushes, fieldfares, European and Iceland redwings and the Alpine ring ouzel. There is considerable difficulty experienced in the identification of tapeworms which often require sophisticated staining and microscopic techniques for specific separation. They can result in quite heavy mortality in birds especially in association with Nematode infections. The Trematode *Leucochloridium macrostomum* has been found in the mistle thrush and fieldfare.

SELECTED BIBLIOGRAPHY

THE TRUE THRUSHES

ALERSTOM, T., and PETTERSON, S. G. (1976). Do birds use waves for orientation when migrating across the sea? *Nature* 259: 205–207

ALLSOPP, E. M. P. (1972). Veery in Cornwall: a species new to Britain and Ireland. *Brit. Birds* 65: 45–49

ANDREW, D. G., NELDER, J. A., and HAWKES, M. (1955). Siberian thrush on the Isle of May: a new British bird. *Brit. Birds* 48: 21–25

ANDREW, R. J. (1961). The displays given by passerines in courtship and reproductive fighting; a review. *Ibis* 103a: 315–348, 549–579

ARHEIMER, O. (1973). (The breeding biology of the redwing (*Turdus iliacus*) in subalpine birch forest, Ammarnäs, Swedish Lapland). *Vår Fågelvarld* 32: 1–10. (Swedish with English summary).

ASH, J. S. (1957). Post-mortem examinations of birds found dead during the cold spells of 1954 and 1956. *Bird Study* 4: 159–166

—— (1960). A study of the Mallophaga of birds with particular reference to their ecology. *Ibis* 102: 93–110

—— (1964). Observations in Hampshire and Dorset during the 1963 cold spell. *Brit. Birds* 57: 221–241

ASHMOLE, M. J. (née GOODACRE) (1962). The migration of European thrushes; a comparative study based on ringing recoveries. *Ibis* 104: 314–346, 522–559

BARRY, M. (1960). Observations from a light-vessel on passerine immigration into the Wash in autumn 1956. *Brit. Birds* 53: 435–443

BATTEN, L. A. (1972). The past and present bird life of the Brent Reservoir and its vicinity. *Lond. Nat.* 50: 8–62

—— (1973). Population dynamics of suburban blackbirds. *Bird Study* 20: 251–258

BATTEN, L. A., and MARCHANT, J. H. (1976). Bird population changes for the years 1973–74. *Bird Study* 23: 11–20

BAWTREE, R. F. (1952). Blackbird's nest in use six times in three successive seasons. *Brit. Birds* 45: 330

BEECHER, W. J. (1951). Adaptations for food-getting in the American blackbirds. *Auk* 68: 411–440

BENGTSON, S. A. (1970). Densities of passerine bird communities in Iceland. *Bird Study* 17: 260–268

BENSON, S. V. (1963). Blackbird breaking snails. *Brit. Birds* 56: 191–192

BENT, A. C. (1964). *Life Histories of North American Thrushes, Kinglets and Their Allies*. New York.

BERNDT, R. (1942). Vom Schlafplatzflug inbesondere der Amseln und Singdrossel (*Turdus m. merula* L. und *T. ericetorum philomelos* Brehm) in Bad Pyrmont. *Orn. Monatsb.* 50: 7–14

BEVEN, G. (1969). Studies of less familiar birds. 152. Rock Thrush. *Brit. Birds* 62: 23–25

BJORKE, T. (1974). (Geographic variation in the song of the redwing, *Turdus iliacus*). *Sterna* 13: 65–76 (Norwegian with English summary).

BLACKMORE, D. K., and KEYMER, I. F. (1969). Cutaneous diseases of wild birds in Britain. *Brit. Birds* 62: 316–331

BOCHÉNSKI, Z. (1968). Nesting of the European members of the genus *Turdus* Linnaeus 1758 (Aves). *Acta zool. cracov.* 13: 349–440

277

BOYD, A. W. (1946). Courtship feeding of mistle thrush. *Brit. Birds* 39: 88

BROOKS-KING, M. (1942). Song form in the thrush family. *Brit. Birds* 36: 82–85

(1946). Courtship feeding of the mistle thrush. *Brit. Birds* 39: 179

BRUNS, H. (1952). Zur massenvermehrung und zum oekologischen Verhalten des Misteldrossel in Nordwesteuropa. *Orn. Mitt.* 4: 97–101

BUCKNILL, J. A. (1900). *The Birds of Surrey*. London.

BULL, P. C. (1946). Notes on the breeding cycle of the thrush and blackbird in New Zealand. *Emu* 46: 198–218

BURKITT, J. P. (1935). An attempt to chart fluctuations in the song of the song thrush, blackbird and chaffinch. *Brit. Birds* 28: 364–367

BURTON, J. F., and MAYER-GROSS, H. (1965). The first 25 years of the Nest Record Scheme. *Bird Study* 12: 100–107

BUTLIN, S. M. (1959). Snail-eating by blackbirds. *Brit. Birds* 52: 315–316

BUTT, D. V. (1949). Unusual display of fieldfare in spring. *Brit. Birds* 42: 328

CALDWELL, H. R., and CALDWELL, J. C. (1931). *South China Birds*. Shanghai.

CAMPBELL, B. (1953). A comparison of bird populations upon "industrial" and "rural" farmland in South Wales. *Rep. Trans. Cardiff Nat. Soc.* 81: 4–65

CAMPBELL, J. W. (1936). Birds and molluscs. *Brit. Birds* 30: 173

(1936). On the food of some British birds. *Brit. Birds* 30: 209–218

CAWKELL, E. M. (1947). 'Injury-feigning' of song-thrush. *Brit. Birds* 40: 249

(1950). Weights of nestling blackbirds. *Brit. Birds* 43: 297

CHAPPUIS, C. (1969). Un cline vocal chez les oiseaux paléarctiques: variation tonale des vocalisations, sous différentes latitudes. *Alauda* 37: 59–71

CLAFTON, F. R. (1963). Gray-cheeked thrush on Bardsey. *Brit. Birds* 56: 192–193

CLAPHAM, P. A. (1957). Helminth parasites in some wild birds. *Bird Study* 4: 193–196

CLARKE, W. E. (1912). *Studies in Bird Migration*. 2 Vols. London and Edinburgh.

COATES, B. J. (1960). Dusky thrush in Co. Durham. *Brit. Birds* 53: 275–276

COLEMAN, R. B. (1958–59). Birds washing and drinking. *34th Rept. Gresham's School Nat. Hist. Soc.*

COLQUHOUN, M. K. (1939). The vocal activity of blackbirds at a winter roost. *Brit. Birds* 33: 44–47

CORNWALLIS, R. K. (1953). The pattern of migration in 1953 at the East Coast Bird Observatories. *Brit. Birds* 47: 423–431

(1955). Heavy immigration of blackbirds and other thrushes. *Brit. Birds* 48: 144

COULSON, J. C. (1961). The post-fledging mortality of the blackbird in Great Britain. *Bird Study* 8: 89–97

CRAMP, S., and TOMLINS, A. D. (1966). The birds of Inner London, 1951–65. *Brit. Birds* 59: 209–233

DAVIES, S. J. J. F., and FRASER ROWELL, C. H. (1956). Observations on the redwing in Swedish Lapland. *Bird Study* 3: 242–248

DAVIES, P. W., and SNOW, D. W. (1965). Territory and food in the song thrush. *Brit. Birds* 58: 161–175

DAVIS, P. (1953). American robin on Lundy. *Brit. Birds* 46: 364–369

(1953). White's thrush on Lundy. *Brit. Birds* 46: 455

(1954). The pattern of migration in 1953 at the Irish Sea Bird Observatories. *Brit. Birds* 47: 414–422

(1958). Black-throated thrush at Fair Isle. *Brit. Birds* 51: 195–197

(1959). A second grey-cheeked thrush at Fair Isle. *Brit. Birds* 52: 316

(1964). Aspects of autumn migration at the bird observatories, 1963. *Bird Study* 11: 77–122

(1965). Aspects of passerine migration at the bird observatories, autumn 1964. *Bird Study* 12: 108–134

(1966). The great immigration of early September 1965. *Brit. Birds* 59: 353–376

DINNENDAHL, L. (1954). Nächtlicher Zug und Windrichtung auf Helgoland. *Vogelwarte* 17: 188–194

DOBINSON, H. M., and RICHARDS, A. J. (1964). The effects of the severe winter of 1962/63 on birds in Britain. *Brit. Birds* 57: 373–434

DROST, R. (1930). Vom Zug der Amsel (*T. merula*). *Vogelzug* 1: 74–85

(1935). Ueber das Zahlverhältnis von Alter und Geschlecht auf dem Herbts und Frühjahrzuge. *Vogelzug* 6: 177–182

DUNSTER, C. W., and TUTT, H. R. (1971). Multiple nesting of pair of mistle thrushes. *Brit. Birds* 64: 461–462

DURAND, A. L. (1961). White-throated sparrow and American robin crossing Atlantic on board ship. *Brit. Birds* 54: 439–440

(1963). A remarkable fall of American land-birds on the *Mauretania*, New York to Southampton, October 1962. *Brit. Birds* 56: 157–164

(1972). Land birds over the North Atlantic; unpublished records 1961–65 and thoughts a decade later. *Brit. Birds* 65: 428–442

D'URBAN, W. S. M., and MATTHEW, M. A. (1895). *The Birds of Devon*. London.

DYRCZ, A. (1969). The ecology of the song thrush (*Turdus philomelos*) and blackbird (*T. merula*) during their breeding season in an area of joint occurrence. *Ekol. pol.*, Ser. A. 17: 735–793

EICHLER, W. (1934). Vom Zuge der Singdrossel (*Turdus ph. philomelos* Brehm). *Vogelzug* 5: 135–143

ENEMAR, A. (1958). On the initiation of incubation in the blackbird (*Turdus merula*). *Vår Fågelv.* 17: 81–103 (Swedish with English summary).

EPPRECHT, W. (1946). Die Verbreitung der Amsel, *Turdus m. merula* L. zur brutzeit in Zürich, 1946. *Orn. Beob.* 43: 97–105

ERZ, W. (1963). Populationsökologische Untersuchungen an der zweier nordwestdeutscher grobstade. *Z. Swiss Zool.* 170 (1/2): 1–111

EYGENRAAM, J. A. (1945). Het roepen der merels in de schemering. *Ardea* 33: 241–250

FAIR ISLE BIRD OBSERVATORY TRUST (1975). Fair Isle Bird Observatory. *Rept.* for 1974

FEARE, C. J. (1967). Terrestrial birds feeding in the littoral zone. *Brit. Birds* 60: 412–414

FLEGG, J. J. M. (1974). Some inter-relationships between breeding season, moult and migratory range. *Proc. 16th Int. Orn. Congr:* 116 (abstract).

FLEGG, J. J. M., and GLUE, D. E. (1975). The nesting of the ring ouzel. *Bird Study* 22: 1–8

FLUX, J. E. C. (1966). Breeding of song thrushes and blackbirds at St Arnaud, Nelson. *Notornis* 13: 142–149

FORMANEK, J. (1958). Tah kosa černého (*Turdus merula*) a droza zpěvneho (*T. ericetorum*) z CSR. *Sylvia* 15: 23–41

FRANK, F. (1952). Sind Misteldrossel-ausbreitung und Feldmausmassenverwechsel gleichartigo erscheinungen? *J. Orn.* 93: 353

FRAPS, R. M. (1955). The varying effects of sex hormones in birds. *Mem. Soc. Endocrinol.* 4. Cambridge.

FURRER, R. K. (1975). (Frequency and effectiveness of the attack-behaviour in the fieldfare, *Turdus pilaris*). *Orn. Beob.* 72: 1–8 (German with English summary).

GÉROUDET, P. (1955). L'évolution de l'avifaune suisse au XXe siècle. *Act. XI Congr. Int. Orn.* 72–80

GERVIS, G. R. (1968). Blackbird feeding in association with mole. *Brit. Birds* 61: 314

GIBB, J. (1947). Sun-bathing by birds. *Brit. Birds* 40: 172–174

GIBB, J., and HARTLEY, P. H. T. (1957). Bird foods and feeding-habits as subjects for amateur research. *Brit. Birds* 50: 278–291

GILLESPIE, J. A. (1927). Singing by migrant gray-cheeked thrush. *Auk* 44: 112

GINN, H. B. (1969). The use of annual ringing and nest record card totals as indicators of bird population levels. *Bird Study* 16: 210–248

GLUE, D. E. (1968). Bird predators feeding at autumn roosts. *Brit. Birds* 61: 526–527

GOODACRE, M. J. (1959–60). The origin of winter visitors to the British Isles. *Bird Study* 6: 37–50; 7: 102–113

GOODACRE, M. J., and LACK, D. (1959). Early breeding in 1957. *Brit. Birds* 52: 74–83

GOODHART, C. B. (1958). Thrush predation on the snail *Cepaea hortensis*. *J. Anim. Ecol.* 27: 47–57

GOODWIN, D. (1957). Remarks on some genera of Turdinae. *Bull. B.O.C.* 77: 110–113
(1967). Some possible functions of sun-bathing in birds. *Brit. Birds* 60: 363–364

GRACZYK, R. (1961). (Studies on variability, biology and economic status of the blackbird *Turdus merula* L.) *Ekol. pol.* Ser. A. 9(23): 453–485

GRUSON, E. S. (1976). *Checklist of the Birds of the World*. London.

GUDMUNDSSON, F. (1951). The effects of the recent climate change on the bird life of Iceland. *Proc. 10th Int. Orn. Congr.*: 502–514

GURR, L. (1954). A study of the blackbird *Turdus merula* in New Zealand. *Ibis* 96: 225–261

HAARTMAN, L. V. (1971). A bird census in a Finnish park. *Ornis. fenn.* 48: 93–100

HALL-CRAGGS, J. (1962). The development of song in the blackbird *Turdus merula*. *Ibis* 104: 277–299

HARDY, E. (1969). Mistle thrushes and mistletoe berries. *Bird Study* 16: 191–192

HARRIS, M. P. (1962). Weights from five hundred birds found dead on Skomer Island in January 1962. *Brit. Birds* 55: 97–103

HARRISON, C. J. O. (1963). Some comments on albinism and melanism. *Brit. Birds* 56: 115–116

HARRISON, J. G. (1967). Grey-cheeked thrush in Morayshire. *Brit. Birds* 60: 55–57

HARTLEY, P. H. T. (1954). Wild fruits in the diet of British thrushes. A study in the ecology of closely allied species. *Brit. Birds* 47: 97–107

HARVEY, B. F. (1946). Display of song thrush. *Brit. Birds* 39: 247–248

HAVLIN, J. (1961). (Consumption and digestion of seeds in the blackbird *Turdus merula* L.) *Zool. Listy* 10: 243–248
(1962). (Variability of somatic characters in the European blackbird, *Turdus merula merula* Linné, 1758). *Zool. Listy* 11: 1–14
(1962). (Age structure and mortality rate in blackbird populations). *Zool. Listy* 11: 279–285
(1962). (Environmental requirements in the blackbird, *Turdus merula* L.) *Prace* 34: 1–48
(1963). (Breeding density in the blackbird, *Turdus merula* Linn.) *Zool. Listy* 12: 1–18
(1963). (Reproduction in the blackbird (*Turdus merula* L.)) *Zool. Listy* 12: 195–216 (All in Czech with English summaries).

HEMMINGSEN, A. M. (1956). Om flerfolding redebygning (serierder) hos solsort (*Turdus merula* L.) og andre fugle. *Dansk. Orn. Foren. Tidsskr.* 3: 179–190 (On multiple nest-building: Danish with English summary).

HEMS, H. A. (1966). Photographs of ring ouzel nests in Derbyshire. *Brit. Birds* 59: 107–108

HENDY, E. W. (1943). *Somerset Birds and Some Other Folk*. London.
(1946). *Wild Exmoor through the Year*. London.

HEPPNER, F. (1965). Sensory mechanisms and environmental clues used by the American robin in locating earthworms. *Condor* 67: 247–256

HESS, G. (1938). Vom Zug der Wacholderdrossel (*Turdus pilaris*). *Orn. Beob.* 35: 150–156

HEYDER, R. (1931). 'Amselbeobachtungen'. *Mitt. Vereins Sächs. Orn.* 3: 105–129
(1950). Studien über Amselrufe. *Zool. Garten* (N.F.). 17: 242–249
(1953). *Die Amsel.* Wittenberg-Lutherstadt.

HINDE, R. A. (1956). The biological significance of the territories of birds. *Ibis* 98: 340–370
(1969). The bases of aggression in animals. *J. psychosom. Res.* 13: 213–219

HODSON, N. L., and SNOW, D. W. (1965). The road deaths enquiry, 1960-61. *Bird Study* 12: 90–99

HÖHN, E. O. (1950). Physiology of the thyroid gland in birds: a review. *Ibis* 92: 464–473
(1960). The endocrine system. In Marshall, A. J. (ed.). *Biology and Comparative Physiology of Birds.* New York and London.

HOLGERSEN, H. (1953). Trostetrekk. *Saertrykk av Stav. Mus. Arbok.* 1953: 91–102
(1962). Grastrupetrost, Turdus obscurus, funnet i Norge. *Sterna* 5: 27–30
(1970). (Ringing and migration of Norwegian *Turdus torquatus*). *Stav. Mus. Arbok.* 1970: 111–116. (Norwegian with English summary).

HOLT, E. G. (1959–60). Redwings breeding in Ross-shire. *Brit. Birds* 52: 315; 53: 358–359
(1966). Redwings breeding in Sutherland. *Brit. Birds* 59: 500–501

HOLYOAK, D. T. (1974). High incidence of plumage abnormalities in London birds. *Brit. Birds* 67: 122–124

HOWARD, E. (1948). *Territory in Bird Life.* London.

JABŁOŃSKI, B. (1963). (Observations on the redwing, *Turdus musicus* L., in the Polish lowlands during the breeding season). *Notatki Ornitologiczne* 4 (4): 38–41 (Polish with English summary).

JACKSON, R. D. (1952). The display of the blackbird. *Brit. Birds* 45: 103–104
(1954). Territory and pair-formation in the blackbird. *Brit. Birds* 47: 123–131

JEFFERIES, D. J., and DAVIS, B. N. K. (1968). Dynamics of dieldrin in soil, earthworms and song thrushes. *J. Wildl. Mgmt.* 32: 441–456

JENNINGS, A. R. (1959). Diseases of wild birds. Fifth Report. *Bird Study* 6: 19–22

JENNINGS, A. R., and SOULSBY, E. J. L. (1957). Diseases of wild birds. Fourth Report. *Bird Study* 4: 216–220

JOGI, A. (1963). (The nesting of thrushes at Puhtu). *Ornitologiline Kogumik* 3: 101–121 (Estonian with English and Russian summaries).

JONES, P. H. (1961). Lieux d'origine des grives de la France méditerranéenne. *Oiseau* 31: 193–213
(1962). Mortality and weights of fieldfares in Anglesey in January 1962. *Brit. Birds* 55: 178–181

KALELA, O. (1949). Changes in geographic ranges in the avifauna of northern and central Europe in relation to recent changes in climate. *Bird Banding* 20: 77–103

KEAR, J. (1968). Plant poisons in the diet of wild birds. *Bull. B.O.C.* 88: 98–102

KENNEDY, R. J. (1968). The role of sunbathing in birds. *Brit. Birds* 61: 320–322
(1969). Sunbathing behaviour of birds. *Brit. Birds* 62: 249–258

KESKPAIK, J. (1963). (Diurnal rhythm of the thrushes when nurturing their young). *Ornitologiline Kogumik* 3: 22–132 (Estonian with English summary).
(1963). (Changes in intensity of gas metabolism in young thrushes). *Ornitologiline Kogumik* 3: 133–147 (Estonian with English summary).

KEYMER, I. F. (1958). A survey and review of the causes of mortality in British birds and the significance of wild birds as disseminators of disease. *Vet. Rec.* 70: 713–720, 736–740

KEYMER, I. F., and BLACKMORE, D. K. (1964). Diseases of the skin and soft parts of wild birds. *Brit. Birds* 57: 175–179

KING, F. (1955). American robin in Co. Kerry. *Brit. Birds* 48: 420–421

KLOMP, H. (1972). Regulation of the size of bird populations by means of territorial behaviour. *Neth. J. Zool.* 22: 456–488

KLUYVER, H. N., and TINBERGEN, L. (1953). Territory and the regulation of density in titmice. *Arch. Neerl. Zool.* 10: 265–286

KREBS, J. R. (1970). Regulation of the numbers in the great tit (Aves: Passeriformes). *J. Zool.* 162: 317–333

——— (1971). Territory and breeding density in the great tit, *Parus major* L. *Ecology* 52: 2–22

——— (1976). Bird song and territorial defence. *New Scientist* 3 June 1976: 534–536

KRÜGER, C. (1940). Nordiske solsorters (*Turdus m. merula*) forekomst og traek. *Dansk Orn. Foren. Tidsskr.* 34: 114–153

LACK, D. (1940). Courtship feeding in birds. *Auk* 57: 169–178

——— (1943). The age of the blackbird. *Brit. Birds* 36: 166–175

——— (1943). The problem of partial migration. *Brit. Birds* 37: 122–170

——— (1947). The significance of clutch-size. *Ibis* 89: 302–352

——— (1949). Family size in certain thrushes (*Turdidae*). *Evolution* 3: 57–66

——— (1950). The breeding seasons of European birds. *Ibis* 92: 288–316

——— (1954). *The Natural Regulation of Animal Numbers*. Oxford.

——— (1958). The significance of the colour of Turdine eggs. *Ibis* 100: 145–166

——— (1960). The influence of the weather on passerine migration. A review. *Auk* 77: 171–209

——— (1960). Migration across the North Sea studied by radar. Part 2. The Spring Departure. *Ibis* 102: 26–57

——— (1960). The height of bird migration. *Brit. Birds* 53: 5–10

——— (1962). Radar evidence on migratory orientation. *Brit. Birds* 55: 139–158

——— (1963). Migration across the southern North Sea studied by radar. Part 4. Autumn. *Ibis* 105: 1–54

——— (1966). *Population Studies of Birds*. Oxford.

——— (1969). Drift migration. A correction. *Ibis* 111: 235–255

LEE, S. L. B. (1963). Migration in the Outer Hebrides studied by radar. *Ibis* 105: 493–515

LOFTS, B., and MARSHALL, A. J. (1957). The interstitial and spermatogenetic tissue of autumn migrants in southern England. *Ibis* 99: 621–627

LØPPENTHIN, B. (1955). Some isolated bird-populations and their possible origin. *Act. XI Congr. Int. Orn.* 394–398

LORD, J., and MUNNS, D. J. (1970). ed. *Atlas of Breeding Birds of the West Midlands*. London.

LUNDEVALL, C.-L. (1952). The bird fauna in the Abisko national park and its surroundings. *Kungl. Svenska Vetenskapsakademiens Avhandlingar i Naturskyddsärenden* No 7.

MACDONALD, J. W. (1962). Mortality in wild birds with some observations on weights. *Bird Study* 9: 147–167

——— (1963). Mortality in wild birds. *Bird Study* 10: 91–108

——— (1965). Mortality in wild birds. *Bird Study* 12: 181–195

MANNS, L. (1967). Leaf litter fauna in the ecology of ground-feeding birds. *Lond. Nat.* 46: 116–125

MARSHALL, A. J. (1949). Weather factors and spermatogenesis in birds. *Proc. Zool. Soc. London* 119: 711–716

——— (1959). Internal and environmental control of breeding. *Ibis* 101: 456–478

——— (1961). Breeding seasons and migration. In Marshall A. J. (ed.). *Biology and Comparative Physiology of Birds*. Vol 2. New York and London.

MAYAUD, N. (1952). Migration de *Turdus viscivorus* et particularités de sa reproduction. *Alauda* 20: 31–38

MAYER-GROSS, H. (1964). Late nesting in Britain in 1960. *Brit. Birds* 57: 102–118

MAYER-GROSS, H., and PERRINS, C. M. (1962). Blackbirds rearing five broods in one season. *Brit. Birds* 55: 189–190

MAYR, E., and AMADON, D. (1951). A classification of recent birds. *Amer. Mus. Nov.*

MEINERTZHAGEN, R. (1948). The birds of Ushant, Brittany. *Ibis* 90: 553–567

MELLANBY, K. (1967). *Pesticides and Pollution.* London.

MESSMER, E., and MESSMER, I. (1956). Die Entwicklung der Lautäusserungen und einiger Verhaltensweisen der Amsel (*Turdus merula* L.) unter naturlichen Bedingungen und nach einzel Aufzucht in schalldichten Raumen. *Z. Tierpsychol.* 13: 341–441

MEUGENS, E. (1947). *La Vie des Merles.* Paris.

MINTON, C. D. Y. (1965). Blackbird and song thrush counts in the West Midlands. *West Mid. Bird Rept.* 32: 8–10

MITCHELL, F. S. (1885). *The Birds of Lancashire.* London.

MOORE, N. W. (1965). Pesticides and birds – a review of the situation in Great Britain in 1965. *Bird Study* 12: 222–252

MOREAU, R. E. (1946). The recording of incubation and fledging periods. *Brit. Birds* 39: 66–70

(1953). Migration in the Mediterranean area. *Ibis* 95: 329–364

(1954). The main vicissitudes of the European avifauna since the Pliocene. *Ibis* 96: 411–431

MORLEY, A. (1937). Some activities of resident blackbirds in winter. *Brit. Birds* 31: 34–41

(1943). Sexual behaviour in British birds from October to January. *Ibis* 85: 132–158

MORRIS, D. (1954). The snail-eating behaviour of thrushes and blackbirds. *Brit. Birds* 47: 33–49

MORTON BOYD, J., and WATERS, W. E. (1963). Rock thrush on St Kilda. *Brit. Birds* 56: 66–67

MYRES, M. T. (1955). The breeding of the blackbird, song thrush and mistle thrush in Great Britain. Part 1. Breeding seasons. *Bird Study* 2: 2–24

(1964). Dawn ascent and re-orientation of Scandinavian thrushes (*Turdus spp.*) migrating at night over the north-eastern Atlantic Ocean in autumn. *Ibis* 106: 7–51

NEWTON, I. (1967). The adaptive radiation and feeding ecology of some British finches. *Ibis* 109: 33–96

(1972). *Finches.* London.

NICHOLSON, E. M. (1951). *Birds and Men.* London.

NIETHAMMER, G. (1970). Clutch sizes of introduced European passerines in New Zealand. *Notornis* 17: 214–222

NISBET, I. C. T. (1963). American passerines in western Europe, 1951-62. *Brit. Birds* 56: 204–217

NOVIKOV, G. A. (1960). Geographical variation in the density of forest birds in the European part of the U.S.S.R. and adjacent countries. *Zool. Zh.* 39: 433–437 (Russian with English summary).

OLNEY, P. (1966). Berries and birds. *Birds* 1: 98–99

OWEN, D. F. (1953). Migration at the Kentish Knock Lightship. *Brit. Birds* 46: 353–364

(1957). *Neottiophillum praeustum* in birds' nests. *Brit. Birds* 59: 160–164

OWEN, D. F., and ASH, J. S. (1955). Additional records of *Protocalliphora* (Diptera) in birds' nests. *Brit. Birds* 48: 225–229

PALMÉR, S., and BOSWALL, J. (1972). *A Field Guide to the Bird Songs of Britain and Europe.* Sveriges Radio. Stockholm.

PARSLOW, J. F. L. (1966). American robins in the Isles of Scilly. *Brit. Birds* 59: 41–42
    (1968). Eye-browed thrushes in Northamptonshire, Hebrides and Scilly; a species new to Britain and Ireland. *Brit. Birds* 61: 218–223
    (1973). *Breeding Birds of Britain and Ireland*. Berkhamsted.
PAYN, W. H. (1962). *The Birds of Suffolk*. London.
PEITZMEIER, J. (1951). Zum ökologischen Verhalten der Misteldrossel (*Turdus v. viscivorus* L.) in Nordwesteuropa. *Bonn Zool. Beitr.* 2: 55–82
PERRINS, C. M. (1970). The timing of birds' breeding seasons. *Ibis* 112: 242–255
PERRY, R. (1946). *A Naturalist on Lindisfarne*. London.
PEUS, F. (1951). Nüchterne Analyse der Massenvermehrung der Misteldrossel (*Turdus viscivorus* L.) in Nordwesteuropa. *Bonn Zool. Beitr.* 2: 55–82
    (1958). Ökologie und historische Einordnung der jüngsten Übervermehrung und Ausbreitung der Misteldrossel (*Turdus viscivorus* L.) in Nordwesteuropa. *J. Orn.* 99: 297–321
PHILIPSON, W. R. (1937). Two contrasting seasons at a redwing roost. *Brit. Birds* 30: 343–345
PHILLIPS, J. H. (1961). Sex and age counts of wintering thrushes. *Brit. Birds* 54: 277–282
PICOZZI, N. (1965). Eye-browed thrush on North Rona. *Scot. Birds* 3: 419–420
PIKULA, J. (1973). The influence of environmental conditions on the breeding of *Turdus philomelos* in Czechoslovakia. *Zool. Listy* 22: 223–233
POULSEN, H. (1958). A study of anting behaviour in birds. *Dansk Orn. Foren. Tidsskr.* 50: 267–298
PUGH, G. J. F. (1972). The contamination of birds' feathers by fungi. *Ibis* 114: 172–177

QUICK, H. (1964). *Birds of the Scilly Isles*.

RADFORD, A. P. (1955). Imitative behaviour of immature blackbirds. *Brit. Birds* 48: 458
RENDAHL, H. (1960). Die Zugverhältnisse schwedischer Drosseln. Mit Berücksichtigung der Ergebnisse von den finnischen und norwegischen Beringungen. *Ark. Zool.* 12: 303–312
RIBAUT, J.-P. (1964). Dynamique d'une population de merles noirs, *Turdus merula* L. *Rev. Suisse Zool.* 71: 816–901
RICHTER, A. (1972). Zum Umfang der Jugendmauser am Flügel der Amsel *Turdus merula*. *Orn. Beob.* 69: 1–16 (English summary).
RIPLEY, S. D. (1952). The Thrushes. *Postilla* (Yale University). No 13. A Taxonomic Study.
    (1964). 'Turdinae'. In *Check List of Birds of the World*. Cambridge, Mass. Vol 10. ed. E. Mayr and R. A. Paynter.
ROBERTSON, A. W. P. (1949). Sub-song of female blackbird. *Brit. Birds* 42: 388–389
ROBSON, W. (1975). Breeding of the ring ouzel. *B.T.O. News Bull.* 75: 6–7
ROLLIN, N. (1948). A note on sun-bathing by birds. *Brit. Birds* 41: 304–305
    (1953). A note on abnormally marked song thrushes and blackbirds. *Trans. Nat. Hist. Soc. Northumb., Durham and Newcastle u.T.*, *N.S.* 10: 183–184
    (1959). White plumage in blackbirds. *Bull. B.O.C.* 79: 92–96
ROLLS, J. C. (1972). Redwings roosting in reed beds. *Brit. Birds* 65: 126–127
ROYAL SOCIETY FOR THE PROTECTION OF BIRDS (1962). *Deaths of birds and mammals from toxic chemicals, January–June 1961*.
RUDEBECK, G. (1950). Studies on bird migration based on field studies in southern Sweden. *Vår Fågelv.* Suppl. 1: 1–148
RUTTLEDGE, R. F. (1966). *Ireland's Birds*. London.
RYVES, B. H. (1946). Courtship feeding of mistle thrush. *Brit. Birds* 39: 179

SAGE, B. L. (1962). Albinism and melanism in birds. *Brit. Birds* 55: 201–225

(1963). The incidence of albinism and melanism in British Birds. *Brit. Birds* 56: 409–416

SALOMONSEN, F. (1948). The distribution of birds and the recent climatic change in the North Atlantic area. *Dansk Orn. Foren. Tidsskr.* 42: 85–90

(1951). The immigration and breeding of the fieldfare (*Turdus pilaris* L.) in Greenland. *Proc. 10th Int. Orn. Congr.*: 515–526

(1955). The evolutionary significance of bird-migration. *Dan. Biol. Medd.* 22 (6): 1–62

SANDSTRÖM, L. A. (1970). (Interbreeding between blackbird *Turdus merula* and fieldfare *Turdus pilaris*). *Vår Fågelv.* 19: 231 (Swedish with English summary).

SAUER, E. G. F. (1961). Further studies on the stellar orientation of nocturnally migrating birds. *Psychol. Forschung* 24: 224–244

SAUERBREI, F. (1926). Amselbeobachtungen. *Orn. Monatsschr.* 51: 65–66

SCHAANNING, T. H. L. (1948). Bjerktrostens (*Turdus pilaris*) trekk og vinterkvarter. *Stav. Mus. Arbok* 1948: 135–146

SCOTT, R. E., ROBERTS, L. J., and CADBURY, C. J. (1972). Bird deaths from power lines at Dungeness. *Brit. Birds* 65: 273–286

SEEBOHM, H., and SHARPE, R. B. (1898–1902). *A Monograph of the Turdidae.* 2 Vols. London.

SHARROCK, J.T.R. (1971). Scarce migrants in Britain and Ireland during 1958–67. *Brit. Birds* 64: 93–113

SHARROCK, J. T. R., GREEN, T. Q., and PRESTON, K. (1973). Olive-backed thrush in Co. Cork. *Brit. Birds* 66: 35–36

SIIVONEN, L. (1939). Zur Oekologie und Verbreitung der Singdrossel, *Turdus ericetorum philomelos* Brehm. *Ann. Zool. Soc. Zool.–Bot. Fenn.* 7: 1–285

SILVA, E. T. (1949). Nest records of the song thrush. *Brit. Birds* 42: 97–111

SIMMONS, K. E. L. (1957). A review of the anting-behaviour of passerine birds. *Brit. Birds* 50: 401–424

(1960). Notes on anting by British passerine birds in the wild. *Brit. Birds* 53: 11–25

(1961) Problems of head-scratching in birds. *Ibis* 103a: 37–49

(1964). 'Feather Maintenance' in Thomson, A. L. (ed.). *New Dict. Birds.* London and New York.

SIMMS, E. (1952). *Bird Migrants.* London.

(1957). *Voices of the Wild.* London.

(1960). Visible migration in the Vaud. *Bird Notes* 29: 45–51

(1962). A study of suburban bird life at Dollis Hill. *Brit. Birds* 55: 1–36

(1965). Effects of the cold weather of 1962/63 on the blackbird population at Dollis Hill. *Brit. Birds* 58: 33–43

(1971). *Woodland Birds.* London.

(1975). *Birds of Town and Suburb.* London.

SMITH, F. R., and THE RARITIES COMMITTEE (1972). Report on rare birds in Great Britain in 1971 (with 1967, 1968, 1969 records). *Brit. Birds* 65: 322–354

(1974). Report on rare birds in Great Britain in 1973. *Brit. Birds* 67: 310–348

SMITH, K. D. (1960). The passage of palaearctic migrants through Eritrea. *Ibis* 102: 536–544

(1965). On the birds of Morocco. *Ibis* 107: 493–526

SNOW, D. W. (1953). Visible migration in the British Isles. A review. *Ibis* 95: 242–270

(1955). The breeding of the blackbird, song thrush and mistle thrush in Great Britain. Part II. Clutch size. Part III. Nesting season. *Bird Study* 2: 72–84, 170–178

(1955). The abnormal breeding of birds in the winter 1953/54. *Brit. Birds* 48: 120–126

(1956). Territory in the blackbird, *Turdus merula. Ibis* 98: 438–447

(1958). The breeding of the blackbird. *Ibis* 100: 1–30

(1958). *A Study of Blackbirds.* London.

(1965). The moult enquiry. *Bird Study* 12: 135–142

(1966). The migration and dispersal of British blackbirds. *Bird Study* 13: 237–255

(1966). The population dynamics of the blackbird. *Nature* 211: 1231–1233

(1967). Population changes in some common birds in gardens. *Brit. Birds* 60: 339–341

(1969). An analysis of breeding success in the blackbird *Turdus merula*. *Ardea* 57: 163–171

(1969). Some vital statistics of British mistle thrushes. *Bird Study* 16: 34–44

(1969). The moult of British thrushes and chats. *Bird Study* 16: 115–129

(1971). Evolutionary aspects of fruit-eating by birds. *Ibis* 113: 194–202

SNOW, D. W., and MAYER-GROSS, H. (1967). Farmland as a nesting habitat. *Bird Study* 14: 43–52

SOUTHERN, H. N. (1954). Tawny owls and their prey. *Ibis* 96: 384–410

SPENCER, K. G. (1956). Albinism related to age. *Brit. Birds* 49: 500

SPENCER, R. (1964). Report on bird ringing for 1963. *Brit. Birds Ringing Supp.* 1964. 57: 525–596

(1975). Changes in the distribution of recoveries of ringed blackbirds. *Bird Study* 22: 176–190

STEENBERGEN, G. V. (1971). (The mortality of the Belgian blackbird population based on recovery data). *Gerfaut* 61: 1–13

STEIN, G. W. (1952). Probleme der Ökologie und der Siedlungsdichte bei der Misteldrossel, *Turdus viscivorus* L. *J. Orn.* 93: 158–171

STEINBACHER, G. (1953). Zur Biologie der Amsel (*Turdus merula* L.). *Biol. Abhand.* 5.

STRESEMANN, E. (1963). The nomenclature of plumages and moults. *Auk* 80: 1–8

SUFFERN, C. (1954). A song thrush's method of holding a snail-shell. *Brit. Birds* 47: 450

SVÄRDSON, G. (1953). Visible migration within Fenno–Scandia. *Ibis* 95: 181–211

(1957). The 'invasion type' of bird migration. *Brit. Birds* 50: 314–349

SVENSSON, S. (1953). Övervintrande taltrast (*Turdus ericetorum*) in Skåne. *Vår Fågelv.* 12: 194

SWANBERG, P. O. (1948). Ringtrastar (*Turdus torquatus*) vinddrivna under vårflyttningen. (Ringdrossels während des Früjahrs–Zuges verschlagen in Västergötland beobachter) *Vår Fågelv.* 7: 45–46

TAYLOR, S. M. (1965). The common birds census – some statistical aspects. *Bird Study* 12: 268–286

TEAGER, C. W. (1967). Birds sun-bathing. *Brit. Birds* 60: 361–363

THIELCKE-POLTZ, H., and THIELCKE, G. (1960). Akutisches lernen verschieden alter schallisolierter Amseln *Turdus merula* L. und die Entwicklung erlernter Motive ohne und mit küntstlichem einfluss von testosteron. *Z. Tierpsychol.* 17: 211–244

THOMSON, A. L. (1950). Factors determining the breeding seasons of birds: an introductory review. *Ibis* 92: 173–184

THORPE, W. H. (1961). *Bird Song: The Biology of Vocal Communication and Expression in Birds*. Cambridge.

THORPE, W. H., and PILCHER, P. M. (1958). The nature and characteristics of sub-song. *Brit. Birds* 51: 509–514

TICEHURST, N. F., and HARTLEY, P. H. T. Report on the effect of the severe winter of 1946-47 on bird-life. *Brit. Birds* 41: 322–334

TINBERGEN, N. (1957). The functions of territory. *Bird Study* 4: 14–27

TRETZEL, E. (1967). Imitation und Transposition menslicher Pfiffe durch Amseln (*Turdus m. merula* L.). Ein weiterer Nachweis relativen Lernens und akutischer Abstraktien bei Vögeln. *Z. Tierpsychol.* 24: 137–161

TUCKER, B. W. (1946). Courtship feeding in thrushes and warblers. *Brit. Birds* 39: 88–89

TURČEK, F. J. (1956). On the bird population of the spruce forest community in Slovakia. *Ibis* 98: 24–33

(1957). The bird succession in the conifer plantations on mat-grass land in Slovakia. *Ibis* 99: 587–593

(1960). Uber das Fehlen der Amsel in den menslichen Siedlungen der Nordslowakei (ŠSR). *Orn. Mitt. Göttingen* 12: 172–173

(1963). Colour preferences in fruit- and seed-eating birds. *Proc XIII Int. Orn. Congr.*: 285–292

TYRVÄINEN, H. (1969). The breeding biology of the redwing (*Turdus iliacus* L.). *Ann. Zool. Fenn.* 6: 1–46

UDDLING, Å. (1951). (Breeding anomalies in the blackbird *Turdus merula*). *Vår Fågelv.* 14: 112–115 (Swedish with English summary).

VARLEY, G. C. (1970). The concept of energy flow applied to a woodland community. In *Animal Populations in Relation to their Food Resources*, ed. A. Watson. Oxford and Edinburgh.
VARLEY, G. C., and GRADWELL, G. R. (1968). 'Population models for the winter moth'. In *Insect Abundance*, ed. T. R. E. Southwood. Oxford and Edinburgh.
VAURIE, C. (1965). *The Birds of the Palaearctic Fauna*. London.
VENABLES, L. S. V., and VENABLES, U. M. (1952). The blackbird in Shetland. *Ibis* 94: 636–653
(1961). Further sex counts of wintering blackbirds. *Brit. Birds* 54: 120–121
VERHEYEN, R. (1953). Étude statistique relative à la biologie de nos trois grives (*Turdus* sp.) indigènes. *Gerfaut* 43: 231–261
(1958). Over de gemiddelde ouderdom van de merel. *Gerfaut* 48: 5–14
VERHEYEN, R., and LE GRELLE, G. (1951). Interprètation des rèsultats du baguage au nid de nos grives (*Turdus*) indigènes. *Gerfaut* 41: 271–280
VOITKEVICH, A. A. (1966). *The Feathers and Plumage of Birds*. London.
VOOUS, K. H. (1960). *Atlas of European Birds*. London.

WALLACE, D. I. M. (1974). The Birds of Regent's Park, London, 1959–68. *Brit. Birds* 67: 449–468
WALLACE, H. J. (1939). Bicknell's thrush, its taxonomy, distribution and life history. *Proc. Boston Soc. Nat. Hist.* 41: 211–402
WARD, P., and ZAHAVI, A. (1973). The importance of certain assemblages of birds as 'information-centre' for food-finding. *Ibis* 115: 517–534
WATSON, A. (1973). A review of population dynamics in birds. *Brit. Birds* 66: 417–437
WEIMANN, R. (1938). Beringungsergebnisse schlesischer und sächsischer Amseln. (*Turdus merula merula* L.) *Ber. Ver. Schles. Orn.* 23: 1–14
WERTH, I. (1947). The tendency of blackbird and song thrush to breed in their birthplaces. *Brit. Birds* 40: 328–330
WHITE, C. M. N. (1937). Notes on Outer Hebridean birds. *Brit. Birds* 31: 230–232
WHITE, M. F. (1971). Unusual display of mistle thrush. *Brit. Birds* 64: 505
WILLIAMS, E. M. (1949). Behaviour of song thrush. *Brit. Birds* 42: 294
WILLIAMS, G. R. (1953). The dispersal from New Zealand and Australia of some introduced European passerines. *Ibis* 95: 676–692
WILLIAMS, R. E. (1947). Courtship feeding of mistle thrush. *Brit. Birds* 40: 52
WILLIAMSON, K. (1951). Fair Isle Bird Observatory. *2nd Ann. Rept.* 1950
(1952). Reports on the movements of some commoner summer migrants at British Bird Observatories in 1951. Ring Ouzel. *Brit. Birds* 45: 251–255
(1954). Gray-cheeked thrush at Fair Isle: a new British bird. *Brit. Birds* 47: 266–267
(1955). Migrational drift. *Act. XI Congr. Int. Orn.* 179–186
(1957). Iceland redwings wintering. *Brit. Birds* 50: 84
(1958). Autumn migration of redwings *Turdus musicus* at Fair Isle. *Ibis* 100: 582–604
(1958). Bergmann's rule and obligatory overseas migration. *Brit. Birds* 51: 209–232
(1959). The September drift movements of 1956 and 1958. *Brit. Birds* 52: 334–377
(1964). Bird census work in woodland. *Bird Study* 11:1–22
(1965). *Fair Isle and its Birds*. Edinburgh and London.
(1967). The bird community of farmland. *Bird Study* 14: 210–226

WILLIAMSON, K., and FERGUSON-LEES, I. J. (1960). Nearctic birds in Great Britain and Ireland in autumn 1958. *Brit. Birds* 53: 369–378
WILLIAMSON, K., and HOMES, R. C. (1964). Methods of preliminary results of the Common Birds Census, 1962-63. *Bird Study* 11: 24–56
WOODWARD, I. (1961). Pied blackbird with symmetrical markings. *Bull. B.O.C.* 81: 20
WYNNE-EDWARDS, V. C. (1959). The control of population-density through social behaviour: a hypothesis. *Ibis* 101: 436–441
(1962). *Animal Dispersion in Relation to Social Behaviour*. Edinburgh and London.

YAPP, W. B. (1962). *Birds and Woods*. London.
YEATES, G. K. (1951). *The Land of the Loon*. London.
YOUNG, H. (1951). Territorial behaviour of the eastern robin. *Proc. Linn. Soc. New York*. 58/62: 1–37

THE CHAT-LIKE THRUSHES

AGATHO, B. (1960–1). De Roodborsttapuit *Saxicola torquata rubicola* L. *Publikaties van bet Natuurhistorisch Geroootschop in Limburg* 12: 97–175
ASH, J. S. (1955). Pied wheatear in Dorset. *Brit. Birds* 48: 130–2
ASH, J. S., and ROOKE, K. B. (1956). Female pied wheatear: the problem of identification. *Brit. Birds* 49: 317–22

BUXTON, J. (1950). *The Redstart*. London.

CONDER, P. J. (1954). The hovering of the wheatear. *Brit. Birds* 47: 76–9
(1956). The territory of the wheatear *Oenanthe oenanthe*. *Ibis* 98: 453–9

DAVIS, P. (1958). Thrush nightingale at Fair Isle. *Brit. Birds* 51: 188
(1962). Robin recaptures on Fair Isle. *Brit. Birds* 55: 225–9
(1966). The great immigration of early September 1965. *Brit. Birds* 59: 353–76
DORST, J. (1961). *The Migrations of Birds*. London.

ECCLES, L. (1955). Whinchats choosing nest-site. *Brit. Birds* 48: 421–2

FITTER, R. S. R. (1965). The breeding status of the black redstart in Great Britain. *Brit. Birds* 58: 481–92
(1971). Black redstarts breeding in Britain in 1964–8. *Brit Birds* 64: 117–24
(1976). Black redstarts breeding in Britain in 1969–73. *Brit. Birds* 69: 9–15

GRAY, D. B. (1973). Whinchats on a deserted railway. *Bird Study* 20: 81–2

HEMPEL, C. (1957). Vom Zug des Steinschmätzers (*Oenanthe oenanthe*). *Vogelwarte* 19: 23–36
HEMPEL, C., and REETZ, W. (1957). Der Zug von Hausrotschwanz (*Phoenicurus ochrurus gibraltariensis*) und Gartenrotschwanz (*Ph. phoenicurus*) nach Beringungsergebnissen. *Vogelwarte* 19: 97–119
HOLME, R. C., and SIMMS, E. (1953). Black-eared wheatear in London. *Brit. Birds* 46: 42–5

JOHNSON, E. D. H. (1961). The pair relationship and polygyny in the stonechat. *Brit. Birds* 54: 213–25
(1971). Observations on a resident population of stonechats in Jersey. *Brit. Birds* 64: 201–13, 267–79

JONES, P. H. (1975). The migration of redstarts through and from Britain. *Ringing and Migration*. Vol. 1. No. 1: 12–17

LACK, D. (1944). The problem of partial migration. *Brit. Birds* 37: 122–30, 143–50
(1946). Clutch and brood size in the robin. *Brit. Birds* 39: 98–109. 130–35
(1946). *The Life of the robin*. (Rev'd.) London
(1948). Further notes on clutch and brood size in the robin. *Brit. Birds* 41: 98–114, 130–7
LLOYD, B. (1933). The courtship and display of wheatears. *Trans. Herts. Nat. Hist. Soc.* 19: 135–9

MAGEE, J. D. (1965). The breeding distribution of the stonechat in Britain and the causes of its decline. *Bird Study* 12: 83–9
MEADOWS, B. S. (1965). Black redstarts along the lower reaches of the River Lea. *Lond. Bird Rept.* 29: 91–4
(1970). Breeding distribution and feeding ecology of the black redstart in London. *Lond. Bird Rept.* 34: 72–9
MEINERTZHAGEN, R. (1953). On the validity of *Saxicola torquata hibernans*. *Bull. B.O.C.* 73: 14–15
MIKKOLA, H. (1973). The red-flanked bluetail and its spread to the west. *Brit. Birds* 66: 3–11

ORR, N. (1976). Studies of less familiar birds. 180. Thrush nightingale. *Brit. Birds* 69: 265–71

PARRINDER, E. R., and PARRINDER, E. D. (1945). Some observations on stonechats in north Cornwall. *Brit. Birds* 38: 362–9
PEAKALL, D. B. (1956). Some notes on the red-spotted bluethroat. *Brit. Birds* 49: 135–9
PETTIT, R. G., and BUTT, D. V. (1950). Dancing display of wheatear. *Brit. Birds* 43: 298
PHILLIPS, J. S. (1968). Stonechat breeding statistics. *Bird Study* 15: 104–5
(1970). Inter-specific competition in stonechat and whinchat. *Bird Study* 17: 320–4
(1973). Stonechats in young forestry plantations. *Bird Study* 20: 82–4

RENDAHL, H., and VESTERGREN, G. (1958). Uber die Zugverhältnisse bei schwedischen Gartenrotschwänzen (*Ph. phoenicurus* L.). *Vogelwarte* 19: 256–65
ROMER, M. L. R. (1955). Black wheatear in Kent. *Brit. Birds* 48: 132

SHARROCK, J. T. R., and SHARROCK, E. M. (1976). *Rare Birds in Britain and Ireland*. Berkhamsted.
SIMMS, E. (1957). *Voices of the Wild*. London.
(1971). *Woodland Birds*. London.
(1975). *Birds of Town and Suburb*. London.
SMITH, K. D. (1971). Notes on *Oenanthe* species in winter in Africa. *Bird Study* 18: 71–9
SNOW, D. W. (1966). Movements of British robins as shown by ringing. *Brit. Birds* 59: 67–74
(1969). The moult of British thrushes and chats. *Bird Study* 16: 115–29
SOUTHERN, H. N. (1938–9). The spring migration of the redstart over Europe. *Brit. Birds* 33: 34–8
STRESEMANN, E. (1948). Die mittlere Erstankunft von *Lanius collurio*, *Muscicapa striata*, *Oriolus oriolus* und *Oenanthe oenanthe* in Europäischen Brutraum. *Vår Fågelvarld* & (1) 1–18

290   SELECTED BIBLIOGRAPHY

STUTTARD, P., and WILLIAMSON, K. (1971). Habitat requirements of the night-
ingale. *Bird Study* 18: 9–14
SZULC-OLECH, B. (1965). The resting period of migrant robins on autumn passage.
Bird Study 12: 1–7

THOMSON, A. L. (1956). The migrations of British chats (*Oenanthe, Saxicola, Phoenicurus*)
as shown by the results of ringing. *Brit. Birds* 49: 63–73
TOOK, G. E. (1948). Incubation and fledging of black redstart. *Brit. Birds* 41: 246
TURNER, B. C. (1950). Dancing display of wheatear. *Brit. Birds* 43: 298–9

VAN HECKE, P. (1965). The migration of the west European stonechat *Saxicola torquata*
L. according to ringing data. *Gerfaut* 55: 164–94

WILLIAMSON, K. (1957). The annual post-nuptial moult in the wheatear *Oenanthe
oenanthe. Bird Banding* 28: 129–35
(1959). The September drift-movements of 1956 and 1958. *Brit. Birds* 52: 334–77
(1965). *Fair Isle and its Birds*. Edinburgh and London.

YOUNGMAN, R. E. (1974). Black redstarts breeding in newly developed town centres.
Brit. Birds 67: 394–5

INDEX

Pages in **bold type** show where the main sections are for each species or topic